Addison-Wesley
Mathematics

Robert E. Eicholz
Phares G. O'Daffer
Charles R. Fleenor

Randall I. Charles
Sharon Young
Carne S. Barnett

Addison-Wesley Publishing Company

Menlo Park, California • Reading, Massachusetts • New York
Don Mills, Ontario • Wokingham, England • Amsterdam • Bonn
Sydney • Singapore • Tokyo • Madrid • Bogotá • Santiago • San Juan

Illustration Acknowledgments

Robert Bausch 392
Cindy Brodie 112, 176 – 177, 178, 219, 234 – 235, 265, 304 – 305, 366
Elizabeth Callen 138, 232 – 233, 338 – 339
Dick Cole 150 – 151, 212
Betsy Day 92
Rae Ecklund 128 – 129, 217, 230 – 231, 356 – 357
Lisa French 284 – 285
Jon Goodell 80 – 81
John E. Hendrick 322 – 323, 370
Roberta Holmes 372
Barbara Hoopes 290 – 291, 295 upper right, 312 – 313
Larry Hughston 24 – 25, 90 – 91, 278 – 279
Susan Jaekel 4, 16, 32 – 33, 48, 74, 102, 122 – 123, 132, 140 – 141, 155, 162, 172 – 173, 188, 199, 220, 246, 272, 294, 300, 316, 335, 352 – 353, 354, 390 – 391, 402, 423, 426
Heather King 228, 252, 258, 260, 262
Dennis Leatherman 8 – 9
Susan Lexa 12 – 13, 68 – 69
Marlene May 174 – 175

Jane McCreary 168, 171, 182, 189, 194 – 195, 297, 326 – 327, 348 – 349, 386, 395
Jim M'Guinness 280 – 281
Masami Miyamoto 88, 254, 288 – 289, 295 upper left, 346 – 347, 350 – 351, 358 – 359, 393, 398 – 399, 403
Debby Morse 70 – 71, 180, 200 – 201, 256 – 257, 270 – 271
Dennis Nolan 60 – 61, 116 – 117
Bill Ogden 86
Sharron O'Neil 242
Kevin O'Shea 82 – 83, 124, 160, 179, 204, 206
Ed Parker 26 – 27
Sandra Popovich 191
Blanche Sims 111, 239, 311, 396 – 397
Doug Smith 1, 23, 30 – 31, 42 – 43, 44 – 45, 53, 79, 107, 137, 146 – 147, 167, 193, 225, 251, 277, 299, 321, 345, 365, 385, 407
Sandra Speidel 38 – 39, 66 – 67
Robert Steele 14
Michael G. Surles 126 – 127

Photograph acknowledgments appear on page 458

ISBN 0-201-23266-9

DEFGHIJKL-KR-8921098

Contents

CHAPTER 9   Fractions: Multiplication and Division, 225

CHAPTER 10   Geometry, 251

CHAPTER 11   Ratio and Proportion, 277

CHAPTER 12   Percent, 299

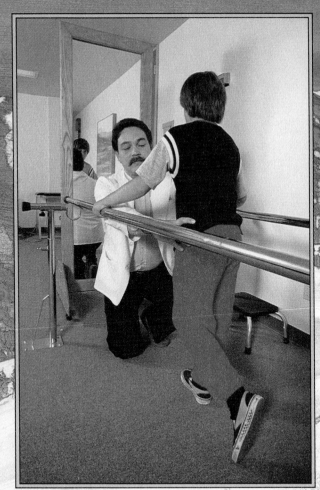

Basic Facts

The afternoon sun was low in the sky, making the snow look flat. Suddenly the tip of Ian's right ski hit a mogul, or bump of snow. He fell, twisting his knee. The ski patrol had to take him down the mountain on their toboggan.

Ian's doctor said he needed physical therapy to strengthen the muscles that support the knee joint. Ian began going to a clinic 3 days a week. A physical therapist helped him exercise his leg with a machine. He did 6 groups of exercises, repeating each exercise 20 times. On the days he didn't go to the clinic, he did leg lifts at home with 180-gram weights.

Once a week, the therapist tested Ian's knee. After 18 weeks, it was almost as strong as his other knee. After that, Ian only needed to exercise at home.

With his doctor's approval, Ian was back skiing the next season. But he kept a sharp eye out for moguls.

Addition and Subtraction

We use **addition** to find the total when two amounts have been **put together**.

We use **subtraction** when **taking away, comparing**, or finding **how many more are needed**.

Megan went on a boat trip to watch the whales migrating north for the summer. She saw 9 adult whales and 7 very young whales. How many whales did she see during their trip?

During an all-day boat trip Eric saw 16 whales. He saw 7 of them in the morning. Can you make up a question about this data that can be answered using the subtraction equation below?

$$\text{Since } \overset{\text{Addend}}{9} + \overset{\text{Addend}}{7} = \overset{\text{Sum}}{16}, \text{ then } \overset{\text{Sum}}{16} - \overset{\text{Addend}}{7} = \overset{\text{Addend}}{9} \leftarrow \text{Difference}$$

Warm Up The letter n in each equation saves a place for the sum or difference. Copy each equation, replacing n with the sum or difference.

1. $6 + 4 = n$ **2.** $7 + 5 = n$ **3.** $8 + 3 = n$ **4.** $9 + 4 = n$

5. $10 - 6 = n$ **6.** $12 - 7 = n$ **7.** $13 - 4 = n$ **8.** $14 - 6 = n$

Add or subtract. Check your subtraction by adding.

9.	**10.**	**11.**	**12.**	**13.**
$\begin{array}{r} 6 \\ +\ 8 \\ \hline \end{array}$	$\begin{array}{r} 4 \\ +\ 7 \\ \hline \end{array}$	$\begin{array}{r} 9 \\ +\ 7 \\ \hline \end{array}$	$\begin{array}{r} 8 \\ +\ 8 \\ \hline \end{array}$	$\begin{array}{r} 5 \\ +\ 9 \\ \hline \end{array}$

14.	**15.**	**16.**	**17.**	**18.**
$\begin{array}{r} 17 \\ -\ 9 \\ \hline \end{array}$	$\begin{array}{r} 16 \\ -\ 7 \\ \hline \end{array}$	$\begin{array}{r} 15 \\ -\ 6 \\ \hline \end{array}$	$\begin{array}{r} 18 \\ -\ 9 \\ \hline \end{array}$	$\begin{array}{r} 13 \\ -\ 5 \\ \hline \end{array}$

Practice Find the sums and differences below. These properties of addition may help.

0 Property	**Commutative (Order) Property**	**Associative (Grouping) Property**
When one addend is 0, the sum is the other addend.	When the order of addends is changed, the sum is the same.	When the grouping of addends is changed, the sum is the same.

1. 8
   + 0

2. 0
   + 9

3. 7
   + 3

4. 3
   + 7

5. 9
   + 4

6. 4
   + 9

7. 0
   + 0

A number subtracted from itself is 0.

8. 9
   − 9

9. 7
   − 7

Subtracting 0 doesn't change a number.

10. 0
    − 0

11. 6
    − 0

12. 9
    + 2

13. 2
    + 9

14. 8
    − 0

15. 7
    + 4

16. 18
    − 9

17. 14
    − 7

18. 8
    + 8

19. 5
     4
   + 6

20. 6
     4
   + 5

21. 8
     6
   + 3

22. 9
     3
   + 7

23. 6
     8
   + 4

24. 5
     7
   + 6

25. 8
     3
   + 8

26. $9 + 7 = n$

27. $6 + 5 = n$

28. $0 + 4 = n$

29. $7 + 7 = n$

30. $6 + 8 = n$

31. $17 − 8 = n$

32. $16 − 9 = n$

33. $15 − 6 = n$

★ 34. $n + 5 = 13$ ★ 35. $n − 8 = 9$

36. What is 7 more than 8?

37. What is the difference of 13 and 9?

Mixed Applications

38. An adult gray whale was 12 meters long. Her calf was 4 meters long. How much longer was the adult whale than the calf?

39. A whale calf was 5 meters long. It grew 7 meters in the next two years. How long was it then?

Think

Logical Reasoning

Copy this figure and write the digits 1, 2, 3, 4, 5, 6, 7, 8, 9 in the circles so that the sum on each side of the triangle is the same.

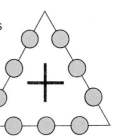

Math

Multiplication

We use **multiplication** to find the **total amount** for a problem when a **certain number** of equal **amounts** are given.

Problem

Jeff sold 7 used video game tapes for $9 each. How much money did he receive?

$7 \times 9 = 63$ Jeff received $63.

Multiplication by whole numbers other than 0 or 1 can be thought of as **repeated addition.**

$$\begin{array}{ccc} \text{Factor} & \text{Factor} & \text{Product} \\ \downarrow & \downarrow & \downarrow \end{array}$$

Since $9 + 9 + 9 + 9 + 9 + 9 + 9 = 63$, then $7 \quad \times \quad 9 \quad = \quad 6\,3$

Warm Up   Copy each equation, replacing n with the product.

1. $2 \times 4 = n$ **2.** $2 \times 3 = n$ **3.** $2 \times 5 = n$ **4.** $2 \times 6 = n$

5. $5 \times 2 = n$ **6.** $5 \times 3 = n$ **7.** $5 \times 4 = n$ **8.** $5 \times 6 = n$

9. $9 \times 2 = n$ **10.** $9 \times 3 = n$ **11.** $9 \times 4 = n$ **12.** $9 \times 5 = n$

Find the products.

13. $\begin{array}{r} 8 \\ \times\ 8 \\ \hline \end{array}$ **14.** $\begin{array}{r} 9 \\ \times\ 9 \\ \hline \end{array}$ **15.** $\begin{array}{r} 6 \\ \times\ 9 \\ \hline \end{array}$ **16.** $\begin{array}{r} 9 \\ \times\ 7 \\ \hline \end{array}$ **17.** $\begin{array}{r} 9 \\ \times\ 8 \\ \hline \end{array}$

18. $\begin{array}{r} 5 \\ \times\ 7 \\ \hline \end{array}$ **19.** $\begin{array}{r} 5 \\ \times\ 8 \\ \hline \end{array}$ **20.** $\begin{array}{r} 2 \\ \times\ 7 \\ \hline \end{array}$ **21.** $\begin{array}{r} 2 \\ \times\ 8 \\ \hline \end{array}$ **22.** $\begin{array}{r} 2 \\ \times\ 9 \\ \hline \end{array}$

Practice Find the products below. These properties of multiplication may help.

0 and 1 Properties	**Commutative (Order) Property**	**Associative (Grouping) Property**
When either factor is 0, the product is 0. When either factor is 1, the product is the other factor.	When the order of the factors is changed, the product is the same.	When the grouping of three factors is changed, the product is the same.

1. 5
    × 0
    ___

2. 0
    × 6
    ___

3. 8
    × 1
    ___

4. 1
    × 8
    ___

5. 3
    × 4
    ___

6. 4
    × 3
    ___

7. 3
    × 9
    ___

8. 9
    × 3
    ___

9. 4
    × 8
    ___

10. 8
    × 4
    ___

11. 3
    × 7
    ___

12. 7
    × 3
    ___

13. 6
    × 5
    ___

14. 5
    × 6
    ___

15. $(4 \times 2) \times 3 = n$

16. $4 \times (2 \times 3) = n$

17. $(4 \times 3) \times 2 = n$

Distributive (Multiplication-Addition) Property
When two products have a common factor, you can add to find another product of the same factor.

Find the first two products. Then add to find the third.

18. 8   8   8
    × 5   × 2 → × 7
    ___   ___   ___

19. 4   4   4
    × 5   × 3 → × 8
    ___   ___   ___

★ Give the number for n.

20. $n \times 9 = 45$

21. $8 \times n = 56$

Mixed Applications

22. Mary bought 8 used video tapes for $8 each. How much did she pay for them?

23. Dina rented 4 video tapes for $15. She could have saved $6 total by renting them at another store. How much would she have paid at the other store?

Think

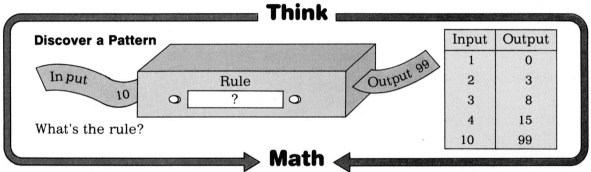

Discover a Pattern

Input 10   Rule ?   Output 99

Input	Output
1	0
2	3
3	8
4	15
10	99

What's the rule?

Math

More Practice, page 427, Set B

division to solve problems that
involve finding **how many equal sets**
there are.

We also use division for problems that
involve finding **how many are in each
equal set.**

Problem 1
Jonita had 56 tubes of paint.
She put 8 tubes in each box.
How many boxes did she use?

$$56 \div 8 = 7$$

Jonita used 7 boxes.

Problem 2
Carl put 56 brushes in 8 boxes.
He put the same number in each. How
many brushes did he put in each box?

$$56 \div 8 = 7$$

Carl put 7 brushes in each box.

Division is related to multiplication as shown below.

$$\text{Since} \quad \underset{\uparrow}{\underset{\text{Factor}}{7}} \times \underset{\uparrow}{\underset{\text{Factor}}{8}} = \underset{\uparrow}{\underset{\text{Product}}{56}}, \text{ then } \underset{\underset{\text{Dividend}}{\uparrow}}{\overset{\overset{\text{Product}}{\downarrow}}{56}} \div \underset{\underset{\text{Divisor}}{\uparrow}}{\overset{\overset{\text{Factor}}{\downarrow}}{8}} = \overset{\overset{\text{Factor}}{\downarrow}}{7} \leftarrow \text{Quotient}$$

Warm Up   Copy each equation, replacing n with the quotient.

$(? \times 3 = 24)$

1. $24 \div 3 = n$ **2.** $12 \div 2 = n$ **3.** $15 \div 5 = n$ **4.** $18 \div 3 = n$

5. $20 \div 4 = n$ **6.** $24 \div 6 = n$ **7.** $27 \div 3 = n$ **8.** $32 \div 8 = n$

9. $35 \div 7 = n$ **10.** $36 \div 6 = n$ **11.** $30 \div 5 = n$ **12.** $40 \div 8 = n$

Find the quotients. Check by multiplying.

13. $8\overline{)64}$ **14.** $3\overline{)24}$ **15.** $9\overline{)72}$ **16.** $6\overline{)54}$ **17.** $7\overline{)56}$

18. $7\overline{)49}$ **19.** $5\overline{)25}$ **20.** $4\overline{)16}$ **21.** $8\overline{)32}$ **22.** $7\overline{)63}$

Practice Divide. Check by multiplying.

Any number divided by 1 is that number.	**1.** $1\overline{)6}$	**2.** $1\overline{)8}$	**3.** $1\overline{)1}$	**4.** $1\overline{)0}$

5. $7\overline{)7}$ **6.** $9\overline{)9}$ **7.** $1\overline{)1}$ **8.** $6\overline{)6}$

Any number other than 0 divided by itself is 1.

9. $5\overline{)0}$ **10.** $8\overline{)0}$

Remember: **WE NEVER DIVIDE BY 0.**

0 divided by another number is 0.

11. $9\overline{)0}$ **12.** $7\overline{)0}$

Check: Check:
$\not{0}\not{)6}$ $? \times 0 = 6$ $\not{0}\not{)0}$ $? \times 0 = 0$
        No solution!   Too many solutions!

13. $3\overline{)27}$ **14.** $5\overline{)30}$ **15.** $7\overline{)49}$ **16.** $6\overline{)48}$ **17.** $9\overline{)63}$

18. $8\overline{)24}$ **19.** $5\overline{)45}$ **20.** $7\overline{)56}$ **21.** $8\overline{)64}$ **22.** $8\overline{)72}$

23. $20 \div 4 = n$ **24.** $21 \div 3 = n$ **25.** $6 \div 1 = n$ **26.** $8 \div 8 = n$

27. $54 \div 6 = n$ **28.** $56 \div 7 = n$ **29.** $0 \div 4 = n$ **30.** $54 \div 9 = n$

★ **31.** $n \div 6 = 9$ ★ **32.** $72 \div n = 8$

33. What is 63 divided by 7?

Mixed Applications

34. At the art store, Alejandro had 42 prints of famous paintings. He put 6 prints in each bin. How many bins did he use?

35. Each box of paint tubes holds 6 tubes. How many paint tubes are in 9 boxes?

Think

Estimation

Choose the best estimate for the total amount of money shown. Explain the reasons for your choice.

Dimes

Nickels

1. $10 **2.** $100 **3.** $1,000 **4.** $10,000

Math

Problem Solving: The 5-Point Checklist

To Solve a Problem

1. **Understand the Question**
2. **Find the needed Data**
3. **Plan what to do**
4. **Find the Answer**
5. **Check back**

QUESTION
DATA
PLAN
ANSWER
CHECK

These five steps can help you solve problems. Follow them to solve this problem.

Neil and 8 friends went to an amusement park. Tickets cost $8 each. How much did the group pay?

1. Understand the Question
What was the total cost of the tickets?

2. Find the needed Data
There were 9 persons (Neil and 8 friends) who bought tickets. The tickets cost $8 each.

3. Plan what to do
Since we want the total for 9 equal amounts, we multiply.

4. Find the Answer
$9 \times 8 = 72$ Neil and his friends paid $72 for tickets.

5. Check back
Read the problem again. The answer $72 seems reasonable.

Solve. Use the 5-Point Checklist.

1. Eddie went on 6 rides an hour for 5 hours. How many rides did he take?

2. Jenny rode 14 rides in the first 3 hours. Nan rode 6 less than this. How many rides did Nan take?

Solve.

1. Marie stayed at the amusement park for 15 hours during 2 days. She stayed 7 hours the first day. How many hours did she stay the second day?

2. Todd spent $8 to get into the park, $4 for gifts, and $6 for food. What was the total amount Todd spent?

3. A rollercoaster ride lasts only 7 minutes. During the first hour, Sam took 6 rides. How many minutes did Sam spend on the roller coaster the first hour?

4. Tim thought he would see more people he knew at the park than Jay would. Tim saw 5 people he knew the first day and 4 people the second. How many did Jay see if he saw 6 more than Tim?

5. On one trip 24 people rode the Runaway Rails Train. There were 4 people on each car. How many cars did the train have?

6. The Giant Caterpillar ride has 9 rows of seats. Each row has seats for 6 people. How many people can the ride carry?

7. Miranda and her sister together spent $16 for food and gifts at the park. Her sister spent $9 of that amount. How much did Miranda spend?

★ 8. Each car of the Log Splash ride holds 9 people. An average of 8 cars are filled every 5 minutes. How many people ride the Log Splash in 10 minutes?

9

Combining Operations

Work with a group. You will need one deck of playing cards.

Part 1

First, remove the jacks, queens, and kings from your deck, and set them aside. Then shuffle the remaining cards, deal three to each player, and turn the next card up.

1. Find ways to make your three cards equal to the top card or come as close to it as possible by using any two math operations: addition, subtraction, multiplication, division. Write your problems as shown, using parentheses and changing the order of the cards as needed.

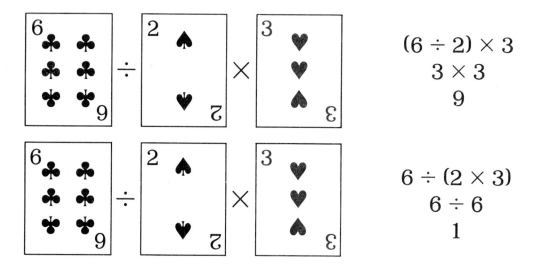

$$(6 \div 2) \times 3$$
$$3 \times 3$$
$$9$$

$$6 \div (2 \times 3)$$
$$6 \div 6$$
$$1$$

- What difference did the parentheses make in each problem?
- When did it make a difference which operation you did first?
- Share your findings with your group.

2. Now deal three cards to each player. Keep the cards in the order they were dealt. Use parentheses and any two math operations to write as many problems as possible.
   - Find pairs of problems that are exactly the same except for parentheses.

   Examples: $(9 - 3) \times 2$ and $9 - (3 \times 2)$
   $(9 + 3) \div 2$ and $9 + (3 \div 2)$
   $(9 \times 3) \times 2$ and $9 \times (3 \times 2)$

10

- Find some pairs where the solutions are the same, and some pairs where the solutions are different.
- Discuss what you notice. Decide which combinations of operations are not affected by parentheses.

Part 2

3. From your deck of cards, select one *6*, two *2s*, and one *4*, and arrange them in the order shown below. Using the operations shown here, how many different solutions can you get by using two sets of parentheses? Compare your results with others in your group.

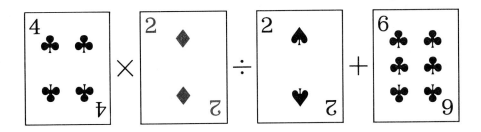

4. Arrange cards with the numbers *1* (ace) through *9* in a row. Use any combination of math operations to make the numbers equal to 100 or come as close to 100 as possible. Keep the nine cards in sequence, but you may put them together to make 2-digit, 3-digit, or larger numbers. Work together to write as many equations as you can. Talk about whether or not using parentheses makes a difference in your solutions and how many parentheses you could use in each equation. Compare your equations with those of other groups.

   Examples: $123 - (4 \times 5) + 6 + 7 - (8 + 9) = 99$
   $1 + 2 + 3 - 4 + 5 + 6 + 78 + 9 = 100$

5. Ivy and Chris decided to experiment with only the *4s* in a deck. They used the four cards with the number *4* and wrote as many equations as they could using any combination of math operations.

   Example: $(4 - 4) \times (4 + 4) = 0$

Try some with your group. Can you write an equation with a solution of 1? of 2? of 3? How far can you continue this pattern of solutions? Share your work with another group.

Problem Solving: Understanding the Question

To solve a problem, you must first **understand the question.**

For each set of data below, complete the following activities:

A Write a question.

B Solve the problem.

C Write a short sentence that answers the question.

Example:
DATA: Nell washed cars to earn money. She washed 7 cars. She received $6 for each car.

A Question: How much did Nell earn?

B Solution: $7 \times 6 = 42$

C Sentence: Nell earned $42 by washing cars.

1. DATA: Eric mows lawns on weekends. He earned $24 for mowing 3 lawns.

2. DATA: Peggy earned $12 for painting a fence. She paid her little sister $3 for helping her.

3. DATA: John earns $8 a day from his paper route. He delivers papers 7 days a week.

4. DATA: Theresa earned $16 by babysitting. Tim earned $9 by babysitting.

5. DATA: Jan agreed to work a total of 15 hours on Friday and Saturday. She worked 6 hours on Friday.

6. DATA: Tom was paid $4 an hour for delivering ads. He earned $36.

7. DATA: Carlos worked as a golf caddy. He earned $5 on Monday, $8 on Tuesday, and $9 on Wednesday.

★ 8. DATA: Dana worked 3 hours at $4 an hour and 2 more hours at $5 an hour.

Problem Solving:
Using Data from an Information Sheet

Sometimes you must search for data needed to solve a problem. Use data from this sheet as needed to solve these problems.

1. How many more points do you get for a bull's eye than for a ring in the green zone?

2. Todd threw 6 rings onto pegs in the red zone. What was his score?

3. What is the highest number of points you can get with two rings that hit pegs in different zones?

4. Sheila played the game 3 times. How many rings did she throw in all?

5. Paul threw a total of 30 rings one afternoon. How many times did he play the game?

6. The first time Allison played, she scored 8 points. The second time, she scored 17 points. How many more points did she score the second time?

7. Darrell made 21 points with rings in the red zone. How many rings did he get in the red zone?

8. Brenda threw 4 rings onto pegs in the green zone. Her other 2 rings fell outside the white zone. What was her score?

Ring-a-Peg Game Direction Sheet

Rules: Players must stand the same distance from the board. Each player throws 6 rings. The player with the highest score wins.

Zone	Points
Gold (Bull's eye)	9
Red	7
Blue	5
Green	3
White	1
Outside White	0

9. Jeff threw 3 rings. He got 1 in the gold zone, 1 in the red zone, and 1 in the white zone. What was the total number of points from the 3 rings?

★ 10. What would be your score if you threw 6 rings and hit a peg in each zone, with 1 ring falling outside the white zone?

Using Basic Facts: Finding Multiples

Batteries are often sold in packages of 4. What are some of the different numbers of batteries you can buy?

To show some different numbers of batteries that can be bought, we can list some **multiples** of 4.

Some multiples of 4:

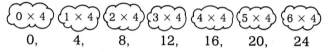

0,   4,   8,   12,   16,   20,   24

> Any number that is a product of 4 and another whole number is a multiple of 4!

You could buy any number of batteries that is a multiple of 4 (0, 4, 8, 12, ...).

We form the multiples of any number by multiplying each of the whole numbers by that number.

Other Examples
Multiples of 3: 0, 3, 6, 9, 12, 15, 18, ...
Multiples of 5: 0, 5, 10, 15, 20, 25, 30, ...

Practice   Write ten multiples of each number, starting with 0.

1. 8   **2.** 6   **3.** 1   **4.** 9   **5.** 7

6. The multiples of 2 are called **even numbers.** Write ten even numbers, starting with 0.

7. Numbers that are 1 more than a multiple of 2 are called **odd numbers.** Write ten odd numbers, starting with 1.

★ Find the Mystery Number.

8. This Mystery Number is the smallest number that is a multiple of 6 and also a multiple of 8.

9. This Mystery Number is the largest number less than 50 that is a multiple of 9 and a multiple of 6.

Using Basic Facts: Finding Factors

To find the factors of 12, Jolene wrote these "product 12" equations. (There are 3 more if you change the order of the factors.)

The **factors** (or divisors) of **12** are **1, 2, 3, 4, 6,** and **12.**

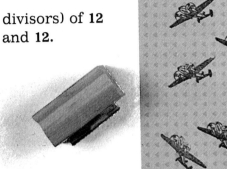

Factor Factor Product

$1 \times 12 = 12$

$2 \times 6 = 12$

$3 \times 4 = 12$

Jolene

Copy and complete the equations. Then list all the factors of the product.

1. $1 \times n = 18$
   $2 \times n = 18$
   $3 \times n = 18$

2. $1 \times n = 14$
   $2 \times n = 14$

3. $1 \times n = 20$
   $2 \times n = 20$
   $4 \times n = 20$
   $5 \times n = 20$

List all the factors of each number.

4. 10   **5.** 15   **6.** 21   **7.** 13   **8.** 16   **9.** 5

10. 8   **11.** 7   **12.** 17   **13.** 4   **14.** 27   **15.** 9

16. 25   **17.** 6   **18.** 22   ★ **19.** 28   ★ **20.** 24   ★ **21.** 36

Skillkeeper

Solve.

1. $16 - 9 = n$ **2.** $6 + 7 = n$ **3.** $12 \div 3 = n$ **4.** $7 \times 5 = n$

5. $32 \div 8 = n$ **6.** $18 - 9 = n$ **7.** $6 \times 9 = n$ **8.** $9 + 8 = n$

9. $15 - 7 = n$ **10.** $45 \div 5 = n$ **11.** $9 + 5 = n$ **12.** $7 \times 6 = n$

Problem-Solving Strategy: Choose the Operations

Some problems can be solved by choosing a single operation (+, −, ×, ÷). For other problems, you may need to use more than one operation. A problem-solving strategy that might help you is called

Choose the Operations

Try This   Tina found that she could make 35 pottery vases in a 5-day week. At this rate, how many vases could she make in a 5-day week and 3 days?

Think about when to use each operation. What does the problem involve?

+
• Finding the total after putting together?

—
• Taking away?   • Comparing?   • Finding how many more are needed?

×
• Finding the total for a number of same-size sets?

÷
• Finding the number of same-size sets?   • Finding the number in each same-size set?

Since I want to know the number of vases Tina can make each day, I divide.

$35 \div 5 = 7$
Tina can make 7 vases each day.

Since I want to find the total for 7 vases a day for 3 days, I multiply.

$7 \times 3 = 21$
In 3 days, Tina can make 21 vases.

Since I want to put together two numbers of vases, I add.

$35 + 21 = 56$
Tina can make 56 vases in a 5-day week and 3 days.

Solve.

1. Waldo bought 9 vases for $27 and sold them for $7 each. How much total profit did he make?

2. Beth received $54 for 9 hours work. Erin received $36 for the same number of hours. How much more did Beth make per hour than Erin?

Chapter Review-Test

Add, subtract, multiply, or divide.

1. $\begin{array}{r} 9 \\ + 7 \\ \hline \end{array}$	**2.** $\begin{array}{r} 13 \\ - 6 \\ \hline \end{array}$	**3.** $\begin{array}{r} 9 \\ \times 7 \\ \hline \end{array}$	**4.** $\begin{array}{r} 8 \\ + 0 \\ \hline \end{array}$	**5.** $\begin{array}{r} 7 \\ \times 1 \\ \hline \end{array}$	**6.** $\begin{array}{r} 9 \\ - 9 \\ \hline \end{array}$

7. $8\overline{)56}$ **8.** $8 + 5$ **9.** 4×9 **10.** $48 \div 6$ **11.** $16 - 7$

12. 7×3 **13.** $8 - 8$ **14.** 8×8 **15.** 6×0 **16.** $4 \div 4$

17. 7×5 **18.** 5×7 **19.** $9 + 6$ **20.** $6 + 9$ **21.** $6\overline{)42}$

22. $8 + 5 + 4$ **23.** $(54 \div 9) + 8$ **24.** $(3 \times 2) \times 4$

25. $3 \times (2 \times 4)$ **26.** $8 + (12 - 7)$ **27.** $(6 \times 6) \div 9$

28. $(3 \times 3) + (18 \div 6)$ **29.** $(4 + 3) \times 7$ **30.** $(2 \times 9) - (27 \div 3)$

31. Give the first five multiples of 4.   **32.** Give the first five multiples of 7.

33. List all the factors of 12.   **34.** List all the factors of 18.

Give the number for n.

35. $9 + 5 = n$ **36.** $8 + 4 = n$ **37.** $15 - 9 = n$

38. $11 - 7 = n$ **39.** $18 - 9 = n$ **40.** $48 \div 8 = n$

41. $7 \times 4 = n$ **42.** $35 \div 5 = n$ **43.** $21 \div 7 = n$

Solve.

44. Gary washed windows 9 hours to make money for a two-day trip to the amusement park. He received $5 an hour. How much did he earn?

45. In a target game you get 9 points for a bull's eye, 7 for a red, 5 for a blue, 3 for a black, and 1 for a white. Cindy scored 2 blacks and 1 bull's eye. How many points did she get?

Another Look

$8 + 4 = 12$, so $4 + 8 = 12$

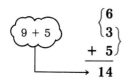

$9 + 5$
$\begin{cases} 6 \\ 3 \\ + 5 \end{cases}$ Add either pair first.

$\rightarrow 14$

—
16
$- 7$
Think about addition to find the difference.

$? + 7 = 16$

×

$3 \times 5 = 15$, so $5 \times 3 = 15$

Factor Factor Product

÷ Think about multiplication to find the quotient.

$6)\overline{54}$

$? \times 6 = 54$

$54 \div 6 = ?$

Add.

1. 8
+ 3

2. 3
+ 8

3. 5
4
+ 6

4. $7 + 0$ **5.** $9 + 9$ **6.** $7 + 2 + 8$

7. $8 + 7$ **8.** $4 + 9$ **9.** $4 + 3 + 9$

Subtract.

10. 12
$- 7$

11. 4
$- 4$

12. 16
$- 8$

13. 14
$- 5$

14. $6 - 0$ **15.** $13 - 6$ **16.** $15 - 8$

17. $13 - 8$ **18.** $16 - 7$ **19.** $17 - 9$

Multiply.

20. 5
$\times 6$

21. 4
$\times 9$

22. 8
$\times 7$

23. 9
$\times 7$

24. 8×0 **25.** 6×8 **26.** 5×8

27. 9×4 **28.** 8×7 **29.** 6×3

30. 4×7 **31.** 6×9 **32.** 8×4

Divide.

33. $8)\overline{24}$ **34.** $7)\overline{42}$ **35.** $5)\overline{0}$

36. $8)\overline{72}$ **37.** $7)\overline{63}$ **38.** $6)\overline{6}$

39. $45 \div 9$ **40.** $5 \div 1$ **41.** $49 \div 7$

42. $36 \div 9$ **43.** $56 \div 7$ **44.** $54 \div 6$

18

Enrichment

Solving Equations Using Mental Math

We **solve** an equation such as $n \times 8 = 56$ by finding a number replacement for n that will make the equation true. You can solve equations **mentally** by thinking about them as shown in this example.

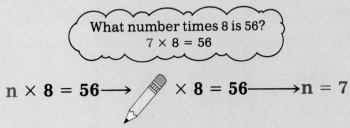

What number times 8 is 56?
$7 \times 8 = 56$

$n \times 8 = 56 \longrightarrow \times 8 = 56 \longrightarrow n = 7$

The solution to the equation is 7.

Decide if the number shown above n is a solution to the equation. Answer **yes** or **no**. If your answer is **no**, give the solution.

| 8? | 4? | 3? | 4? | 8? |

1. $7 + n = 15$ **2.** $12 - n = 9$ **3.** $n \times 9 = 27$ **4.** $28 \div n = 7$ **5.** $n + 4 = 13$

Solve mentally. Write the equation with the solution included.

6. $n + 3 = 12$
$ + 3 = 12$

7. $16 - n = 9$
$16 - = 9$

8. $8 \times n = 48$
$8 \times = 48$

9. $n \div 4 = 5$
$ \div 4 = 5$

Solve mentally. Write the equation and the solution as shown in the example.
Example: Solve: $9 + n = 12$. You write: $9 + n = 12$
$n = 3$

10. $6 + n = 11$ **11.** $n + 9 = 13$ **12.** $8 + n = 17$ **13.** $n + 7 = 12$ **14.** $5 + n = 14$

15. $12 - n = 8$ **16.** $n - 9 = 6$ **17.** $16 - n = 8$ **18.** $n - 4 = 9$ **19.** $14 - n = 9$

20. $6 \times n = 18$ **21.** $n \times 5 = 20$ **22.** $4 \times n = 24$ **23.** $n \times 8 = 32$ **24.** $9 \times n = 36$

25. $12 \div n = 4$ **26.** $n \div 2 = 7$ **27.** $24 \div n = 8$ **28.** $n \div 4 = 8$ **29.** $30 \div n = 6$

30. $15 = n + 7$ **31.** $8 = n - 6$ **32.** $48 = n \times 8$ **33.** $8 = n \div 7$ **34.** $n \times 9 = 72$

Calculator

Using a Calculator

A calculator is a tool that can help us solve problems. We must carefully enter the correct numbers and arithmetic operations on the calculator because it does only what we tell it to do.

How the Calculator Works

A calculator has the ability to "remember," or store, numbers for future use. For example, when a number is entered and an operation key such as $+$ is pushed, the calculator stores the number and "remembers" that it is to add that number to the next number entered. Also, the sum of two numbers can be stored and later added to another number. The memory ability of a calculator helps it do computations quickly and accurately.

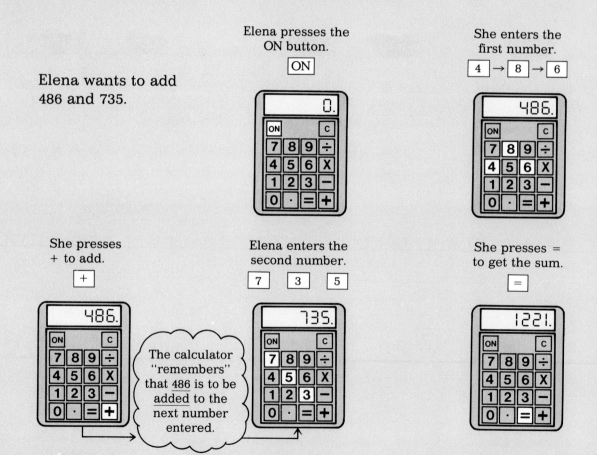

Elena wants to add 486 and 735.

Elena presses the ON button.

ON

She enters the first number.

$4 \rightarrow 8 \rightarrow 6$

She presses + to add.

+

The calculator "remembers" that 486 is to be added to the next number entered.

Elena enters the second number.

7 3 5

She presses = to get the sum.

=

Example

One summer Nils, a mountain climber, climbed the Matterhorn 6 times, the Eiger 4 times, and Dufour Peak 9 times. Use a calculator to find the total number of meters Nils climbed that summer.

Mountain	Height (m)
Matterhorn	4,478
Eiger	3,970
Dufour Peak	4,634

First, multiply to find how many meters Nils climbed on each mountain.

Matterhorn $\underline{4478 \times 6}$ = 26868 ←

Eiger $\underline{3970 \times 4}$ = 15880 ←

Dufour Peak $\underline{4634 \times 9}$ = 41706 ←

Record these products.

Then add: 26868 + 15880 + 41706 = 84454

Nils climbed a total of 84,454 m.

Use a calculator to help solve these problems. Follow these steps:

Write the problem.

Estimate the answer mentally.

Find the answer using the calculator.

Compare the answer to your estimate.

1. $(75 \times 8) + (59 \times 4) + (98 \times 9) = n$

2. $(795 + 3{,}685 - 1{,}020) - 5 = n$

3. $(391 \div 17) + (48 \times 29) = n$

4. Gretchen climbed 1,306 m the first day and 948 m the second. How much farther did she climb the first day than she climbed the second?

5. For their hiking trip Duffy's family needed to buy 4 backpacks, 4 sleeping bags, and a first aid kit. The backpacks cost $18 each, the sleeping bags cost $47 each, and the first aid kit cost $9. What was the total cost?

6. In June a ranger took 23 groups of visitors on hikes. There were 18 in each group. In July she took 38 groups on hikes, with 14 in each group. How many more did she take in one month than in the other?

Cumulative Review

Add.

1.
```
    3
  + 7
```
A 9
B 10
C 15
D not given

2. 5 + 4
A 6
B 9
C 10
D not given

3.
```
    3
    0
  + 9
```
A 0
B 10
C 11
D not given

Subtract.

4.
```
   16
  - 8
```
A 9
B 8
C 4
D not given

5.
```
   17
  - 9
```
A 5
B 8
C 7
D not given

6. 15 − 8
A 9
B 6
C 7
D not given

Multiply.

7.
```
    5
  × 0
```
A 50
B 10
C 5
D not given

8.
```
    7
  × 7
```
A 7
B 70
C 49
D not given

9. 4 × 9
A 24
B 32
C 36
D not given

Divide.

10. 72 ÷ 9
A 6
B 8
C 9
D not given

11. 8)‾40‾
A 8
B 10
C 4
D not given

12. 7)‾56‾
A 5
B 7
C 8
D not given

13. Sue has 32 large stamps to put in her album. Each page will hold 8 stamps. How many pages will she fill?

A 2
B 4
C 9
D not given

14. Tomás worked 2 hours at his father's store on Thursday. He worked 3 hours on Friday and 6 hours on Saturday. How many hours did he work in all?

A 10
B 9
C 11
D not given

2

Addition
and Subtraction

Bailey took a step forward and jolted the heavy sled into
motion. Barney began pulling steadily. Working together,
they pulled 6,500 pounds a distance of 72 inches to win the
contest. Of course Bailey and Barney weigh quite a bit them-
selves. These horses have a total weight of 3,050 pounds.

Many county fairs have contests called horse pulls. Teams
of two horses, guided by three handlers, pull sleds weighed
down with cement blocks. These large horses are called
draft horses. Some of them weigh over a ton each. (In comparison, an average saddle horse weighs between 900 and
1,200 pounds.) Some teams can pull up to 16,000 pounds.

In the days before trucks and tractors, draft horses pulled
plows and wagons, and sleds loaded with logs. Today's horse
pulls remind us of the great amount of work that horses did
in our country's past.

Place Value: Thousands

You can think about the number for Earhart's trip as shown below.

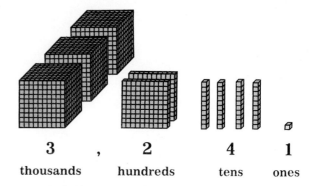

3	,	2	4	1
thousands		hundreds	tens	ones

In the number for the moon trip, each group of three digits, called a **period,** is separated by a comma as shown below.

Thousands Period Ones Period ← Periods

We write, in
standard form: →

3	7	6	,	2	8	4	
hundred thousands	ten thousands	thousands		hundreds	tens	ones	← Place Values

We read: "three hundred seventy-six thousand, two hundred eighty-four"

We can write, in **expanded form:**

$$300,000 + 70,000 + 6,000 + 200 + 80 + 4$$

Warm Up Read each number. Use place value to tell what each red digit means.

1. 3,574
2. 6,384
3. 3,596
4. 23,329
5. 45,204
6. 72,521
7. 425
8. 197,600
9. 647,938
10. 502,749
11. 86,074
12. 986,240

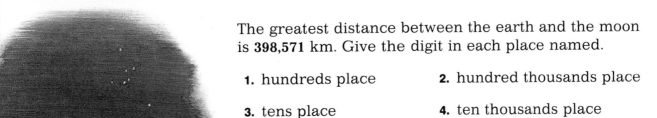

The greatest distance between the earth and the moon is **398,571** km. Give the digit in each place named.

1. hundreds place   **2.** hundred thousands place

3. tens place   **4.** ten thousands place

5. ones place   **6.** one thousands place

Write the number in standard form.

7. 500,000 + 60,000 + 4,000 + 300 + 20 + 8

8. 8,000 + 70,000 + 200 + 50 + 3 + 400,000

9. 90,000 + 400 + 80 + 7

10. 3 + 800,000 + 4,000

11. two hundred forty-five thousand, nine hundred sixty-five

12. 568 thousand   **13.** 864 thousand 637

Write in expanded form.

14. 376   **15.** 6,376   **16.** 28,341   **17.** 687,924

18. 207   **19.** 4,029   **20.** 30,560   **21.** 700,903

Write in words.

22. 247   **23.** 5,620   **24.** 12,306

25. 34,029   **26.** 86,492   **27.** 374,982

★ **28.** Write the largest number and the smallest number that use the digits 0 through 6 exactly once.

Think

Place Value—Guess and Check

Find the largest 6-digit number in which

- the thousands period contains three different odd digits with sum 21

and
- the ones period contains three different even digits with sum 18.

Math

Millions and Billions

At one time during a recent year, the sales of phonograph records in the United States amounted to the number shown here.

The periods and place values for this number are shown below.

Periods	Billions				Millions				Thousands				Ones		
Place Values	hundred billions	ten billions	billions	hundred millions	ten millions	millions	hundred thousands	ten thousands	thousands	hundreds	tens	ones
	2 ,	4	3	9 ,	5	1	7 ,	6	8	0

We think about the periods and read: "two **billion**, four hundred thirty-nine **million**, five hundred seventeen **thousand**, six hundred eighty"

Warm Up Give the digits in the period named. Then read each number.

1. 467,398,275
(thousands)

2. 367,248,204
(millions)

3. 86,240,302,617
(billions)

4. 9,460,300,480
(ones)

5. 68,943,287,400
(millions)

6. 975,837,246,781
(billions)

Read each number. Then use place value to tell what each red digit means.

7. 59,876,476

8. 864,327,413

9. 362,470,198

10. 5,468,294,300

11. 42,385,297

12. 3,576,284

13. 57,936,485,800

14. 684,362,943,702

15. 1,743,849

16. 59,241,708

17. 165,376,240

18. 463,807,620,700

Practice Write the digits in the period named.

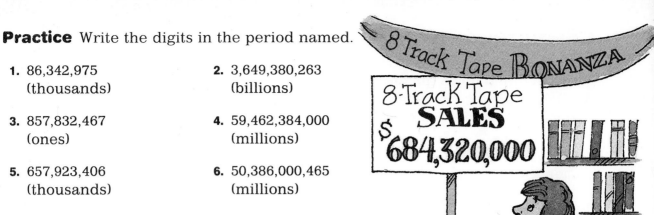

1. 86,342,975
(thousands)

2. 3,649,380,263
(billions)

3. 857,832,467
(ones)

4. 59,462,384,000
(millions)

5. 657,923,406
(thousands)

6. 50,386,000,465
(millions)

Use the number shown for 8-track tape sales. Which digit is in the place named?

7. ten millions

8. thousands

9. hundred thousands

10. ten thousands

11. hundred millions

12. millions

Write the number that has these digits in the periods shown.

13. billions: 376; thousands: 724; ones: 325; millions: 423

14. thousands: 204; billions: 217; millions: 749; ones: 200

15. ones: 461; millions: 613; thousands: 209; billions: 24

Write in standard form.

16. 5,000,000 + 300,000 + 80,000 + 4,000 + 600 + 2

17. 3,000,000,000 + 400,000,000 + 70,000,000 + 1,000,000

18. Three billion, seven hundred six million, five hundred forty thousand

19. 836 billion

20. 792 million

21. How many zeros are in the number one thousand? one million? one billion?

★ 22. Write the largest number and the smallest number that use the digits 0 through 9 exactly once.

Think

Calculator—Estimation

How old is someone who is a million minutes old? About

A 2 months?   **B** 2 years?

C 20 years?   **D** 200 years?

Estimate first. Then check using your calculator.

Math

Comparing and Ordering

Which stadium holds the greater number of people, Schaefer Stadium or Candlestick Park?

We **compare** two numbers by deciding which is greater.

Stadium Capacities	
Stadium	Capacity
Soldier Field, Chicago	58,064
Candlestick Park, San Francisco	61,246
Atlanta-Fulton Stadium, Atlanta	60,489
Texas Stadium, Dallas	65,101
Schaefer Stadium, Foxboro, Mass.	61,297
Memorial Stadium, Baltimore	60,020

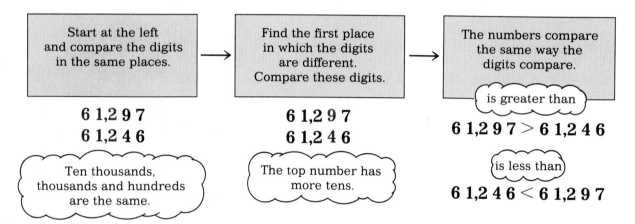

Start at the left and compare the digits in the same places. → Find the first place in which the digits are different. Compare these digits. → The numbers compare the same way the digits compare.

6 1,2 9 7
6 1,2 4 6

Ten thousands, thousands and hundreds are the same.

6 1,2 9 7
6 1,2 4 6

The top number has more tens.

is greater than

6 1,2 9 7 > 6 1,2 4 6

is less than

6 1,2 4 6 < 6 1,2 9 7

Schaefer stadium holds the greater number of people.

We **order** numbers by listing them from least to greatest or from greatest to least. We do this by comparing them two at a time.

65,101 ← greatest
61,297
61,246
60,489
60,020
58,064 ← least

Warm Up Which stadium capacity is greater?
Use greater than (>) to compare the numbers.

1. Oakland-Alameda Stadium: 54,615
   San Diego Stadium: 52,552

2. R. F. Kennedy Stadium, Washington, D.C.: 55,031
   Milwaukee County Stadium: 55,958

3. Lambeau Field, Green Bay: 56,267
   Riverfront Stadium, Cincinnati: 56,200

4. Order the stadium capacities in exercises 1 through 3 from least to greatest.

Practice Write $>$, $<$, or $=$ for each ▥ .

1. 973 ▥ 898
2. 7,436 ▥ 7,440
3. 1,000 ▥ 999
4. 10,000 ▥ 99,999
5. 78,604 ▥ 78,640
6. 863,426 ▥ 86,526
7. 9,743,800 ▥ 9,743,008
8. 65,000 ▥ 64,999
9. 784,946 ▥ 946,784
10. 1,010,000 ▥ 1,001,100
11. 475 thousand ▥ 475,000
12. 42 million ▥ 23 billion
13. 800,000 ▥ 8 million
14. 764 billion ▥ 698 billion

Use $>$ or $<$ to compare the top number with the bottom number.

15. 946,627
    938,576

16. 95,606
    95,599

17. 3,467,936,800
    3,468,107,400

18. 367,432,567
    367,432,498

19. Which holds more people, Yankee Stadium or Tiger Stadium?

20. Order the capacities of these baseball parks by listing them from the greatest to least.

Order from least to greatest.

21. 7,983; 7,979; 7,899; 7,958

22. 57,384; 57,099; 57,401

23. 5,396,238; 5,396,229; 5,401,107; 5,396,199

Write the number that is

24. 1,000 less than 37,398.

25. 1,000,000 more than 18,365,421.

26. 100,000 less than 367,548,219.

Baseball Park	Capacity
Tiger Stadium, Detroit	54,220
Three Rivers Stadium, Pittsburgh	50,230
Yankee Stadium, New York	54,208
Busch Memorial Stadium, St. Louis	50,101
Veterans Stadium, Philadelphia	56,581

Think

Discovering Patterns

These dots should help you see why 3, 6, and 10 are sometimes called triangular numbers.

3 ∴   6 ∷∴   10 ∷∷∴

Give the next 5 triangular numbers.

Math

Rounding

A bathyscaph went to a depth of 31,829 ft. This is greater than the height of the world's highest mountain! What is this number of feet rounded to the nearest thousand?

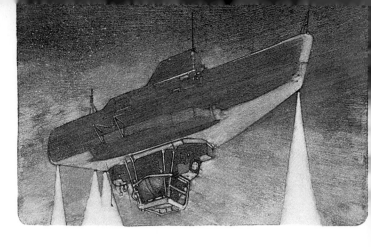

The number line helps us understand how to round numbers.

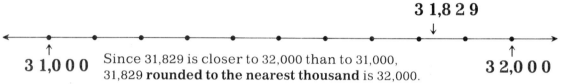

3 1,8 2 9
↓

3 1,0 0 0   Since 31,829 is closer to 32,000 than to 31,000, 31,829 **rounded to the nearest thousand** is 32,000.   3 2,0 0 0

We can round a number to any desired place as shown below.

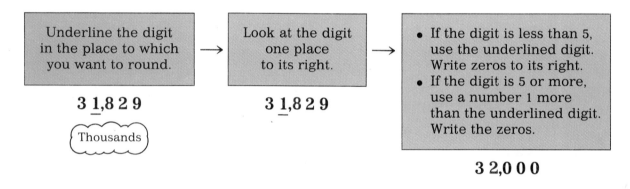

| Underline the digit in the place to which you want to round. | → | Look at the digit one place to its right. | → | • If the digit is less than 5, use the underlined digit. Write zeros to its right.
• If the digit is 5 or more, use a number 1 more than the underlined digit. Write the zeros. |

3 1,8 2 9

(Thousands)

3 1,8 2 9

3 2,0 0 0

Other Examples

9,645 rounded to the **nearest hundred** is 9,600.

9,645 rounded to the **nearest ten** is 9,650. (When the digit is **5**, we round **up**.)

74,962 rounded to the **nearest ten thousand** is 70,000.

$8.65 rounded to the **nearest dollar** is $9.

Warm Up   Round to the place indicated.

1. 683
(nearest ten)

2. 7,285
(nearest hundred)

3. 34,725
(nearest thousand)

4. $4.55
(nearest dollar)

5. 86,398
(nearest thousand)

6. 9,453
(nearest hundred)

7. $19.75
(nearest dollar)

8. 8,366
(nearest ten)

9. 85,382
(nearest ten thousand)

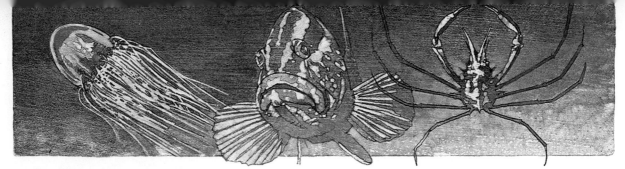

Practice Round to the nearest ten. Then round to the nearest hundred.

1. 764   **2.** 495   **3.** 976   **4.** 8,652   **5.** 9,374

6. 15,643   **7.** 27,386   **8.** 607   **9.** 9,338   **10.** 10,655

Round to the nearest thousand.

11. 4,374   **12.** 9,568   **13.** 10,246   **14.** 24,872   **15.** 37,594

16. 7,249   **17.** 18,076   **18.** 79,423   **19.** 236,472   **20.** 178,537

Round to the nearest ten thousand.

21. 74,652   **22.** 36,478   **23.** 35,350   **24.** 140,985   **25.** 68,370

26. 15,863   **27.** 267,840   **28.** 345,659   **29.** 229,780   **30.** 369,010

Round to the nearest dollar.

31. $3.45   **32.** $5.69   **33.** $9.51   **34.** $12.19   **35.** $36.79

36. Round 763,984 to the nearest hundred thousand.

37. Round 34,579,643 to the nearest million.

★ **38.** Give 4 numbers that give 16,000 when rounded to the nearest thousand.

★ **39.** A newspaper headline reported, "BATHYSCAPH REACHES A DEPTH OF 36,000 FEET." If this number has been rounded to the nearest thousand, what are the smallest and largest possibilities for the actual depth?

Skillkeeper

Add or subtract.

1.   50
     + 70

2.   90
     − 60

3. $70
     − 20

4.   800
     + 400

5.   1,500
     − 600

6. $9,000
     + 7,000

Estimating Sums and Differences Using Rounding

Mr. Gonzales owns a restaurant. He uses a calculator to find the answers to questions such as these. He makes estimates to see if the calculated answers are reasonable.

48 chairs in one area. 72 chairs in another. About how many?

Took in $318 at lunch. Took in $589 at dinner. About how much?

To estimate an answer, you can round and find a simpler sum or difference.

Round to the nearest ten.

$$\begin{array}{r} 4\,8 \to 5\,0 \\ +\,7\,2 \to +\,7\,0 \\ \hline \end{array}$$

Estimate: 120

About 120 chairs

Round to the nearest hundred.

$$\begin{array}{r} \$3\,1\,8 \to \$3\,0\,0 \\ +\,5\,8\,9 \to +\,6\,0\,0 \\ \hline \end{array}$$

Estimate: $900

About $900

Other Examples

Round to the nearest thousand.

$$\begin{array}{r} \$9,7\,6\,5 \to \$1\,0,0\,0\,0 \\ -\quad 3,4\,5\,6 \to -\quad 3,0\,0\,0 \\ \hline \end{array}$$

Estimate: $ 7,000

Round to the nearest dollar.

$$\begin{array}{r} \$1\,2.2\,5 \to \$1\,2 \\ -\quad 8.9\,5 \to -\quad 9 \\ \hline \end{array}$$

Estimate: $ 3

Warm Up Estimate the sums or differences.

Round to the nearest ten:

1. 87 + 55

2. 123 − 47

Round to the nearest hundred:

3. 389 + 841

4. 1,276 − 653

Round to the nearest thousand:

5. 8,638 + 9,299

6. 15,386 − 6,899

Round to the nearest dollar:

7. $9.27 + $5.89

8. $13.53 − $8.39

32

Practice Estimate by rounding to the nearest ten.

1.	94	2.	78	3.	123	4. 86 + 75
	+ 46		+ 45		− 58	5. 134 − 69

Estimate by rounding to the nearest hundred.

6.	456	7.	875	8.	1,358	9. 1,423 − 777
	+ 809		− 299		+ 367	10. 647 + 869

Estimate by rounding to the nearest thousand.

11.	15,562	12.	8,436	13.	11,906	14. 5,323 + 4,576
	− 9,274		+ 8,597		− 5,888	15. 13,099 − 3,644

Estimate by rounding to the nearest dollar.

16.	$6.75	17.	$15.39	18.	$13.64	19. $9.27 + $8.65
	+ 8.23		− 8.89		− 7.99	20. $16.72 − $8.54

Estimate. Decide whether to round to the nearest thousand or the nearest ten thousand.

21. 7,653 − 3,999　　　22. 4,432 + 6,579　　　23. 56,342 − 28,476

Mixed Applications

24. Advertising costs for a restaurant were $376 in May and $857 in June. Estimate the difference in those costs.

25. Restaurant income was as follows: January, $4,436; February, $4,737; March, $7,526. Estimate the total income.

More Practice, page 428, Set C

Think

Logical Reasoning

Start with 20 counters. Two players take turns and each may pick up 1, 2, or 3 counters. The player who picks up the last counter loses the game.

Try the game! Can you always win if you start first?

Math

QUESTION
DATA
PLAN
ANSWER
CHECK

Problem Solving: Using Estimation

The amount of electricity we use is measured in kilowatt-hours (kWh). A kilowatt-hour is the amount of electrical power needed to light ten 100-watt bulbs for 1 hour.

Estimate the answer to each problem. Then find the exact answer with a calculator. Does the calculator answer seem reasonable?

1. An air conditioner uses 805 kWh per month. A water heater uses 578 kWh. About how many more kilowatt-hours does the air conditioner use than the water heater?

2. A color TV uses 395 kWh in a year. A black and white TV uses 109 kWh. How many kilowatt-hours do the two TV sets use in a year?

3. A water heater uses 578 kWh per month, a refrigerator uses 141 kWh, and a clothes dryer uses 96 kWh. About how many kilowatt-hours is this per month altogether?

4. A space heater uses 6,936 kWh per year. An air conditioner uses 9,660 kWh. About how many more kilowatt-hours does the air conditioner use than the heater?

5. In a year, two television sets used 595 kWh of electricity. Electric lights used double this amount. About how many kilowatt-hours did the lights use?

6. For one month electricity costs are $3.68 for lights, $1.07 for a color TV, and $7.98 for a space heater. About how much do all three cost together?

7. The Pecks' electric bill for May was $14.79. The bill for June was $3.29 less than for May. The July bill was $4.82 more than the June bill. How much was the July bill?

8. **Strategy Practice** The first 300 kWh of electricity cost $11.89. The second 300 kWh cost $17.89. The total cost for 900 kWh was $56.67. What did the third 300 kwh cost? Hint: Choose the operations.

Problem Solving: Using a Data Bank

A **data bank** is any source of information or **data.**

A microcomputer (or larger computer) can store large amounts of data on disks. When specific data is needed, the computer searches for it and a printer prints it on paper. Data stored in a computer can be passed to another computer over the telephone. This makes it possible for people all over the world to use data stored in a central library, or data bank.

Starting on page 423, a **Data Bank** has been printed for your use. Use it to find the data needed to solve the problems below and other Data Bank problems throughout the book.

1. Estimate how much longer the L1011 is than the 737.

2. Estimate how much greater the usual gross weight of the 747 is than that of the 707.

3. Estimate the total number of passengers carried when a DC8, a DC9, and a DC10 leave on a trip.

4. Order the maximum lengths of all the transport planes listed in the Data Bank from the shortest to the longest.

5. Order the 6 fastest plane speeds from greatest to least. Include each different speed only once.

6. Estimate how much faster the maximum speed of the L1011 is than the speed of a plane that flies 695 km/h.

7. Order the gross weights of all the planes listed in the Data Bank from the heaviest plane to the lightest plane.

8. **Strategy Practice** There were 398 men, women, and children on a 747. There were two times as many women as there were men. There were 103 men. Estimate the number of children.

Adding Whole Numbers

The different kinds of animals drawn on the walls of caves in Europe were counted. In one sample, there were 275 deer or bison and 189 horses. How many of these kinds of animals were there?

Since we want to find the combined number of animals, we add.

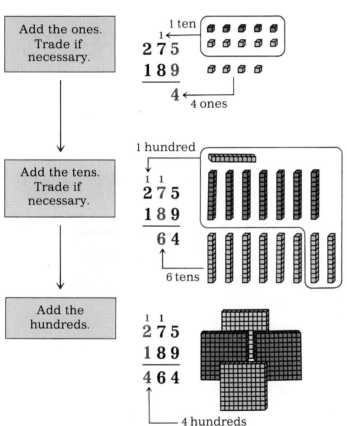

Add the ones. Trade if necessary.

```
      1 ten
    1
  2 7 5
  1 8 9
      4      4 ones
```

Add the tens. Trade if necessary.

```
  1 hundred
  1 1
  2 7 5
  1 8 9
    6 4
      6 tens
```

Add the hundreds.

```
  1 1
  2 7 5
  1 8 9
  4 6 4
      4 hundreds
```

There were 464 of the animals in the sample.

Other Examples

```
    1 1            1 1 1           1     1            1 1 1
    8 6 4          9,6 8 4         5 6,3 8 4          $ 1 6.7 9
  + 7 5 9        +   9 1 9       + 9 5,4 3 0        +     3.4 3
  ─────────      ─────────       ───────────        ───────────
  1,6 2 3        1 0,6 0 3       1 5 1,8 1 4         $ 2 0.2 2
```

To add money, add as with whole numbers. Then write the answer as dollars and cents.

Warm Up   Add.

1.	2.	3.	4.	5.
369 + 423	974 + 38	3,468 + 2,769	27,397 + 59,876	$15.26 + 27.98

Practice Add.

1. 864
   + 119

2. 368
   + 576

3. 965
   + 847

4. 759
   + 86

5. 8,468
   + 970

6. 5,436
   + 2,849

7. 7,652
   + 5,896

8. 9,786
   + 4,528

9. 9,657
   + 879

10. 16,756
    + 8,439

11. 18,765
    + 3,479

12. 24,621
    + 36,569

13. 38,570
    + 46,238

14. 79,684
    + 86,598

15. 98,729
    + 67,365

16. $7.59
    + 3.86

17. $25.68
    + 13.49

18. $54.95
    + 39.89

19. $327.58
    + 269.29

20. $896.69
    + 436.74

21. 754 + 398

22. 6,874 + 876

23. 9,863 + 7,476

24. 25,937 + 9,836

25. 34,943 + 26,875

26. 59,086 + 74,397

27. Estimate, then find: 6,743 + 8,635

28. Estimate, then find: 879 + 654

Mixed Applications

29. An art historian took 9,678 photos of cave art in Europe. She took 6,395 photos of cave art in Africa. How many photos did she take in all?

30. Write a question that can be answered using the data below. Then solve the problem.

    A collection of cave art had 978 pictures of elephants and 567 pictures of rhinoceroses.

More Practice, page 429, Set A

Think

Logical Reasoning

Every row, column, and diagonal of a MAGIC SQUARE has the same "magic sum."

152		
	155	
154		158

Draw a grid like this and complete a magic square using the numbers 151 through 159. What is the "magic sum?"

Math

Column Addition

Hal went on a 4-week canoe trip in Canada. His group traveled these distances on different lakes and rivers:

Trout Lake—97 km
Otter Lake—164 km
Contact Lake—26 km
Churchill River—285 km

How far did the group travel? Since we want to find the total distance traveled, we add.

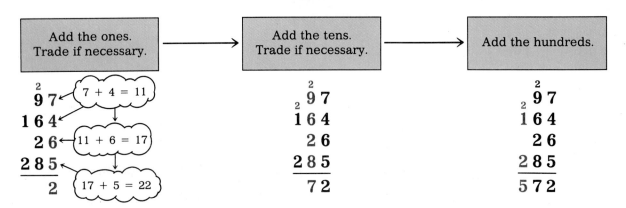

Add the ones. Trade if necessary.	Add the tens. Trade if necessary.	Add the hundreds.

```
  2                          2                        2
  9 7   7 + 4 = 11         2 9 7                    2 9 7
1 6 4                      1 6 4                    1 6 4
  2 6   11 + 6 = 17          2 6                      2 6
2 8 5                      2 8 5                    2 8 5
─────                      ─────                    ─────
    2   17 + 5 = 22          7 2                    5 7 2
```

The group traveled 572 km.

Other Examples

```
                  1 1              2 3 2              2 2 2 2 3
    5           6 7 4            7,4 3 7          $  8,6 5 0.7 9
    9           3 9 8            8,3 9 6             3,5 9 6.3 8
    7         + 4 0 7            2 4 8 0               4 7 4.6 7
  + 6         ───────         + 1 6,7 8 9         +  1 5,9 6 8.4 9
  ───           1,4 7 9        ─────────          ──────────────
    2 7                         3 3,1 0 2          $ 2 8,6 9 0.3 3
```

Warm Up   Add.

1.	2.	3.	4.	5.
276	5,963	18,365	78,349	$9,346.38
89	286	744	63,258	647.89
+ 147	4,932	7,638	91,340	521.70
	+ 694	+ 24,502	+ 67,536	+ 6,487.39

Practice Add.

1.	674	**2.**	576	**3.**	5,643	**4.**	17,863	**5.**	$236.59
	39		380		796		9,748		87.65
	+ 897		+ 998		+ 8,321		+ 3,675		+ 479.23

6.	9,863	**7.**	28,648	**8.**	96,700	**9.**	75,309	**10.**	$375.75
	469		7,379		68,488		64,752		463.23
	527		15,648		34,599		37,867		550.88
	+ 8,436		+ 32,571		+ 67,347		+ 59,346		+ 795.69

11. 23,468 + 847 + 9,635

12. 65,479 + 5,638 + 978 + 747

13. 68,666 + 7,435 + 8,627

14. 43,999 + 27,364 + 9,765

15. Estimate, then find the sum of 7,246, 8,907, and 3,549.

Mixed Applications

16. Make up a story problem about this map of 3 lakes. Then solve the problem.

17. Linda's group took these canoe trips: Hale Lake—119 km; Hunter Bay—57 km; Hidden Lake—96 km; Lynx Lake—9 km; Otter Lake—274 km. How far did the group travel?

18. Is the total area of the five Great Lakes more than or less than 275,000 km² (square kilometers)? Estimate first. Then find the exact answer. Compare it with your estimate.

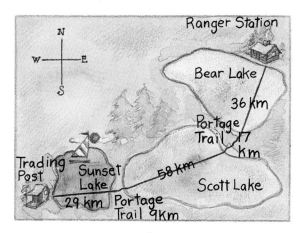

Areas of the Great Lakes (km²)

Superior 82,414	Huron 59,596
Michigan 58,016	Erie 25,719
Ontario 19,477	

Think

Mental Math

If the letter A = $1, B = $2, C = $3, . . . , Z = $26, what is the "value" of a name?

S U S A N
$19 $21 $19 $1 $14

"Susan" has a value of $74. List the letter values. Use mental math to find the value of your name.

Can you find some names worth $100 or more?

Math

Subtracting Whole Numbers

A recent record for distance traveled in a large hot-air balloon was 611 km. The record for a small hot-air balloon was 369 km. How much farther did the large balloon travel?

Since we want to compare the distances, we subtract.

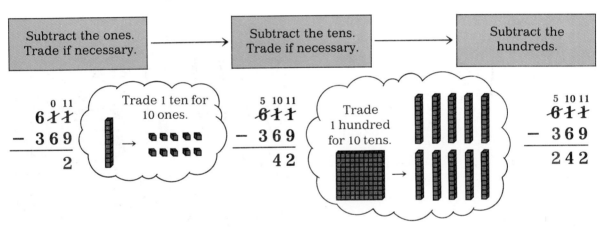

Subtract the ones. Trade if necessary.	→	Subtract the tens. Trade if necessary.	→	Subtract the hundreds.

The large balloon traveled 242 km farther.

Other Examples

$$
\begin{array}{r}
{\scriptstyle 7\ 12\ 15} \\
8\,3\,5 \\
-\ 7\,9\,6 \\
\hline
3\,9
\end{array}
\qquad
\begin{array}{r}
{\scriptstyle 5\ 13\ 11\ 11} \\
6\,4\,2\,1 \\
-\ \ \ 9\,7\,5 \\
\hline
5{,}4\,4\,6
\end{array}
\qquad
\begin{array}{r}
{\scriptstyle 4\ 12\ 16} \\
7\,5{,}3\,6\,4 \\
-\ 3\,4{,}7\,8\,0 \\
\hline
4\,0{,}5\,8\,4
\end{array}
\qquad
\begin{array}{r}
{\scriptstyle 5\ 12\ 11\ 15} \\
\$\,6\,3.2\,5 \\
-\ \ \ 2\,4.6\,9 \\
\hline
\$\,3\,8.5\,6
\end{array}
$$

To subtract money, subtract as with whole numbers. Then write the answer as dollars and cents.

Warm Up   Subtract. Check by adding.

1.	2.	3.	4.	5.
847 − 269	653 − 576	8,637 − 789	83,216 − 29,457	$37.75 − 19.98

Practice Subtract.

1.	527 − 188	**2.**	963 − 879	**3.**	7,432 − 865	**4.**	8,276 − 5,498	**5.**	6,213 − 5,654
6.	4,136 − 1,874	**7.**	7,238 − 6,450	**8.**	16,342 − 9,237	**9.**	27,641 − 19,506	**10.**	56,375 − 37,588
11.	87,465 − 59,387	**12.**	93,274 − 8,680	**13.**	$9.75 − 3.98	**14.**	$18.25 − 7.56	**15.**	$256.45 − 97.75

16. 742 − 578   **17.** 9,534 − 806   **18.** 7,316 − 4,857

19. 17,386 − 9,419   **20.** 78,211 − 65,879   **21.** $56.32 − $38.49

22. Estimate, then find: 7,219 − 3,899   **23.** Estimate, then find: 925 − 478

Mixed Applications

24. The record altitude (height above sea level) for an AX-2 balloon was 3,477 m. The record for an AX-3 balloon was 4,642 m. How much greater was the second record?

25. Make up the missing information and solve the problem. An old record distance for a helium balloon was 3,339 km. What was the distance flown by the balloon that set the new record?

26. DATA BANK How much greater is the altitude for an AX-10 balloon than for an AX-7 balloon? than for an AX-3 balloon? (See Data Bank, page 425.)

Think

Logical Reasoning

Copy each problem and supply the missing digits.

A.	**B.**	**C.**	**D.**
▮,6▮▮▮ + 5,▮1 2 9,5 0 6	▮,6 1▮ − 2,8▮9 2,▮7 8	▮,▮7▮ − 3▮6 7,6 7 8	▮,3▮9 + 6,5 4▮ ▮0,▮0 2

Math

Subtracting with Zeros

If we follow the safety rules in our sports activities, we can have fun with fewer accidents!

How many more injuries per 100,000 participants were there in baseball than in soccer?

Sports Injuries
(per one hundred thousand participants in a recent year)

Baseball—9,807	Soccer—4,158
Football—9,587	Snow Skiing—1,101
Ice Hockey—8,082	Ice Skating—505
Basketball—5,383	Tennis—429

Since we want to compare the two numbers, we subtract.

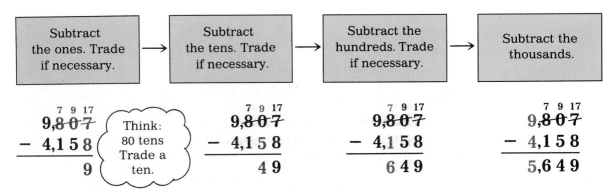

Subtract the ones. Trade if necessary.	→	Subtract the tens. Trade if necessary.	→	Subtract the hundreds. Trade if necessary.	→	Subtract the thousands.

```
   7 9 17              7 9 17            7 9 17            7 9 17
  9,8̶0̶7̶              9,8̶0̶7̶            9,8̶0̶7̶            9,8̶0̶7̶
- 4,1 5 8           - 4,1 5 8         - 4,1 5 8         - 4,1 5 8
─────────          ─────────         ─────────         ─────────
        9               4 9             6 4 9           5,6 4 9
```

Think: 80 tens Trade a ten.

There were 5,649 more injuries per 100,000 participants in baseball than in soccer.

Other Examples

```
   69 10             6 15 10           4 9 9 12          5 9 9 9 10
  7̶0̶0̶              7,̶6̶0̶5            5,̶0̶0̶2̶           6̶0̶,0̶0̶0̶
-  3 5 6           - 2,9 7 2         - 2,6 8 4         - 4 6,5 2 1
─────────          ─────────         ─────────         ───────────
    3 4 4             4,6 3 3           2,3 1 8           1 3,4 7 9
```

Warm Up   Subtract. Check by adding.

1.	508	**2.**	900	**3.**	7,065	**4.**	8,007	**5.**	36,000
	− 169		− 367		− 3,897		− 3,669		− 17,386

42

Practice Subtract.

1.	702 − 256	**2.**	600 − 176	**3.**	5,303 − 2,748	**4.**	4,704 − 2,381	**5.**	3,024 − 867
6.	6,004 − 5,789	**7.**	8,000 − 4,237	**8.**	4,009 − 2,765	**9.**	2,900 − 1,435	**10.**	26,082 − 7,395
11.	98,004 − 67,385	**12.**	80,000 − 36,594	**13.**	$10.05 − 3.69	**14.**	$30.00 − 17.49	**15.**	$40.27 − 23.79

16. 608 − 79

17. 900 − 462

18. 5,036 − 2,178

19. 6,805 − 3,677

20. 7,004 − 5,666

21. 42,000 − 36,784

22. Estimate, then find how many more 16,201 is than 8,898.

Mixed Applications

Use the table on page 42 for problems 23 and 24.

23. How many more injuries per 100,000 participants were there in ice hockey than in basketball?

24. How much more or less is the number of injuries in basketball and soccer combined than in football?

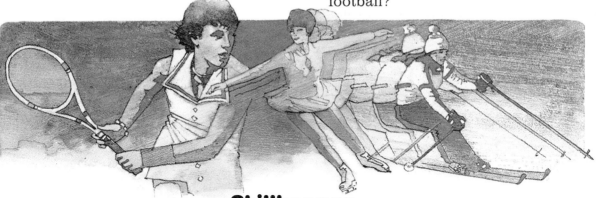

Use the table on page 42 for problems 23 and 24.

Skillkeeper

Use place value to tell what each red digit means.

1. 35,278   **2.** 420,356   **3.** 634,219   **4.** 75,341,892

Write the standard number.

5. 30,000 + 6,000 + 500 + 10 + 9   **6.** 200,000 + 9,000 + 300 + 40 + 1

7. 5,000,000,000 + 2,000,000 + 8,000 + 700 + 8

Estimating Sums: Using Front-End Estimation

We can estimate sums using a technique called **front-end estimation**. First add the "front-end" digits and then use the rest of the number to make a closer estimate.

Example 1

Add the front-end digits.   Make a closer estimate.

$$\begin{array}{r} \underline{5}\ 6\ 8 \\ \underline{4}\ 3\ 5 \\ \underline{2}\ 8\ 7 \\ \underline{3}\ 1\ 9 \end{array}$$ 1,400

5 **6 8** ← About 100
4 **3 5** ←
2 **8 7** ← About 100
3 1 9 ←

Final estimate: About **1,600**

Example 2

Add the front-end digits: $\underline{3}56 + \underline{4}75 + \underline{7}49$ About 1,400

Make a closer estimate: $3\underline{56} + 4\underline{75} + 7\underline{49}$ Final estimate: About **1,600**

About 200

Practice   Estimate. Use the front-end method.

1. 468 + 726	**2.** 383 + 527	**3.** 478 388 + 695	**4.** 985 423 + 98	**5.** 658 475 + 845
6. $9.58 + 4.45 About $1	**7.** $6.84 + 7.24	**8.** $9.06 5.23 + 7.75	**9.** $8.57 6.36 + 4.29	**10.** $6.47 3.89 + 7.58

11. 735 + 869   **12.** 459 + 803 + 943   **13.** 674 + 287 + 828 + 717

14. $8.67 + $6.45   **15.** $12.24 + $8.86 + $5.78   **16.** 945 + 238 + 754 + 379

Mixed Applications Estimate the answer using the front-end method.

17. Tim's class collected 439 aluminum cans to recycle. Jill's class collected 871 cans, and Nan's class collected 664. How many cans did the three classes collect?

Problem Solving: Mixed Practice

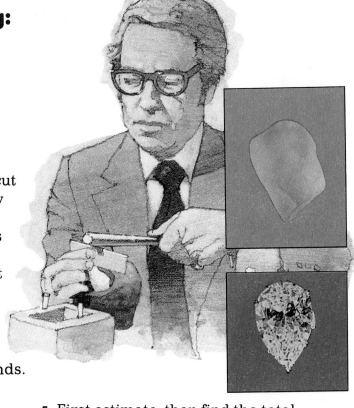

Diamond cutting is a very time-consuming process. Every step must be done with great care. The cutter must decide the best way to cut the stone to make the gem as nearly perfect as possible. The weights of diamonds and other precious stones are given in units called carats. Before it was cut, the world's largest rough diamond, the *Cullinan* diamond, weighed 3,106 carats.

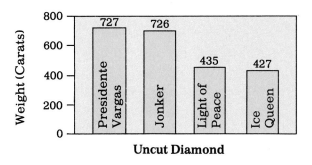

Solve these problems about diamonds.

1. Two famous uncut diamonds were the *Star of Sierra Leone,* which weighed 968 carats, and the *Great Mogul,* which weighed 787 carats. First estimate, then find the total weight of these diamonds. How much less or greater is your estimate than the exact total?

2. The *Excelsior* diamond was the world's second-largest rough diamond. It weighed 995 carats. How much less did it weigh than the 3,106-carat *Cullinan*?

3. A good half-carat diamond might cost $600. What would be the cost of 8 of these diamonds?

4. The *Excelsior* diamond was found in South Africa in 1893. How many years ago was this?

5. First estimate, then find the total weight of the diamonds shown on the bar graph. How much greater or less is your estimate than the exact total?

Bar graph: Weight (Carats) vs. Uncut Diamond

Uncut Diamond	Weight (Carats)
Presidente Vargas	727
Jonker	726
Light of Peace	435
Ice Queen	427

6. **Strategy Practice** A cutter started with an uncut stone that weighed 726 carats. The cutter got 8 gems from it. The largest of these was 128 carats and the smallest was 9 carats. How many carats of the rough diamond were lost in the cutting if the other gems averaged 60 carats each?

Problem Solving:
Using a Calculator

You can open a checking account by depositing money in a bank or a savings and loan company. You fill out a **deposit slip** when you put money in your account. After you write a check, you record the amount of the check in a checkbook record.

Study these examples. Then use a calculator to solve the problems below.

DEPOSIT SLIP		
List Checks by Bank Number	Dollars	Cents
Currency	96	00
Coin	4	75
Checks	467	98
Total Deposit	568	73

Checkbook Record

Check number	Date	Description of transaction	Payment	Deposit	Balance
	2/15			1,000.00	1,000.00
101	2/20	Dr. Ruth Hauser	50.00		950.00
102	2/22	Genuine Insurance Co.	325.00		625.00
103	2/26	Corner Grocery	47.87		577.13
	2/27	Deposit		100.00	677.13

1. Jean filled out a deposit slip with these amounts: Currency, $156.00; Coin, $4.96; Checks, $388.36. What was the total amount deposited?

2. A banker received a deposit slip with this information: Currency $5,976.00; Checks $3,749.56; Total $10,765.25. The amount of coins was blotted out. What was the amount of coins?

3. Mr. Gilmore had a balance of $3,675.54 in his account. What was his new balance after a deposit of $2,988.97?

4. Ms. Wilmont had a balance of $6,273.08 in her account. What was her new balance after she wrote a check for $3,495.79?

5. **Strategy Practice**   Mr. Rich started with a balance of $5,362. He wrote a check for $864.73, deposited $1,729.58, and wrote another check for $1,167.39. What is the largest check he can write next if he wants to keep a balance of no less than $1,000?

Roman Numerals

Roman numerals use alphabet letters to name numbers. They were developed by the Romans many centuries ago and are still sometimes used today. The values of the basic symbols are added or subtracted to show all numbers.

Basic Symbols	I	V	X	L	C	D	M
	1	5	10	50	100	500	1,000

Using Addition	II	XX	CC	MM	VI	LX	DC
	2	20	200	2,000	6	60	600

5 – 1

Using Subtraction	IV	IX	XL	XC	CD	CM
	4	9	40	90	400	900

Practice Write as a standard number.

Subtract when a letter with a smaller value is to the left of a letter with a larger value.

1. VII   **2.** XIII   **3.** LV   **4.** CL   **5.** DXX

6. XIV   **7.** LIX   **8.** XLIV   **9.** XCI   **10.** CCCIV

11. MMMD   **12.** XXIX   **13.** CCXCV   **14.** MCDXCII   **15.** MMCMLXIV

Write as a Roman numeral.

16. 3   **17.** 8   **18.** 11   **19.** 15   **20.** 21   **21.** 56

22. 54   **23.** 39   **24.** 204   **25.** 549   **26.** 92   **27.** 45

28. 454   **29.** 961   **30.** 747   **31.** 1,176   **32.** 2,001   **33.** 3,336

34. Write your age and the current year using Roman numerals.

★ **35.** The date 1888 uses 13 letters as a Roman numeral. Can you write it?

★ **36.** A bar over a basic symbol multiplies its value by 1,000. For example, $\overline{V} = 5,000$. Can you write the standard number for $\overline{X}DCXL$?

Problem-Solving Strategy: Guess and Check

To solve a problem like this, you must do more than just decide whether to add, subtract, multiply, or divide. A problem-solving **strategy** which will help you is called

Guess and Check

Try This Nancy spent $78 for 10 tickets to a play. The main floor seats cost $9 and the balcony seats cost $5. How many of each kind did she buy?

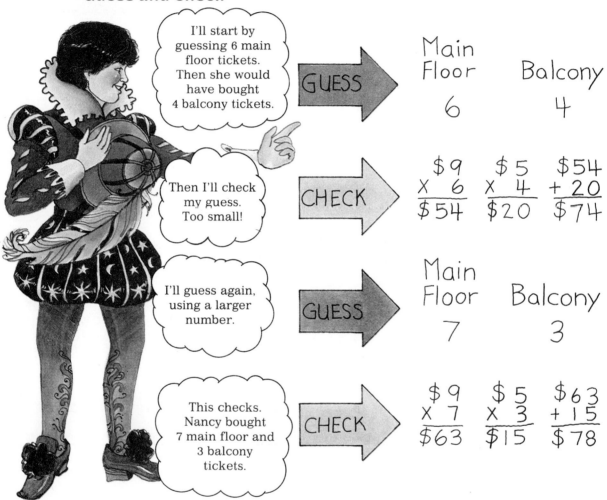

I'll start by guessing 6 main floor tickets. Then she would have bought 4 balcony tickets.

GUESS

Main Floor — 6   Balcony — 4

Then I'll check my guess. Too small!

CHECK

$$\begin{array}{cc} \$9 \\ \times\ 6 \\ \hline \$54 \end{array} \quad \begin{array}{cc} \$5 \\ \times\ 4 \\ \hline \$20 \end{array} \quad \begin{array}{cc} \$54 \\ +\ 20 \\ \hline \$74 \end{array}$$

I'll guess again, using a larger number.

GUESS

Main Floor — 7   Balcony — 3

This checks. Nancy bought 7 main floor and 3 balcony tickets.

CHECK

$$\begin{array}{cc} \$9 \\ \times\ 7 \\ \hline \$63 \end{array} \quad \begin{array}{cc} \$5 \\ \times\ 3 \\ \hline \$15 \end{array} \quad \begin{array}{cc} \$63 \\ +\ 15 \\ \hline \$78 \end{array}$$

Solve.

1. A test had 10 questions worth 3 points and 10 worth 5 points. Scott had 15 correct answers and a total score of 57 points. How many questions of each kind did he answer correctly?

2. Paula is 6 years old. Her Uncle Steve is 4 times as old. How old will Paula be when she is half as old as her uncle?

Chapter Review-Test

Give the digits of this number in the place or period named.

$$4, 3\ 6\ 8, 5\ 9\ 7, 1\ 0\ 2$$

1. millions place

2. ten thousands place

3. hundreds place

4. billions place

5. millions period

6. thousands period

7. Write in standard form: 40,000 + 200 + 8,000 + 9 + 30.

8. Write in expanded form: 5,674.

Write >, <, or = for each ▒ .

9. 8,888 ▒ 999

10. 9,999 ▒ 10,000

11. 378,296 ▒ 378,902

Estimate. Round as indicated.

12. Nearest ten

```
   63
+  89
```

13. Nearest hundred

```
  705
- 296
```

14. Nearest thousand

```
  8,016
+ 6,786
```

15. Nearest dollar

```
$12.89
-  5.24
```

Add or subtract.

16.
```
  6,784
+ 2,597
```

17.
```
  15,365
-  9,407
```

18.
```
  603
- 286
```

19.
```
  65,384
   9,768
+ 23,602
```

20.
```
  36,748
     899
+  3,407
```

21.
```
$57.34
+ 26.59
```

22.
```
  8,003
- 4,657
```

23.
```
$186.42
-  97.68
```

24. 964 + 83,795 + 6,948

25. Estimate using front-end estimation: 467 + 234 + 388 + 618

26. Write 454 as a Roman numeral.

27. Write MLXVI as a standard number.

28. A 747 flies from San Francisco to Chicago and from there to New York. It is 2,990 km from San Francisco to Chicago, and 1,147 km from Chicago to New York. How far does the plane travel?

29. Mrs. Blake has a balance of $3,106 in a checking account. Then she writes a check for $967, makes a deposit of $489, and writes another check for $2,627. How much does she have left in her account?

Another Look

Place Value

Periods

Billions Millions Thousands Ones

5 8 3 , 2 7 6 , 4 9 1 ,5 0 8

These places repeat in each period.

hundreds ——
tens ——
ones ——

Comparing

Find the first place where the digits are different.

↓   ↓
8 4,**9** 6 5   8 4,**8** 9 5

> greater than
< less than

9 > 8 , so

84,965 > 84,895

Rounding

Find the digit to the right of the place to which you want to round.

- If the digit is less than 5, round down.
- If the digit is 5 or greater, round up.

6,**7** 5 4   6,754 rounded to the
  ↑   nearest hundred is 6,800.

Adding, Subtracting

Think about pennies and add as with whole numbers.

Write the answer in dollars and cents.

```
  3,9 4 5 ¢
+ 2,4 1 9 ¢
```

4 thousands = 400 tens
400 tens = 399 tens and 10 ones

```
  $ 3 9.4 5
+   2 4.1 9
  $ 6 3.6 4
```

```
    3 9 9 13
  4,0̶0̶3̶
- 1,8 4 7
  2,1 5 6
```

Read each number. Tell what each red digit means.

1. 5,3**6**8

2. 25,**9**75

3. 864,3**6**2

4. 7,**3**65,947

5. 48,**9**73,862

6. **6**73,829,437

7. 9,4**6**5,382,647

8. 54,**3**84,107,298

Write >, <, or = for each ||||| .

9. 3,568 ||||| 3,509

10. 27,462 ||||| 2,846

11. 999 ||||| 1,000

12. 368,247 ||||| 368,251

Round to the nearest place named.

13. 294 (tens)

14. 842 (hundreds)

15. 7,536 (thousands)

16. 384,596 (ten thousands)

17. $49.09 (nearest dollar)

Add or subtract.

18.
```
  876
+ 497
```

19.
```
  57,347
+ 29,208
```

20.
```
  5,365
- 2,819
```

21.
```
  8,002
- 5,496
```

22.
```
  $25.75
+  19.95
```

23.
```
  $36.50
-  19.98
```

50

Computer Literacy

Modern computers use these ideas to remember and work with numbers:

A switch **on** can represent 1.
A switch **off** can represent 0.

The numbers 0 and 1 are called **binary digits** or **bits.**

For example, if we group by twos instead of by our usual tens and use place value, a panel of lights can show a number.

two × two × two ×   two × two × two ×   two × two × twos   two × twos   twos   ones
two × twos place (32)   twos place (16)   place (8)   place (4)   place (2) place (1)

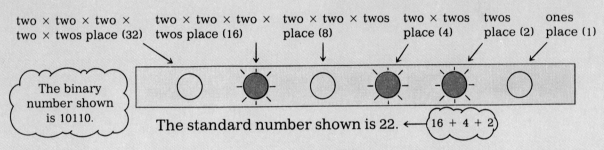

The binary number shown is 10110.

The standard number shown is 22. ← 16 + 4 + 2

What standard number is shown by each panel of lights?

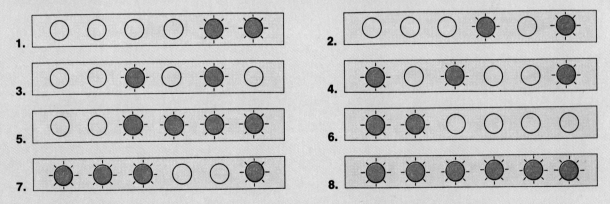

1.
2.
3.
4.
5.
6.
7.
8.

Can you draw a panel of lights to show these numbers?

9. 4   **10.** 9   **11.** 17   **12.** 26   ★ **13.** 100

51

Cumulative Review

Add or subtract.

1.
```
   7     A 15
 + 9     B 17
         C 16
         D not given
```

2.
```
  13     A 9
 - 5     B 6
         C 7
         D not given
```

Multiply or divide.

3. 9)54
```
         A 7
         B 6
         C 60
         D not given
```

4.
```
   8     A 48
 × 6     B 56
         C 42
         D not given
```

Give the standard numeral.

5. nine hundred fifteen thousand, two hundred thirty-one

   A 915,031   B 915,231
   C 900,151   D not given

6. 3,000,000 + 70,000 + 6,000 + 800 + 50 + 3

   A 3,706,853
   B 3,760,853
   C 3,076,853
   D not given

Add or subtract.

7.
```
   32     A 41
 -  9     B 23
          C 33
          D not given
```

8.
```
   57     A 130
 +83      B 134
          C 140
          D not given
```

9.
```
   417    A 219
 - 198    B 319
          C 229
          D not given
```

10.
```
 $27.50    A $63.48
 + 46.98   B $74.38
           C $73.42
           D not given
```

11.
```
 $40.15    A $30.32
 - 9.87    B $30.28
           C $30.38
           D not given
```

12. Irina bought a new bike horn that cost $3.79 and a new seat cushion that cost $6.55. What was the cost for both items?
   A $10.34   B $9.24
   C $9.34   D not given

13. Pat jogged 4 km each day for 7 days. How many kilometers was that in all?
   A 11   B 24
   C 28   D not given

3

Decimals: Addition and Subtraction

In some areas of the earth, there is hot rock close to the earth's surface. When water sinks into the ground, it is heated by these rocks. The water often returns to the surface as steam. This hot water or steam is a source of energy. It is called *geothermal energy* because *geo-* means "earth" and *thermal* means "heat."

Several countries use geothermal power. It is not usually a major source of power, however. In the United States, for example, it represents only 0.01 of our total energy use.

In Iceland, however, geothermal energy is very important. About 0.75 of the Icelanders have inexpensive central heating from geothermal energy. Geothermal energy also provides Icelanders with electricity, power for manufacturing, and heat for their greenhouses and swimming pools.

cimal Place Value: Tenths and Hundredths

Carla and Vince started stamp collections. Carla has filled
1 whole page and part of another page. Vince has filled less
than 1 whole page. How can they use fractions and decimals
to tell the number of pages they have filled?

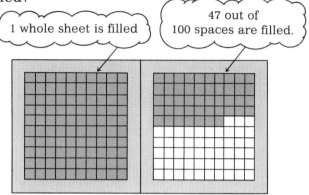

1 whole sheet is filled

47 out of
100 spaces are filled.

Using a fraction   **Using a decimal**

$$1\frac{47}{100} \quad = \quad 1.47$$

We read: "one and forty-seven
hundredths"

Carla can say she filled 1.47 pages.

Carla

Using a fraction   **Using a decimal**

$$\frac{7}{10} \quad = \quad 0.7$$

or

$$\frac{70}{100} \quad = \quad 0.70$$

$$\frac{70}{100} = \frac{7}{10} \text{ or } 0.70 = 0.7$$

We read: "seven **tenths**" or "seventy
hundredths"

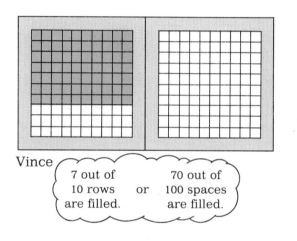

Vince

7 out of
10 rows   or
are filled.

70 out of
100 spaces
are filled.

Vince can say he filled 0.7 or 0.70 pages.

Other Examples

	ones	tenths	hundredths
We think:	0	0	8

We write: 0.08

We read: "eight hundredths"

	ones	tenths	hundredths
We think:	2	3	

We write: 2.3

We read: "two and three tenths"

Write and read the decimal
for the amount shaded in
each picture.

1.

2.

3.

4.

5.

6.

Use place value to tell what each red digit means.

7. 16.1   **8.** 0.49   **9.** 12.15   **10.** 8.08

11. 23.44   **12.** 0.02   **13.** 0.60   **14.** 4.25

Write the decimal.

15. thirty-two hundredths   **16.** five and two tenths   **17.** seven hundredths

18. one and fifty hundredths   **19.** nine tenths   **20.** twelve and twelve hundredths

Write the word name for
each decimal.

21. 0.4   **22.** 0.63

23. 1.25   **24.** 0.05

25. 2.10   **26.** 0.58

27. 1.07   **28.** 5.3

Think

A Line Segment Puzzle

Draw 4 straight line segments
to pass through all 9 dots. Each
segment must be connected to
an endpoint of at least one
other segment.

• • •

• • •

• • •

Math

Thousandths

A **micrometer** is a tool that can be used to measure objects very accurately. For example, with a metric micrometer, Rhonda found that the thickness of a leaf was 0.243 cm. We can use graph paper as a model to show this decimal.

We see this model:

We think:

0	2	4	3
ones	tenths	hundredths	thousandths

We write: 0.243   **We read:** "two hundred forty-three **thousandths**"

We write in expanded form: 0.2 + 0.04 + 0.003

Read each decimal. Use place value to tell what each red digit means.

1. 4.286
2. 0.753
3. 0.042
4. 1.54
5. 7.008

6. 25.34
7. 4.622
8. 18.531
9. 0.427
10. 0.050

Write in expanded form.

11. 0.356
12. 4.23
13. 0.875
14. 7.068
15. 24.79

Write the word name for each decimal.

16. 0.323
17. 0.041
18. 1.21
19. 1.210
20. 8.62

21. 12.602
22. 1.003
23. 0.037
24. 14.206
25. 32.275

Write the decimal.

26. four hundred twenty-five thousandths
27. one and one hundred eight thousandths
28. thirty-nine thousandths

56

Place Value Through Hundred-Thousandths

Ms. Reilly uses her home computer to calculate and record the average amount of gas used in her home each day. The screen shows the daily average use for the three coldest months. What was the average number of therms (units of heat) used per day in January?

```
MONTH    AVERAGE NUMBER OF
         THERMS USED PER DAY

DECEMBER    3.97651
JANUARY     4.03682
FEBRUARY    4.35768
```

We think:

4	0	3	6	8	2
ones	tenths	hundredths	thousandths	ten-thousandths	hundred-thousandths

We write: 4.03682

We read: "four and three thousand, six hundred eighty-two **hundred-thousandths**"

The average number of therms used per day in January was 4.03682.

Read each decimal. Use place value to tell what each red digit means.

1. 6.205
2. 0.72364
3. 15.3834
4. 9.45002

5. 9.2
6. 126.365
7. 18.006
8. 0.99999

Write in expanded form.

9. 0.0157
10. 1.43628
11. 0.56329
12. 4.4035

Write the word name for each decimal.

13. 0.4256
14. 1.2005
15. 0.00645
16. 14.02

17. 6.007
18. 8.45
19. 12.0054
20. 0.32624

Write the decimal.

21. nine hundred forty-five thousandths
22. five and fifteen ten-thousandths
23. two hundred six hundred-thousandths

Comparing and Ordering Decimals

A welder is cutting pieces of steel bars to a length as close as possible to 18.125 in. (inches). The welder has cut five pieces. Is piece 1 longer or shorter than piece 2?

Welder's Record Sheet

Piece Number	Length
1	18.186
2	18.1806
3	18.085
4	18.0728
5	18.1472

Compare the length of piece 1 to the length of piece 2 to decide which of the two pieces has the greater length.

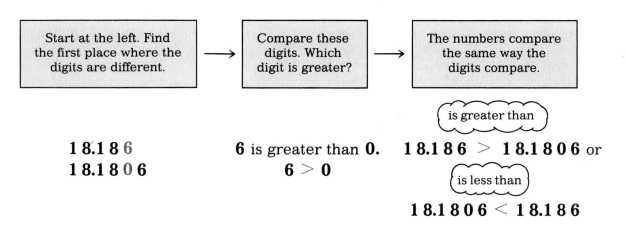

Start at the left. Find the first place where the digits are different.	→	Compare these digits. Which digit is greater?	→	The numbers compare the same way the digits compare.

18.186
18.1806

6 is greater than 0.
6 > 0

is greater than
18.186 > 18.1806 or
is less than
18.1806 < 18.186

The length of piece 1 is greater than the length of piece 2.

Order the lengths of the pieces by listing them from greatest to least. Do this by comparing them two at a time.

18.186 ← greatest
18.1806
18.1472
18.085
18.0728 ← least

Warm Up   Write >, <, or = for each ▥ .

1. 6.5 ▥ 6.2

2. 26.4 ▥ 27.4

3. 0.5 ▥ 0.62

4. 423 ▥ 420

5. 0.052 ▥ 0.0520

6. 6.07353 ▥ 6.074

7. 0.009 ▥ 0.02

8. 10.01 ▥ 100.1

Practice Write, >, <, or = for each ▥ .

1. 7.8 ▥ 7.7

2. 0.67 ▥ 0.68

3. 0.742 ▥ 7.40

4. 50.3 ▥ 5.30

5. 9.32 ▥ 9.3

6. 832 ▥ 840

7. 16.2 ▥ 6.2

8. 0.006 ▥ 0.0060

9. 0.1 ▥ 0.01

10. 0.977 ▥ 0.978

11. 3.0740 ▥ 3.047

12. 9.500 ▥ 9.6

13. 0.76 ▥ 0.8

14. 14.050 ▥ 14.05

15. 0.503 ▥ 0.508

16. 4.7 ▥ 4.6999

17. 2.0234 ▥ 2.0243

18. 0.00006 ▥ 0.0006

19. 12.0640 ▥ 1.064

20. 63.95 ▥ 63.81

21. 40.2 ▥ 40.02

22. 0.7502 ▥ 0.752

23. 165.25 ▥ 165.3

24. 400.5 ▥ 40.55

25. Order the hole sizes from greatest to least.

Drill Sizes	
Drill number	Hole size (in inches)
1	0.531
2	0.422
3	0.484
4	0.594
5	0.578

26. Order the diameters of the wires from least to greatest.

Electrical Wires for Cars	
Wire number	Diameter (in inches)
1	0.01
2	0.0126
3	0.007
4	0.0179
5	0.0089

27. Which of the five lengths of pieces shown in the table on page 58 were less than 18.125 in.?

28. A welder cut a steel rod that measured 12.5043 in. The needed length was 12.543 in. Was the piece cut longer or shorter than the needed length?

Think

Logical Reasoning

Use all of the digits 5, 1, 6, 2, 0, and 4 to write these numbers. Use each digit only once.

1. the largest number less than 1

2. the smallest number less than 1

3. the largest number between 5 and 6

Math

Rounding Decimals

The measurements of a bowling pin are very precise. For example, the neck of a bowling pin has a diameter of 4.564 cm. What is this diameter to the nearest **tenth** of a centimeter?

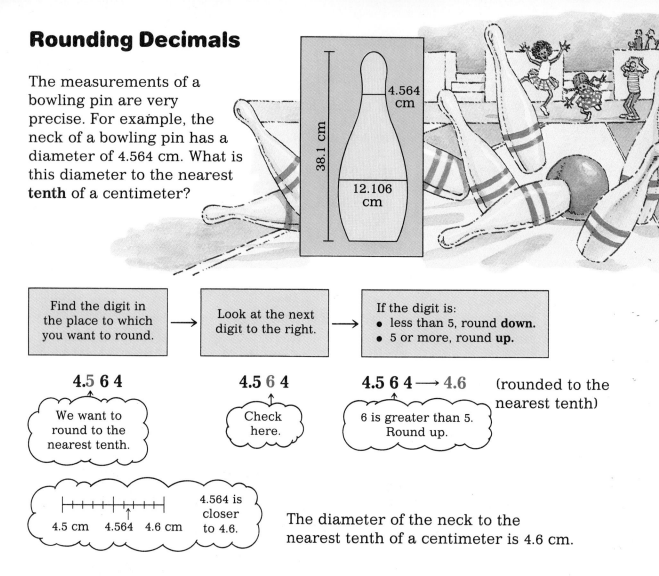

| Find the digit in the place to which you want to round. | → | Look at the next digit to the right. | → | If the digit is:
• less than 5, round **down.**
• 5 or more, round **up.** |

4.5 6 4

We want to round to the nearest tenth.

4.5 6 4

Check here.

4.5 6 4 → 4.6

6 is greater than 5. Round up.

(rounded to the nearest tenth)

4.5 cm   4.564   4.6 cm

4.564 is closer to 4.6.

The diameter of the neck to the nearest tenth of a centimeter is 4.6 cm.

Other Examples

Nearest **whole number**

2.3 7 → 2

3 < 5, round down.

Nearest **hundredth**

0.0 1 5 → 0.0 2

5 or more, round up.

Nearest **tenth**

1 2.8 0 2 → 1 2.8

0 < 5, round down.

Warm Up

Round to the nearest tenth.

1. 0.74   **2.** 6.553   **3.** 0.98

Round to the nearest hundredth.

4. 7.006   **5.** 0.519   **6.** 12.2021

Round to the nearest whole number.

7. 3.72   **8.** 21.08   **9.** 0.59   **10.** 19.6

Practice Round to the nearest tenth.

1. 2.67	**2.** 7.319	**3.** 0.884	**4.** 48.42
5. 365.55	**6.** 0.093	**7.** 1.89	**8.** 32.462
9. 4.95	**10.** 0.504	**11.** 12.85	**12.** 49.96

Round to the nearest hundredth.

13. 5.478	**14.** 2.828	**15.** 0.258	**16.** 0.048
17. 14.172	**18.** 165.642	**19.** 7.445	**20.** 18.066
21. 0.514	**22.** 64.064	**23.** 2.996	**24.** 3.502

Round to the nearest whole number.

25. 8.27	**26.** 42.81	**27.** 69.866	**28.** 2.845
29. 54.2	**30.** 10.904	**31.** 76.05	**32.** 146.49
33. 0.705	**34.** 9.824	**35.** 8.083	**36.** 12.457

37. What is the height of the bowling pin shown on page 60 to the nearest whole centimeter?

38. The diameter of a bowling pin at its widest point is 12.106 cm. What is this measurement to the nearest hundredth of a centimeter?

39. What is the diameter of a bowling pin at its narrowest point, to the nearest hundredth of a centimeter? (See page 60.)

40. DATA BANK What is the length of a bowling alley lane to the nearest meter? (See the Data Bank, page 426.)

Skillkeeper

Use place value to tell what each red digit means.

1. 3,549	**2.** 27,830
3. 216,349	**4.** 5,391,672
5. 736,294	**6.** 86,792
7. 94,026,153	**8.** 864,301

More Practice, page 430, Set C

Estimating Sums and Differences: Using Rounding

The planet Jupiter takes 11.862 years to revolve around the sun one time. Saturn takes 29.458 years. Estimate how many more years it takes Saturn to revolve around the sun.

Since we want to compare the times, we subtract.

To **estimate** the difference, we can round each number to the **nearest whole number** and subtract.

$$
\begin{array}{r}
2\,9.4\,5\,8 \rightarrow 2\,9 \\
-\ 1\,1.8\,6\,2 \rightarrow -\ 1\,2 \\
\hline
1\,7 \leftarrow \text{estimate}
\end{array}
$$

It takes Saturn about 17 more years to revolve around the sun than it takes Jupiter to revolve around the sun.

Other Examples

Round to the **nearest whole number** to estimate the sum.

$$
\begin{array}{r}
7.0\,2\,6 \rightarrow 7 \\
1\,2.8 \ \rightarrow 1\,3 \\
+\ \ 4.5\,4 \rightarrow +\ \ 5 \\
\hline
2\,5 \leftarrow \text{estimate}
\end{array}
$$

Round to the **nearest dollar** to estimate the difference.

$$
\begin{array}{r}
\$4\,2.8\,5 \rightarrow \$4\,3 \\
-\ \ 3\,0.3\,4 \rightarrow -\ \ 3\,0 \\
\hline
\$1\,3 \leftarrow \text{estimate}
\end{array}
$$

Estimate each sum or difference by rounding to the nearest whole number.

1. $\begin{array}{r}7.63\\+\ 4.71\\\hline\end{array}$	**2.** $\begin{array}{r}9.055\\-\ 4.41\\\hline\end{array}$	**3.** $\begin{array}{r}12.4\\-\ 10.66\\\hline\end{array}$	**4.** $\begin{array}{r}\$19.52\\+\ \ \ 4.89\\\hline\end{array}$	**5.** $\begin{array}{r}23.328\\-\ 19.720\\\hline\end{array}$
6. $\begin{array}{r}\$42.79\\-\ \ 23.19\\\hline\end{array}$	**7.** $\begin{array}{r}0.72\\+\ 4.53\\\hline\end{array}$	**8.** $\begin{array}{r}64.23\\-\ 19.59\\\hline\end{array}$	**9.** $\begin{array}{r}\$139.52\\+\ \ \ 29.61\\\hline\end{array}$	**10.** $\begin{array}{r}24.66\\-\ 14.22\\\hline\end{array}$
11. $\begin{array}{r}9.215\\8.804\\+\ 7.521\\\hline\end{array}$	**12.** $\begin{array}{r}4.623\\19.55\\+\ 20.46\\\hline\end{array}$	**13.** $\begin{array}{r}8.47\\6.3\\+\ 39.5\\\hline\end{array}$	**14.** $\begin{array}{r}\$60.45\\41.95\\+\ \ \ 9.88\\\hline\end{array}$	**15.** $\begin{array}{r}\$124.50\\59.95\\+\ 100.40\\\hline\end{array}$

QUESTION
DATA
PLAN
ANSWER
CHECK

Problem Solving: Using Estimation

Estimate the answers by rounding to the nearest whole number.

1. It takes Uranus 84.013 years to revolve around the sun. It takes Neptune 164.794 years. About how much longer does it take Neptune to revolve around the sun?

2. One day on Earth is 23.933 hours. One day on Jupiter is 9.833 hours. About how much longer is a day on Earth?

3. A person who weighs 67.5 kg on Earth would weigh 10.8 kg on the moon. About how much less would the person weigh on the moon?

4. It takes Mars 1.888 years to revolve around the sun once. About how many years would it take Mars to revolve around the sun 5 times?

5. A round-trip flight by rocket to Saturn could take 12.2 years. A round-trip flight to Mars could take 1.41 years. About how much longer is the round-trip flight to Saturn?

6. One year on Earth is 365.26 days. One year on Mercury is 87.97 days. About how much shorter is one year on Mercury than on Earth?

7. An object on Jupiter weighs 2.6 times as much as on Earth. About how much would a 2.25 kg math book weigh on Jupiter?

8. **Strategy Practice** A rocket traveled 1,400 km in 7 minutes. If it flew 50 km more each minute than the minute before, how many kilometers did it travel during each minute of the flight? Hint: Guess and check.

Adding with Decimals

The table shows the weights of the elements that make up an average human body. Carbon and oxygen make up the greatest part of the weight. How many kilograms of carbon and oxygen are in the average human body?

Elements in the Human Body (in kilograms)							
calcium	1.27	sulphur	0.11	nitrogen	2.09	iron	0.46
fluorine	0.01	carbon	14.33	potassium	0.15	oxygen	41.91
magnesium	0.02	hydrogen	6.62	chlorine	0.51	sodium	0.05
						phosphorus	0.64

Since we want the total, we add.

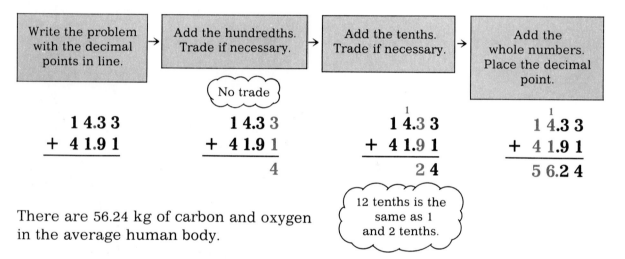

Write the problem with the decimal points in line.	→	Add the hundredths. Trade if necessary.	→	Add the tenths. Trade if necessary.	→	Add the whole numbers. Place the decimal point.

No trade

$$
\begin{array}{r} 14.33 \\ +\ 41.91 \\ \hline \end{array}
\qquad
\begin{array}{r} 14.33 \\ +\ 41.91 \\ \hline 4 \end{array}
\qquad
\begin{array}{r} \overset{1}{1}4.33 \\ +\ 41.91 \\ \hline 24 \end{array}
\qquad
\begin{array}{r} \overset{1}{1}4.33 \\ +\ 41.91 \\ \hline 56.24 \end{array}
$$

12 tenths is the same as 1 and 2 tenths.

There are 56.24 kg of carbon and oxygen in the average human body.

Other Examples

$$
\begin{array}{r} \overset{1\ 1}{1}4.75 \\ +\ 12.88 \\ \hline 27.63 \end{array}
\qquad
\begin{array}{r} \overset{1\ 1}{0}.0039 \\ +\ 0.0087 \\ \hline 0.0126 \end{array}
\qquad
\begin{array}{r} \overset{1\ 1}{2}4.72 \\ +\ \ \ 8.634 \\ \hline 33.354 \end{array}
$$

24.72 is the same as 24.720.

$$
\begin{array}{r} \overset{1}{7}.4\overset{1}{1}9 \\ 0.25 \\ +\ 1.8264 \\ \hline 9.4954 \end{array}
$$

Warm Up Find the sum.

1.
$$
\begin{array}{r} 4.0054 \\ +\ 6.0239 \\ \hline \end{array}
$$

2.
$$
\begin{array}{r} 0.68 \\ +\ 0.4 \\ \hline \end{array}
$$

3.
$$
\begin{array}{r} 63.852 \\ +\ 24.188 \\ \hline \end{array}
$$

4.
$$
\begin{array}{r} \$19.85 \\ +\ \ \ 4.72 \\ \hline \end{array}
$$

5.
$$
\begin{array}{r} \$10.04 \\ 9.80 \\ +\ 24.58 \\ \hline \end{array}
$$

6. $5.371 + 4.635$

7. $2.8403 + 0.965$

8. $\$48.96 + \$67.89 + \$0.65$

Practice Add.

1. 4.7 + 8.6	**2.** 0.55 + 0.78	**3.** 47.5 + 26.4	**4.** 6.472 + 1.131	**5.** 0.082 + 0.69
6. 622.8 + 67.3	**7.** 0.045 + 0.264	**8.** 61.0 + 9.71	**9.** 172.61 + 148.94	**10.** 3.472 + 2.5188
11. 0.4263 + 0.6178	**12.** 80.06 + 14.67	**13.** 4.2572 + 0.628	**14.** 0.52 + 0.6897	**15.** 12.5265 + 24.6982
16. 4.251 5.324 + 6.786	**17.** 0.2621 0.545 + 0.8259	**18.** $ 6.75 12.64 + 9.49	**19.** $ 4.45 8.70 + 14.85	**20.** $26.95 48.49 + 14.78

21. 6.234 + 0.567

22. 0.472 + 0.6598

23. 12.62 + 26.074

24. 0.245 + 0.68 + 0.2987

25. $14.75 + $12.08 + $9.75

26. $28.15 + $16.95

27. Estimate, then find: 9.375 + 8.86

28. Estimate, then find: 29.34 + 61.827

Mixed Applications

29. How many kilograms of hydrogen and nitrogen are included in a typical person's weight? See page 64.

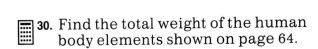 **30.** Find the total weight of the human body elements shown on page 64.

31. In Leona's school the average weight for boys is 43 kg. The average weight for girls is 5 kg less. What is the average weight for girls?

32. Estimate how many more kilograms of an average human body are oxygen than are carbon.

Skillkeeper

Solve.

1. 3 + 6 + 2 = n

2. 5 + 4 + 5 = n

3. 7 + 2 + 5 = n

4. (6 + 2) × 3 = n

5. 6 + (2 × 3) = n

6. (8 − 3) × 2 = n

7. 8 − (3 × 2) = n

8. (16 ÷ 4) × 2 = n

9. 16 ÷ (4 × 2) = n

Subtracting with Decimals

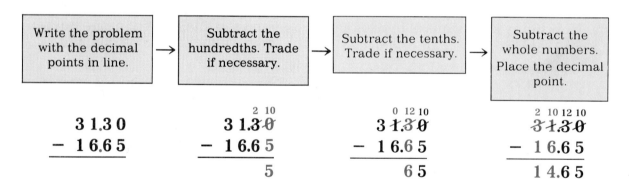

A college basketball court is 16.65 m wide and 31.30 m long. How much greater is the length of the court than the width?

Since we want to compare the length and the width, we subtract.

Write the problem with the decimal points in line.	Subtract the hundredths. Trade if necessary.	Subtract the tenths. Trade if necessary.	Subtract the whole numbers. Place the decimal point.

$$\begin{array}{r} 31.30 \\ -\ 16.65 \\ \hline \end{array}$$

$$\begin{array}{r} {\scriptstyle 2\ 10} \\ 31.3\cancel{0} \\ -\ 16.65 \\ \hline 5 \end{array}$$

$$\begin{array}{r} {\scriptstyle 0\ 12\ 10} \\ 31.30 \\ -\ 16.65 \\ \hline 65 \end{array}$$

$$\begin{array}{r} {\scriptstyle 2\ 10\ 12\ 10} \\ \cancel{31.30} \\ -\ 16.65 \\ \hline 14.65 \end{array}$$

The length is 14.65 m greater than the width.

Other Examples

$$\begin{array}{r} {\scriptstyle 6\ 13} \\ 0.7\cancel{3} \\ -\ 0.36 \\ \hline 0.37 \end{array}$$

$$\begin{array}{r} 7.5 \\ -\ 4.26 \\ \hline \end{array} \rightarrow \begin{array}{r} {\scriptstyle 4\ 10} \\ 7.5\cancel{0} \\ -\ 4.26 \\ \hline 3.24 \end{array}$$

$$\begin{array}{r} {\scriptstyle 7\ 9\ 9\ 10} \\ \cancel{8.000} \\ -\ 3.824 \\ \hline 4.176 \end{array}$$

$$\begin{array}{r} {\scriptstyle 1\ 9\ 14} \\ \$12.0\cancel{4} \\ -\quad 6.59 \\ \hline \$5.45 \end{array}$$

Warm Up Subtract.

1. $\begin{array}{r} 18.43 \\ -\ 7.26 \\ \hline \end{array}$

2. $\begin{array}{r} 7.5 \\ -\ 6.8 \\ \hline \end{array}$

3. $\begin{array}{r} 0.806 \\ -\ 0.448 \\ \hline \end{array}$

4. $\begin{array}{r} 265.3 \\ -\ 121.44 \\ \hline \end{array}$

5. $\begin{array}{r} \$1.00 \\ -\ 0.63 \\ \hline \end{array}$

Practice Subtract.

1. 9.2
    − 2.6

2. 0.61
    − 0.17

3. 4.63
    − 3.55

4. 0.518
    − 0.245

5. 7.546
    − 2.485

6. 0.73
    − 0.42

7. 2.585
    − 2.499

8. 0.7655
    − 0.4645

9. 1.42
    − 1.265

10. 4.7642
    − 1.5887

11. 12.76
    − 4.854

12. 8.6523
    − 4.516

13. 0.62
    − 0.5203

14. 21.5628
    − 19.4731

15. 42.05
    − 25.05

16. $4.85
    − 2.32

17. $0.83
    − 0.29

18. $42.35
    − 21.48

19. $60.05
    − 21.48

20. $185.44
    − 97.85

21. 18.33 − 6.47

22. 0.983 − 0.494

23. 42.1 − 35.42

24. $1.75 − $0.49

25. $14.48 − $12.95

26. $40.00 − $13.43

27. Estimate, then find: 15.372 − 8.94

28. Estimate, then find: 59.04 − 21.562

Mixed Applications

29. A tennis court is 10.97 m wide and 23.77 m long. How much greater is the length than the width?

30. A men's soccer field is 119.88 m long. A women's soccer field is 19.98 m shorter. Both fields are 68.05 m wide. How much greater is the length of the women's field than the width of the women's field?

31. **DATA BANK** How much greater is the length of a bowling alley lane than the width of a bowling alley lane? (See Data Bank, page 426.)

Think

Magic Square

Complete this decimal **magic square.** Each row, column, and diagonal must have the same sum.

	0.9	1.0
0.7	1.1	
1.2		0.8

What is the magic sum?

Math

More Practice, page 431, Set B

67

More Estimating Sums and Differences

Dorian has $1.50 to spend for lunch. She wants to have an egg sandwich, soup, and milk. Estimate whether she has enough money to pay for the items she wants.

Lunch Specials

Soup of the Day	$0.38
Cheese Sandwich	0.42
Tuna Sandwich	0.79
Egg Sandwich	0.65
Green Salad	0.48
Milk	0.24
Fruit Juice	0.37

Since we want to find the total cost, we add.

To **estimate** the sum, we can round each number **to the nearest ten cents** (**tenth** of a dollar) and add.

$$
\begin{aligned}
\$\,0.3\,8 &\rightarrow \quad \$\,0.4\,0 \\
0.6\,5 &\rightarrow \quad 0.7\,0 \\
+\quad 0.2\,4 &\rightarrow +\quad 0.2\,0 \\
\hline
& \quad \$\,1.3\,0 \quad \leftarrow \text{estimate}
\end{aligned}
$$

Since $1.50 is more than $1.30, Dorian has enough money to pay for the items she wants.

Other Examples

Estimate the sum by rounding to the nearest **ten dollars.**

$$
\begin{aligned}
\$\,4\,4.7\,5 &\rightarrow \quad \$\,4\,0 \\
+\quad 2\,8.2\,0 &\rightarrow +\quad 3\,0 \\
\hline
& \quad \$\,7\,0 \quad \leftarrow \text{estimate}
\end{aligned}
$$

Estimate the difference by rounding to the nearest **ten cents.**

$$
\begin{aligned}
\$\,1.4\,9 &\rightarrow \quad \$\,1.5\,0 \\
-\quad 0.6\,2 &\rightarrow -\quad 0.6\,0 \\
\hline
& \quad \$\,0.9\,0 \quad \leftarrow \text{estimate}
\end{aligned}
$$

Estimate by rounding to the nearest ten cents.

1.	2.	3.	4.	5.
$0.46	$0.75	$1.19	$0.72	$1.47
+ 0.62	− 0.39	− 0.52	0.88	2.14
			+ 0.16	+ 1.25

Estimate by rounding to the nearest ten dollars.

6.	7.	8.	9.	10.
$17.35	$53.95	$78.50	$40.50	$57.25
+ 62.60	− 29.95	− 43.15	18.75	22.95
			+ 31.40	+ 68.90

Problem Solving: Using Estimation

For problems 1–4, estimate by rounding to the nearest ten cents. Use the list of prices on page 68.

1. About how much more does a tuna sandwich cost than a cheese sandwich?

2. Maury had a tuna sandwich, green salad, and milk for lunch. About how much did his lunch cost?

3. Val had soup, a cheese sandwich, and fruit juice for lunch. Roberto had a tuna sandwich, green salad, and milk. About how much more or how much less did Val's lunch cost than Roberto's?

4. Harriet's lunch cost $1.17. Luann's lunch cost $1.51. About how much more did Luann's lunch cost than Harriet's lunch?

For problems 5 and 6, estimate by rounding to the nearest ten dollars.

5. The lunch room took in $93.45 on Thursday and $68.72 on Friday. About how much more did the lunch room take in on Thursday than on Friday?

6. On Tuesday lunch room sales were $37.50 greater than on Monday. On Monday the sales totaled $62.75. About how much did the sales total on Tuesday?

7. For the last three years the lunch room sales were $4,919.75, $5,076.38, and $4,954.78. Estimate, then find the total sales for these years.

8. **DATA HUNT** About how much would a bowl of soup, a salad, and a container of milk cost in your school's lunch room? Estimate the total by rounding the cost of each item to the nearest ten cents.

9. **Strategy Practice** Clark and Lee each had a Hot Plate Special. The Specials cost $1.50 each. Clark also had a glass of lemonade that cost $0.35. Lee had a glass of juice that cost $0.45. Clark paid for both lunches with a $10 bill. How much change should Clark have received?

Money: Making Change

Aaron works in a bookstore. A customer bought a backpack for $6.70 and gave Aaron a $10 bill. How much change should Aaron give the customer?

Aaron starts with the cost of the backpack and counts out coins and bills to bring the total to $10.

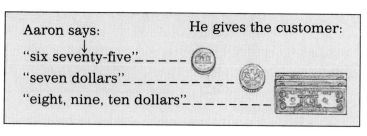

Aaron says: He gives the customer:
↓
"six seventy-five"_ _ _ _ _
"seven dollars"_ _ _ _ _ _ _ _ _
"eight, nine, ten dollars"_ _ _ _ _ _ _ _

Count the coins and bills Aaron gave the customer to find the total amount of change.

Then check by subtracting.

$$\begin{array}{r} \overset{9\ 10}{\$ \cancel{10}.0\,0} \\ -\quad 6.7\,0 \\ \hline \$\quad 3.3\,0 \end{array}$$

Aaron should give the customer $3.30 change.

List in order each coin or bill you would count out as change. Use the fewest possible coins and bills.

1. Cost $0.65. Customer paid with $1.00.

2. Cost $1.25. Customer paid with $2.00.

3. Cost $1.83. Customer paid with $5.00.

4. Cost $2.40. Customer paid with $5.00.

5. Cost $3.95. Customer paid with $10.00.

6. Cost $11.45. Customer paid with $15.

7. Cost $14.75. Customer paid with two $10 bills.

8. Cost $22.18. Customer paid with $50.

9. Cost $17.88. Customer paid with one $20 bill.

10. Cost $37.95. Customer paid with two $20 bills.

Problem Solving: Mixed Practice

Solve.

1. A pad of notebook paper was on sale for $0.85. It regularly costs $1.39. How much do you save if you buy the paper on sale?

2. Maria worked in the bookstore 24.25 hours last week. This week she worked 30.5 hours. How many more hours did she work this week than last week?

3. Mazi bought a school T-shirt for $3.95 and gym shorts for $1.50. How much change should she get if she paid with a $10 bill?

4. Eduardo bought a pen for $0.65, an eraser for $0.45, and colored pencils for $1.09. How much did he spend altogether?

5. Wes bought a photo album for $2.35. How much change should he get from a $5 bill?

6. Pete bought 3 felt-tip pens for $2 each and a calendar for $1.75. How much did he spend altogether?

7. Stephanie wants to buy a book bag for $4.95 and a school flag for $3.50. So far, she has saved $6 from her allowance. How much more does she need to buy the book bag and flag?

8. Heather saves $4 each week from her allowance. She wants to buy a school jacket that costs $24.59. She has been saving for 4 weeks. How much more does she need to save to buy the jacket?

9. **Strategy Practice** Pencils were on sale for 20¢. Pens were on sale for 30¢. Steve bought a total of 11 pens and pencils and spent $2.80. How many items of each kind did he buy? Hint: Guess and check.

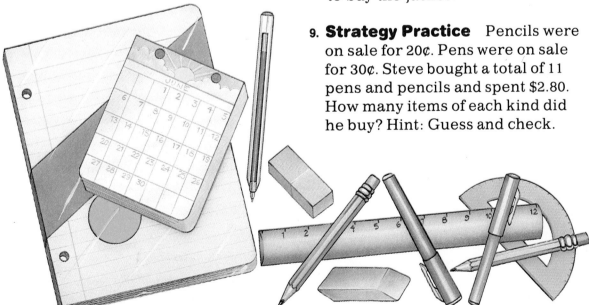

Estimating Sums: Using Compatible Numbers

Often the best way to estimate a sum is by finding pairs of numbers that "go together" or are **compatible**. Sometimes it helps to look at the first digits of the numbers.

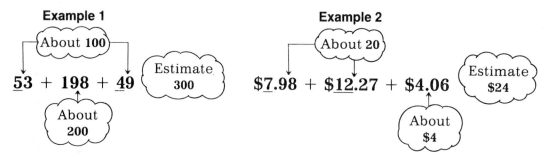

Example 1

About 100

$\underline{53} + \underline{198} + \underline{49}$ Estimate 300

About 200

Example 2

About 20

$\$\underline{7}.98 + \$\underline{12}.27 + \$4.06$ Estimate $24

About $4

Practice   Estimate. Look for numbers that go together to make about 100 or about 1,000.

1. 48 + 97 + 54

2. 51 + 76 + 26

3. 83 + 19 + 151

4. 45 + 89 + 56

5. 24 + 47 + 78 + 53

6. 61 + 79 + 42 + 96

7. 498 + 209 + 512

8. 587 + 799 + 218

9. 751 + 516 + 248

10. 915 + 98 + 487

11. 619 + 524 + 478

12. 299 + 435 + 726 + 584

Estimate. Look for amounts that go together to make about $10.

13. $6.95 + $9.98 + $3.15

14. $7.95 + $5.16 + $4.84

15. $2.53 + $1.89 + $8.24

Estimate. Look for compatible numbers.

16. 56 + 197 + 46

17. 509 + 299 + 717 + 468

18. $19.98 + $8.15 + $1.97

Mixed Applications

Estimate the answers. Look for compatible numbers.

19. Carla's family drove these distances on their trip: Monday, 518 mi; Tuesday, 297 mi; Wednesday, 486 mi. How many miles did they drive altogether?

20. Mrs. Gove kept these price tags from her purchases at the hotel gift shop. How much did she spend?

$3.98

$29.69

$6.24

QUESTION · DATA · PLAN · ANSWER · CHECK

Problem Solving: Using Data from a Tour Book

Amanda works in a travel agency. She uses a tour book to find the cost of rooms in hotels. Use data from Amanda's tour book table to solve the problems below.

Name of Hotel	Single	Standard Double	Deluxe Double	Extra Person*
Cliffside	$43.25	$52.75	$68.50	$5.00
Beachfront	65.00	72.00	85.50	8.00
Grandview	58.95	62.95	78.95	6.50
Seaside	60.75	65.75	80.75	7.00
Pearl Cove	62.50	67.50	84.50	7.50
Moontide	70.00	76.00	94.00	8.00

*Under 6 years old, no charge

1. Mr. Harding stayed one night each in a single room at the Cliffside and at the Grandview. The third night he stayed in a deluxe double at the Moontide. Estimate the total cost of his rooms for these three nights.

2. Tax on a single room for one night at the Grandview is $2.36. What is the cost of the room for one night including the tax?

3. How much less is the rate for a deluxe double at the Seaside than at the Moontide?

4. What is the cost per night of a deluxe double with 2 extra persons at the Beachfront?

5. Which costs less at the Grandview—a deluxe double room or a standard double with 1 extra person? How much less?

6. Mr. and Mrs. Ito have two children. One child is 2 years old, the other is 7. What is the cost of a standard double room for this family at the Moontide?

7. A travel agent checked out the six hotels on the list. She stayed in a single room in each hotel for one night. Estimate the total cost of her rooms.

8. **Strategy Practice** A person who cleans rooms at the Grandview found 58¢ under a bed. Altogether, there were 9 coins, and none of the coins was a half dollar or a quarter. What coins did the person find?

Problem-Solving Strategy: Draw a Picture

When you are trying to solve a problem, it is often very helpful to

Draw a Picture

Try This Five boys ran in a 100-m dash. Len came in first. Jerry came in last. If Phil was ahead of Nico and Fred was just behind Nico, who came in second?

I'll start by drawing the race track.

Start   Finish

I know who came in first and who came in last.

Start   Finish

Jerry   Len

Now I'll add the other information.

Start   Finish

Jerry Fred Nico Phil   Len

Fred was behind Nico.   Phil was ahead of Nico.

Phil must have been second!

1. Five girls ran in a 100-m dash. Debbie finished ahead of Carmen, and Carmen was not last. Betty finished far ahead of Carmen, and Evelyn finished just behind Betty. If Darlene finished last, which girl finished next to last?

2. Derek has a ribbon 180 cm long. He wants to cut the ribbon into pieces 20 cm long. How many cuts will he have to make?

Chapter Review-Test

Use place value to tell what each red digit means.

1. 2.45   **2.** 0.673   **3.** 41.05   **4.** 1.0057   **5.** 26.709

Write the word name for each decimal.

6. 0.246   **7.** 5.00732   **8.** 18.0502

Write >, <, or = for each ⦿ .

9. 4.20 ⦿ 4.2   **10.** 12.705 ⦿ 12.715   **11.** 0.96 ⦿ 0.096

12. 1.40 ⦿ 11.40   **13.** 82.4 ⦿ 8.24   **14.** 0.5213 ⦿ 0.5321

15. Write in order from greatest to least.   2.640   2.099   2.85   2.605   2.5

Round each number to the place given.

16. 25.43 (tenths)   **17.** 0.545 (hundredths)   **18.** 14.61 (whole number)

19. Estimate the sum by rounding to the nearest tenth.

$$\begin{array}{r} 4.02 \\ 12.58 \\ +\ 1.98 \\ \hline \end{array}$$

20. Estimate the difference by rounding to the nearest dollar.

$$\begin{array}{r} \$29.48 \\ -\ 14.65 \\ \hline \end{array}$$

Add.

21.
$$\begin{array}{r} 0.527 \\ +\ 0.822 \\ \hline \end{array}$$

22.
$$\begin{array}{r} 1.4905 \\ +\ 6.070 \\ \hline \end{array}$$

23.
$$\begin{array}{r} 12.06 \\ 18.7 \\ +\ 4.99 \\ \hline \end{array}$$

24.
$$\begin{array}{r} 64.203 \\ 9.74 \\ +\ 8.7 \\ \hline \end{array}$$

25.
$$\begin{array}{r} \$62.95 \\ +\ 49.95 \\ \hline \end{array}$$

Subtract.

26.
$$\begin{array}{r} 17.64 \\ -\ 9.86 \\ \hline \end{array}$$

27.
$$\begin{array}{r} 0.402 \\ -\ 0.186 \\ \hline \end{array}$$

28.
$$\begin{array}{r} 96.4 \\ -\ 14.55 \\ \hline \end{array}$$

29.
$$\begin{array}{r} 126.424 \\ -\ 86.63 \\ \hline \end{array}$$

30.
$$\begin{array}{r} \$124.85 \\ -\ 64.90 \\ \hline \end{array}$$

31. Look for compatible numbers and estimate: 49 + 79 + 53 + 24

32. Juanita ran the 100-m race in 16.5 seconds. Sharon ran the same race in 14.35 seconds. How much faster did Sharon run the race than Juanita?

33. Maury's ticket for the movie cost $3.25. He bought a cup of juice for $0.75 and a bag of peanuts for $0.85. How much money did Maury spend?

Another Look

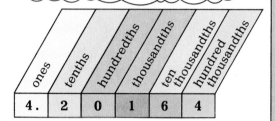

Each digit has a place value.

ones	tenths	hundredths	thousandths	ten thousandths	hundred thousandths
4.	2	0	1	6	4

"Four and twenty thousand,
one hundred sixty-four
hundred-thousandths."

Since 5 > 2,
0.265 > 0.262

0.265 > 0.262

RULE: Find the first place where
the digits are different. The
numbers compare as these digits
compare.

Round to the nearest **tenth.**

tenths
↓
6.3 4 5 →round→ 6.3
to
↑
check
here

Round down
since
4 < 5.

```
  1   1              3 10
  7.409          0.5 4 0 ← ( 0.5 4 = 0.5 4 0 )
+ 6.687        − 0.326
 14.096          0.214
```

RULE: Add or subtract as with
whole numbers. Write the decimal
point in the answer.

**Use place value to tell
what each red digit means.**

1. 0.063   **2.** 41.5   **3.** 1.7524

4. 29.26   **5.** 8.60   **6.** 5.00244

Write the word name.

7. 0.26   **8.** 0.0050   **9.** 7.7

Write >, <, or = for each ▐ .

10. 0.45 ▐ 4.5   **11.** 0.607 ▐ 0.0609

12. 4.22 ▐ 4.202   **13.** 0.95 ▐ 0.950

14. 8.99 ▐ 9.009   **15.** 12.0056 ▐ 12.0064

16. 4.050 ▐ 4.05   **17.** 1.1010 ▐ 1.0101

Round to the nearest tenth.

18. 0.46   **19.** 7.251   **20.** 12.64

Round to the nearest hundredth.

21. 1.551   **22.** 0.8392   **23.** 6.497

Round to the nearest whole number.

24. 8.52   **25.** 0.626   **26.** 11.4

Add or subtract.

```
27.    0.645   28.    2.05   29.    18.6
     + 0.372        + 1.98          9.545
                                + 12.064

30.    4.364   31.   0.627   32.    1.5
     − 3.187        − 0.35         − 0.36
```

Enrichment

Logical Reasoning

The words **and**, **or**, **not**, and **if-then** are used to express ideas in a clear, **logical** manner.

A **Venn diagram** is a drawing used to show and analyze logical relationships among sets of objects.

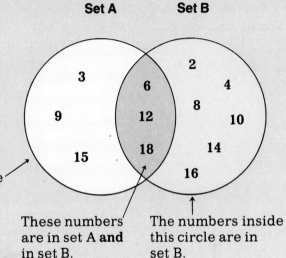

Set A   Set B

The numbers inside this circle are in set A.

These numbers are in set A **and** in set B.

The numbers inside this circle are in set B.

1. List all the numbers in set A.

2. List all the numbers in set B.

3. Which numbers are in set A but **not** in set B?

4. Which numbers are in set B but **not** in set A?

5. Which numbers are in both set A **and** set B?

6. **If** Carol chose an odd number, **then** she must have chosen the number from which of the sets?

7. Nancy wanted to choose a number that is a multiple of 2 and a multiple of 3. How many choices did she have?

8. Jeff made this "Who Am I" card about the numbers in the diagram above. Can you find the number described on his card?

9. Make a "Who Am I" card and give it to a classmate to solve.

---

1. I'm a multiple of 2 AND a multiple of 3.

2. I'm NOT a single-digit number.

3. IF you divide me by 9, THEN you will get a remainder that is not 0.

WHO AM I?

Cumulative Review

Add, subtract, multiply, or divide. Watch the signs.

1. 13
  – 8

A 4
B 5
C 21
D not given

2. 9
  + 7

A 48
B 17
C 16
D not given

3. 7 × 8

A 48
B 15
C 78
D not given

4. 6
  × 9

A 54
B 63
C 15
D not given

5. 8)72

A 8
B 9
C 12
D not given

6. Give the digits in the millions period:
123,456,789,101

A 123   B 456
C 789   D not given

7. Use place value to tell what the 8 means in 1,268,374.

A 8 thousands
B 8 hundreds
C 80 thousands
D not given

8. Which symbol (>, <, or =) goes in the ||||| ?

57,389 ||||| 57,839

A >   B <   C =

9. Round 62,184 to the nearest thousand.

A 60,000 B 62,200
C 63,000 D not given

Add or subtract.

10. 738
  + 295

A 923
B 443
C 1,033
D not given

11. 6,243
  – 1,706

A 5,547
B 4,537
C 7,949
D not given

12. 14,331
  + 62,284

A 76,515
B 63,516
C 47,953
D not given

13. One stereo costs $549. Another costs $638. What is the difference in price?

A $1,187 B $89
C $99 D not given

14. A shirt costs $24.89. A sweater costs $46.68. What is the cost of both items?

A $71.57 B $70.47
C $21.79 D not given

4

Multiplication

When Rita heard her voice on the radio commercial, she hardly recognized herself. Hers was one of the voices in the background of a series of ads for the local skating rink.

The advertising agency that had created the ads had decided to direct them to teenagers. The ads were broadcast on the two local rock music stations before and after school hours. The agency figured that each station had about 100,000 listeners. For the first 3 weeks of the campaign, the 60-second ads were on the radio 20 times a week. Each of Rita's friends heard the ads at least 3 times during the first week. Judging by her friends alone, Rita thought the advertising agency had done a good job of reaching their "targeted audience" of teenagers.

Using Multiplication Facts: Mental Math

A small theater at an amusement park holds 500 people when it is full. How many people attended 3 shows if the theater was full for each show?

Since each show was attended by the same number of people, we multiply.

$$3 \times 5 = 15$$
so $3 \times 5\,0\,0 = 1{,}5\,0\,0$ ←

We can use **multiplication facts** and the **grouping property** to find products like this.

$3 \times (5 \times 100) = (3 \times 5) \times 100$

A total of 1,500 people attended the shows.

Other Examples

$6 \times 5 = 30$
so $6 \times 5\,0 = 3\,0\,0$

$8 \times 1 = 8$
so $8 \times 1\,0\,0 = 8\,0\,0$

$9 \times 7 = 6\,3$
so $9{,}0\,0\,0 \times 7 = 6\,3{,}0\,0\,0$

Find the products using mental math.
Use pencils for answers only.

1. 6 × 1
 6 × 10
 6 × 100
 6 × 1,000

2. 4 × 8
 4 × 80
 4 × 800
 4 × 8,000

3. 9 × 6
 9 × 60
 9 × 600
 9 × 6,000

4. 8 × 5
 8 × 50
 8 × 500
 8 × 5,000

5. 9 × 10

6. 8 × 100

7. 4 × 1,000

8. 100 × 3

9. 6 × 80

10. 7 × 40

11. 3 × 20

12. 40 × 6

13. 3 × 800

14. 9 × 500

15. 7 × 600

16. 400 × 7

17. 4,000 × 8

18. 2,000 × 9

19. 8 × 7,000

20. 4 × 6,000

Special Products: Mental Math

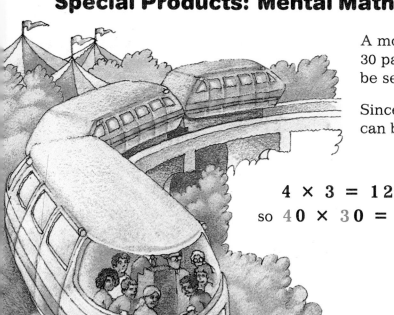

A monorail car has enough seats for 30 passengers. How many people can be seated during 40 trips?

Since the same number of passengers can be seated each time, we multiply.

$$4 \times 3 = 12$$
so $40 \times 30 = 1{,}200$

> We can use **multiplication facts** and **basic properties** to find larger products.
> $40 \times 30 = 4 \times 10 \times 3 \times 10$
> $= 12 \times 100$
> $= 1{,}200$

During 40 trips 1,200 passengers can be seated.

Other Examples

$8 \times 5 = 40$	$9 \times 6 = 54$	$8 \times 3 = 24$
so $80 \times 50 = 4{,}000$	so $90 \times 600 = 54{,}000$	so $800 \times 300 = 240{,}000$
	and $90 \times 6{,}000 = 540{,}000$	

Find the products using mental math.

1. 7×4	**2.** 6×8	**3.** 9×8	**4.** 5×6
70×4	6×80	90×8	5×60
70×40	60×80	90×80	50×60
70×400	60×800	900×80	50×600
$70 \times 4{,}000$	$60 \times 8{,}000$	$9{,}000 \times 80$	$50 \times 6{,}000$
700×400	600×800	900×800	500×600

5. 10×10 **6.** 100×10 **7.** $10 \times 1{,}000$ **8.** 100×100

9. 90×40 **10.** 30×70 **11.** 60×30 **12.** 80×60

13. 40×600 **14.** 800×40 **15.** $4{,}000 \times 20$ **16.** 500×200

17. 600×700 **18.** $4{,}000 \times 90$ **19.** $5{,}000 \times 40$ **20.** 600×600

nating Products: ing Rounding

An estimated answer is often all that is needed to solve an everyday problem.

Gasoline costs 39¢ a liter. Will $20 be enough to fill a 49-liter gas tank on a small car?

To solve this problem, round the numbers to the nearest ten.

$$\begin{array}{r} 49 \rightarrow 50 \\ \times\ 39¢ \rightarrow \times\ 40¢ \\ \hline 2{,}000¢, \text{ or } \$20.00 \end{array}$$

Since each number was rounded up, $20 is enough to fill the tank.

Other Examples

7 × 814   25 × 319   462 × 536
   ↓   ↓   ↓   ↓   ↓
7 × 800 = 5,600   30 × 300 = 9,000   500 × 500 = 250,000

Estimate these products by rounding 2-digit numbers to the nearest ten and 3-digit numbers to the nearest hundred.

1. 6 × 72   **2.** 4 × 98   **3.** 8 × 53   **4.** 5 × 894   **5.** 3 × 456

    (6 × 70)   (5 × 900)

6. 7 × 634   **7.** 2 × 279   **8.** 9 × 852   **9.** 29 × 74   **10.** 38 × 43

11. 39 × 71   **12.** 19 × 389   **13.** 82 × 415   **14.** 68 × 720   **15.** 316 × 493

16.   75   **17.**   92   **18.**   47   **19.**   76   **20.**   97
     × 46   × 78   × 23   × 37   × 64

21.   783   **22.**   507   **23.**   378   **24.**   741   **25.**   823
     × 45   × 49   × 57   × 986   × 456

QUESTION
DATA
PLAN
ANSWER
CHECK

Problem Solving: Using Estimation

Estimate the answers to these problems.

1. A family bought a new television set by paying $24 a month for 36 months. About what was the total amount paid?

2. A service club wants to raise $150,000 to give to local charities. Has the goal been reached when 519 people have given an average of $305 each?

3. A bag of grass seed will cover an area of 425 m² (square meters). A yard has an area of 1,568 m². Will 4 bags of seed be enough to cover it?

4. A savings account pays interest daily. About how many days of interest will be paid on money left in the account for 5 years?

5. You can buy 3 records for $5.98. Is this a better price than $2.45 for one record?

6. The highway distance from Chicago to St. Louis is 465 km. If you leave Chicago at 8 a.m. and drive at an average speed of 78 km/h, can you reach St. Louis by 1:00 p.m.?

7. **DATA HUNT** About how many breaths do you take in an hour? Count the number you take in a minute. Then find the number for a week. Estimate to find whether your answer is reasonable.

8. **Strategy Practice** In an auto race, Auto number 67 finished 1 second ahead of Auto 34. Auto 34 was not the last place auto. Auto 25 finished 7 seconds ahead of Auto 46, which finished 3 seconds behind Auto 67. Auto 67 finished 7 seconds behind Auto 50. What was the finishing order of the autos? Hint: Draw a picture.

Multiplying by a 1-Digit Factor

On an average July day at Yellowstone National Park there might be 7,693 people camping. If 4 different groups this size were in the park during a week, how many people were there that week?

Since we want to find the total for several equal amounts, we multiply.

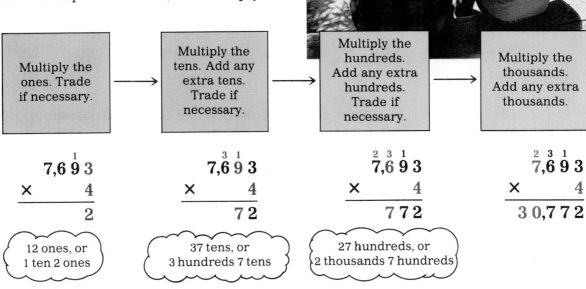

Multiply the ones. Trade if necessary.	Multiply the tens. Add any extra tens. Trade if necessary.	Multiply the hundreds. Add any extra hundreds. Trade if necessary.	Multiply the thousands. Add any extra thousands.

$$\begin{array}{r} \overset{1}{7{,}6\,9\,3} \\ \times\qquad 4 \\ \hline 2 \end{array}$$

$$\begin{array}{r} \overset{3\ \ 1}{7{,}6\,9\,3} \\ \times\qquad 4 \\ \hline 7\,2 \end{array}$$

$$\begin{array}{r} \overset{2\ 3\ 1}{7{,}6\,9\,3} \\ \times\qquad 4 \\ \hline 7\,7\,2 \end{array}$$

$$\begin{array}{r} \overset{2\ 3\ 1}{7{,}6\,9\,3} \\ \times\qquad 4 \\ \hline 3\,0{,}7\,7\,2 \end{array}$$

12 ones, or 1 ten 2 ones

37 tens, or 3 hundreds 7 tens

27 hundreds, or 2 thousands 7 hundreds

There were 30,772 campers.

Other Examples

$$\begin{array}{r} \overset{6}{8\,9\,0} \\ \times\quad 7 \\ \hline 6{,}2\,3\,0 \end{array}$$

$$\begin{array}{r} \overset{3\ 3}{9{,}0\,7\,6} \\ \times\quad 5 \\ \hline 4\,5{,}3\,8\,0 \end{array}$$

$$\begin{array}{r} \overset{5\ 5\ 4\ 2}{3\,8{,}9\,7\,4} \\ \times\qquad 6 \\ \hline 2\,3\,3{,}8\,4\,4 \end{array}$$

$$\begin{array}{r} \overset{3\ 3\ 2}{\$5\,8.7\,6} \\ \times\qquad 4 \\ \hline \$2\,3\,5\,0\,4 \end{array}$$

Multiply as with whole numbers. Estimate to help you write the answer in dollars and cents.

About 4 × $60, or $240

Warm Up Multiply.

1. $\begin{array}{r} 787 \\ \times\quad 9 \\ \hline \end{array}$

2. $\begin{array}{r} 3{,}498 \\ \times\quad 7 \\ \hline \end{array}$

3. $\begin{array}{r} 5{,}036 \\ \times\quad 8 \\ \hline \end{array}$

4. $\begin{array}{r} 49{,}658 \\ \times\quad 4 \\ \hline \end{array}$

5. $\begin{array}{r} \$61.79 \\ \times\quad 6 \\ \hline \end{array}$

Practice Multiply.

1. $\begin{array}{r} 87 \\ \times\ 3 \\ \hline \end{array}$	**2.** $\begin{array}{r} 62 \\ \times\ 5 \\ \hline \end{array}$	**3.** $\begin{array}{r} 86 \\ \times\ 8 \\ \hline \end{array}$	**4.** $\begin{array}{r} 75 \\ \times\ 7 \\ \hline \end{array}$	**5.** $\begin{array}{r} 86 \\ \times\ 4 \\ \hline \end{array}$
6. $\begin{array}{r} 678 \\ \times\ 7 \\ \hline \end{array}$	**7.** $\begin{array}{r} 394 \\ \times\ 5 \\ \hline \end{array}$	**8.** $\begin{array}{r} 275 \\ \times\ 6 \\ \hline \end{array}$	**9.** $\begin{array}{r} 607 \\ \times\ 8 \\ \hline \end{array}$	**10.** $\begin{array}{r} 1{,}980 \\ \times\ 2 \\ \hline \end{array}$
11. $\begin{array}{r} 6{,}038 \\ \times\ 9 \\ \hline \end{array}$	**12.** $\begin{array}{r} 7{,}954 \\ \times\ 3 \\ \hline \end{array}$	**13.** $\begin{array}{r} 5{,}009 \\ \times\ 4 \\ \hline \end{array}$	**14.** $\begin{array}{r} 32{,}947 \\ \times\ 8 \\ \hline \end{array}$	**15.** $\begin{array}{r} 27{,}306 \\ \times\ 7 \\ \hline \end{array}$
16. $\begin{array}{r} 19{,}417 \\ \times\ 5 \\ \hline \end{array}$	**17.** $\begin{array}{r} 68{,}506 \\ \times\ 2 \\ \hline \end{array}$	**18.** $\begin{array}{r} \$9.65 \\ \times\ 6 \\ \hline \end{array}$	**19.** $\begin{array}{r} \$31.98 \\ \times\ 3 \\ \hline \end{array}$	**20.** $\begin{array}{r} \$49.23 \\ \times\ 4 \\ \hline \end{array}$

21. 6×417 **22.** 5×947 **23.** $9 \times 3{,}208$

24. $8{,}628 \times 4$ **25.** $6{,}305 \times 7$ **26.** $8 \times 37{,}946$

27. What is the product when the factors are 7 and 364?

28. Estimate, then find: 6×792 **29.** Estimate, then find: $3{,}975 \times 8$

Mixed Applications

30. Each of the 7,693 campers at Yellowstone on an average day creates about 3 kg of trash. About how many kilograms of trash is this in all?

31. Make up a story problem about Yellowstone National Park that can be solved with this number sentence:
$$6{,}729 + 755 = 7{,}484$$

32. Each visitor to Yellowstone costs the National Park Service an average of $2.74. In a recent year 2,487,084 people visited the park. What was the cost to the Service that year, to the nearest dollar?

Think

Mental Math

Use the distributive property to find the products below mentally. For example:

To find 3×24

Think: 3×20 is $\underline{60}$. 3×4 is $\underline{12}$.

So 3×24 is $\underline{60 + 12}$, or 72.

1. 3×32 2. 2×48 3. 4×18

4. 5×26 5. 3×35 6. 4×54

7. 5×17 8. 6×18 9. 2×14

Math

Multiplying by Multiples of 10, 100, and 1,000

Did you know that an average of about 400 babies are born every hour in the United States?

There are 672 hours in the month of February (except in a leap year). How many babies, on the average, are born in February?

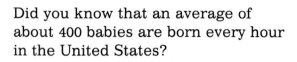

Since we want to find the total for a number of equal amounts, we multiply.

Multiply by the ones.	Multiply by the tens.	Multiply by the hundreds.

$$
\begin{array}{r} 672 \\ \times\ 400 \\ \hline 0 \end{array}
\qquad
\begin{array}{r} 672 \\ \times\ 400 \\ \hline 00 \end{array}
\qquad
\begin{array}{r} \overset{2}{6}72 \\ \times\ 400 \\ \hline 268,800 \end{array}
$$

Remember the 0 property!

An average of 268,800 babies are born during February.

Other Examples

$$
\begin{array}{r} \overset{4}{5}6 \\ \times\ 70 \\ \hline 3,920 \end{array}
\quad
\begin{array}{r} \overset{1}{1}\overset{1}{5}6 \\ \times\ 30 \\ \hline 4,680 \end{array}
\quad
\begin{array}{r} \overset{\ 2}{7}04 \\ \times\ 500 \\ \hline 352,000 \end{array}
\quad
\begin{array}{r} \overset{121}{4,3}75 \\ \times\ 300 \\ \hline 1,312,500 \end{array}
\quad
\begin{array}{r} \overset{\ \ 1}{3,2}46 \\ \times\ 2,000 \\ \hline 6,492,000 \end{array}
$$

Shortcut: Just write the zeros in the product and multiply by the other number.

Warm Up   Multiply.

1.
$$
\begin{array}{r} 83 \\ \times\ 50 \\ \hline \end{array}
$$

2.
$$
\begin{array}{r} 237 \\ \times\ 20 \\ \hline \end{array}
$$

3.
$$
\begin{array}{r} 876 \\ \times\ 300 \\ \hline \end{array}
$$

4.
$$
\begin{array}{r} 3,582 \\ \times\ 600 \\ \hline \end{array}
$$

5.
$$
\begin{array}{r} 4,158 \\ \times\ 4,000 \\ \hline \end{array}
$$

Practice Multiply.

1.	38 × 20	**2.**	79 × 40	**3.**	94 × 30	**4.**	78 × 50	**5.**	39 × 80
6.	504 × 40	**7.**	716 × 30	**8.**	638 × 60	**9.**	840 × 70	**10.**	496 × 90
11.	1,906 × 70	**12.**	4,387 × 40	**13.**	9,052 × 60	**14.**	$8.98 × 40	**15.**	437 × 100
16.	803 × 500	**17.**	$7.48 × 600	**18.**	1,654 × 800	**19.**	8,754 × 3,000	**20.**	9,540 × 6,000

21. 10 × 89

22. 10 × 563

23. 9,345 × 10

24. 59 × 40

25. 84 × 70

26. 365 × 60

27. 743 × 500

28. 400 × 608

29. 2,000 × 9,571

30. Estimate, then find: 800 × 2,987

31. Estimate, then find 517 multiplied by 400.

Mixed Applications

32. There were 325 girls and 278 boys born in one year at Park Hospital. How many babies were born in the hospital that year?

33. It is estimated that the world's population increases at the rate of about 140 people each minute. About how much does the world's population increase in an hour?

Skillkeeper

Use place value to tell what each red digit means.

1. 0.37

2. 1.0008

3. 3.95

4. 0.02146

5. 6.051

6. 0.47

7. 6.32

8. 0.0143

Write >, <, or = for each ⦀ .

9. 0.309 ⦀ 0.039

10. 6.88 ⦀ 6.808

11. 0.47 ⦀ 0.470

12. 0.92 ⦀ 9.2

13. 7.070 ⦀ 7.07

14. 3.05 ⦀ 3.5

Multiplying by a 2-Digit Factor

The *Titanic* was the largest ship in the world when it was built. For a movie about the ship, a 55-ft (foot) scale model was built. The *Titanic* was actually 16 times as long as the model. How long was the *Titanic*?

Since we want to find the total for the same amount repeated several times, we multiply.

Multiply by the ones.	→	Multiply by the tens.	→	Add the products.

Use the multiplication-addition property.

$$\begin{array}{r} 5\,5 \\ \times\ 1\,6 \\ \hline 3\,3\,0 \end{array}$$ (6 × 55)

$$\begin{array}{r} 5\,5 \\ \times\ 1\,6 \\ \hline 3\,3\,0 \\ 5\,5\,0 \end{array}$$ (10 × 55)

$$\begin{array}{r} 5\,5 \\ \times\ 1\,6 \\ \hline 3\,3\,0 \\ 5\,5\,0 \\ \hline 8\,8\,0 \end{array}$$ (16 × 55)

The *Titanic* was 880 ft (feet) long.

Other Examples

$$\begin{array}{r} 9\,5 \\ \times\ 3\,7 \\ \hline 6\,6\,5 \\ 2\,8\,5\,0 \\ \hline 3{,}5\,1\,5 \end{array}$$

Shortcut: Leave out the zero! Be sure to line up the products below the digit you're multiplying by!

$$\begin{array}{r} 5\,0\,7 \\ \times\ \ 4\,6 \\ \hline 3\,0\,4\,2 \\ 2\,0\,2\,8 \\ \hline 2\,3{,}3\,2\,2 \end{array}$$

$$\begin{array}{r} 2{,}3\,1\,4 \\ \times\ \ \ 6\,7 \\ \hline 1\,6\,1\,9\,8 \\ 1\,3\,8\,8\,4 \\ \hline 1\,5\,5{,}0\,3\,8 \end{array}$$

Warm Up   Multiply.

1.	2.	3.	4.	5.
86 × 29	174 × 68	309 × 45	986 × 87	3,528 × 23

Practice Multiply.

1. 52
    × 23

2. 48
    × 16

3. 79
    × 20

4. 88
    × 55

5. 96
    × 74

6. 132
    × 46

7. 263
    × 21

8. 374
    × 65

9. 507
    × 34

10. 747
    × 26

11. 999
    × 44

12. 850
    × 37

13. 900
    × 56

14. 1,537
    × 28

15. 3,605
    × 18

16. 4,032
    × 71

17. 8,743
    × 54

18. 9,400
    × 78

19. $57.36
    × 24

20. $19.95
    × 12

21. 74 × 25

22. 86 × 32

23. 27 × 205

24. 590 × 62

25. 54 × 618

26. 1,370 × 69

27. 83 × 2,431

28. 5,046 × 29

29. 6 × 8 × 12

30. 7 × 7 × 7

31. 5 × 5 × 5

32. 10 × 10 × 10

33. What is the product when 426 is multiplied by 33?

34. Estimate, then find: 379 × 42

35. Estimate, then find: 79 × 53

Mixed Applications

36. Suppose a full-size ship is 28 times the length of a scale model that will be used in a movie. If the model is 12 ft long, how long is the actual ship?

37. Tracy built a model that was 9 inches long. Rae's model was 5 inches more than 3 times as long as Tracy's. How long was Rae's model?

38. **DATA BANK** The model of one of the world's largest passenger ships is 22 feet long. The actual ship is 45 times that length. What is the name of the ship? (See Data Bank, page 424.)

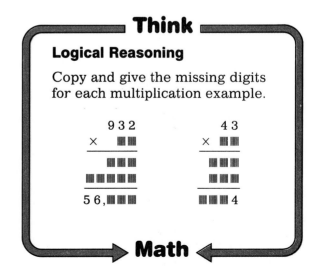

Think

Logical Reasoning

Copy and give the missing digits for each multiplication example.

```
  9 3 2                4 3
×  ▓▓ ▓▓             ×  ▓▓ ▓▓
  ▓▓ ▓▓               ▓▓ ▓▓
 ▓▓ ▓▓ ▓▓            ▓▓ ▓▓
5 6,▓▓ ▓▓            ▓▓ ▓▓ 4
```

Math

Problem Solving: Using the 5-Point Checklist

To Solve a Problem

1. **Understand the Question**
2. **Find the needed Data**
3. **Plan what to do**
4. **Find the Answer**
5. **Check back**

These 5 steps can help you solve problems. Follow them to solve this problem.

Jack traveled 4 hours at an average speed of 88 km/h (kilometers per hour). Then he traveled 3 more hours at a speed of 82 km/h. How far did he travel?

1. Understand the Question
What was the total number of kilometers traveled?

2. Find the needed Data
4 hours at 88 km/h   3 hours at 82 km/h

3. Plan what to do
Distance = rate × time. Since we know the rates and times, we must multiply. Then we add the distances.

4. Find the Answer
4 × 88 = 352   3 × 82 = 246   352 + 246 = 598
Jack traveled 598 km.

5. Check back
Reread the problem. Estimate the answer.
4 × 90 = 360, 3 × 80 = 240, and 360 + 240 = 600, so 598 km seems reasonable.

Solve. Use the 5-Point Checklist.

1. A bicycle rider averaged 24 km/h for 8 hours. How far did she travel?

2. The average speed of the winning car in a 4-hour race was 249 km/h. How far did the car travel?

Solve.

1. A high-speed train in France travels 380 km/h. If a train could travel across the United States at this speed, could it cover the 4,885 km distance from New York to San Francisco in 13 hours?

2. The record speed for a space vehicle is 68 times as fast as the record speed for a jet plane. The fastest jet plane flew 3,529 km/h. What is the record space vehicle speed?

3. The record speed for a car is 1,001 km/h. The record speed for a power boat is 219 km/h. How many more kilometers per hour is the record auto speed than the record power boat speed?

4. Light travels about 300 thousand km/s (kilometers per second). If it takes 311 seconds for the light from a sunspot flare-up to travel to the earth and be seen, about how far is it from the earth to the sun?

5. Sound travels 1,460 m/s (meters per second) in sea water. It takes sound waves 7 seconds to reach the bottom of a deep part of the Pacific Ocean. How deep is it?

6. Sound travels 331 m/s through the air. The sound of a foghorn reached a fishing boat in 6 seconds. The sound reached an oil tanker in 14 seconds. How much farther away from the foghorn was the oil tanker than the fishing boat?

7. As passengers on Spaceship Earth, we travel around the sun at a speed of 107,211 km/h. How far do we travel during a 24-hour day?

8. **Strategy Practice** The highway distance from Boston to Cleveland is 1,028 km. A car leaves Boston averaging 88 km/h at the same time a car leaves Cleveland averaging 77 km/h. How far apart will the cars be when they have traveled toward each other for 6 hours? Hint: Draw a picture.

Understanding Exponents

Life begins as a single cell. This cell splits rapidly into 2 parts, which in turn continue dividing. The human body is composed of about 10,000,000,000,000 cells.

Part 1

Experiment with your group by folding paper to see how numbers can multiply rapidly.

1. Let a large, unfolded sheet of paper represent one cell. Label this model: 0 folds, 1 cell. (The 0 means you did not fold your cell.)

   Fold another paper into 2 parts to show the cell splitting once. Open your paper to see two cells. Label this model: 1 fold, 2 cells.

   Continue to split your original cell by folding sheets of paper. Make a table to record this information.

2. Talk about any patterns you see in your papers and your tables.
   - How many cells would there be if you folded your original cell 6 times? 10 times?
   - Share your findings with the class.

Number of Times You Fold into 2	Number of Cells
0	1
1	2
2	
3	
4	
5	

Part 2

The patterns that you have developed can be expressed in another way. The cell pattern showed the number 2 being used as a **factor** several times. An **exponent** tells how many times the number, called the **base,** is used as a factor.

$$2 \times 2 \times 2 = 2^3$$

3 Factors   Exponent   Base

92

3. On a table like the one below, make entries until you have more than 100 as the number of units. Then label your models with their exponential names.

Number of Times You Fold into 2	Factors (expanded notation)	Exponential Name (base with exponent)	Number of Units
0	—	2^0	1
1	2	2^1	2
2	2×2	2^2	4
3	$2 \times 2 \times 2$	2^3	8

Part 3

4. Do the same experiment, this time folding the paper into 3 parts each time instead of 2.

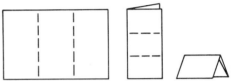

5. Continue the table until you have more than 200 as the number of units. Then label your models with their exponential names.

Number of Times You Fold into 3	Factors (expanded notation)	Exponential Name (base with exponent)	Number of Units
0	—	3^0	1
1	3	3^1	3
2	3×3	3^2	9

6. Look at your tables from Parts 2 and 3. Which has more units, 2^3 or 3^2? Can you prove this using your folded papers?

Part 4

Use what you have learned to fill in the table using 10 as a base.

?	Factors (expanded notation)	Exponential Name (base with exponent)	Number of Units
0			
1			
2			
3			

What could you call the first column?

Counting Possibilities

Mr. Kim had 2 tickets to a new computer-animation movie. He told the Computer Club, "I want to give 1 ticket to a seventh-grader and 1 to a sixth-grader. There are 10 seventh-graders and 12 sixth-graders in the club. The first student in each grade who can tell me how many different pairs of students I could send to the movie wins a ticket."

"That's easy," said Arthur. He whispered the solution to Mr. Kim. The others took longer. Most of them started by making a tree diagram or an organized list.

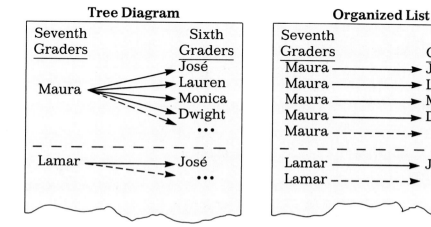

"Arthur couldn't have made a tree diagram in his head," Lauren thought. "There must be a pattern."

Work with a group.

Part 1

1. Write a statement, in your own words, that describes the problem the Computer Club is trying to solve. Share your statement with your group.

2. If you completed the diagram or list, how many names would be matched with Maura's? With Lamar's?

3. How could you show all the possible pairs of students if there were 2 seventh-graders and 3 sixth-graders in the club? If there were 3 seventh-graders and 3 sixth-graders? If there were 3 seventh-graders and 5 sixth-graders?
   • In each case, how many possible pairs are there?
   • Talk about the patterns you notice.

4. Use the patterns you noticed to help you write a statement describing a method for counting possibilities.
   - Use your method to decide how many different ways Mr. Kim could have distributed the tickets.
   - Compare your method and solution with another group's results.

"Suppose I had a third ticket for a fifth-grader in the club," said Mr. Kim. "Could you use your method to find the number of different ways I could distribute the 3 tickets?"

5. If there were 9 fifth-graders, how many different ways could Mr. Kim distribute the tickets? Explain your reasoning.

6. How could you apply your counting method to situations involving 3 things being done together? More than 3 things? Explain. Use examples to show why this is true.

Part 2

In each of the following situations, discuss how your counting method might be helpful in finding the information asked for. Explain your reasoning.

7. Customers at a department store may choose sweaters from among 4 sizes, 6 colors, and 3 styles. How many different combinations can they choose?

8. Seventeen girls are at a school dance. If each girl dances once with each boy, and there are 255 possible pairs, how many boys are at the dance?

9. Blake can make 144 different running outfits by combining his various running shoes, socks, T-shirts, and shorts. If he has 4 pairs of socks, 6 T-shirts, and 2 pairs of shorts, how many pairs of running shoes does he have?

10. Write a problem similar to the ones you have been solving. Trade problems with someone in your group. Solve the problems and compare solutions and methods.

Practice: Multiplying

Find the products.

1.	96 × 4	**2.**	347 × 8	**3.**	609 × 6	**4.**	1,735 × 5
5.	38,964 × 7	**6.**	174 × 80	**7.**	78 × 49	**8.**	36 × 27
9.	503 × 26	**10.**	479 × 87	**11.**	560 × 74	**12.**	906 × 80
13.	700 × 59	**14.**	1,364 × 28	**15.**	5,789 × 54	**16.**	627 × 123
17.	484 × 251	**18.**	645 × 230	**19.**	729 × 407	**20.**	868 × 474
21.	979 × 777	**22.**	806 × 485	**23.**	1,364 × 274	**24.**	3,547 × 676

25. $6 \times 8 \times 9$ **26.** $7 \times 7 \times 7$ **27.** $5 \times 4 \times 8 \times 6$

28. $24 \times 61 \times 13$ **29.** $56 \times 21 \times 43$ **30.** $79 \times 46 \times 58$

31. $9 \times 6 \times 8 \times 674$ **32.** $27 \times 3 \times 826$ **33.** $56 \times 57 \times 428$

34. Find this product: (your age) $\times$ 37 $\times$ 91 $\times$ 3
Try this using a different age.

★ Try finding these larger products.

35.	5,738 × 4,659	**36.**	2,084 × 8,136	**37.**	64,968 × 4,387	**38.**	89,477 × 5,638

★ Use estimation and a calculator to find which three of the
four factors given can be used to give the product in the
blue box. Use the fewest multiplications possible.

39. 42, 79, 18, 53 | 40,068 | **40.** 23, 88, 52, 98 | 198,352 |

41. 679, 95, 124, 496 | 7,998,620 | **42.** 9, 57, 185, 378 | 629,370 |

Estimating Sums: Using Clustering

When we have addends that are "close to" or cluster around a certain number, we can multiply that number by the number of addends to estimate the sum. We call this method **clustering**.

Example 1

$$589 + 613 + 598 + 607$$

These <u>4</u> addends cluster around <u>600</u>.

Estimate: <u>4</u> × <u>600</u>, or 2,400

Example 2

$$4,875 + 5,236 + 4,983$$

These <u>3</u> addends cluster around <u>5,000</u>.

Estimate: <u>3</u> × <u>5,000</u>, or 15,000

Practice Look for clusters of addends that are close to a multiple of 10, 100, or 1,000. Estimate the sum.

1. 69 + 72 + 67

2. 85 + 83 + 76 + 78 + 75 + 79

3. 46 + 48 + 54 + 52

4. 32 + 28 + 34 + 29 + 26

5. 396 + 413 + 425

6. 695 + 726 + 683 + 709

7. 179 + 243 + 195 + 209

8. 478 + 486 + 497 + 523 + 547

9. 285 + 318 + 289 + 299 + 335

10. 913 + 925 + 906 + 919 + 897 + 886

11. 6,123 + 6,087 + 5,976

12. 6,895 + 7,346 + 6,999 + 6,855 + 7,279

13. 5,009 + 4,998 + 4,563 + 4,777

14. 8,994 + 9,068 + 8,975 + 9,159

15. 9,766 + 9,804 + 10,276

16. 2,567 + 3,333 + 3,208 + 2,799 + 2,918

★ 17. 53 + 49 + 89 + 92 + 94 + 88

★ 18. 19 + 23 + 48 + 54 + 49 + 53 + 24

★ 19. 99 + 295 + 307 + 289 + 104

★ 20. 195 + 689 + 209 + 723 + 187 + 693

Mixed Applications

Estimate the answers. Use clustering.

21. A school play was presented 3 times. 423 people attended the first performance, 396 the second, and 387 the last. How many came to see the play?

22. Janette has a sticker collection. She has 185 stickers in one book, 237 in another, 196 in a third, and 207 in a fourth book. How many stickers are there in her collection?

More Practice, page 432, Set C

Problem Solving: Using Data from a Graph

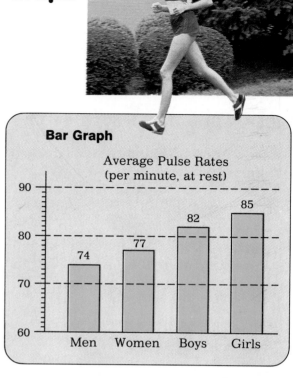

A Look at Pulse Rates

Solve.

1. A sprinter in excellent health might have a pulse rate of 58 beats per minute. How much less is this than the rate for the average man?

2. What is the average pulse rate per **hour** for girls?

3. A woman's pulse rate after jogging was 46 beats per minute greater than before jogging. What would that rate be for the average woman?

4. The pulse rate for a normal mouse is about 6 times the rate for a boy. What is the mouse's pulse rate?

5. By how much does a child's pulse rate decrease from birth to age 10?

6. How many more times does a newborn baby's heart beat during a 15-minute period than does a 6 year-old child's heart?

7. Find how many times the average man's heart beats in a year (365 days).

8. **DATA HUNT**   How many times does your heart beat during a 24-hour day? (Count for 1 minute, then calculate.)

Bar Graph

Average Pulse Rates
(per minute, at rest)

- Men: 74
- Women: 77
- Boys: 82
- Girls: 85

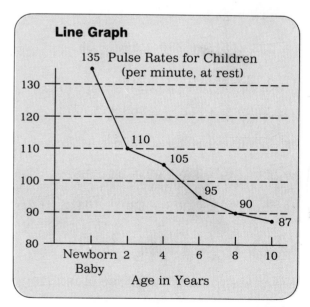

Line Graph

135 Pulse Rates for Children
(per minute, at rest)

- Newborn Baby: 135
- 2: 110
- 4: 105
- 6: 95
- 8: 90
- 10: 87

Age in Years

9. **Strategy Practice**   The difference between Joe's pulse rate before exercise and his rate after exercise is 47. The sum of the two rates is 183. What are the two rates?

98

QUESTION
DATA
PLAN
ANSWER
CHECK

Problem Solving: Multiple-Step Problems

Human Body Facts

Solve.

1. A person's heart pumps about 5 L of blood every minute. How many liters is this per day?

2. The eyes of an average person blink 25 times per minute. How many is this per day? per year?

3. Every extra kilogram of fat a person carries takes about 708 more kilometers of capillaries. If Jo's weight increases from 47 kg to 51 kg, how many extra kilometers of capillaries are needed?

4. An adult usually has 4 canine teeth. He or she has twice as many incisors and twice as many premolars as canines. He or she also has 3 times as many molars as canines. How many teeth does an adult have?

5. A person may take 25 breaths per minute while working and 18 breaths per minute while resting. At this rate, how many more breaths per hour are taken while working than while resting?

6. A person's total body weight is about twice the weight of the person's skin combined with 3 times the weight of the person's bones. How much does a person weigh whose bones weigh 9 kg and whose skin weighs 14 kg?

7. The height of a 6-year-old boy is about 6 times the distance from the bottom of his chin to the top of his head. The height of an adult man is about 8 times this distance. This distance on a certain man was 22 cm. On a boy it was 19 cm. How much taller was the man?

8. **Strategy Practice**   A person's hair grows about 15 cm each year. A child's hair was 31 cm long on her fourth birthday. She cut off 5 cm of hair on her fifth birthday and 7 cm on her seventh birthday. How long was her hair on her ninth birthday?

Mixed Skills Practice

Computation

Find the answers.

1. $596 + 427$

2. $819 + 67$

3. $606 + 278$

4. $3{,}745 + 437$

5. $7{,}839 + 6{,}458$

6. $782 - 538$

7. $804 - 728$

8. $9{,}567 - 3{,}407$

9. $36{,}503 - 24{,}268$

10. $56{,}002 - 9{,}573$

11. $\$16.89 + 43.65$

12. $\$605.37 - 368.49$

13. $2{,}456.7 - 873.38$

14. $534.347 \\ 79.39 \\ + 8.689$

15. $3{,}565.674 + 473.49$

16. 58×67

17. $45{,}376 \times 9$

18. $\$56.37 \times 8$

19. $5{,}054 \times 17$

20. 468×347

Mental Math

Write only the answers.

21. $30 + 50$

22. $80 + 40$

23. $600 + 900$

24. $8{,}000 + 7{,}000$

25. $70 - 40$

26. $150 - 80$

27. $1{,}600 - 900$

28. $17{,}000 - 9{,}000$

29. $25 + 45$

30. $86 + 7$

31. $78 - 24$

32. $53 + 26$

33. 6×80

34. 40×60

35. 800×30

36. 500×600

Estimation

Estimate.

37. $89 + 37$

38. $76 - 38$

39. $632 - 297$

40. $794 - 488$

41. $52 + 96 + 49$

42. $98.2 + 47.3 + 54.8$

43. $62.3 + 38 + 19.5 + 79 + 98.3$

44. $648 + 275 + 553$

45. $475 + 819 + 927$

46. $638 + 226 + 765 + 975$

47. $63 + 59 + 65 + 54 + 61 + 57$

48. $617 + 587 + 624 + 596 + 579 + 609$

Applied Problem Solving

Your grandmother has asked you to help her choose a new telephone. You have looked at 3 models. You need to decide whether your grandmother should buy a telephone or plan to lease (rent) one.

Some Things to Consider

- The costs of the models are as shown.
- If you buy a telephone and it breaks, you must pay to have it repaired.
- If you lease a telephone and it breaks, you do not have to pay for repairs.
- People sometimes want to change phones after a few years.

Model	Purchase Price	Lease per month
Touchtone desk-top	$ 55.95	$2.85
Rotary-dial slim	$ 49.95	$3.25
Cordless touchtone	$109.95	Not Available

Some Questions to Answer

1. How much would it cost to lease the touchtone desk-top model for 1 year? For 4 years?

2. Suppose your grandmother bought the touchtone desk-top model and found that she wanted to buy a new one at the end of 3 years. Would it have been cheaper to lease this model for 3 years?

3. How much would it cost to lease the rotary-dial model for 1 year? For 4 years?

4. How much would be saved in 4 years leasing the touchtone rather than the rotary-dial?

5. What are some advantages and disadvantages of buying the cordless telephone?

What Is Your Decision?

Which telephone model would you suggest your grandmother choose? Would you advise her to buy or lease the telephone?

101

Problem-Solving Strategy: Make a Table

To solve a problem like this it sometimes helps to put the data in a table. This problem solving strategy is called

Make a Table

Try This Julie delivers 2 out of every 5 papers on a paper route. Her older brother, Ben, delivers the others. There are 40 customers on the route. How many papers does each carrier deliver?

I'll use the data in the problem and make a table.

Julie	2					
Ben						
Total	5					

Label↑ carefully.   ↑ Data from the problem

I'll complete as much of the table as needed to solve the problem.

Answers to the problem ↓

Julie	2	4	6	8	10	12	14	16
Ben								24
Total	5	10	15	20	25	30	35	40

Data from the problem ↑

Julie delivers 16 papers and Ben delivers 24.

Solve.

1. One out of every 3 seats on a small bus is empty. If 14 passengers are on the bus, how many empty seats are there?

2. The body of a tropical fish is twice as long as its tail. The total length of the fish is 24 cm. How long is the fish's tail?

Chapter Review-Test

Multiply.

1. 8 × 600

2. 40 × 9

3. 6,000 × 5

4. 6 × 100

5. 20 × 80

6. 10 × 700

7. 600 × 900

8. 8,000 × 50

Estimate the products. Round 2-digit numbers to the nearest ten and 3-digit numbers to the nearest hundred.

9. 4 × 389

10. 61 × 38

11. 74 × 652

12. 813 × 496

Multiply.

13.
$$\begin{array}{r} 426 \\ \times \quad 5 \\ \hline \end{array}$$

14.
$$\begin{array}{r} 5{,}943 \\ \times \quad 6 \\ \hline \end{array}$$

15.
$$\begin{array}{r} 63{,}078 \\ \times \quad 9 \\ \hline \end{array}$$

16.
$$\begin{array}{r} 83 \\ \times \ 20 \\ \hline \end{array}$$

17.
$$\begin{array}{r} 564 \\ \times \ 40 \\ \hline \end{array}$$

18.
$$\begin{array}{r} 396 \\ \times \ 500 \\ \hline \end{array}$$

19.
$$\begin{array}{r} 94 \\ \times \ 36 \\ \hline \end{array}$$

20.
$$\begin{array}{r} 97 \\ \times \ 48 \\ \hline \end{array}$$

21.
$$\begin{array}{r} 368 \\ \times \ 24 \\ \hline \end{array}$$

22.
$$\begin{array}{r} 6{,}439 \\ \times \quad 67 \\ \hline \end{array}$$

Multiply and give the number in standard form.

23. 2^3

24. 3^2

25. 5^4

26. 10^3

27. 7^5

28. 10^6

Write using exponents.

29. 2 × 2 × 2 × 2 × 2 × 2

30. 10,000

31. 10,000,000

Multiply.

32.
$$\begin{array}{r} 508 \\ \times \ 345 \\ \hline \end{array}$$

33.
$$\begin{array}{r} 295 \\ \times \ 406 \\ \hline \end{array}$$

34.
$$\begin{array}{r} 386 \\ \times \ 124 \\ \hline \end{array}$$

35.
$$\begin{array}{r} 809 \\ \times \ 341 \\ \hline \end{array}$$

36.
$$\begin{array}{r} 4{,}102 \\ \times \quad 506 \\ \hline \end{array}$$

37. Estimate using clustering and multiplication: 389 + 418 + 397 + 424 + 379

38. A spacecraft in orbit around the earth might travel 28,163 km/h. How far would it travel in 8 hours?

39. Dale's pulse rate at rest is 76 beats per minute. During fast jogging, his rate is 123 beats per minute. How many more times does Dale's heart beat during a 25-minute jog than during 25 minutes at rest?

Another Look

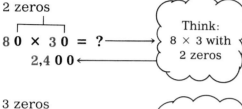

Use basic facts to find special products.

2 zeros

$80 \times 30 = ?$ → Think: 8×3 with 2 zeros

$2,400$ ←

3 zeros

$600 \times 50 = ?$ → Think: 6×5 with 3 zeros

$30,000$ ←

Multiply.

1. 5×30 2. 400×9

3. $8 \times 6,000$ 4. 100×8

5. 40×70 6. 900×30

7. 10×300 8. 600×900

9. 500×800 10. $3,000 \times 70$

11. $8,000 \times 40$ 12. 700×700

Estimate products by rounding factors.

6×87
↓   ↓
$6 \times 90 = 540$

nearest ten

8×536
↓   ↓
$8 \times 500 = 4,000$

nearest hundred

25×620
↓   ↓
$30 \times 600 = 18,000$

Estimate the product by rounding to the nearest ten or the nearest hundred.

13. 4×68 14. 37×42

15. 6×382 16. 93×8

17. 56×72 18. 34×875

19. 8×379 20. 68×23

21. 41×526 22. 619×88

Use the multiplication-addition property.

$$
\begin{array}{r}
736 \\
\times 842 \\
\hline
1472 \leftarrow 2 \times 736 \\
29440 \leftarrow 40 \times 736 \\
588800 \leftarrow 800 \times 736 \\
\hline
619,712 \leftarrow 842 \times 736
\end{array}
$$

Find the products.

23	176 × 8	24.	4,365 × 9	25.	57,384 × 6
26.	73 × 28	27.	547 × 56	28.	3,459 × 38
29.	924 × 186	30.	708 × 567	31.	4,836 × 941

Enrichment

History of Mathematics

A method of multiplying two numbers that was used in Europe centuries ago is shown here. It is called **Russian Peasant Multiplication**.

Use this method to find the product 49×63. Here's how!

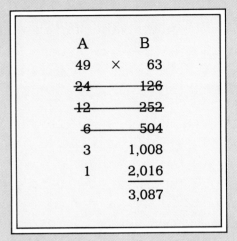

A		B
49	×	63
~~24~~		~~126~~
~~12~~		~~252~~
~~6~~		~~504~~
3		1,008
1		2,016
		3,087

Divide the number in column A by 2. Drop the remainder.	→	Double the number in column B.	→	Repeat until you get 1 in column A.	→	Draw lines through rows with an even number in column A.	→	Add the numbers left in column B.

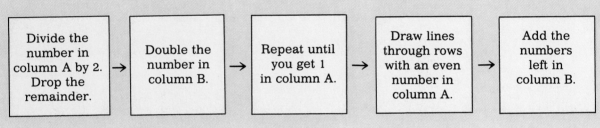

A	B		A	B		A	B		A	B		A	B
49 × 63			49 × 63			49 × 63			49 × 63			49 × 63	
24			24	126		24	126		~~24~~	~~126~~		~~24~~	~~126~~
						12	252		~~12~~	~~252~~		~~12~~	~~252~~
						6	504		~~6~~	~~504~~		~~6~~	~~504~~
						3	1,008		3	1,008		3	1,008
						1	2,016		1	2,016		1	2,016
													3,087

The product of 49×63 is 3,087.

Use Russian Peasant Multiplication to find these products.
Check by multiplying the usual way.

1. 12×42 **2.** 23×35 **3.** 37×53 **4.** 43×71

5. 54×73 **6.** 18×49 **7.** 36×67 **8.** 78×96

9. 101×101 **10.** 365×42 **11.** 627×143 **12.** 546×695

105

1. Use place value to tell what the 4 means in 234,601.

   A 4 hundreds   **B** 4 thousands
   C 4 ten thousands **D** not given

2. Use place value to tell what the 6 means in 826,471,395.

   A 6 ten thousands **B** 6 billions
   C 6 thousands   **D** not given

Which symbol (>, <, or =) goes in each ▒ ?

3. 36,209 ▒ 36,029
   A <   **B** >   **C** =

4. 417,298 ▒ 471,289
   A <   **B** >   **C** =

Add or subtract.

5.
   $$\begin{array}{r} 6{,}785 \\ + 2{,}619 \end{array}$$
   A 4,166
   B 8,394
   C 9,404
   D not given

6.
   $$\begin{array}{r} 2{,}308 \\ - 194 \end{array}$$
   A 2,214
   B 2,114
   C 1,402
   D not given

7. Use place value to tell what the 5 means in 2.3651.

   A 5 hundredths   **B** 5 thousandths
   C 5 tenths   **D** not given

8. Use place value to tell what the 3 means in 0.0362.

   A 3 tenths   **B** 3 thousandths
   C 3 hundredths **D** not given

Which symbol (>, <, or =) goes in each ▒ ?

9. 0.38 ▒ 3.8
   A <   **B** >   **C** =

10. 0.72 ▒ 0.720
    A <   **B** >   **C** =

Add or subtract.

11.
    $$\begin{array}{r} 9.02 \\ - 5.34 \end{array}$$
    A 3.68
    B 4.78
    C 4.36
    D not given

12.
    $$\begin{array}{r} 5.1 \\ 2.56 \\ + 1.4 \end{array}$$
    A 8.07
    B 8.61
    C 8.06
    D not given

13. Barbara drove 378 km one week and 504 km the next week. How many kilometers did she drive in the two weeks?

    A 882 km   **B** 126 km
    C 927 km   **D** not given

14. Andy bought a record for $7.29. How much change did he receive from a $10 bill?

    A $17.29   **B** $2.71
    C $3.81   **D** not given

5

Division

Jane's birthday, February 29, comes only in leap years. Leap years have 366 days instead of the usual 365 days. This puzzled Jane, and she decided to find out about our calendar.

Jane learned that since ancient times the positions of the sun, moon, and stars have been used to make calendars. Our calendar began in ancient Egypt. The Egyptian calendar had 12 equal months, which totaled 360 days. Five festival days were added to make a total of 365 days.

A year, or the time it takes the earth to go around the sun, is almost $365\frac{1}{4}$ days, however. In the time of Julius Caesar, the calendar was changed. A leap year was added every fourth year. In 1582, a more accurate leap year system was developed. Years that are evenly divisible by 4 are leap years, except that century leap years (such as 1600) must be evenly divisible by 400. England and the American colonies began using the new calendar in 1752. This is the calendar we use today.

Using Division Facts: Mental Math

The 8 horses on the Buckaroo Ranch drink a total of about 320 L of water each day. About how much water is this for each horse?

Since we want to find the size of 1 of 8 equal amounts, we divide.

$$32 \div 8 = 4$$
so $$320 \div 8 = 40$$

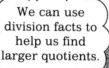

We can use division facts to help us find larger quotients.

Check: $40 \times 8 = 320$, so the answer is correct.

Each horse drinks about 40 L of water.

Other Examples

$$48 \div 6 = 8$$
so $$4,800 \div 6 = 800$$

$$40 \div 5 = 8$$
so $$40,000 \div 5 = 8,000$$

$$9\overline{)63}^{\,7}, \quad \text{so} \quad 9\overline{)630}^{\,70}$$

Practice   Find the quotients. Use pencils for answers only.

1. $32 \div 4$
   $320 \div 4$
   $3,200 \div 4$
   $32,000 \div 4$

2. $72 \div 9$
   $720 \div 9$
   $7,200 \div 9$
   $72,000 \div 9$

3. $42 \div 6$
   $420 \div 6$
   $4,200 \div 6$
   $42,000 \div 6$

4. $30 \div 5$
   $300 \div 5$
   $3,000 \div 5$
   $30,000 \div 5$

5. $210 \div 7$

6. $180 \div 3$

7. $560 \div 7$

8. $2,700 \div 9$

9. $4,800 \div 8$

10. $45,000 \div 5$

11. $4,000 \div 8$

12. $8,100 \div 9$

13. $3,600 \div 4$

14. $140 \div 2$

15. $54,000 \div 6$

16. $3,500 \div 5$

17. $6\overline{)300}$

18. $4\overline{)3,600}$

19. $3\overline{)15,000}$

20. $8\overline{)64,000}$

108

Special Quotients: Mental Math

Sara feeds her horse 1 kg of grain for every 90 kg the horse weighs. If the horse weighs 540 kg, how much grain does it get?

Since we want to find the number of same-size amounts in the total, we divide.

> Division facts also help us divide with multiples of 10, 100, or 1,000.

$$54 \div 9 = 6$$
so $$540 \div 90 = 6$$

Check: $6 \times 90 = 540$, so the answer is correct.

The horse gets 6 kg of grain.

Other Examples

$$36 \div 4 = 9$$
so $$3,600 \div 40 = 90$$

$$30 \div 6 = 5$$
so $$30,000 \div 60 = 500$$

$$9 \div 1 = 9$$
so $$900 \div 10 = 90$$

$$8)\overline{56}^{\,7}$$
so $$800)\overline{5,600}^{\,7}$$

Practice Find the quotients. Use pencils for answers only.

1. $35 \div 7$
   $350 \div 70$
   $3,500 \div 70$
   $35,000 \div 70$

2. $45 \div 9$
   $450 \div 90$
   $4,500 \div 90$
   $45,000 \div 90$

3. $72 \div 8$
   $720 \div 80$
   $7,200 \div 80$
   $72,000 \div 80$

4. $40 \div 8$
   $4,000 \div 800$
   $40,000 \div 800$
   $400,000 \div 800$

5. $420 \div 70$

6. $540 \div 60$

7. $3,600 \div 40$

8. $6,300 \div 90$

9. $18,000 \div 60$

10. $27,000 \div 30$

11. $210 \div 70$

12. $2,800 \div 40$

13. $24,000 \div 40$

14. $5,600 \div 800$

15. $4,500 \div 500$

16. $72,000 \div 900$

17. $60)\overline{360}$

18. $50)\overline{2,000}$

19. $80)\overline{48,000}$

20. $90)\overline{6,300}$

109

Estimating Quotients: Using Compatible Numbers

When estimating quotients, it often helps to replace a given number with another, more **compatible** number so that you can estimate using a basic fact. (Compatible numbers are those that go together and are easy to work with.)

$$532 \div 6$$
$$540 \div 6 = 90$$
Estimate

$$3{,}740 \div 9$$
$$3{,}600 \div 9 = 400$$
Estimate

$$23{,}465 \div 82$$
$$24{,}000 \div 80 = 300$$
Estimate

Practice Choose the best replacement for the bold number so that a basic fact can be used to estimate the quotient. Give the estimate.

1. **249** ÷ 6
   - A 200
   - B 240
   - C 250

2. **174** ÷ 3
   - A 170
   - B 180
   - C 190

3. **274** ÷ 40
   - A 270
   - B 280
   - C 300

4. **259** ÷ 50
   - A 250
   - B 260
   - C 270

5. **3,437** ÷ 7
   - A 3,000
   - B 3,400
   - C 3,500

6. **4,906** ÷ 8
   - A 4,800
   - B 4,900
   - C 5,000

7. **6,234** ÷ 9
   - A 6,000
   - B 6,200
   - C 6,300

8. **55,658** ÷ 6
   - A 54,000
   - B 55,000
   - C 56,000

Choose compatible numbers and use basic facts to estimate the quotients.

9. $3\overline{)125}$

10. $6\overline{)427}$

11. $2\overline{)163}$

12. $50\overline{)306}$

13. $70\overline{)342}$

14. $8\overline{)3{,}372}$

15. $9\overline{)4{,}567}$

16. $4\overline{)3{,}517}$

17. $90\overline{)6{,}400}$

18. $60\overline{)4{,}325}$

19. $6\overline{)54{,}631}$

20. $8\overline{)62{,}479}$

21. $5\overline{)46{,}235}$

22. $60\overline{)29{,}437}$

23. $70\overline{)54{,}896}$

Mixed Applications

Estimate the answers. Use compatible numbers.

24. Rex used 72 L of gasoline to travel 639 km. When he divided on his calculator to find the number of kilometers he had traveled on a liter of gas, the calculator looked like this. Is the answer reasonable?

25. Mary used 62 L of gas to travel 251 km. How many kilometers per liter was this?

110

Problem Solving: Using Estimation

Give your estimate for the answer to each problem. Write
R (Reasonable) or **NR** (Not Reasonable) for the answer given.

1. A record store sold $3,451 worth of record albums during a special sale. At $7 per album, how many records were sold?

   Answer: 493

2. How much farther would you travel during an 8-hour trip at 79 km/h (kilometers per hour) than during a 7-hour trip at 89 km/h?

   Answer: 100 km

3. A pro basketball player made 2,365 points in 80 games. How many points did he average per game?

   Answer: 29.6

4. A clerk earned $245 for 48 hours' work. How much did the clerk earn per hour?

   Answer: $5.10

5. How many egg cartons that hold 1 dozen eggs each are needed to hold 612 eggs?

   Answer: 61

6. A tennis ball manufacturer put 3 balls in each of 897 cans during a 2-hour period. How many balls were put in cans?

   Answer: 300

7. A full school bus holds 43 children. If 119 children from one school and 162 from another are to be taken on a field trip, how many buses are needed?

   Answer: 7

8. **Strategy Practice** Nick spends twice as much time practicing basketball as practicing his horn. One week his total practice time was 24 hours. How many hours did he practice his horn? Hint: Make a table.

1-Digit Divisors

Ken earned $75 in a "Swim for Charity." He divided it equally among 3 charities. How much did each charity receive?

$75

Since the money is shared equally, we divide.

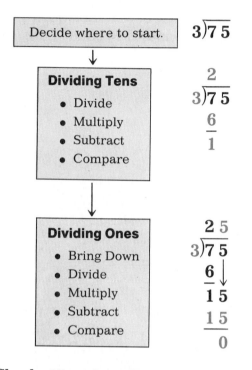

| Decide where to start. | $3\overline{)75}$ |

$3 < 7$
Divide the tens.

Dividing Tens
- Divide
- Multiply
- Subtract
- Compare

$$\begin{array}{r} 2 \\ 3\overline{)75} \\ \underline{6} \\ 1 \end{array}$$

Dividing Ones
- Bring Down
- Divide
- Multiply
- Subtract
- Compare

$$\begin{array}{r} 25 \\ 3\overline{)75} \\ \underline{6}\downarrow \\ 15 \\ \underline{15} \\ 0 \end{array}$$

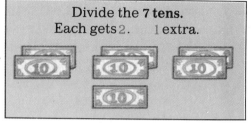

Divide the 7 tens.
Each gets 2.   1 extra.

Trade the extra ten for 10 ones.

These 10 ones and the other 5 ones make 15 ones.

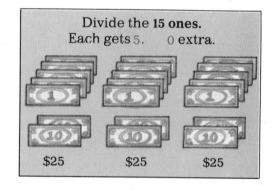

Divide the 15 ones.
Each gets 5.   0 extra.

$25 $25 $25

Check: $25 \times 3 = 75$

Each charity received $25.

Other Examples

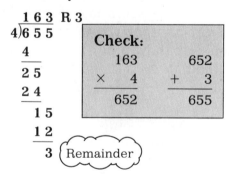

$$\begin{array}{r} 163 \ \text{R}\,3 \\ 4\overline{)655} \\ \underline{4} \\ 25 \\ \underline{24} \\ 15 \\ \underline{12} \\ 3 \end{array}$$

3 Remainder

Check:

$$\begin{array}{r} 163 \\ \times \quad 4 \\ \hline 652 \end{array} \qquad \begin{array}{r} 652 \\ + \quad 3 \\ \hline 655 \end{array}$$

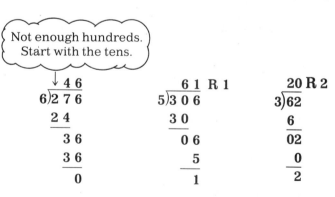

Not enough hundreds. Start with the tens.

$$\begin{array}{r} 46 \\ 6\overline{)276} \\ \underline{24} \\ 36 \\ \underline{36} \\ 0 \end{array} \qquad \begin{array}{r} 61 \ \text{R}\,1 \\ 5\overline{)306} \\ \underline{30} \\ 06 \\ \underline{5} \\ 1 \end{array} \qquad \begin{array}{r} 20 \ \text{R}\,2 \\ 3\overline{)62} \\ \underline{6} \\ 02 \\ \underline{0} \\ 2 \end{array}$$

Warm Up   Divide. Check by multiplying.

1. $2\overline{)49}$ **2.** $3\overline{)87}$ **3.** $6\overline{)199}$ **4.** $8\overline{)985}$ **5.** $7\overline{)359}$

Practice Divide.

1. $2\overline{)28}$ 2. $6\overline{)84}$ 3. $3\overline{)86}$

4. $5\overline{)59}$ 5. $9\overline{)198}$ 6. $7\overline{)164}$

7. $3\overline{)175}$ 8. $8\overline{)576}$ 9. $4\overline{)332}$

10. $6\overline{)97}$ 11. $6\overline{)380}$ 12. $5\overline{)406}$

13. $3\overline{)139}$ 14. $8\overline{)216}$ 15. $7\overline{)96}$

16. $7\overline{)476}$ 17. $2\overline{)836}$ 18. $9\overline{)432}$

19. $4\overline{)731}$ 20. $5\overline{)87}$ 21. $2\overline{)179}$

22. $4\overline{)636}$ 23. $9\overline{)478}$ 24. $2\overline{)972}$

25. $8\overline{)608}$ 26. $7\overline{)875}$ 27. $5\overline{)297}$

28. $222 \div 3$ 29. $364 \div 5$ 30. $497 \div 7$

31. $334 \div 4$ 32. $557 \div 6$ 33. $96 \div 8$

34. Estimate, then find: $345 \div 5$

35. Estimate, then find: $718 \div 9$

Mixed Applications

36. Shari earned $176 in the "Swim for Charity." She divided it equally among 4 charities. How much did each charity get?

37. Darlene and 2 friends each earned $64 in the "Swim for Charity." What was the total amount earned by Darlene and her friends?

38. Matthew can swim 6 meters in 5 seconds. At this rate, how far can he swim in one minute?

Remember!

Divide

↓

Multiply
Subtract
Compare

↓

Bring
down

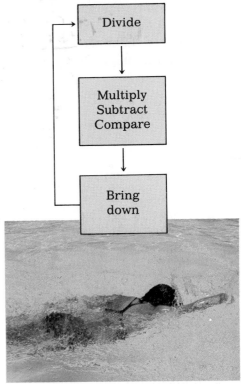

Think

Factor Trees

Here is a **factor tree** for 60.

$$60$$
$$6 \times 10$$
$$2 \times 3 \times 2 \times 5$$

Can you make factor trees for 24, 30, 72, and 140?

Math

1-Digit Divisors: Larger Quotients

On a trip from Honolulu, Hawaii, to Los Angeles, California, a plane traveled 4,256 km in 7 hours. What was its speed in kilometers per hour (km/h)?

Since we want to find the number of kilometers traveled per hour, we divide.

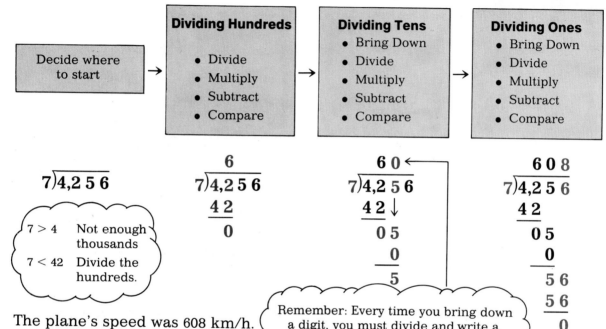

| Decide where to start | → | **Dividing Hundreds**
• Divide
• Multiply
• Subtract
• Compare | → | **Dividing Tens**
• Bring Down
• Divide
• Multiply
• Subtract
• Compare | → | **Dividing Ones**
• Bring Down
• Divide
• Multiply
• Subtract
• Compare |

```
7)4,256
```

7 > 4   Not enough thousands
7 < 42   Divide the hundreds.

```
        6
7)4,2 5 6
  4 2
    0
```

```
      6 0 ←
7)4,2 5 6
  4 2 ↓
    0 5
    0
    5
```

Remember: Every time you bring down a digit, you must divide and write a digit (sometimes 0) in the quotient.

```
      6 0 8
7)4,2 5 6
  4 2
    0 5
    0
    5 6
    5 6
      0
```

The plane's speed was 608 km/h.

Other Examples

```
    3 5 0 R 5
8)2,8 0 5
  2 4
    4 0
    4 0
      0 5
        0
        5
```

```
    2,6 2 4
6)1 5,7 4 4
  1 2
    3 7
    3 6
      1 4
      1 2
        2 4
        2 4
          0
```

```
    $9.2 6 ←
7)$6 4.8 2
  6 3
    1 8
    1 4
      4 2
      4 2
        0
```

Think about pennies and divide as for whole numbers. Estimate to help you write the quotient as dollars and cents.

Warm Up   Divide.

1. 3)621   **2.** 7)2,823   **3.** 5)17,735   **4.** 4)36,864   **5.** 8)$39.12

Practice   Divide and check.

1. 3)547
2. 6)278
3. 7)963
4. 2)587
5. 4)689

6. 9)3,476
7. 8)1,920
8. 5)4,115
9. 3)607
10. 6)1,218

11. 2)1,876
12. 4)2,836
13. 7)4,760
14. 5)2,076
15. 9)4,996

16. 8)9,872
17. 6)27,366
18. 2)19,712
19. 4)25,548
20. 3)9,072

21. 6)19,248
22. 5)22,510
23. 7)45,500
24. 8)$57.84
25. 9)$6.66

26. 804 ÷ 3
27. 3,604 ÷ 4
28. 2,880 ÷ 6
29. 30,065 ÷ 5

30. Estimate, then find: 4,242 ÷ 7
31. Estimate, then find: 2,760 ÷ 4

Mixed Applications

32. A plane flew 3,520 km from San Francisco to Cleveland in 4 hours. What was the rate of speed?

33. A plane flew for 6 hours at an average speed of 870 km/h. How far did it fly?

34. Make up a question involving this data. Solve the problem. On 5 flights a large passenger jet carried a total of 2,145 passengers.

Skillkeeper

Multiply.

1. 7 × 40
2. 600 × 8
3. 5 × 2,000
4. 100 × 3

5. 50 × 90
6. 300 × 40
7. 10 × 700
8. 800 × 800

Write each number in standard form.

9. 3^3
10. 10^4
11. 8^3
12. 2^4
13. 10^6
14. 4^5

Short Division

A company paid $2,850 for 6 minutes of prime time advertising on radio. How much did the company pay per minute?

Since we want to separate the total into equal amounts, we divide.

Decide where to start.	→	Divide the hundreds. Write the remainder by the tens.	→	Divide the tens. Write the remainder by the ones.	→	Divide the ones.

$$\begin{array}{r} 4 \\ 6\overline{)2{,}8\,5\,0} \end{array}$$

Not enough thousands 6 < 28 Divide the hundreds.

$$\begin{array}{r} 4 \\ 6\overline{)2{,}8^{4}5\,0} \end{array}$$

28 ÷ 6 = 4, R4

$$\begin{array}{r} 4\ 7 \\ 6\overline{)2{,}8^{4}5^{3}0} \end{array}$$

45 ÷ 6 = 7, R3

$$\begin{array}{r} 4\ 7\ 5 \\ 6\overline{)2{,}8^{4}5^{3}0} \end{array}$$

30 ÷ 6 = 5, R0

The company paid $475 per minute for the advertising.

Other Examples

$$\begin{array}{r} 2\ 6\ 9 \\ 3\overline{)8^{2}0^{2}7} \end{array} \qquad \begin{array}{r} 8\ 0\ 6 \\ 7\overline{)5{,}6\,4\,2} \end{array} \qquad \begin{array}{r} 4{,}5\ 9\ 4\ \text{R }4 \\ 6\overline{)2\ 7^{3}5^{5}6^{2}8} \end{array} \qquad \begin{array}{r} \$4.7\ 3 \\ 8\overline{)\$3\ 7^{5}8^{2}4} \end{array}$$

Warm Up   Divide. Use short division.

1. $2\overline{)576}$ 2. $5\overline{)2{,}307}$ 3. $6\overline{)1{,}830}$ 4. $9\overline{)7{,}836}$ 5. $3\overline{)2{,}408}$

6. $7\overline{)16{,}563}$ 7. $8\overline{)24{,}076}$ 8. $4\overline{)65{,}384}$ 9. $7\overline{)\$9.73}$ 10. $6\overline{)\$136.26}$

Practice Divide and check. Use short division.

1. $4\overline{)172}$ 2. $3\overline{)483}$ 3. $6\overline{)867}$ 4. $3\overline{)832}$ 5. $5\overline{)945}$

6. $2\overline{)8,765}$ 7. $9\overline{)1,927}$ 8. $7\overline{)2,520}$ 9. $3\overline{)2,953}$ 10. $5\overline{)3,105}$

11. $7\overline{)25,494}$ 12. $9\overline{)28,890}$ 13. $2\overline{)13,178}$ 14. $4\overline{)24,136}$ 15. $6\overline{)31,224}$

16. $8\overline{)92,146}$ 17. $3\overline{)57,183}$ 18. $2\overline{)46,872}$ 19. $4\overline{)73,946}$ 20. $5\overline{)28,970}$

21. $7\overline{)71,848}$ 22. $6\overline{)\$8.46}$ 23. $9\overline{)\$74.70}$ 24. $8\overline{)\$146.56}$ 25. $6\overline{)\$98.70}$

26. $1,876 \div 7$ 27. $3,745 \div 9$ 28. $42,324 \div 5$ 29. $2,432 \div 4$

30. $32,364 \div 6$ 31. $45,382 \div 8$ 32. $71,057 \div 7$ 33. $18,054 \div 9$

34. Estimate, then find: $23,574 \div 6$ 35. Estimate, then find: $8,865 \div 3$

Mixed Applications

36. A company paid $556 a minute for 5 minutes of advertising during a show. What was the total cost of their advertising during that show?

37. The advertising cost for 4 minutes of radio time was $2,032. What was the cost per minute?

38. In a recent year, the record charge for television advertising was about $250,000 per minute. At this rate, about how many minutes could be bought with $1,550,000?

Think

Prime Numbers

A **prime number** is a number that has exactly two factors, the number itself and 1. Other whole numbers (except 0 and 1) are **composite**.

- 7 is a prime number, since it is the product of the two factors 1 and 7 and no others.
- 6 is a composite number, since it is the product of 3 and 2 as well as 1 and 6.

Can you list the prime numbers up to 50?

→ **Math** ←

Finding Averages

The graph shows Nina's scores on 5 mathematics tests. What is her average score?

To find the average of a set of numbers, we add the numbers and divide the sum by the number of addends.

Scores on 5 Mathematics Tests

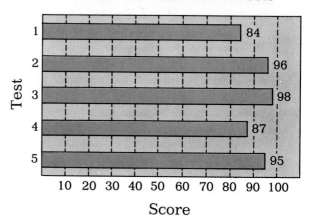

| Find the sum of the numbers. | → | Divide by the number of addends. | → | The quotient is the **average** of the numbers. |

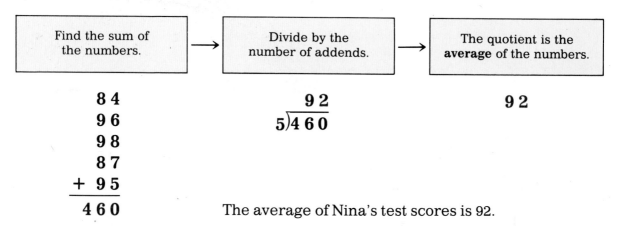

```
   8 4
   9 6
   9 8
   8 7
 + 9 5
 ─────
   4 6 0
```

```
      9 2
 5)4 6 0
```

9 2

The average of Nina's test scores is 92.

Other Examples

Find the average of these test scores.

Test	1	2	3	4
Score	79	87	93	86

```
   7 9
   8 7
   9 3
 + 8 6
 ─────
   3 4 5
```

```
       8 6 R 1
 4)3 4²5
```

The remainder, 1, is closer to 0 than to the divisor, 4, so the average, to the nearest whole number, is 86.

Practice Find the average of these test scores, to the nearest whole number.

1. 76, 84, 96, 80   2. 98, 91, 86, 92   3. 99, 89, 83   4. 58, 70, 63, 49

5. 67, 74, 86, 92, 95   6. 71, 75, 86, 94, 82, 74   7. 84, 98, 79, 83, 78

8. 92, 88, 96, 98, 99, 100   9. 74, 86, 91, 82, 79   10. 64, 69, 71, 62

11. 78, 82, 69, 73, 90   12. 89, 86, 87, 84, 91, 92   13. 70, 68, 60

Problem Solving:
Using Data from Tables

Solve.

1. What is Jorge's average bowling score for the 3 games?

2. How much higher is Jorge's highest bowling score than his average?

3. What is the average height of the students? the average weight?

4. What is the difference between the average height of the girls and the average height of the boys?

5. By how much does the average weight of the children in the table differ from the average weight of 37 kg for children their age?

6. What is the average speed for the race car on the 4 time trials?

7. By how much does the average time trial speed differ from the time trial record speed of 325 km/h?

8. **DATA BANK** To the nearest whole number, what is the average number of clear days per year in the six sunniest cities in the United States? (See Data Bank, page 424.)

9. **DATA HUNT** Suppose you write the names of the students in your class on slips of paper and put them in a hat. Then you draw 5 names. What is the average height of those students in centimeters? Guess first, then find out.

Jorge's Bowling Scores	
Game	Score
1	174
2	190
3	158

Name	Height (cm)	Weight (kg)
Doug	149	40
Carol	148	38
Bret	143	35
Ann	152	42
Art	145	37
Joan	155	39

Time Trial	Race Car Speed (km/h)
1	314
2	295
3	318
4	301

10. **Strategy Practice** During a 30-day month there were 2 rainy days for every 3 clear days. How many of the days were clear? Hint: Make a table.

Dividing by Multiples of 10

A guidebook suggests that you can average 30 km a day on a 362-km raft trip on the Colorado River through the Grand Canyon. About how many days will the trip take?

Since we want to find how many equal amounts in the total, we divide.

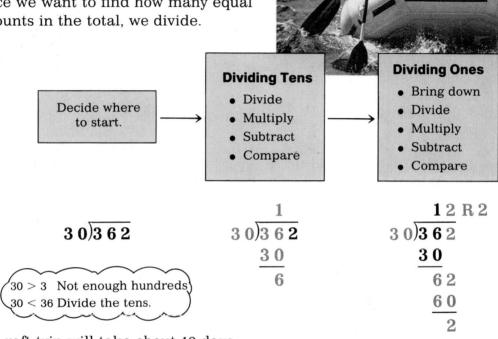

| Decide where to start. | → | **Dividing Tens**
• Divide
• Multiply
• Subtract
• Compare | → | **Dividing Ones**
• Bring down
• Divide
• Multiply
• Subtract
• Compare |

$$30\overline{)362}$$

30 > 3 Not enough hundreds.
30 < 36 Divide the tens.

$$\begin{array}{r} 1 \\ 30\overline{)362} \\ \underline{30} \\ 6 \end{array}$$

$$\begin{array}{r} 12\ \text{R}\,2 \\ 30\overline{)362} \\ \underline{30} \\ 62 \\ \underline{60} \\ 2 \end{array}$$

The raft trip will take about 12 days.

Other Examples

$$\begin{array}{r} 8\ \text{R}\,32 \\ 40\overline{)352} \\ \underline{320} \\ 32 \end{array}$$

$$\begin{array}{r} 324 \\ 60\overline{)19{,}440} \\ \underline{180} \\ 144 \\ \underline{120} \\ 240 \\ \underline{240} \\ 0 \end{array}$$

$$\begin{array}{r} 4{,}053\ \text{R}\,8 \\ 20\overline{)81{,}068} \\ \underline{80} \\ 10 \\ \underline{0} \\ 106 \\ \underline{100} \\ 68 \\ \underline{60} \\ 8 \end{array}$$

Check:
Find the product of the quotient and the divisor and add the remainder.

$$\begin{array}{r} 40 \\ \times\ 8 \\ \hline 320 \end{array} \qquad \begin{array}{r} 320 \\ +\ 32 \\ \hline 352 \end{array}$$

Warm Up   Divide and check.

1. $30\overline{)284}$ **2.** $50\overline{)467}$ **3.** $70\overline{)4{,}480}$ **4.** $20\overline{)9{,}260}$ **5.** $40\overline{)84{,}756}$

Practice Divide and check.

1. $20\overline{)174}$ 2. $60\overline{)252}$ 3. $40\overline{)362}$

4. $30\overline{)291}$ 5. $70\overline{)572}$ 6. $50\overline{)1,226}$

7. $80\overline{)4,560}$ 8. $40\overline{)2,743}$ 9. $30\overline{)2,520}$

10. $90\overline{)5,895}$ 11. $20\overline{)1,560}$ 12. $60\overline{)4,182}$

13. $50\overline{)4,199}$ 14. $70\overline{)2,600}$ 15. $80\overline{)7,492}$

16. $90\overline{)28,260}$ 17. $20\overline{)13,140}$ 18. $40\overline{)12,200}$

19. $60\overline{)43,858}$ 20. $80\overline{)53,298}$ 21. $30\overline{)15,600}$

22. $50\overline{)106,700}$ 23. $70\overline{)434,280}$ 24. $90\overline{)128,250}$

25. $40\overline{)241,697}$ 26. $60\overline{)308,765}$ 27. $80\overline{)250,240}$

28. $565 \div 60$ 29. $337 \div 40$ 30. $2,856 \div 70$

31. $50,960 \div 80$ 32. $20,700 \div 30$ 33. $474,390 \div 90$

34. Estimate, then find: $1,756 \div 60$.

35. Estimate, then find: $2,439 \div 80$.

Mixed Applications

36. A motor boat can average 50 km a day on the 362-km river trip through the Grand Canyon. About how many days will the trip take?

37. One group of rafters averaged 25 km a day on their trip. If they traveled for 5 days, how far did they travel?

38. If there were 30 people on the boat trip described on page 120 and 60 dozen eggs were eaten, how many eggs per person per day were eaten?

Think

Logical Reasoning

On the scale the large blocks weigh the same. Each small block weighs 1 g (gram). What is the weight of each large block?

GRAMS   997

Math

2-Digit Divisors: 1-Digit Quotients

Marguerite's hobby is designing and making stained glass pictures. She gave some to friends and sold others for $72 each. Her earnings were $432. How many did she sell?

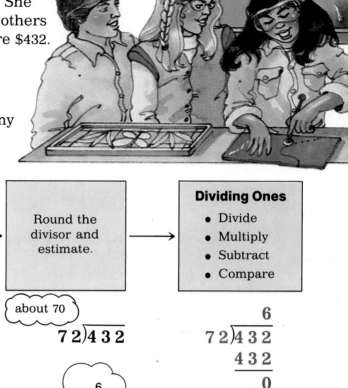

Since we want to find how many equal amounts in the total, we divide.

Decide where to start.	→	Round the divisor and estimate.	→	**Dividing Ones** • Divide • Multiply • Subtract • Compare

about 70

$$72\overline{)432}$$

$$72\overline{)432}$$

$$\begin{array}{r} 6 \\ 72\overline{)432} \\ \underline{432} \\ 0 \end{array}$$

Not enough hundreds
Not enough tens
72 < 432 Divide
the ones.

$$\begin{array}{r} 6 \\ 7\overline{)43} \\ \underline{42} \\ 1 \end{array}$$

Try 6.

Marguerite sold 6 pictures.

Other Examples

40
$$\begin{array}{r} 6 \text{ R } 15 \\ 39\overline{)249} \\ \underline{234} \\ 15 \end{array}$$

60
$$\begin{array}{r} 7 \\ 64\overline{)448} \\ \underline{448} \\ 0 \end{array}$$

50
$$\begin{array}{r} 6 \text{ R } 38 \\ 45\overline{)308} \\ \underline{270} \\ 38 \end{array}$$

Warm Up Divide and check.

1. $21\overline{)175}$ **2.** $49\overline{)267}$ **3.** $52\overline{)312}$ **4.** $78\overline{)578}$ **5.** $33\overline{)231}$

6. $87\overline{)579}$ **7.** $64\overline{)348}$ **8.** $36\overline{)281}$ **9.** $35\overline{)241}$ **10.** $53\overline{)424}$

Practice Divide and check.

1. $42\overline{)252}$ 2. $67\overline{)217}$ 3. $38\overline{)284}$ 4. $23\overline{)138}$ 5. $41\overline{)205}$

6. $75\overline{)328}$ 7. $83\overline{)664}$ 8. $56\overline{)360}$ 9. $34\overline{)238}$ 10. $62\overline{)558}$

11. $29\overline{)223}$ 12. $48\overline{)150}$ 13. $72\overline{)360}$ 14. $91\overline{)648}$ 15. $55\overline{)262}$

16. $84\overline{)504}$ 17. $42\overline{)378}$ 18. $38\overline{)296}$ 19. $71\overline{)497}$ 20. $67\overline{)443}$

21. $53\overline{)425}$ 22. $44\overline{)396}$ 23. $29\overline{)205}$ 24. $76\overline{)532}$ 25. $94\overline{)567}$

26. $164 \div 18$ 27. $448 \div 56$ 28. $337 \div 42$ 29. $439 \div 73$

30. $123 \div 37$ 31. $496 \div 62$ 32. $360 \div 51$ 33. $362 \div 48$

34. $286 \div 65$ 35. $744 \div 93$ 36. $558 \div 62$ 37. $504 \div 84$

38. Estimate, then find: $328 \div 82$

39. Estimate, then find: $354 \div 49$

Mixed Applications

40. Marguerite uses $26 worth of supplies to make 1 "picture." How many "pictures" can she make for $234?

41. Marguerite sold some large stained glass pictures for an average of $94 each. Her earnings fell $30 short of $500. How many pictures did she sell?

42. Marguerite made 7 stained-glass pictures. The pictures usually sell for $65 each, but she gives her friends a $6 discount. If she sold all 7 of her pictures to friends, how much did she earn?

Think

Discovering Some Patterns

1. Use short division to find this quotient:

   $9\overline{)11,111,111,010}$

   What patterns do you see?

2. Divide 427,427 by 7. Divide the first quotient by 11, then divide the second quotient by 13. What is the result? Does this work for any number like 427,427?

Math

2-Digit Divisors: Changing Estimates

In the early 1900s the most popular car in America was the Model T Ford. Les and Eve solved these problems about the Model T.

The Model T could make a 212-mile trip on one tank of gas. If its average speed was 35 miles per hour, how long would the trip have taken?

Les

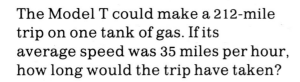

$$35\overline{)212} \rightarrow 35\overline{)212}$$

about 40

$$\begin{array}{r} 5 \\ 35\overline{)212} \\ 175 \\ \hline 37 \end{array} \rightarrow \begin{array}{r} 6\,R2 \\ 35\overline{)212} \\ 210 \\ \hline 2 \end{array}$$

Les's first estimated quotient was too small. How did he know it must be larger?

A factory assembly line could turn out 1 Model T every 93 minutes. At this rate how many cars could the line turn out in a 450-minute shift?

Eve

about 90

$$\begin{array}{r} 5 \\ 93\overline{)450} \\ -465 \end{array} \rightarrow \begin{array}{r} 4\,R78 \\ 93\overline{)450} \\ 372 \\ \hline 78 \end{array}$$

Eve's first estimated quotient was too large. How did she know it must be smaller?

Divide. Watch for estimates that need to be changed.

Remember!

Divide → Multiply Subtract Compare → Bring Down

1. $34\overline{)166}$
2. $76\overline{)460}$
3. $68\overline{)342}$

4. $21\overline{)128}$
5. $45\overline{)364}$
6. $36\overline{)108}$

7. $54\overline{)350}$
8. $63\overline{)315}$
9. $77\overline{)330}$

10. $39\overline{)285}$
11. $86\overline{)520}$
12. $25\overline{)196}$

13. $19\overline{)152}$
14. $42\overline{)285}$
15. $84\overline{)756}$
16. $93\overline{)452}$
17. $66\overline{)539}$

18. $75\overline{)378}$
19. $33\overline{)231}$
20. $27\overline{)174}$
21. $68\overline{)642}$
22. $45\overline{)352}$

More Practice, page 433, Set C

Problem Solving: Multiple-Step Problems

QUESTION
DATA
PLAN
ANSWER
CHECK

Solve.

1. A Model T cost $850 in 1908. In 1985 a low-cost compact car cost 8 times as much. How much greater was the cost of the 1985 car?

2. A Model T went 315 miles on 15 gallons of gasoline. How many miles could it go on the gasoline in a 5-gallon can?

3. The first gasoline-driven auto was patented in 1886. An American automobile was first built in 1892. The Model T Ford was built 16 years later. How long after the first gasoline auto patent was the Model T built?

4. An auto company in 1903 made a total of 900 cars in 6 months. How many cars did they make per day?

5. In 1914 a worker in an automobile factory earned $5.04 for 8 hours' work. Some automobile factory workers today earn $96 for 8 hours' work. How much more per hour does today's worker earn?

6. Henry Ford set a record in 1904 when his racing car, the Arrow, reached a speed of 92 miles per hour. About 75 years after that, a rocket-powered car reached a speed 8.41 miles per hour less than 6 times as fast as the Arrow's record. What was the speed of the rocket-powered car?

7. In 1900 about 350 autos were built each month. 50 years later, 1,909 times as many were built. How many autos were built that year?

8. **Strategy Practice** In an antique car tour, Felipe started at the park and drove 20 km west, 15 km north 55 km east, and 70 km south. If all roads run north and south or east and west only, what is the shortest route Felipe can take to return to the park? Give the direction and distances he must travel.

2-Digit Divisors: Larger Quotients

A trip for the 46 members of the school marching band cost a total of $6,578. What was the cost per band member?

Since we want to find how much in each part when the total is separated equally, we divide.

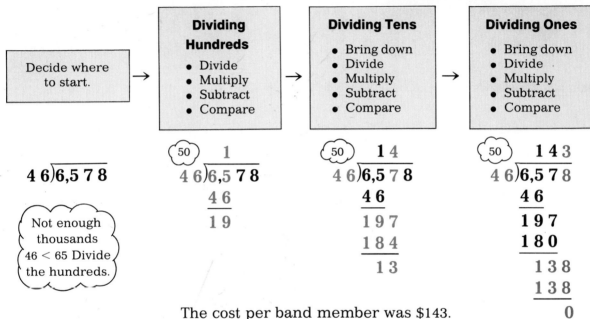

| Decide where to start. | → | **Dividing Hundreds**
• Divide
• Multiply
• Subtract
• Compare | → | **Dividing Tens**
• Bring down
• Divide
• Multiply
• Subtract
• Compare | → | **Dividing Ones**
• Bring down
• Divide
• Multiply
• Subtract
• Compare |

$$46\overline{)6{,}578}$$

Not enough thousands 46 < 65 Divide the hundreds.

```
        1
 46)6,578
    46
    19
```
(50)

```
       14
 46)6,578
    46
    197
    184
     13
```
(50)

```
       143
 46)6,578
    46
    197
    180
    138
    138
      0
```
(50)

The cost per band member was $143.

Other Examples

```
     21 R5
 23)488
    46
    28
    23
     5
```

```
      2,317
 37)85,729
    74
    117
    111
     62
     37
    259
    259
      0
```

```
      $3.95
 45)$177.75
    135
    427
    405
    225
    225
      0
```

Warm Up   Divide.

1. $34\overline{)782}$ **2.** $68\overline{)9{,}658}$ **3.** $75\overline{)94{,}725}$ **4.** $29\overline{)7{,}016}$ **5.** $46\overline{)\$114.54}$

Practice Divide and check.

1. $43\overline{)2{,}322}$ 2. $68\overline{)1{,}564}$ 3. $54\overline{)918}$ 4. $27\overline{)1{,}975}$ 5. $31\overline{)2{,}666}$

6. $78\overline{)11{,}076}$ 7. $85\overline{)27{,}540}$ 8. $46\overline{)9{,}752}$ 9. $92\overline{)37{,}998}$ 10. $57\overline{)19{,}762}$

11. $36\overline{)14{,}796}$ 12. $62\overline{)58{,}967}$ 13. $25\overline{)2{,}495}$ 14. $77\overline{)6{,}622}$ 15. $86\overline{)10{,}234}$

16. $91\overline{)112{,}294}$ 17. $37\overline{)78{,}218}$ 18. $55\overline{)200{,}475}$ 19. $49\overline{)\$316.05}$ 20. $28\overline{)\$691.32}$

21. $1{,}836 \div 27$ 22. $2{,}700 \div 58$ 23. $7{,}875 \div 35$ 24. $48{,}269 \div 79$

25. Estimate, then find: $3{,}967 \div 48$ 26. Estimate, then find: $64{,}276 \div 79$

Mixed Applications

27. New uniforms for a school band cost $5,167.50 for 50 students. What did each uniform cost?

 28. New hats for the 65 members of a band cost $1,784.25. Coats cost $4,371.25. How much greater was the cost per coat than per hat?

29. **DATA HUNT** Use a newspaper, magazine, or catalog to find out how much it would cost to buy a band instrument. If you paid in 12 monthly installments (no interest), how much would each payment be?

Skillkeeper

Add or subtract.

1.	2.	3.	4.	5.
$3.14 + 5.27	$7.12 − 3.56	$8.75 + 6.49	$26.60 − 13.78	$38.98 + 17.42

Find the products.

6.	7.	8.	9.	10.
$2.42 × 8	$69.22 × 4	$2.03 × 47	$36.51 × 12	$4.28 × 317

Zeros in the Quotient

After Lisa worked an exercise incorrectly, her teacher asked her to show it on graph paper and correct her mistake.

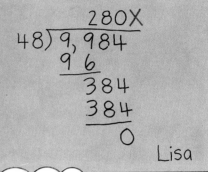

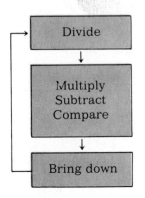

Remember:

Every time you bring down a digit you must divide and write a digit (sometimes 0) in the quotient.

Other Examples

```
      7 0
6 8)4,7 6 0
    4 7 6
      0 0
        0
        0
```

```
       4 3 0  R 9
2 6)1 1,1 8 9
    1 0 4
        7 8
        7 8
          0 9
            0
            9
```

```
        2,0 0 7
3 1)6 2,2 1 7
    6 2
      0 2
        0
        2 1
          0
          2 1 7
          2 1 7
              0
```

Remember!

→ Divide
↓
Multiply
Subtract
Compare
↓
Bring down

Divide.

1. 43)2,580   2. 67)6,045   3. 53)3,551   4. 32)6,562

5. 89)9,970   6. 74)7,548   7. 26)6,240   8. 20)1,030

9. 38)9,984   10. 22)8,866   11. 19)6,097   12. 41)8,407

13. 91)7,957   14. 75)8,175   15. 46)9,245   16. 13)13,949

17. 27)21,762 18. 34)21,270 19. 53)34,450 20. 74)37,000

More Practice, page 434, Set A

3-Digit Divisors

Sometimes we need to divide by a 3-digit number. For larger divisors or quotients we often use a calculator or estimate the quotient.

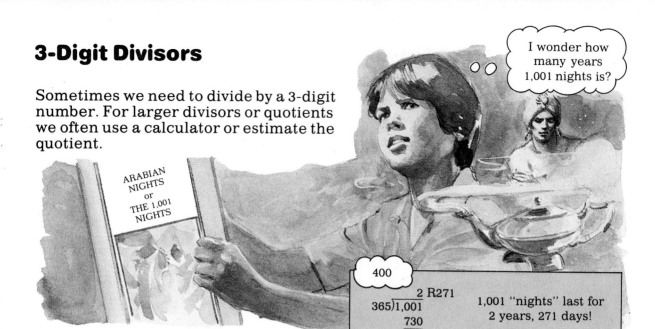

ARABIAN NIGHTS or THE 1,001 NIGHTS

I wonder how many years 1,001 nights is?

400

$$\begin{array}{r} 2 \text{ R271} \\ 365\overline{)1,001} \\ 730 \\ \hline 271 \end{array}$$

1,001 "nights" last for 2 years, 271 days!

Practice Divide.

1. $365\overline{)2,920}$ 2. $402\overline{)2,412}$ 3. $231\overline{)1,850}$ 4. $225\overline{)1,325}$ 5. $527\overline{)2,179}$

6. $648\overline{)3,888}$ 7. $747\overline{)2,641}$ 8. $635\overline{)5,965}$ 9. $243\overline{)1,701}$ 10. $516\overline{)1,432}$

11. $860\overline{)3,480}$ 12. $326\overline{)4,564}$ 13. $215\overline{)4,945}$ 14. $375\overline{)12,750}$ 15. $678\overline{)8,136}$

16. $365\overline{)90,520}$ 17. $813\overline{)531,702}$ 18. $764\overline{)1,767,896}$ 19. $453\overline{)1,631,706}$

Think

Using a Calculator for Dividing

Here's how to use a calculator to find the **quotient** and **remainder** for 87,152 ÷ 365.

Divide. The whole number part is the quotient.	Multiply the quotient by the divisor.	Subtract the product from the dividend to find the remainder.

$$\begin{array}{r} 238 \\ 365\overline{)87,152} \end{array}$$ `238.7726`

$$\begin{array}{r} 238 \\ 365\overline{)87,152} \\ 86870 \end{array}$$ `86870`

$$\begin{array}{r} 238 \\ 365\overline{)87,152} \\ -86870 \\ \hline 282 \end{array}$$ `282`

Try these: 1. $476\overline{)127,875}$ 2. $387\overline{)276,947}$ 3. $967\overline{)389,486}$

Math

Problem Solving:
Using Data from a Map

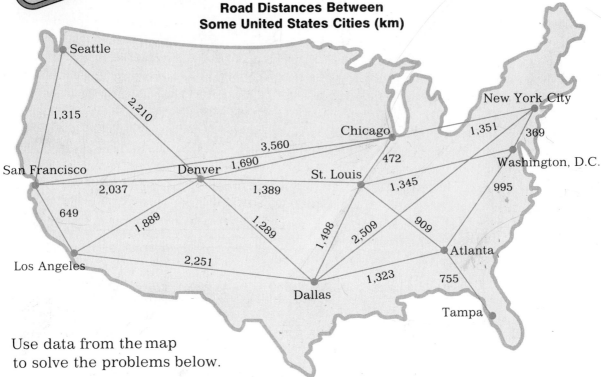

**Road Distances Between
Some United States Cities (km)**

Seattle

1,315

2,210

New York City

San Francisco

Chicago   1,351   369

Denver   3,560

1,690   Washington, D.C.

2,037   1,389   St. Louis   472

649   995

1,889   1,289   1,498   2,509   909   1,345

Los Angeles   2,251   Atlanta

Dallas   1,323   755

Tampa

Use data from the map
to solve the problems below.

1. Stuart's family wants to drive direct
from Chicago to San Francisco in
4 days. How many kilometers must
they average per day?

2. About how many kilometers per
hour must you average to drive
from Washington, D.C., to Atlanta,
Georgia, in 12 hours?

3. Find how much farther it is from
San Francisco through Denver to
St. Louis than from San Francisco
through Los Angeles to Dallas.

4. About how many times as far is it
from Los Angeles to Denver as it is
from New York to Washington,
D.C.?

5. Clea Jenkins drove to Tampa
from Washington, D.C., by way
of Atlanta, and returned to
Washington by the same route.
The trip took her 7 days. What was
the average number of kilometers
she drove each day?

6. What one trip is closest in distance
to two round trips between Chicago
and St. Louis?

7. **Strategy Practice**   Mark went to
New York from Los Angeles. He drove
through two other cities on the way.
He traveled a total of 5,560 km.
Describe his trip.

QUESTION
DATA
PLAN
ANSWER
CHECK

Problem Solving:
Understanding the Operations

Here is a review of the four basic operations.

Add **+**	• **Put together** How many in all?

Multiply **×**	• **Put together a number of same-size sets** How many in all?

Subtract **—**	• **Take away** How many are left? • **Compare** How many more or less than? • **Missing amount** How many more are needed?

Divide **÷**	• **Put the same number into a given number of sets** How many in each set? • **Put into sets of a given size** How many sets?

Tell which operation or operations you would use
to solve the problems below if the numbers were given.

1. Oakdale School has ▥ students. Hoose School has ▥. How many more students does Oakdale have than Hoose?

2. Brigham School took ▥ bus loads of students on a field trip. A total of ▥ students went on the trip. About how many students rode on each bus?

3426

3. The ▥ band members from Glenn School joined the ▥ band members from Field School for a concert. How many members were in the combined band?

4. At Sugar Creek School there are an average of ▥ students per class. There are ▥ classes. How many students are in the school?

5. All but ▥ of the ▥ middle grade children at Fairview School played on a soccer team. Each team had ▥ players. How many teams were there?

6. Sande sold ▥ student tickets to the school play at $▥ each and ▥ adult tickets at $▥ each. How much were her total sales?

7. **Strategy Practice** Bent School has an average of 28 students per class. It has 20 classes. The numbers of students in Stevenson, Washington, and Centennial Schools are 614, 555, and 598. How much greater is the average number of students in these three schools than the number of students in Bent School?

131

Problem-Solving Strategy: Make an Organized List

To solve some problems, it helps to write all the possibilities for the situation in a certain order. This problem-solving strategy is called

Make an Organized List

Try This Al, Bob, Connie, Debra, and Earl are having playoff matches to decide who plays number 1, number 2, and so forth, on a tennis team. How many matches must they play so that each person plays every other person just once?

First, I'll write all the people Al plays.

Then I'll write all the people Bob, Connie, Debra, and Earl play who haven't already been listed.

Bob has already played Al.

A plays B, C, D, E.   4

A plays B, C, D, E.   4
B plays C, D, E.   3
C plays D, E.   2
D plays E.   1

They must play a total of 4 + 3 + 2 + 1, or 10 matches.

Solve.

1. Shelly has white, tan, and gray shorts. She has brown, red, blue, and green shirts. How many different outfits can she wear?

2. How many different playing orders are possible for 4 players on a tennis team? (If the players are Angie, Brigid, Curtis, and Dano, one order is A, B, C, D. Another is B, D, A, C.)

Chapter Review-Test

Find the quotients mentally. Write only the answer.

1. 360 ÷ 9   **2.** 4,200 ÷ 60   **3.** 5,600 ÷ 800   **4.** 4,000 ÷ 8   **5.** 3,200 ÷ 10

6. 810 ÷ 90   **7.** 3,500 ÷ 7   **8.** 4,800 ÷ 80   **9.** 5,400 ÷ 6   **10.** 6,300 ÷ 70

Estimate the quotient by choosing numbers so you can use basic facts.

11. 538 ÷ 6   **12.** 334 ÷ 8   **13.** 447 ÷ 5   **14.** 739 ÷ 92   **15.** 6,295 ÷ 71

Divide.

16. $4\overline{)344}$ **17.** $6\overline{)2,838}$ **18.** $5\overline{)2,010}$ **19.** $3\overline{)10,843}$ **20.** $8\overline{)71,739}$

21. $6\overline{)5,148}$ **22.** $9\overline{)4,617}$ **23.** $7\overline{)8,192}$ **24.** $5\overline{)3,840}$ **25.** $4\overline{)27,386}$

Find the average of these sets of numbers to the nearest whole number.

26. 318, 459, 296   **27.** 75, 63, 82, 94, 71

28. 11, 8, 14, 9, 12, 18   **29.** 516, 497, 501, 528, 476

Divide.

30. $30\overline{)1,455}$ **31.** $70\overline{)25,270}$ **32.** $41\overline{)287}$ **33.** $59\overline{)374}$ **34.** $34\overline{)1,923}$

35. $78\overline{)5,400}$ **36.** $92\overline{)\$345.00}$ **37.** $67\overline{)\$75.04}$ **38.** $185\overline{)840}$ **39.** $342\overline{)3,078}$

Solve.

40. During a vacation trip Akim and his family drove 1,106 km in 14 hours. What was the average distance they traveled in an hour?

41. The total cost of Tracy's trombone was $345.80. She paid for it with 52 weekly payments. How much did she pay each week?

Another Look

After you **decide where to start**, use these steps to divide in each place.

Divide
↓
Multiply
Subtract
Compare
↓
Bring down

Divide and check.

1. 7)406
2. 2)194
3. 6)2,720
4. 5)3,123
5. 8)50,808
6. 4)774
7. 9)56,957
8. 3)9,162
9. 9)2,947
10. 8)20,917

To find the **average** of a list of numbers: 21, 33, 29, 36

1. Find the sum.

2. Divide the sum by the number of addends.

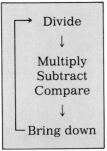

```
2 1
3 3        4          2 9  R 3 → 3 0
2 9     (addends)   4)1 1 9
3 6                   8          Average to
                      3 9        the nearest
1 1 9                 3 6        whole number
                       3
```

Find the average of each set of numbers to the nearest whole number.

11. 15, 19, 11, 22

12. 68, 79, 56, 74, 83

13. 311, 514, 476, 343, 417

14. 48, 53, 39, 45, 58, 61

15. 254, 351, 277, 316, 335

Round the divisor to estimate the quotient.

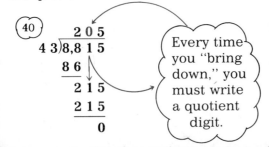

```
 40        2 0 5
       4 3)8,8 1 5    Every time
           8 6        you "bring
           2 1 5      down," you
           2 1 5      must write
               0      a quotient
                      digit.
```

Divide and check.

16. 32)256
17. 76)685
18. 59)1,593
19. 43)2,686
20. 64)12,992
21. 25)21,000
22. 87)127,281
23. 94)192,324
24. 27)2,200
25. 89)12,575

Enrichment

Number Relationships

We say 864 is **divisible by** 2 because the remainder is 0 when 864 is divided by 2. Here are some easy-to-use **divisibility tests.**

- A number is divisible by **2** if its last digit is 0, 2, 4, 6, or 8.
- A number is divisible by **5** if its last digit is 0 or 5.

- A number is divisible by **3** if the sum of its digits is divisible by 3.
- A number is divisible by **9** if the sum of its digits is divisible by 9.

I just look at the last digit!

9,436 is divisible by 2.
87,965 is divisible by 5.

3 + 8 + 6 + 4 = 21

21 is divisible by 3, so 3,864 is divisible by 3!

3,864

21 isn't divisible by 9, so neither is 3,864!

- A number is divisible by **4** if twice its tens digit plus its ones digit is divisible by 4.

- A number is divisible by **6** if it is divisible by 2 and by 3.

(2 × 5) + 6 = 16

16 is divisible by 4, so 4,756 is divisible by 4!

4,756

This number is divisible by 2 and by 3, so it is divisible by 6!

3,282

Try the divisibility tests on the numbers below.
Give the number or numbers (2, 3, 4, 5, 6, 9) each is divisible by.

1. 570 **2.** 2,684 **3.** 7,926 **4.** 417 **5.** 1,260

6. 2,340 **7.** 56,879 **8.** 492,657 **9.** 246,904 **10.** 1,376,844

135

Cumulative Review

1. Use place value to tell what the 9 means in 294,362.

   A 9 ten thousands   B 9 thousands
   C 9 ten millions   D not given

2. Which symbol (>, <, or =) goes in the ▒ ?

   637,218 ▒ 607,218
   A <   B >   C =

3. Round 429,375 to the nearest hundred.

   A 430,000   B 429,000
   C 429,400   D not given

Add or subtract.

4.
   $$646 + 389$$
   A 257
   B 925
   C 1,035
   D not given

5.
   $$7,000 - 434$$
   A 6,676
   B 6,566
   C 7,434
   D not given

6.
   $$\$42.75 - 18.83$$
   A $61.58
   B $23.92
   C $34.92
   D not given

7. Use place value to tell what the 8 means in 3.581.

   A 8 tenths   B 8 hundredths
   C 8 thousandths   D not given

8. Which symbol (>, <, or =) goes in the ▒ ?
   1.101 ▒ 1.011
   A >   B <   C =

Multiply.

9.
   $$461 \times 8$$
   A 3,288
   B 3,598
   C 3,678
   D not given

10.
    $$3,785 \times 6$$
    A 2,271
    B 21,610
    C 22,710
    D not given

11.
    $$71 \times 24$$
    A 1,704
    B 1,724
    C 2,471
    D not given

12.
    $$322 \times 265$$
    A 85,330
    B 85,930
    C 8,533
    D not given

13. A jacket cost $44.80. How much change would you receive from $50.00?

    A $45.52   B $5.52
    C $39.80   D not given

14. There are 48 cans in a case. How many cans are there in 24 cases?

    A 1,152   B 2,016
    C 484   D not given

6
Decimals: Multiplication and Division

Young men and women who want careers at sea often are trained on sailing ships called schoolships. Although these young people will not work on sail-powered ships, sail training gives them an excellent education. They learn about the sea, and they also learn the value of working together as a team.

The largest of the schoolships are the square-rigged *tall ships*. The American *Eagle,* for example, is 89.8 m long, and has a maximum width of 11.99 m and a sail area of 1,982.95 m². There are also many smaller ships. Some are only about 15 m long.

Every two years, the Sail Training Association invites the schoolships to a race involving ships from many nations. In 1976, the race began in Plymouth, England, and finished in Newport, Rhode Island. The ships then formed a "Parade of Sail" from Newport to New York, which was one of the most exciting parts of the American Bicentennial celebration.

Estimating Decimal Products and Quotients

Rick used a calculator to solve some decimal multiplication and division problems. Then he checked to see if the calculator answers were reasonable. To do this, he rounded the numbers or replaced them with compatible numbers so that he could estimate using a basic fact.

$$\begin{array}{r} 8.5\,6 \\ \times\ 6.2\,5 \\ \hline \end{array}$$

$$3.9\overline{)2\,8\,2.7\,5}$$

$$4\,1\,2.8\,8\ \div\ 5.2$$

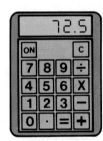

Round to the **nearest whole number.**

Round the divisor to the **nearest whole number.** Round the dividend to the **nearest ten.**

Round the divisor to the **nearest whole number.** Round the dividend to the **nearest hundred.**

$$\begin{array}{rcr} 8.5\,6 & \rightarrow & 9 \\ \times\ 6.2\,5 & \rightarrow & \times\ 6 \\ \hline & & 5\,4 \end{array}$$

$$3.9\overline{)2\,8\,2.7\,5} \longrightarrow 4\overline{)2\,8\,0}\ \ (70)$$

$$\begin{array}{ccc} 4\,1\,2.8\,8 & \div & 5.2 \\ \downarrow & & \downarrow \\ 4\,0\,0 & \div & 5 = 8\,0 \end{array}$$

The calculator answer seems reasonable.

The calculator answer seems reasonable.

The calculator answer does not seem reasonable.

Warm Up   Estimate by rounding so that you can use a basic fact.

1.
$$\begin{array}{r} 7.58 \\ \times\ 3.24 \\ \hline \end{array}$$

2.
$$\begin{array}{r} 4.736 \\ \times\ \ \ 8.5 \\ \hline \end{array}$$

3.
$$\begin{array}{r} 56.287 \\ \times\ \ \ \ 7.3 \\ \hline \end{array}$$

4.
$$\begin{array}{r} 89.76 \\ \times\ 38.2 \\ \hline \end{array}$$

5.
$$\begin{array}{r} \$787.53 \\ \times\ \ \ \ \ \ 6 \\ \hline \end{array}$$

6. $2.8\overline{)273.5}$

7. $7.4\overline{)62.96}$

8. $5\overline{)\$379.86}$

9. $6.9\overline{)35.68}$

10. $3\overline{)11.777}$

138

Practice Estimate the products or quotients by rounding so that you can use a basic fact.

1.	3.7 × 8.3	**2.**	6.47 × 7.19	**3.**	8.96 × 4	**4.**	5.94 × 8.36	**5.**	9.08 × 6.89

6.	$48.36 × 5	**7.**	71.794 × 8.6	**8.**	67.46 × 39.28	**9.**	319.38 × 86.759	**10.**	$809.36 × 6.2

11. 7.4 × 3.826 **12.** 9.324 × 6.7 **13.** 57.8 × 9.15

14. 6.45 × 8.591 **15.** 68.9 × 7.38 **16.** $486.25 × 7.75

17. 66.57 × 23.69 **18.** 398.6 × 27.43 **19.** 687.4 × 719.6

20. 4)283.64 **21.** 6)478.34 **22.** 8)724.62 **23.** 3)$265.98

24. 3.2)14.862 **25.** 7.6)322.47 **26.** 5.8)355.93 **27.** 9.1)$536.71

28. 55.982 ÷ 7.8 **29.** 483.7 ÷ 6.3 **30.** 34.967 ÷ 4.7

Replace the decimals with compatible numbers so that you can estimate by using a basic fact.

31. 55.36 ÷ 9.25 **32.** 470.56 ÷ 8.35 **33.** 410.3 ÷ 49.6

34. 366.38 ÷ 3.5 **35.** 310.29 ÷ 5.2 **36.** 624.57 ÷ 8.9

Mixed Applications

 37. Superdogs are 29.2 cm long. How long a table would you need in order to place 52 Superdogs end to end in a single row on the table top? Estimate, then check by finding the exact answer.

 38. Suppose a club sandwich is 4.9 cm high. Estimate how many sandwiches you would need to make a stack as tall as the World Trade Center in New York. The Trade Center is 41,000 cm tall. Check by finding the exact answer.

Think

Logical Reasoning

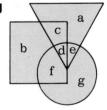

Give the letter or letters that are

1. in ☐ or ◯, but not ▽.

2. in ☐ and ◯ but not ▽.

3. in ☐ and ◯ and ▽.

4. in ☐ and ▽ but not ◯.

Math

Multiplying Decimals

The inside distance between the rails on some model railroads is about 1.6 cm. If we use the scale given below, about how far apart are the rails on a real railroad?

Scale: 1 cm on the model is about 0.9 m on a real railroad.

Since each centimeter on the model stands for the same actual distance, we multiply.

Multiply as with whole numbers.	→	Write the product so it has as many decimal places as the sum of the decimal places in the factors.

$$
\begin{array}{r}
1.6 \\
\times\ 0.9 \\
\hline
1\,4\,4
\end{array}
$$

$$
\begin{array}{r}
1.6 \leftarrow 1 \text{ decimal place} \\
\times\ 0.9 \leftarrow 1 \text{ decimal place} \\
\hline
1.4\,4 \leftarrow 2 \text{ decimal places}
\end{array}
$$

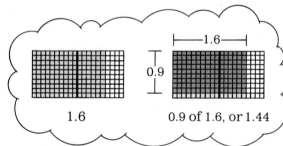

1.6

0.9

1.6

1.6

0.9 of 1.6, or 1.44

The rails on a real railroad are about 1.44 m apart.

Other Examples

$$
\begin{array}{r}
9.4\,3 \leftarrow 2 \text{ decimal places} \\
\times\ \ \ 0.6 \leftarrow 1 \text{ decimal place} \\
\hline
5.6\,5\,8 \leftarrow 3 \text{ decimal places}
\end{array}
$$

$$
\begin{array}{r}
0.2\,7\,6 \leftarrow 3 \text{ places} \\
\times\ \ \ \ \ \ \ 3 \leftarrow 0 \text{ places} \\
\hline
0.8\,2\,8 \leftarrow 3 \text{ places}
\end{array}
$$

$$
\begin{array}{r}
1.3\,2 \leftarrow 2 \text{ places} \\
\times\ 0.8\,7 \leftarrow 2 \text{ places} \\
\hline
9\,2\,4 \\
1\,0\,5\,6 \\
\hline
1.1\,4\,8\,4 \leftarrow 4 \text{ places}
\end{array}
$$

Warm Up   Multiply.

1.	2.	3.,	4.	5.
4.27 × 0.7	1.374 × 6	2.41 × 0.68	9.4 × 6.8	46.75 × 8.68

6. 3.14 × 1.2   7. 6.35 × 9   8. 7.2 × 0.45   9. 5.26 × 8.21

140

Practice Multiply.

1.   3.4
    × 0.6

2.   2.8
    × 5.9

3.   0.35
    × 6

4.   4.28
    × 9

5.   26.5
    × 0.46

6.   1.765
    ×   8

7.   3.46
    × 2.9

8.   2.78
    × 4.6

9.   437.9
    × 26.4

10. $7.23
    × 4.5

11.   0.58
    × 8.41

12.   9.67
    × 4.5

13.   2.75
    × 1.89

14.   6.461
    ×   28

15. $9.45
    × 0.9

16. 6.8 × 3.2

17. 9.7 × 0.56

18. 4.75 × 0.9

19. 5.62 × 3.84

20. Estimate, then find: 6.8 × 4.2

21. Estimate, then find: 38.67 × 72.46

Mixed Applications

22. A scale model caboose is 12.2 cm long. Each centimeter on the model is exactly 0.87 m on the actual caboose. How long is the actual caboose?

24. Some needed data is missing from the problem below. Make up the needed data and solve the problem.

A six-car model train is 73.2 cm long. How long is the actual train?

25. DATA BANK   Give the actual lengths of these train cars: box car, auto-loader, tank car, passenger car. (See Data Bank, page 423.)

23. Model railroad track sections 23 cm long cost $2.75 each. What will be the cost for a 299-cm section of track?

Think

Mental Math

Use the distributive property to find decimal products mentally.

To find **6.2 × 3**

Think: **6 × 3 is** <u>18</u>.   **0.2 × 3 is** <u>0.6</u>
        The product is <u>18.6</u>.

1. 4.3 × 2   **2.** 5.2 × 4

3. 6.4 × 2   **4.** 8.3 × 3

5. 6.4 × 3   **6.** 5.6 × 2

7. 8.5 × 3   **8.** 9.3 × 5

Math

More Multiplying Decimals

Gold can be hammered into leaves with a thickness of only 0.000009 cm (9 millionths of a centimeter). A gold layer about 675 times this thick has been used as a protective coating on the outside of space vehicles. How thick is this layer?

Since we want to find the total of several equal amounts, we multiply.

$$
\begin{array}{r}
6\,7\,5 \leftarrow \mathbf{0} \text{ places} \\
\times\ 0.0\,0\,0\,0\,0\,9 \leftarrow \mathbf{6} \text{ places} \\
\hline
0.0\,0\,6\,0\,7\,5 \leftarrow \mathbf{6} \text{ places}
\end{array}
$$

> Write as many extra zeros as are needed to show the correct number of places in the product.

The gold layer is 0.006075 cm thick.

Other Examples

$$
\begin{array}{r}
0.0\,8 \\
\times\ \ \ 0.4 \\
\hline
0.0\,3\,2
\end{array}
\qquad
\begin{array}{r}
0.0\,3 \\
\times\ \ 0.0\,2 \\
\hline
0.0\,0\,0\,6
\end{array}
\qquad
\begin{array}{r}
4\,3\,5 \\
\times\ 0.0\,0\,0\,2 \\
\hline
0.0\,8\,7\,0
\end{array}
\qquad
\begin{array}{r}
\$\,0.7\,3 \\
\times\ \ 0.0\,5 \\
\hline
\$\,0.0\,3\,6\,5
\end{array}
$$
or $\$0.04$
(rounded to the
nearest cent)

Warm Up   Multiply. Write extra zeros in the product as needed.

1. $\begin{array}{r}0.06\\ \times\ \ 0.3\end{array}$	**2.** $\begin{array}{r}0.04\\ \times\ 0.02\end{array}$	**3.** $\begin{array}{r}57\\ \times\ 0.003\end{array}$	**4.** $\begin{array}{r}590\\ \times\ 0.0001\end{array}$	**5.** $\begin{array}{r}\$0.59\\ \times\ \ 0.06\end{array}$
6. $\begin{array}{r}2.05\\ \times\ 0.02\end{array}$	**7.** $\begin{array}{r}0.006\\ \times\ \ 0.05\end{array}$	**8.** $\begin{array}{r}2.3\\ \times\ 0.004\end{array}$	**9.** $\begin{array}{r}8.1\\ \times\ 0.06\end{array}$	**10.** $\begin{array}{r}\$0.47\\ \times\ \ 0.03\end{array}$

Practice Multiply.

1. 4.3
    × 5.7

2. 0.05
    × 0.09

3. 3.2
    × 0.004

4. 5.765
    × 8.6

5. 4.8
    × 0.0005

6. 1.3
    × 0.04

7. 6.375
    × 0.02

8. 0.009
    × 4.3

9. 5.67
    × 2.98

10. $5.77
    × 0.05

11. 7.38
    × 0.06

12. 0.76
    × 0.003

13. 50
    × 0.8

14. 0.015
    × 2.6

15. $46.06
    × 0.06

16. 0.0012
    × 4.6

17. 179
    × 0.01

18. 67.86
    × 0.0003

19. $9.65
    × 0.15

20. 0.080
    × 0.005

21. 4.3 × 0.007

22. 5.7 × 0.18

23. 3.04 × 0.016

24. 0.09 × 0.015

25. 4.86 × 9.573

26. 0.0054 × 0.025

27. 0.075 × $3.45

28. 1.34 × 5.062

29. 0.105 × $9.67

30. What is the product when 0.016 is multiplied by 0.025?

31. Estimate, then find the product of the factors 3.87 and 19.605.

Mixed Applications

32. The thickest gold plating on the outside of some spacecraft is 0.006 cm thick. The thinnest plating is only 0.2 times that thick. What is the thickness of the thinnest gold plating?

33. Write a question about this data and solve the problem. Certain parts of an astronaut's helmet must be coated with 3 layers of gold film. Each layer is 0.0012 cm thick.

Skillkeeper

Divide.

1. 6)540

2. 8)496

3. 5)254

4. 7)875

5. 3)726

6. 9)819

7. 6)4,270

8. 5)26,385

9. 40)1,757

10. 70)18,760

11. 43)3,827

12. 55)$70.40

13. 125)6,275

14. 36)2,052

15. 230)5,750

16. 65)$81.25

Multiplying Decimals by 10, 100, and 1,000: Mental Math

The owner of a jewelry store sells a very popular digital watch for $29.95. What will the store's total amount of sales be for 10 watches? 100 watches? 1,000 watches? Are these calculator answers reasonable?

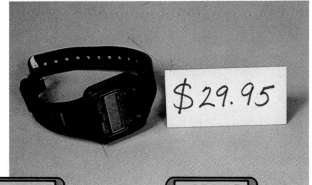

$29.95

10 watches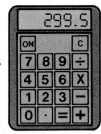

100 watches

1,000 watches

10 × 29.95	100 × 29.95	1,000 × 29.95
↓	↓	↓
10 × 30 = 300	100 × 30 = 3,000	1,000 × 30 = 30,000

The calculator answer seems reasonable.

The calculator answer seems reasonable.

The calculator answer seems reasonable.

To multiply by **10**, move the decimal point **1 place right**. 29.9͜5	To multiply by **100**, move the decimal point **2 places right**. 29.95͜	To multiply by **1,000**, move the decimal point **3 places right**. 29.950͜

Multiply. Write only the answers.

1. 3.54 × 10

2. 4.8 × 10

3. 0.65 × 10

4. 10 × 7.372

5. 10 × 0.8

6. 2.74 × 100

7. 0.68 × 100

8. 1.765 × 100

9. 54.8 × 100

10. 100 × 0.9

11. 4.376 × 1,000

12. 7.28 × 1,000

13. 0.762 × 1,000

14. 1,000 × 0.81

15. 1,000 × 6.7

16. 2.7 × 100

17. 0.64 × 1,000

18. 9.2 × 10

19. 28.4 × 1,000

20. 676 × 100

More Practice, page 435, Set C

Practice: Multiplying Decimals

Multiply.

1. $\begin{array}{r} 9.7 \\ \times\ 6.8 \\ \hline \end{array}$
2. $\begin{array}{r} 57 \\ \times\ 3.6 \\ \hline \end{array}$
3. $\begin{array}{r} 4.076 \\ \times\ \ \ 2.9 \\ \hline \end{array}$
4. $\begin{array}{r} 7.25 \\ \times\ 3.46 \\ \hline \end{array}$
5. $\begin{array}{r} 8.76 \\ \times\ 100 \\ \hline \end{array}$

6. $\begin{array}{r} 0.075 \\ \times\ \ \ 4.9 \\ \hline \end{array}$
7. $\begin{array}{r} 0.096 \\ \times\ 0.003 \\ \hline \end{array}$
8. $\begin{array}{r} 4.56 \\ \times\ \ 7.3 \\ \hline \end{array}$
9. $\begin{array}{r} 7.042 \\ \times\ \ \ \ 10 \\ \hline \end{array}$
10. $\begin{array}{r} 6.432 \\ \times\ 0.003 \\ \hline \end{array}$

11. $\begin{array}{r} 8.6 \\ \times\ 0.0004 \\ \hline \end{array}$
12. $\begin{array}{r} 9.47 \\ \times\ 0.68 \\ \hline \end{array}$
13. $\begin{array}{r} 9.674 \\ \times\ 1,000 \\ \hline \end{array}$
14. $\begin{array}{r} 3.75 \\ \times\ 0.08 \\ \hline \end{array}$
15. $\begin{array}{r} 0.792 \\ \times\ \ 1.46 \\ \hline \end{array}$

16. $\begin{array}{r} 3.4 \\ \times\ 100 \\ \hline \end{array}$
17. $\begin{array}{r} 7.214 \\ \times\ \ 29.6 \\ \hline \end{array}$
18. $\begin{array}{r} \$37.58 \\ \times\ \ \ 0.07 \\ \hline \end{array}$
19. $\begin{array}{r} \$4.57 \\ \times\ 0.20 \\ \hline \end{array}$
20. $\begin{array}{r} \$35.64 \\ \times\ \ \ 0.25 \\ \hline \end{array}$

21. 4.75×3.2

22. 8.67×100

23. 3.047×9.2

24. $1,000 \times 0.46$

25. 29.07×8.6

26. 10×9.472

27. 543×0.86

28. 100×0.7

29. $9.72 \times 1,000$

30. Estimate, then find the product when 8.743 is multiplied by 6.075.

31. Estimate, then find the product of the factors 286.38 and 75.2.

Multiply. Write only the answers.

32. 2.65×10

33. 10×0.73

34. 100×2.8

35. 0.62×100

36. $0.571 \times 1,000$

37. $1,000 \times 5.4$

38. Solve these equations. Then write the equation that would come next in each list.

$0.1089 \times 9 = n$ $\quad$ $0.2178 \times 4 = n$

$0.10989 \times 9 = n$ $\quad$ $0.21978 \times 4 = n$

$0.109989 \times 9 = n$ $\quad$ $0.219978 \times 4 = n$

Think

Greatest-Product Game

Put slips of paper containing the digits 0 through 9 in a hat.

Draw boxes like this on your paper. As a digit is drawn from the hat, write it in a square of your choice. Then find the product. Greatest product wins!

Math

145

Problem Solving: Using Estimation

What is the cost? First choose the best estimate. Then find the exact answer.

Auto Repair

1. A car repair ratesbook lists 2.5 hours as the time needed for a tuneup of an 8-cylinder auto. Suppose the hourly labor charge is $24.75. What is the total cost?
  A under $75　　**B** about $90
  C over $90

Electricity

2. A color TV set might use 540 kWh (kilowatt-hours) of electricity per year. If electricity costs 3.2 cents for 1 kWh, what is the yearly cost?
  A under $15　　**B** over $18
  C between $15 and $18

Heat

3. It might take 119 million B.T.U.s (British thermal units) of natural gas to heat a house for 1 year. A million B.T.U.s might cost $3.94. What would be the total yearly cost?
  A about $40　　**B** about $400
  C about $4,000

Water

4. Water might cost $0.48 for 1,000 L. A family might use 50,000 L in one month. What would that amount of water cost?
  A about $2.50　　**B** about $25
  C about $250

Want Ad

5. A 4-line ad that runs for 6 days in a newspaper might cost $1.93 per line per day. What would the total cost be?
  A less than $50　　**B** more than $60
  C between $50 and $60

Telephone

6. A weekday telephone call from San Francisco to New York City might cost $2.95 for the first 3 minutes and $0.41 for each additional minute. How much would a 24-minute call cost?
  A about $17　　**B** about $15
  C about $11

7. DATA HUNT How much more would it cost to run an ad like this in your local paper for 7 days than for 3 days?

> Used mini bike. Good condition.
> 5 hp. Good tires. Only $125

8. Strategy Practice How many 3-digit telephone number area codes can there be if the first digit is 4 and the other two digits are less than 4? Hint: Make an organized list.

146

Problem Solving: Mixed Practice

Kremer Prize—50,000 British Pounds

This prize was offered for the first completely man-powered flight of a heavier-than-air machine over a set course around two towers a half-mile apart. The plane had to cross both the start line and finish line at least 10 feet above the ground.

The Kremer Prize was won in 1977 by Dr. Paul MacCready of Pasadena, California, when Bryan Allen pedaled MacCready's plane, the *Gossamer Condor,* around the course and maintained the required height.

Solve.

1. When MacCready won the prize, a British pound was worth $1.90 American dollars. How much was the Kremer Prize worth in dollars at that time?

2. The prize was first offered in 1959. It was won in 1977. How many years after it was first offered was the prize won?

3. If the Kremer prize money was given out in equal monthly payments for 1 year, how large would each payment be (to the nearest pound)?

4. The wingspan of the *Gossamer Condor* is 96 feet. The greatest wingspan on record was 224 feet more than this. How many feet was the greatest wingspan?

5. The *Gossamer Condor* made 430 flights in 10 months. What was the average number of flights it made each week? (Use 30 days per month and 7 days per week, and round to the nearest whole number.)

6. The plane covered the course in 6 minutes 23 seconds. Its speed was 0.003 miles per second. How long was the course (to the nearest hundredth of a mile)?

7. In 1979 Bryan Allen pedaled another MacCready plane across the English Channel in 2 hours 40 minutes. How many seconds did the flight last?

8. **Strategy Practice** How many possible orders are there for four test planes to take off one at a time from an airfield? Hint: Make an organized list.

147

ding a Decimal by a Whole Number

ympic team ran the 400-m relay in 38.32 s (seconds). Each of the team members ran 100 m. What was the average time for 100 m?

Since we want to find the average, we divide.

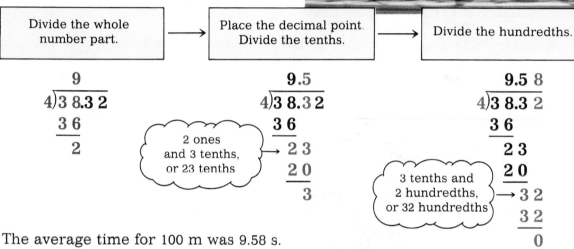

| Divide the whole number part. | → | Place the decimal point. Divide the tenths. | → | Divide the hundredths. |

$$\begin{array}{r} 9 \\ 4\overline{)3\,8.3\,2} \\ \underline{3\,6} \\ 2 \end{array}$$

2 ones and 3 tenths, or 23 tenths →

$$\begin{array}{r} 9.5 \\ 4\overline{)3\,8.3\,2} \\ \underline{3\,6} \\ 2\,3 \\ \underline{2\,0} \\ 3 \end{array}$$

3 tenths and 2 hundredths, or 32 hundredths →

$$\begin{array}{r} 9.5\,8 \\ 4\overline{)3\,8.3\,2} \\ \underline{3\,6} \\ 2\,3 \\ \underline{2\,0} \\ 3\,2 \\ \underline{3\,2} \\ 0 \end{array}$$

The average time for 100 m was 9.58 s.

Other Examples

$$\begin{array}{r} 7.1\,2 \\ 8\overline{)5\,6.9\,6} \\ \underline{5\,6} \\ 0\,9 \\ \underline{8} \\ 1\,6 \\ \underline{1\,6} \\ 0 \end{array}$$

Check
$$\begin{array}{r} 7.12 \\ \times \quad 8 \\ \hline 56.96 \end{array}$$

$$\begin{array}{r} 0.2\,9\,2 \\ 3\overline{)0.8\,7\,6} \\ \underline{6} \\ 2\,7 \\ \underline{2\,7} \\ 0\,6 \\ \underline{6} \\ 0 \end{array}$$

$$\begin{array}{r} 0.5\,0\,4 \\ 2\,6\overline{)1\,3.1\,0\,4} \\ \underline{1\,3\,0} \\ 1\,0 \\ \underline{0} \\ 1\,0\,4 \\ \underline{1\,0\,4} \\ 0 \end{array}$$

Warm Up   Divide. Check your answers.

1. $4\overline{)25.92}$ **2.** $7\overline{)2.555}$ **3.** $5\overline{)1.535}$ **4.** $8\overline{)49.04}$.   **5.** $32\overline{)\$45.76}$

6. $6\overline{)20.58}$ **7.** $9\overline{)5.166}$ **8.** $13\overline{)\$59.93}$ **9.** $62\overline{)22.196}$ **10.** $54\overline{)144.72}$

Practice Divide. Check your answers.

1. $2\overline{)7.24}$
2. $4\overline{)31.76}$
3. $3\overline{)17.52}$
4. $5\overline{)30.15}$
5. $7\overline{)63.84}$

6. $6\overline{)2.898}$
7. $8\overline{)8.344}$
8. $9\overline{)0.5733}$
9. $4\overline{)93.04}$
10. $3\overline{)168.6}$

11. $2\overline{)19.6}$
12. $7\overline{)17.738}$
13. $5\overline{)1.835}$
14. $8\overline{)288.24}$
15. $6\overline{)340.2}$

16. $19\overline{)28.5}$
17. $24\overline{)59.28}$
18. $43\overline{)165.55}$
19. $26\overline{)244.4}$
20. $35\overline{)819.7}$

21. $37\overline{)9.361}$
22. $85\overline{)158.95}$
23. $73\overline{)\$33.58}$
24. $3\overline{)\$50.25}$
25. $24\overline{)\$245.28}$

26. $61.38 \div 9$
27. $9.506 \div 7$
28. $68.8 \div 8$
29. $4.737 \div 3$
30. $4.842 \div 6$

31. Estimate, then find: $8.763 \div 3$

32. Estimate, then find: $362.16 \div 9$

Mixed Applications

33. The time for one woman in the Olympic 800-m run was 114.96 s. What was the average time for each 100 m of this race?

35. Tell what data is not needed in this problem. Then solve.
The U.S. women's speed skating record time for 500 m is 42.76 s. For 1,500 m it is 140.85 s. What is the average time for 100 m of the 500-m race?

34. Each of the 4 runners on a relay team ran an average of 10.8 seconds during a race. What was the total running time for the team?

Think

Logical Reasoning

How many moves do you need to move the four coins (dime, penny, nickel, quarter) to square C?

| A | B | C |

Rules:
1. You may move only a top coin, and only one coin at a time.

2. You may use square B, but you may not place a larger coin on top of a smaller one.

Math

Rounding Decimal Quotients

In a 4-H Club basketball game Tina scored goals on 7 of the 13 shots she took. What was her shooting average?

To find a basketball shooting average, we divide the number of baskets made by the number of shots taken and give the answer to the nearest thousandth.

Divide.	Divide to one place beyond the place to which you are rounding.	Round the quotient. If the last digit is • less than 5, drop it. • 5 or more, drop it and round up.

```
  0.5 3 8
13)7.0 0 0     Write zeros
  6 5          as needed to
  ─────        complete the
    5 0        dividing.
    3 9
  ─────
    1 1 0
    1 0 4
  ─────
        6
```

```
  0.5 3 8 4
13)7.0 0 0 0
  6 5
  ─────
    5 0
    3 9
  ─────
    1 1 0
    1 0 4
  ─────
        6 0
        5 2
      ─────
          8
```

$0.5384 \rightarrow 0.538$

(rounded to the nearest thousandth)

Tina's shooting average was 0.538.

Other Examples

Find $3 ÷ 8 to the nearest cent (hundredth of a dollar).

```
  $ 0.3 7 5
8)$ 3.0 0 0
    2 4
  ─────
      6 0
      5 6
    ─────
        4 0
        4 0
      ─────
          0
```

$\$ 0.375 \rightarrow \$ 0.38$

(nearest cent or hundredth)

Find 10.3 ÷ 7 to the nearest tenth.

```
    1.4 7
7)1 0.3 0
  7
  ─────
    3 3
    2 8
  ─────
      5 0
      4 9
    ─────
        1
```

$1.47 \rightarrow 1.5$

(nearest tenth)

Warm Up

1. Find 24 ÷ 9 to the nearest tenth.

2. Find $25.43 ÷ 7 to the nearest cent.

3. Find 8 ÷ 17 to the nearest thousandth.

Practice Find the quotients. Round to the nearest tenth.

1. 3)11

2. 7)5,600

3. 9)4

4. 6)13

5. 8)3

6. 14)7.34

7. 18)6.45

8. 25)3

9. 27)96

10. 43)287

Find the quotients. Round to the nearest hundredth or cent.

11. 6)5

12. 6)31

13. 7)5

14. 19)6

15. 28)87.2

16. 8)$10.06

17. 3)$19.06

18. 7)$3.94

19. 25)$64.75

20. 36)$38.93

Find the averages in this table. Round
to the nearest thousandth.

	Player	Goals	Shots Taken	Average
21.	Sally	5	11	
22.	Arnold	8	17	
23.	Glenna	11	21	
24.	Wing	6	19	
25.	Orlando	3	7	
26.	Roger	9	21	

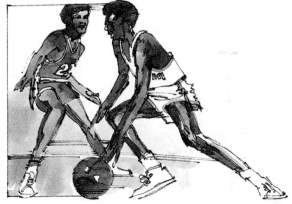

Mixed Applications

27. Renata made 6 baskets and 3 free
throws. Baskets count 2 points and
free throws count 1 point. How
many points did she score?

28. Chris missed on 9 shots but made
5 shots. What was his shooting
average?

29. Aram scored goals on 108 of the
235 shots he took during the
season. Brendan scored on 111 of
251 shots taken. Find their
averages to the nearest
thousandth. How much greater is
the higher average?

Think

Using a Calculator

You can give a decimal
for a fraction by
dividing.

$\frac{3}{8}$ = 3 ÷ 8 = 0.375

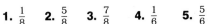

Write decimals for
the fractions below.

Round to the nearest
thousandth when
necessary.

1. $\frac{1}{8}$ **2.** $\frac{5}{8}$ **3.** $\frac{7}{8}$ **4.** $\frac{1}{6}$ **5.** $\frac{5}{6}$

6. $\frac{1}{3}$ **7.** $\frac{2}{3}$ **8.** $\frac{1}{12}$ **9.** $\frac{5}{12}$ **10.** $\frac{1}{16}$

Math

...ling Decimals by 10, 100, ...,000: Mental Math

A pilot whale weighed 734.83 kg. This is 10 times an average man's weight, 100 times a small dog's weight, and 1,000 times a guinea pig's weight. To find these weights, we divide. Are these calculator answers reasonable?

Man's Weight = Whale's Weight ÷ 10	Dog's Weight = Whale's Weight ÷ 100	Guinea Pig's Weight = Whale's Weight ÷ 1,000

 73.483   7.3483    0.73483

7 3 4.8 3 ÷ 1 0	7 3 4.8 3 ÷ 1 0 0	7 3 4.8 3 ÷ 1,0 0 0
↓	↓	↓
7 0 0 ÷ 1 0 = 7 0	7 0 0 ÷ 1 0 0 = 7	7 0 0 ÷ 1.0 0 0 = 0.7

The calculator answer seems reasonable.

The calculator answer seems reasonable.

The calculator answer seems reasonable.

To divide by **10**, move the decimal point **1 place left**. 73.4.83	To divide by **100**, move the decimal point **2 places left**. 7.34.83	To divide by **1,000**, move the decimal point **3 places left**. .734.83

Divide. Write only the answers.

1. 9.6 ÷ 10   **2.** 27.54 ÷ 10   **3.** 0.7 ÷ 10   **4.** 75 ÷ 10

5. 34.2 ÷ 100   **6.** 8.7 ÷ 100   **7.** 536.5 ÷ 100   **8.** 278 ÷ 100

9. 496.4 ÷ 1,000   **10.** 387.25 ÷ 1,000   **11.** 86.3 ÷ 1,000   **12.** 0.9 ÷ 1,000

13. 68.3 ÷ 100   **14.** 29.74 ÷ 10   **15.** 456.8 ÷ 1,000   **16.** 9.4 ÷ 100

More Practice, page 436, Set C

Practice: Dividing Decimals

Divide.

1. $4\overline{)11.48}$
2. $6\overline{)45.924}$
3. $3\overline{)187.41}$
4. $5\overline{)1.545}$

5. $8\overline{)3.824}$
6. $2\overline{)130.94}$
7. $9\overline{)0.783}$
8. $7\overline{)258.3}$

9. $3\overline{)2.067}$
10. $5\overline{)219.35}$
11. $7\overline{)5.439}$
12. $9\overline{)62.01}$

13. $42\overline{)68.46}$
14. $64\overline{)37.568}$
15. $36\overline{)11.088}$
16. $18\overline{)46.44}$

17. $57\overline{)780.9}$
18. $86\overline{)398.18}$
19. $74\overline{)9.102}$
20. $95\overline{)\$605.15}$

21. $31.23 \div 9$
22. $\$56.70 \div 10$
23. $\$29.28 \div 8$

24. $562.8 \div 1,000$
25. $\$747 \div 100$
26. $\$3.50 \div 5$

Divide. Round to the nearest hundredth or cent.

27. $8\overline{)5}$
28. $23\overline{)67}$
29. $9\overline{)\$32.10}$
30. $35\overline{)\$170.21}$

31. Estimate, then find 63.63 divided by 8.

32. Estimate, then find the quotient when the dividend is 144.69 and the divisor is 23.

33. If an average sixth grade student weighs 39 kg and an average elephant weighs 6,343 kg, how many average sixth grade students would be needed to equal the weight of an average elephant? (Round to the nearest whole number.)

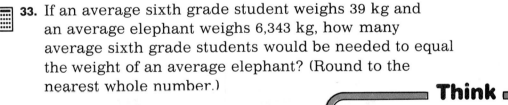

Think

Discovering a Pattern

Here is a magic square. The sum in each row, column, and diagonal is the same. If you divide each number by 10 (or by 100), is it still a magic square?

36	31	38
37	35	33
32	39	34

Math

Problem Solving: Using Data from Several Sources

Solve these problems about reaction times. For some of these problems more than the needed data is given. For other problems you must find needed data in the data source shown beside the problem.

1. The stick had fallen 18 cm when Michael caught it. What was his reaction time (in seconds)?

2. The stick fell from the 16 cm mark to the 31 cm mark before Janine caught it. What was her reaction time?

3. On her first try Rosaura's reaction time was 0.65 s (seconds). On the second try it was 0.58 s. Her best time was equal to the time for her first try divided by 2. What was her best time?

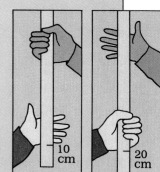

Data Source:
An Experiment

1. Hold a meter stick. Have someone be ready to catch it as quickly as possible.

2. Drop the meter stick. How far did it fall before it was caught?

A person's approximate reaction time (in seconds) can be found as follows:
1. Multiply the fall distance by 4.
2. Add 90.
3. Divide by 1,000.

4. The total stopping distance is the sum of the reaction distance and the braking distance. How much greater is the total stopping distance at 100 km/h than at 80 km/h?

5. If use of a medicine caused a person's reaction distance to be 1.25 as great as the average reaction distance, what would be the reaction distance at 100 km/h?

Data Source: A graph from a driver's book

Reaction and Braking Distances

Automobile speed

☐ Reaction distance
☐ Braking distance

Speed	Reaction distance	Braking distance
40 km/h	8.38 m	9.97 m
80 km/h	16.76 m	40.66 m
100 km/h	20.85 m	68.36 m

↑ Driver sees animal in the road.   ↑ Driver applies brakes.   ↑ Driver stops.

6. Margie's best reaction time on the tone-light test was at the break between "Excellent" and "Good." Her first time was 4 times as great as her best time. What was her first time?

7. Matt's times, in order, were 0.24, 0.18, 0.15, 0.16, 0.12, 0.09. What was his average time for his first 5 tries?

Data Source:
A science museum display

As the tone sounds, tiny bulbs begin to light up in order from bottom to top. The goal is to push the button as fast as possible when you hear the tone to stop the "climbing light" as quickly as possible.

Seconds

Poor
0.25
0.20 — Average
0.15
0.10 — Good
0.05
Excellent
0

8. At what age range is the clapping hands reaction time the shortest?

9. What is the average reaction time for all ages? (Round to the nearest thousandth.)

10. **DATA HUNT** What is the difference between your shortest and longest reaction times in the stick-catching experiment on page 154?

11. **Strategy Practice** Terry's slowest reaction time in the tone-light test above was 3 times her fastest time. The difference in the times was 0.12 s. What was her fastest time?

Data Source:
A table from a reference book

Time needed to clap hands together from a distance of 80 cm when a light flashes

Age	Average Reaction Time (seconds)
6–8	0.466
9–13	0.411
14–19	0.344
20–29	0.344
30–39	0.335
40–49	0.357
50–59	0.391
60+	0.431

Dividing by a Decimal

Work with a group. You will need graph paper cut into 10-by-10 grids, scissors, index cards, and a calculator.

Your class has been invited to help plan an expedition to some archaeological sites. Each site will be divided, for exploration, into several plots of equal size. Here are the site sizes:

Site	Size
Site A	2.32 acres
Site B	3.4 acres
Site C	1.83 acres
Site D	4.0 acres

Part 1

Choose one of the sites for your group to explore.

1. Each person should use 10-by-10 grids to represent the site. Let each whole grid represent one acre. On your own grids, mark off some squares to represent a plot of your choice. Think about dividing the whole site into plots of that size. What decimal division problem shows the way you plan to divide the site? Record the problem on a card.

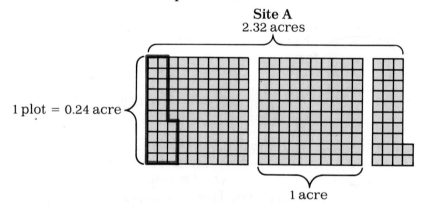

Site A
2.32 acres

1 plot = 0.24 acre

1 acre

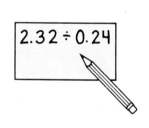

$2.32 \div 0.24$

2. Share your cards in your group. Look at the cards and think about the plots as you discuss these questions:
   - Which choice of plot size do you think will produce the greatest number of plots? Explain your reasoning.
   - For each card, how would you choose an estimate for the number of plots? Record an estimate on each card.

$2.32 \div 0.24$

About 9 plots

3. Decide how you could use your grid model from exercise 1 to find the actual number of plots. Then find the actual number and compare it with the estimate on the card.

4. Share the results with your group. Did your group correctly predict which plot size would produce the greatest number of plots?

5. Working as a group, make a chart like the one shown here and record how each of you divided the site into plots. What relationship do you notice between the plot sizes and the number of plots?

Size of Site	Size of Plots	Number of Plots	Left Over
2.32 acres	0.24 acre	9	0.16 acre
2.32 acres			

6. With your group, choose a plot size and think about dividing each of Sites A through D into plots of that size.
   - Record the division problems on cards.
   - Predict which site will have the greatest number of plots.
   - Estimate the number of plots and record as before.
   - Make models and fill in the chart. What relationships do you notice between the site sizes and the number of plots?

Part 2

7. Discuss each of these pairs of division problems. Using what you have learned about estimating quotients, decide which problem of each pair would have the larger quotient. Give reasons for your choices. Use models to check.

   $3 \div 0.1$ or $3 \div 0.02$

   $5.4 \div 0.05$ or $3.8 \div 0.05$

   $2.81 \div 0.3$ or $2.8 \div 0.4$

   Use what you have discovered to continue to explore dividing by decimals.

8. With your group, choose a decimal dividend and enter it into a calculator. A member of your group chooses a decimal divisor and enters it. Before pressing the equals key, your group decides on an estimate of the quotient. Record the dividend and each divisor, group estimate, and calculator answer in a chart like the one shown. Stop when each member has had a turn to choose a divisor.

Dividend	Divisor	Estimated Quotient	Calculated Quotient
10.9	3.2	3.1	3.41
10.9	0.6	The quotient will be a little more than 3. Let's try 3.1.	

   - Repeat the activity for three other dividends. Record the information in your chart.
   - For each dividend in your chart, find some decimal divisors that give quotients greater than the dividend. What do you notice about these divisors? Find some decimal divisors that give quotients less than 1. What do you notice about these divisors?

More Practice, page 437, Set A

More Dividing by A Decimal

Work in a group. You will need calculators and twelve cards.

Part 1

The Mathemagician says: "I can multiply the dividend and divisor by the same number, and the quotient will not change. It works every time!"

1. With your group, talk about the Mathemagician's "magic." Test it with several basic fact division problems.
   • Does the Mathemagician's magic seem to work?
   • Do you think it works with all division problems? Why or why not?

2. Look at the decimal division problems in the charts below. Do you think the mathemagic will work with them? Try multiplying the dividends and divisors by different numbers. Record at least five tries for each problem, using mental math or a calculator to do the multiplication and the division.

Multipliers	$0.05 \overline{)11}$ (220)
× 2	$0.1 \overline{)22}$ (220)
× 5	$0.25 \overline{)55}$ (220)
× 10	$0.5 \overline{)110}$ (220)
× 100	
× 1,000	

Multipliers	$0.7 \overline{)16.1}$ (2 3)
× 4	

Multipliers	$0.002 \overline{)6.04}$ (3 020)

Multipliers	$1.4 \overline{)5.6}$ (4)

3. Discuss the charts in your group.
   • Does the Mathemagician's magic seem to work with these problems?
   • Which of the multipliers you tried are easiest to multiply in your head?

- In which cases did the multipliers you tried change a decimal divisor into a whole number?
- What pattern do you notice in the way the position of the decimal point changes when you multiply both the dividend and the divisor by 10? by 100? by 1,000? When is it necessary to add zeros to the dividend?

4. How might you use the Mathemagician's magic to make dividing by decimals easier?

Part 2

Label ten cards with the numbers 0 to 9 and two cards with decimal points.

Shuffle the number cards and use six cards to make a division problem.

5. Work with your group to find ways to place the two decimal-point cards so that the quotient is
   a. between 100 and 1,000.
   b. between 10 and 100.
   c. between 1 and 10.
   d. less than 1.

   Record on a chart each way you find.

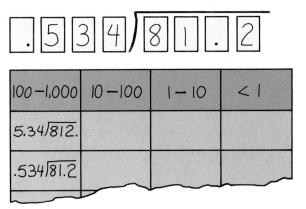

	100–1,000	10–100	1–10	< 1
	$5.34\overline{)812.}$			
	$.534\overline{)81.2}$			

6. Talk about different methods you used to decide where to place the decimal points.

7. Repeat, shuffling the number cards and using a different set of cards to make a division problem. Record your results on a chart.

8. Examine the chart and discuss the results.
   - Look at the decimal problems you listed in each column of the chart. How are the problems related?
   - How can you position the decimal points to produce the largest quotient? The smallest quotient?

Practice: Decimals

Multiply.

1.	2.	3.	4.	5.
7.8 × 0.3	9.6 × 8.5	7.59 × 3.84	0.057 × 35	19.46 × 0.008

Divide.

6. 7)25.2   7. 6)2.52   8. 4)15   9. 22)0.550

10. 12)1.80   11. 3.5)176.05   12. 0.84)63   13. 0.007)3.5

Multiply or divide.

14. 5.92 ÷ 8   15. 3.46 × 7   16. 0.546 ÷ 6

17. 8.75 × 4.02   18. 0.378 ÷ 6.3   19. 9.47 × 0.005

Divide. Round to the nearest tenth.

20. 7 ÷ 4   21. 5.2 ÷ 6

Divide. Round to the nearest hundredth.

22. 13 ÷ 8   23. 2.75 ÷ 76

24. Estimate, then find the quotient: 63.911 divided by 7.9.

25. Estimate, then find the product: 9.97 times 6.08.

26. Which costs more per kilogram, a ham that costs $31.35 and weighs 5 kg or a small car that costs $6,492 and weighs 1,200 kg?

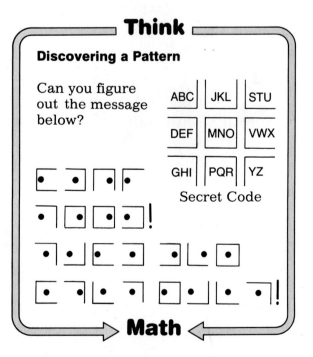

Think

Discovering a Pattern

Can you figure out the message below?

Secret Code

ABC	JKL	STU
DEF	MNO	VWX
GHI	PQR	YZ

Math

160

Problem Solving: Choosing a Calculation Method

Your choice!

Pencil-Paper • Mental Math
Estimation • Calculator

You may use any of these methods, but use each method at least once when solving these **unit price** problems.

Example

A box of 25 greeting cards costs $4.62. What does one card cost?

Solution

Choose a calculator for a quick, accurate answer.

$4.62 ÷ 25 | 0.1848 |

Round the answer to the nearest cent.

$0.1848 $0.18

Unit price: $0.18 per card

1. A box of 25 friendship cards sells for $5.00. What is the price per card?

2. When you buy a package of 3 bars of soap for $1.49, you get an extra bar free. What is your cost per bar?

3. The total cost of having a magazine sent to you each week for 52 weeks is $51.75. Is this cost per copy more than or less than the newsstand cost of $1.25 per copy?

4. Which charge for developing 35-mm film is cheaper, 36 pictures for $7.56 or 24 pictures for $3.12?

5. A dozen large eggs cost $1.10. A dozen medium eggs cost $0.98. How much more per egg do the larger eggs cost?

6. A sports store buys baseballs from the manufacturer for $467 a gross (144). If the store sells each ball for $4.72, how much greater is their selling price than their cost for each ball?

7. A set of 6 books on gardening costs $42.00. A single copy of each book, bought separately, costs $8.25. How much less is the cost per copy if you buy the set?

8. **Strategy Practice**   For every $800 worth of goods sold, a store owner has expenses of $700. What would the owner's profit (sales minus expenses) be for sales totaling $4,000?

Problem-Solving Strategy: Use Logical Reasoning

QUESTION
DATA
PLAN
ANSWER
CHECK

Solving some problems involves more than simply deciding whether to add, subtract, multiply, or divide. To solve such problems, we may use a strategy called

Use Logical Reasoning

A chart can help you keep a record of what you know. It can help you reason logically.

First, I'll write what I know in a chart.

	Soccer	Tennis	Bowling	Softball
Carla		no		
José			yes	
Fran				no
Ron	no			no

Then I'll use what I know to find more information.

	Soccer	Tennis	Bowling	Softball
Carla		no	no	
José		no	yes	
Fran	yes	no	no	no
Ron	no	yes	no	no

Hmm... Now I know that Carla likes softball!

	Soccer	Tennis	Bowling	Softball
Carla		no	no	yes
José		no	yes	
Fran	yes	no	no	no
Ron	no	yes	no	no

Try This Carla, José, Fran, and Ron each have different favorite sports: soccer, tennis, bowling, and softball. The favorite sport of Carla's best friend in the group is tennis. Fran and Ron do not like softball. José's favorite sport is bowling. Ron used to like soccer but no longer does. Which sport is Carla's favorite?

Solve.

1. Four turtles—Lightning, Swifty, Flash, and Rocket—came in first, second, third, and fourth (not in that order) in a race. Lightning was second and Swifty was not fourth. If Flash was third, where did Rocket finish?

2. Beverly, Ralph, and Ginny each wore a blue, red, or green T-shirt with Benton, Ridgeville, or Georgetown on it. No two shirts had the same color or school name. No person's shirt had a color or school name with the same first letter as the person's name. Ginny wore a blue Ridgeville shirt. What shirts did Beverly and Ralph wear?

Chapter Review-Test

Estimate the product or quotient by choosing numbers
so that you can use a basic fact.

1.   6.3
    × 7.8

2.   5.91
    × 3.2

3.   9.43
    × 7.59

4. $5\overline{)39.6}$

5. $7.47\overline{)63.26}$

Multiply.

6.   7.6
    × 2.8

7.   8.5
    × 0.7

8.   28.3
    × 7

9.   0.64
    × 9

10.   5.03
    × 2.75

11.   0.14
    × 0.6

12.   0.0041
    × 0.02

13.   0.0012
    × 13

14.   76.3
    × 1.07

15.   8.63
    × 0.009

16. 3.56 × 10

17. 0.472 × 100

18. 5.743 × 1,000

Divide. Check by multiplying.

19. $5\overline{)12.80}$

20. $8\overline{)25.6}$

21. $37\overline{)155.03}$

22. $23\overline{)16.1}$

Divide. Round the quotient to the place named.

23. 1.6 ÷ 3 (nearest tenth)

24. 2 ÷ 7 (nearest hundredth)

25. 32.3 ÷ 97 (nearest thousandth)

26. $2.47 ÷ 9 (nearest cent)

Divide.

27. 4.7 ÷ 10

28. 56.3 ÷ 100

29. 2.78 ÷ 100

30. 748 ÷ 1,000

31. $3.4\overline{)20.4}$

32. $0.03\overline{)0.174}$

33. $0.009\overline{)0.72}$

34. $0.34\overline{)18.7}$

Solve.

35. One of the first land speed records
was 63.15 km/h. A more recent
record is 15.86 times as fast. How
fast is the more recent record?

36. Which is a better buy, 4 batteries
in a package for $2.88 or 2
batteries in a package for $1.38?
What is the difference in the price
per battery?

Another Look

To multiply by	move the decimal point
1 0	1 place right.
1 0 0	2 places right.
1,0 0 0	3 places right.

To divide by	move the decimal point
1 0	1 place left.
1 0 0	2 places left.
1,0 0 0	3 places left.

Find the product or quotient.

1. 3.46×100 **2.** $4.89 \div 10$

3. $8.347 \times 1{,}000$ **4.** 100×0.46

5. $93.3 \div 1{,}000$ **6.** $0.472 \times 1{,}000$

7. 0.56×10 **8.** 9.42×100

9. $43.8 \div 1{,}000$ **10.** 6.9×100

---

2 decimal places $\longrightarrow$ 7.6 4
1 decimal place $\longrightarrow$ × 3.2
3 decimal places $\longrightarrow$ 1 5 2 8
2 2 9 2
2 4.4 4 8

about 8
about × 3
24

The answer should be about 24.

Multiply.

11. 2.9
× 0.6

12. 3.8
× 0.06

13. 7.5
× 3.8

14. 2.76
× 0.08

15. 0.478
× 0.016

16. 24.95
× 423

1.4
3.2⟌4.4.8
3 2
1 2 8
1 2 8
0

Multiply by 10 to make this a whole number.

Multiplying the dividend and divisor by the same number does not change the quotient.

Divide. Check by multiplying.

17. $8\overline{)25.6}$ **18.** $4\overline{)260.4}$

19. $7\overline{)4.27}$ **20.** $4.8\overline{)14.4}$

21. $0.6\overline{)2.1}$ **22.** $0.59\overline{)0.7729}$

23. $0.07\overline{)0.0406}$ **24.** $0.014\overline{)0.9436}$

Enrichment

Number Relationships

The table shows the numbers 1 through 100. Read the descriptions of the special kinds of numbers and answer the questions below.

A **prime number** has exactly 2 different factors—the number itself and 1. All other whole numbers (except 0 and 1) are **composite**.

1	2	3	4	5	6	7	8	9	10
11	12	13	14	15	16	17	18	19	20
21	22	23	24	25	26	27	28	29	30
31	32	33	34	35	36	37	38	39	40
41	42	43	44	45	46	47	48	49	50
51	52	53	54	55	56	57	58	59	60
61	62	63	64	65	66	67	68	69	70
71	72	73	74	75	76	77	78	79	80
81	82	83	84	85	86	87	88	89	90
91	92	93	94	95	96	97	98	99	100

An **even** number is a multiple of 2. An **odd** number is 1 more or 1 less than an even number.

A **twin prime** is one of a pair of prime numbers whose difference is 2 (like 17 or 19).

A prime number that produces another prime number when its digits are reversed (like 13) is sometimes called a **reversal prime.**

If all the factors of a number (except the number itself) add up to the number, the number is called **perfect.**

1. How many even numbers are in the table? How many odd numbers?

2. How many prime numbers are in the table? How many composite?

3. How many reversal primes can you find? List them.

4. How many even primes are there?

5. How many pairs of twin primes can you find? List them.

6. There are only 2 perfect numbers in the table. One is less than 10. The other is between 25 and 30. Can you find them?

Cumulative Review

1. Use place value to tell what the 5 means in 27,361.752.
   - **A** 5 tens
   - **B** 5 tenths
   - **C** 5 hundredths
   - **D** not given

2. Which symbol (>, <, or =) goes in the ▦ ?
   7.468 ▦ 7.668
   - **A** >
   - **B** <
   - **C** =

3. Round 5.782 to the nearest tenth.
   - **A** 5.7
   - **B** 5.79
   - **C** 6
   - **D** not given

Add, subtract, or divide. Watch the signs.

4. 3.45 + 6.29
   - **A** 9.74
   - **B** 97.4
   - **C** 974
   - **D** not given

5. 5.266 − 4.197
   - **A** 9.463
   - **B** 1.299
   - **C** 1.069
   - **D** not given

6. 56.905 + 47.098
   - **A** 93.993
   - **B** 104.003
   - **C** 103.903
   - **D** not given

7. 7.013 + 8.99
   - **A** 16.003
   - **B** 15.903
   - **C** 90.613
   - **D** not given

8. 0.942 − 0.16
   - **A** 0.782
   - **B** 0.926
   - **C** 0.958
   - **D** not given

9. 7)328
   - **A** 46
   - **B** 47
   - **C** 46 R2
   - **D** not given

10. 4)2,224
   - **A** 456
   - **B** 556
   - **C** 565
   - **D** not given

11. 15)375
   - **A** 25
   - **B** 15
   - **C** 31
   - **D** not given

12. 23)4,762
   - **A** 206 R22
   - **B** 207 R9
   - **C** 207
   - **D** not given

13. Jeff has 7.9 m of wire fence. If he needs 12 m of fence, how much more does he need?
   - **A** 4.1
   - **B** 4.9
   - **C** 3.9
   - **D** not given

14. A fruit packer has 3,060 apples. If 36 apples are put in each box, how many boxes are needed?
   - **A** 100
   - **B** 85
   - **C** 60
   - **D** not given

Measurement

Erin walked carefully along the rocky coastline. She was carrying a meter stick, and her backpack contained a notebook, a pencil, and a thermometer, along with fresh fruit and water. She walked until she came to an area containing two tide pools, which she had discovered a few days before.

Clouds were reflected in the first tide pool, and it looked as deep as the sky. Erin was surprised when she measured its depth, for it was only 12.5 cm deep. The other pool was 60 cm deep.

Next, Erin measured the temperatures of the pools. The deeper pool was 18°C, but the shallower one was an amazing 32°C.

Erin spent the morning drawing and measuring the snails, urchins, anemones, and other tide pool animals. Then the tide started coming in, bringing lunch to some of the tide pool inhabitants. Erin went home to have lunch, too.

Length: Metric Units

The **meter (m)** is the basic metric unit of length.

The **decimeter (dm)** is one tenth of a meter.

10 dm = 1 m

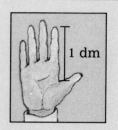

deci- means **one tenth.**

The **centimeter (cm)** is one hundredth of a meter.

100 cm = 1 m

10 cm = 1 dm

centi- means **one hundredth.**

The **millimeter (mm)** is one thousandth of a meter.

1,000 mm = 1 m

100 mm = 1 dm

10 mm = 1 cm

milli- means **one thousandth.**

← dm

← cm

← mm

Meter Stick

Warm Up   Give the number for each ▥.

1. A meter is ▥ centimeters long.

2. A meter is ▥ millimeters long.

3. A meter is ▥ decimeters long.

4. A decimeter is ▥ centimeters long.

5. A decimeter is ▥ millimeters long.

6. A centimeter is ▥ millimeters long.

Practice Choose the measure that is most reasonable.

1. length of a pencil

   19 mm   19 cm   19 dm

2. length of a housefly

   9 mm   9 cm   9 m

3. height of a child

   12 cm   12 dm   12 m

4. height of a flag pole

   9 cm   9 dm   9 m

5. height of the Statue of Liberty

   93 m   93 dm   93 cm

6. length of a small paper clip

   28 m   28 cm   28 mm

7. thickness of a writing tablet

   6 cm   6 m   6 mm

8. length of a basketball court

   26 dm   26 m   26 cm

Which unit (**m, cm,** or **mm**) would you use to measure

9. the width of your book?

10. the length of a soccer field?

11. the height of a tree?

12. the thickness of a quarter?

13. the length of a dollar bill?

14. the length of your shoe?

15. the height of a mountain?

16. the width of a shoelace?

Give the number for each ▥.

17. 1 m = ▥ cm

18. 1 m = ▥ dm

19. 1 m = ▥ mm

20. 1 dm = ▥ mm

21. 1 cm = ▥ mm

22. ▥ cm = 1 dm

23. ▥ mm = 1 m

24. ▥ dm = 1 m

25. 1,000 mm = ▥ m

Give the missing unit.

26. 10 ? = 1 dm

27. 10 ? = 1 m

28. 100 ? = 1 m

29. 1 dm = 100 ?

30. 1 m = 10 ?

31. 1,000 ? = 1 m

32. Name and measure an object you would measure using each of these units: m, cm, and mm.

Think

Metric Prefixes

Suppose metric prefixes (deci-, centi-, and milli-) were used for time.

How many minutes would there be in

1. a deciday?   2. a centiday?

3. a milliday?

Math

169

Measuring with Metric Units of Length

Work with a group. You will need metric rulers, meter sticks, or metric tape measures.

Part 1

1. Try this Metric Scavenger Hunt. Make a score sheet like the one below. Find some objects in the classroom that you estimate are close to the target lengths. Discuss your reasons and agree on one object for each target length. Record them on the score sheet.

Metric Scavenger Hunt Score Sheet			
Target Length	Name of Object	Measured Length	Difference
10 cm			
2 m			
30 cm			
3 mm			
1 m			
50 cm			
6 cm			
70 cm			
3 m			
5 mm			
		Total Difference	

Rules for Each Group

- For each object, measure and record the length. Then calculate the difference between the target length and the measured length. (Be sure to include the unit of measure.)
- After you have measured all the objects, find the total of all the differences. The group with the smallest total difference is the winner.

2. Share your work with the class.
   - Discuss your strategies for finding objects closest to the target lengths.
   - What did you have to think about when you were finding the total difference? Explain the methods you used.

Part 2

With your group, discuss and solve these problems involving estimation and measurement.

3. How can you find the approximate thickness of one page of your math book? Discuss whether or not you can estimate it visually. Then have each person calculate the approximate thickness of a page. Begin by measuring the thickness of your math book and comparing measurements in your group.
   - How do the measurements vary? How do you account for the differences?
   - How can you use your measurements to find the approximate thickness of one page? Try it and compare results with those of other groups.

4. Estimate how many paces it would take you to walk one kilometer. Then measure the length of one pace. Calculate a new estimate.
   - How close was your first estimate to your calculated estimate of the number of paces?
   - Why might this calculation *not* be the actual number of paces?
   - With your group, suggest some ways to make more exact estimates and calculations.

5. How long is your classroom? Make an estimate. Then measure the length of one person's shoe. That person carefully steps the length of the classroom. Use that information to calculate another estimate of the distance.
   - Compare your calculated estimate to your first estimate.
   - Then agree on an estimate for the length of the **diagonal** of your classroom.
   - Step the distance and calculate an estimate.
   - Compare your calculated estimates with those of other groups. Discuss any differences.
   - What might you do to improve your estimates?

6. With the class, discuss different ways to estimate distances and ways you can improve your estimates.

ic Units and Decimals

n use decimals to compare metric units.

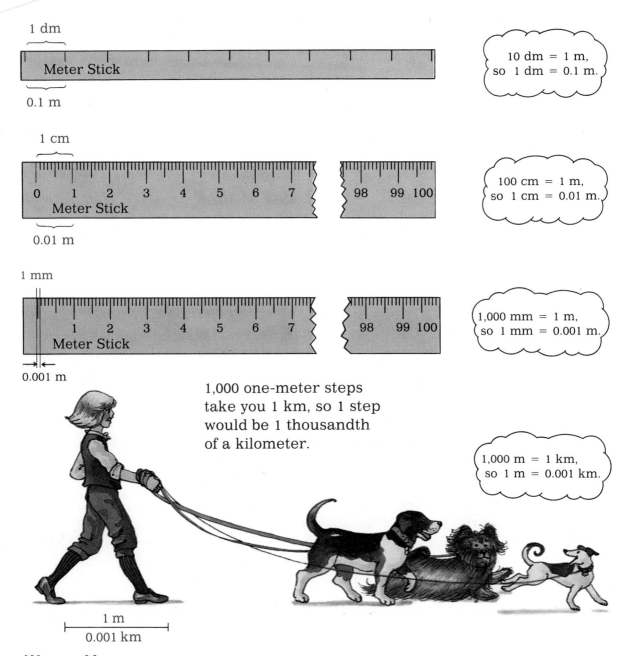

1 dm

Meter Stick

0.1 m

10 dm = 1 m,
so 1 dm = 0.1 m.

1 cm

| 0 | 1 | 2 | 3 | 4 | 5 | 6 | 7 | | 98 | 99 | 100 |

Meter Stick

0.01 m

100 cm = 1 m,
so 1 cm = 0.01 m.

1 mm

| 1 | 2 | 3 | 4 | 5 | 6 | 7 | | 98 | 99 | 100 |

Meter Stick

0.001 m

1,000 mm = 1 m,
so 1 mm = 0.001 m.

1,000 one-meter steps
take you 1 km, so 1 step
would be 1 thousandth
of a kilometer.

1,000 m = 1 km,
so 1 m = 0.001 km.

1 m

0.001 km

Warm Up   Give the missing numbers or units.

1. 1 cm = ▦ m

2. 1 m = ▦ km

3. 1 mm = ▦ m

4. 1 dm = ▦ m

5. 1 cm = ▦ dm

6. 1 mm = ▦ cm

7. 1 ▦ = 0.01 m

8. 1 ▦ = 0.001 m

9. 1 mm = 0.01 ▦

Since both the place-value system and the metric system
are based on 10, we can use decimals to show measurements
that fall between whole numbers of units.

A small flower garden
is 2 m 54 cm or 2.54 m
long.

Since 100 cm = 1 m,
54 cm = 0.54 m.

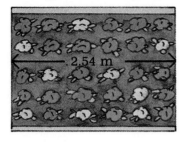

A hole-digger can dig
holes 9 cm 5 mm or
9.5 cm deep.

Since 10 mm = 1 cm,
5 mm = 0.5 cm.

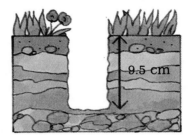

A walk from home to the
garden store is 3 km 725 m
or 3.725 km.

Since 1,000 m = 1 km,
725 m = 0.725 km.

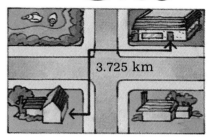

Practice   Give the decimal for each ▥.

1. 5 m 23 cm = ▥ m

2. 8 cm 3 mm = ▥ cm

3. 2 km 465 m = ▥ km

4. 9 mm = ▥ cm

5. 4 km 983 m = ▥ km

6. 6 m 87 cm = ▥ m

7. 43 cm = ▥ m

8. 9 m 4 cm = ▥ m

9. 1 km 86 m = ▥ km

10. 3 m 7 dm = ▥ m

11. 6 m 72 cm = ▥ m

12. 6 m 9 dm = ▥ m

13. 3 km 100 m = ▥ km

14. 8 m 50 cm = ▥ cm

15. 4 dm 9 cm = ▥ m

16. 3.76 m = ▥ m ▥ cm

17. 3.7 dm = ▥ dm ▥ cm

18. 2.375 km = ▥ km ▥ m

19. 4.6 m = ▥ m ▥ cm

20. 9.4 cm = ▥ cm ▥ mm

21. 1.128 km = ▥ km ▥ m

22. 4.23 m = ▥ m ▥ cm

23. 8.9 cm = ▥ cm ▥ mm

★**24.** 3.086 km = ▥ m ▥ cm

Skillkeeper

Divide.

1. 5)‾43‾

2. 9)‾68‾

3. 7)‾96‾

4. 6)‾126‾

5. 8)‾3,410‾

6. 20)‾89‾

7. 32)‾384‾

8. 27)‾1,325‾

9. 52)‾4,529‾

10. 76)‾16,654‾

Changing Units by Multiplying: Mental Math

Yasmin built a birdhouse with an entrance just 3.8 cm wide so that birds larger than bluebirds cannot get into it. What is this width in millimeters?

Each centimeter unit is 10 mm long, so to change from centimeters to millimeters, we multiply by 10, or simply move the decimal point 1 place to the right.

$$3.8 \text{ cm} = 38 \text{ mm}$$

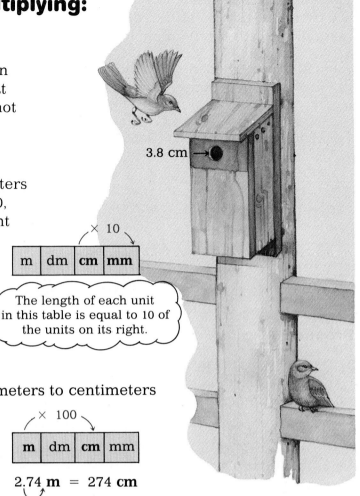

3.8 cm →

× 10

m	dm	cm	mm

The length of each unit in this table is equal to 10 of the units on its right.

Other Examples

meters to decimeters

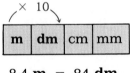

× 10

m	dm	cm	mm

$$8.4 \text{ m} = 84 \text{ dm}$$

meters to centimeters

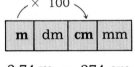

× 100

m	dm	cm	mm

$$2.74 \text{ m} = 274 \text{ cm}$$

meters to millimeters

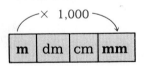

× 1,000

m	dm	cm	mm

$$9.367 \text{ m} = 9,367 \text{ mm}$$

kilometers to meters

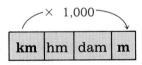

× 1,000

km	hm	dam	m

$$5.465 \text{ km} = 5,465 \text{ m}$$

Give the number for each changed unit.

1. 3.6 m = ▥ dm

2. 3.64 m = ▥ dm

3. 3.64 m = ▥ cm

4. 3.642 m = ▥ mm

5. 5.876 km = ▥ m

6. 4.3 m = ▥ dm

7. 9.68 m = ▥ cm

8. 2.75 m = ▥ mm

9. 0.86 m = ▥ cm

10. 7.8 km = ▥ m

11. 4.9 dm = ▥ cm

12. 8.04 m = ▥ cm

13. 4.65 dm = ▥ mm

14. 12.2 m = ▥ cm

15. 8.4 cm = ▥ mm

Changing Units by Dividing: Mental Math

The diameter of the entrance to a bird house for a purple martin should be 57 mm across. What is this measure in centimeters?

It takes 10 mm to make 1 cm, so to change from millimeters to centimeters we divide by 10, or simply move the decimal point 1 place to the left.

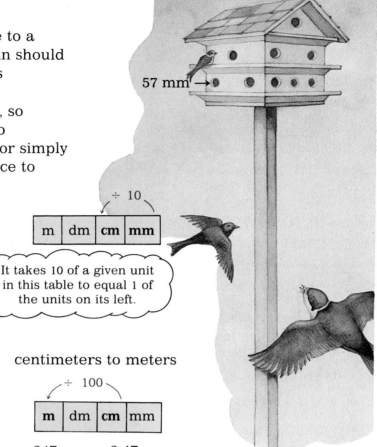

57 mm →

57 mm = 5.7 cm

÷ 10

| m | dm | cm | mm |

It takes 10 of a given unit in this table to equal 1 of the units on its left.

Other Examples

decimeters to meters

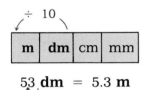

÷ 10

| m | dm | cm | mm |

53 dm = 5.3 m

centimeters to meters

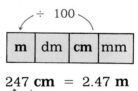

÷ 100

| m | dm | cm | mm |

247 cm = 2.47 m

millimeters to meters

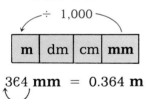

÷ 1,000

| m | dm | cm | mm |

364 mm = 0.364 m

meters to kilometers

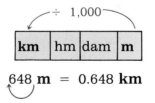

÷ 1,000

| km | hm | dam | m |

648 m = 0.648 km

Give the number for each changed unit.

1. 68 dm = ▦ m

2. 369 cm = ▦ m

3. 867 m = ▦ km

4. 743 mm = ▦ m

5. 147 dm = ▦ m

6. 48 cm = ▦ m

7. 98 m = ▦ km

8. 56 mm = ▦ m

9. 47 mm = ▦ dm

10. 376 cm = ▦ m

11. 1,264 m = ▦ km

12. 9,467 mm = ▦ m

13. 2,876 m = ▦ km

14. 157 dm = ▦ m

15. 137 mm = ▦ dm

Problem Solving: Using Data from a Reference Book

Solve. Change units when necessary.

1. The diameter of a long-playing phonograph record is about 0.3 m. About how much larger is the diameter of a squid's eye than the diameter of the record?

2. The diameter of a human's eye is about 0.05 times the diameter of a giant squid's eye. About how many millimeters is this?

3. If the clam grows the same amount every year, how long will it be when it is 50 years old? 25 years old? How long will it take for the clam to grow to be 1 cm long?

4. A recent men's world record for a long jump is 8.90 m. How many meters longer is that men's record than the frog's jump?

5. The longest wingspan of any airplane was about 26.85 times as long as the wingspan of the wandering albatross. About how many meters was the airplane's wingspan?

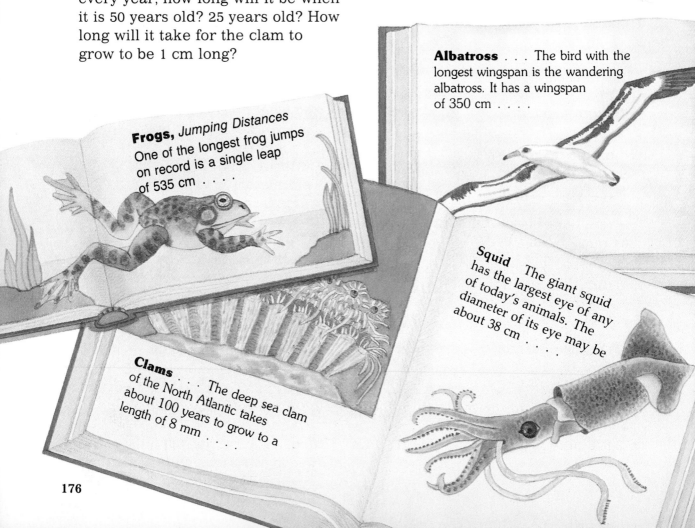

Albatross . . . The bird with the longest wingspan is the wandering albatross. It has a wingspan of 350 cm . . . .

Frogs, *Jumping Distances* One of the longest frog jumps on record is a single leap of 535 cm . . . .

Squid The giant squid has the largest eye of any of today's animals. The diameter of its eye may be about 38 cm . . . .

Clams . . . The deep sea clam of the North Atlantic takes about 100 years to grow to a length of 8 mm . . . .

Butterflies . . . The smallest known butterfly is the dwarf blue of South Africa. Its wingspan is 13.97 mm.

Mountains Mt. Everest, a peak in South Central Asia, is the world's highest mountain. Its height has been found to be 8.8473 km (plus or minus 7.6 m).

6. What are the upper and the lower limits for the height of Mt. Everest (in meters)?

7. The deepest known part of any ocean is the Marianas Trench, 10,912 m deep. How much greater is this depth than the height of Mt. Everest (8.8473 km) in meters?

8. The giant swallowtail butterfly is one of the largest butterflies found in North America. The giant swallowtail's wingspan may be as great as 13 cm. How many millimeters greater is this wingspan than the wingspan of the smallest known butterfly?

9. The world's largest butterfly is the Queen Alexandra birdwing of New Guinea. Its wingspan is about 20 times that of the smallest butterfly. About how many centimeters is the wingspan of the largest butterfly?

10. **Strategy Practice** Bill Brown, Cindy Cole, Denise Downs, and Ed Evans are editors. One is the sports editor, one the science editor, one the geography editor, and one the politics editor. The sports editor is a woman who rides to work with Cindy Cole. Neither Bill Brown nor Cindy Cole has any interest in geography. Cindy Cole is the science editor's cousin. Which job does each person have? Hint: Use logical reasoning.

ume and Capacity

olume of a container is the number of cubic units of space it encloses. Metric units of volume are usually used for very accurate, scientific measurements.

The units of **capacity** are used in everyday measurements to describe how much a container will hold.

cubic unit

Volume = 12 cubic units

The **liter** (L) is the basic unit of capacity.

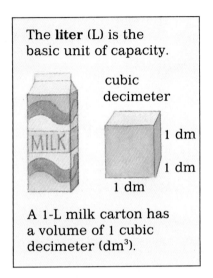

cubic decimeter

1 dm
1 dm
1 dm

A 1-L milk carton has a volume of 1 cubic decimeter (dm³).

A **milliliter** (mL) is one thousandth of a liter.

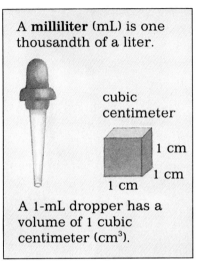

cubic centimeter

1 cm
1 cm
1 cm

A 1-mL dropper has a volume of 1 cubic centimeter (cm³).

A **kiloliter** (kL) is one thousand liters.

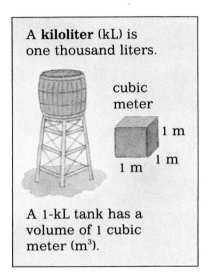

cubic meter

1 m
1 m
1 m

A 1-kL tank has a volume of 1 cubic meter (m³).

1,000 mL = 1 L	1 mL = 0.001 L	1,000 L = 1 kL	1 L = 0.001 kL

Choose the best estimate for the capacity of each container.

1. can of juice

825 mL   825 L   825 kL

2. tablespoon

15 mL   15 L   15 kL

3. bathtub

225 mL   225 L   225 kL

4. city water storage tank
2,000 mL   2,000 L   2,000 kL

5. goldfish tank
40 mL   40L   40kL

6. small can of soup
200 mL   200 L   200 kL

Give the number for each changed unit.

Think about this table.

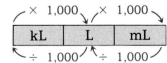

	× 1,000	× 1,000
kL	L	mL
	÷ 1,000	÷ 1,000

7. 3 kL = ▦ L

8. 7 L = ▦ mL

9. 0.250 kL = ▦ L **10.** 0.750 L = ▦ mL

11. 1,435 L = ▦ kL **12.** 2,374 mL = ▦ L **13.** 476 L = ▦ kL **14.** 375 mL = ▦ L

Problem Solving:
Mixed Practice (Capacity)

Solve.

1. How many cups with a capacity of 250 mL can you fill from a 1-L bottle of milk?

2. How many 5-mL teaspoons does it take to fill a 250-mL cup?

3. About how many tablespoons with a capacity of 15 mL can you fill from a 250-mL cup? (Round to the nearest whole number.)

6. The tank on a truck used to ship milk holds 15 kL of milk. How many 1-L bottles can be filled with this milk?

7. A large water cooler holds 16 L of water. About how many water coolers does it take to hold 1 kL of water? (Round to the nearest whole number.)

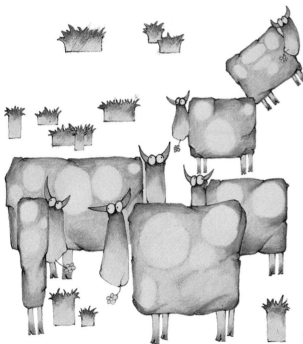

8. A large bottle holds 3.785 L of juice. How many milliliters does it hold?

9. A can of frozen grape juice has a capacity of 177 mL. How much more or less than a liter of liquid do you have after you add 3 cans of water to the juice?

4. A pitcher has 2 L of juice in it. How many 200-mL glasses can you fill with this amount of juice?

5. A bottle of apple juice contains 1.5 L of juice. How many milliliters is this?

10. **Strategy Practice**   Here are two pails. There are no markings on either pail. How can you use the pails to get 4 L of water in the larger pail?

3 L   8 L

Weight

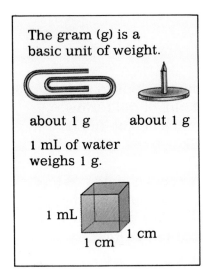

The gram (g) is a basic unit of weight.

about 1 g   about 1 g

1 mL of water weighs 1 g.

1 mL
1 cm   1 cm

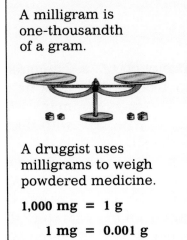

A milligram is one-thousandth of a gram.

A druggist uses milligrams to weigh powdered medicine.

1,000 mg = 1 g

1 mg = 0.001 g

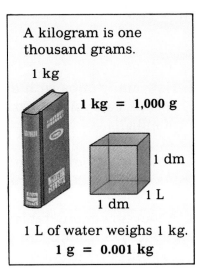

A kilogram is one thousand grams.

1 kg

1 kg = 1,000 g

1 dm
1 dm   1 L

1 L of water weighs 1 kg.

1 g = 0.001 kg

Choose the best estimate of the weight.

1. A bowling ball

7 mg   7 g   7 kg

2. A nickel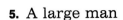

5 mg   5 g   5 kg

3. A drop of water

50 mg   50 g   50 kg

4. A baseball bat

1 mg   1 g   1 kg

5. A large man

90 mg   90 g   90 kg

6. A ballpoint pen

15 mg   15 g   15 kg

7. A horse

500 mg   500 g   500 kg

8. A pin

125 mg   125 g   125 kg

9. A bicycle

12 mg   12 g   12 kg

Give the number for each changed unit.

Think about this table.

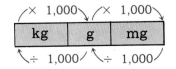

10. 5 kg = ▦ g

11. 12 g = ▦ mg

12. 0.250 kg = ▦ g

13. 0.500 g = ▦ mg

14. 8,346 g = ▦ kg

15. 1,765 mg = ▦ g

16. 425 mg = ▦ g

17. 750 g = ▦ kg

18. 56 kg = ▦ g

19. 1.3 g = ▦ mg

★ **20.** 1 kg = ▦ mg

★ **21.** 4,000,000 mg = ▦ kg

QUESTION
DATA
PLAN
ANSWER
CHECK

Problem Solving:
Mixed Practice (Weight)

Solve.

1. The powdered cocoa in a box weighs 120 g and makes 24 cups of cocoa. How many grams of cocoa are needed for each cup?

2. A package of crackers weighs 539 g. There are 36 crackers in the box. What is the weight of each cracker to the nearest gram?

3. How many pieces of sausage that weigh 250 g each can be cut from a large piece that weighs 1 kg?

4. A baking potato weighs 245 g. How many kilograms does a bag of 6 potatoes weigh?

5. There are 250 mg of sodium in each 30-g serving of a certain cereal. How much would a serving of the cereal that contains 1 g of sodium weigh?

6. A raisin weighs about 500 mg. If there are 28 raisins in a box, what is the total weight of the raisins in grams?

7. A family-size package of ground beef weighs 2.486 kg. If each hamburger patty made from the beef weighs 113 g, how many patties can be made?

8. A giant box of washing powder weighs 3.2 kg. It takes 60 g of the powder to wash a load of dishes. How many loads of dishes can be washed with a box of the powder? (Round to the nearest whole number.)

9. **Strategy Practice**   An apple and a banana together weigh 417 g. The apple weighs 73 g less than the banana. How much does each piece of fruit weigh?

Temperature

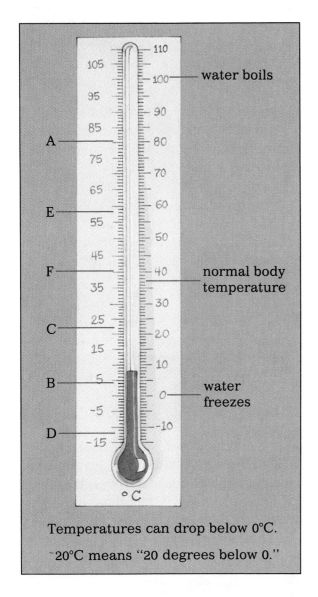

The **degree Celsius** (°C) is the basic unit of temperature.

Give the letter for the temperature on the thermometer that best fits each condition or object pictured below.

1. High fever

2. Hot soup

3. Frozen yogurt

4. Cold water

5. Comfortable room temperature

6. Hottest air temperature recorded on earth

In the thermometer diagram:
- water boils — 100
- normal body temperature — 40
- water freezes — 0

Temperatures can drop below 0°C.

⁻20°C means "20 degrees below 0."

Choose the better temperature estimate.

7. Hot drink

    18°C   81°C

8. Crushed ice

    0°C   30°C

9. Drinking water

    12°C   92°C

10. Hot oven

    40°C   190°C

11. Inside a refrigerator

    4°C   40°C

12. Snowy day

    ⁻5°C   25°C

13. Your classroom

    2°C   20°C

14. Hot bath

    45°C   95°C

Read and write the temperature shown on each thermometer.

1.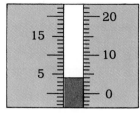

Cold milk

2.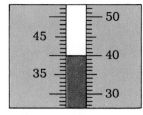

Very warm day

3.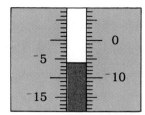

Inside a freezer

4.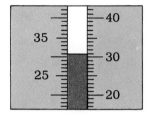

Butter melts

5.

Broiled steak

6.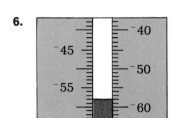

Record cold day

7. This temperature graph shows a normal temperature for each season in San Antonio, Texas. What is the average of these temperatures?

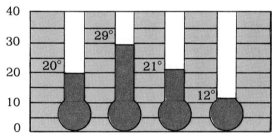

8. The temperature at which water boils changes with the altitude (height above sea level). At sea level water boils at 100°C. At the top of Mt. Everest water boils at a temperature only 0.71 times as great. By how many degrees do these two temperatures differ?

9. DATA BANK How many degrees would the world's record cold temperature have to rise to reach the record high temperature? (See Data Bank, page 424.)

Time: Basic Units

Here are some commonly used
devices and units for measuring time.

Clock   Digital Clock

minute
hand

hour
hand

second
hand

Hours between midnight and
noon are **a.m.** Hours between
noon and midnight are **p.m.**

60 seconds (s)	=	1 minute (min)
60 minutes	=	1 hour (h)
24 hours (h)	=	1 day (d)

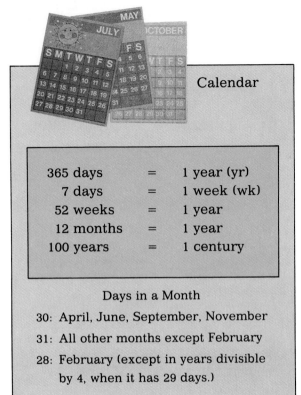

Calendar

365 days	=	1 year (yr)
7 days	=	1 week (wk)
52 weeks	=	1 year
12 months	=	1 year
100 years	=	1 century

Days in a Month

30: April, June, September, November

31: All other months except February

28: February (except in years divisible
by 4, when it has 29 days.)

We can change from one time unit
to another as shown in the examples below.

Example A:
Jenny was on vacation for 3 wk 4 d.
How many days was this?

3 wk = 3 × 7, or 21 d
21 + 4 = 25

Answer: 25 d

Example B:
Byron recorded music for 135 min.
How many hours and minutes
was this?

135 ÷ 60 = 2 R15

Answer: 2 h 15 min

Give the missing numbers.

1. 5 h = ▦ min

2. 4 min = ▦ s

3. 6 wk = ▦ d

4. 4 yr = ▦ mo

5. 3 yr = ▦ d

6. 5 yr = ▦ wk

7. 20 centuries = ▦ yr

8. 180 min = ▦ h

9. 240 s = ▦ min

10. 6 min 24 s = ▦ s

11. 5 h 25 min = ▦ min

12. 3 d 8 h = ▦ h

13. 65 mo ▦ yr ▦ mo

14. 85 h = ▦ d ▦ h

15. 340 min = ▦ h ▦ min

Adding and Subtracting Time

Juan worked at the hospital
3 h 25 min in the morning and
2 h 45 min in the afternoon.

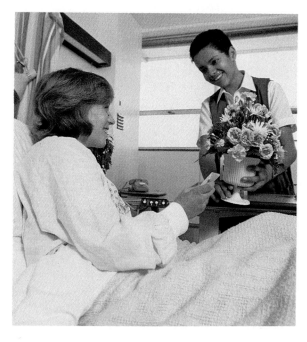

A. How long did Juan work that day?

$$
\begin{array}{r}
3 \text{ h } 25 \text{ min} \\
+ \; 2 \text{ h } 45 \text{ min} \\
\hline
5 \text{ h } 70 \text{ min}
\end{array}
$$

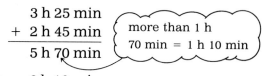
more than 1 h
70 min = 1 h 10 min

or   6 h 10 min

Juan worked 6 h 10 min.

B. How much longer did Juan work in the morning than in the afternoon?

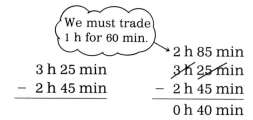
We must trade
1 h for 60 min.

$$
\begin{array}{r}
3 \text{ h } 25 \text{ min} \\
- \; 2 \text{ h } 45 \text{ min} \\
\hline
\end{array}
\qquad
\begin{array}{r}
2 \text{ h } 85 \text{ min} \\
\cancel{3 \text{ h } 25 \text{ min}} \\
- \; 2 \text{ h } 45 \text{ min} \\
\hline
0 \text{ h } 40 \text{ min}
\end{array}
$$

Juan worked 40 min longer in the morning.

Add or subtract.

1. 3 h 45 min + 4 h 30 min	**2.** 4 h 55 min + 2 h 35 min	**3.** 5 h 37 min + 16 h 23 min	**4.** 3 min 25 s + 2 min 44 s
5. 4 min 29 s + 8 min 46 s	**6.** 9 min 55 s + 6 min 42 s	**7.** 8 h 20 min − 3 h 45 min	**8.** 12 h 10 min − 7 h 50 min
9. 8 h 4 min − 2 h 19 min	**10.** 6 min 15 s − 4 min 45 s	**11.** 9 min 12 s − 3 min 20 s	**12.** 12 min 24 s − 7 min 56 s

Think

Estimation

Guess which answer is greatest and which is smallest. Calculate to check your guesses!

A. 1 h = ▦ s

B. 1 yr = ▦ h

C. 1 wk = ▦ min

Math

Time Zones

The world is divided into 24 different time zones. Because of the earth's shape and rotation, the sun may appear in a city in one time zone while it is still dark in a city in another zone. Here are the six time zones in the United States.

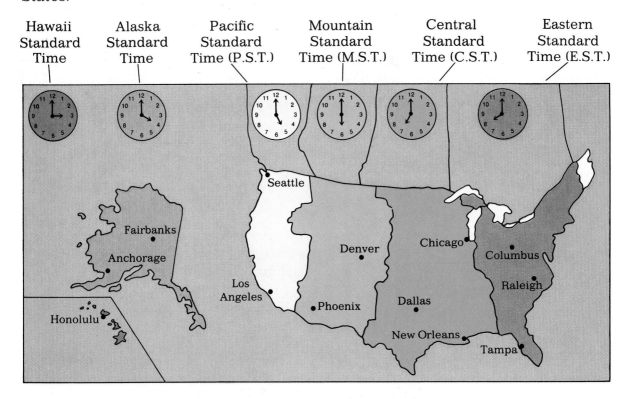

Hawaii Standard Time | Alaska Standard Time | Pacific Standard Time (P.S.T.) | Mountain Standard Time (M.S.T.) | Central Standard Time (C.S.T.) | Eastern Standard Time (E.S.T.)

Give the missing times. Use the map above.

1. When it is 9:00 p.m. Eastern time, it is __?__ Central time and __?__ Pacific time.

2. When it is 6:00 p.m. Hawaii time, it is __?__ Mountain time.

3. The voting polls close in Fairbanks at 6:00 p.m. At that time it is __?__ in Columbus and __?__ in Phoenix.

4. When Kirk made a phone call to Raleigh, it was 7:00 p.m. Denver time. The Raleigh time was __?__.

5. When it is 12:00 midnight in New Orleans, it is __?__ in Anchorage and __?__ in Tampa.

6. The World Series game begins at 5:00 p.m. in Los Angeles. To watch it in Dallas, turn on your TV at __?__.

7. A flight from Chicago to Seattle takes 4 h. If a plane leaves at 10:00 a.m. Chicago time, it arrives at __?__ Seattle time.

186

Problem Solving: Using Mental Math

Try to do these problems without using pencil and paper.

Example: A soccer match started at 1:30 p.m. and ended 2 h 35 min later. When did the match end?

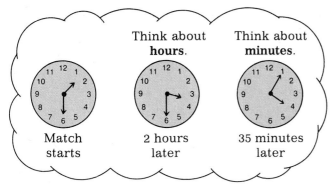

Think about **hours**. Think about **minutes**.

Match starts   2 hours later   35 minutes later

The soccer match was over at 4:05 p.m.

1. Roger's music lesson will begin at 8:00 a.m. He wants to get up 1 h and 15 min earlier than this. What time should he get up?

Think: 1 hour earlier than 8:00 is what time?   15 minutes earlier than this is what time?

2. Lila's family left home at 12:15 p.m. At 2:30 p.m. they arrived at the beach. How long did the trip take?

Think: 12:15 to 2:15 is how many hours?   2:15 to 2:30 is how many minutes?

3. A school baseball game started at 2:15 p.m. and finished 2 h 40 min later. At what time was it over?

4. Jim started work at 1:30 p.m. Tad started work 1 h 20 min earlier. When did Tad start work?

5. Marie planned to finish her project at 4:30 p.m., but actually finished 2 h 45 min earlier. When was that?

6. School starts at 8:30 a.m. and ends at 3:15 p.m. How long is this?

★ 7. A plane left St. Louis at 3:15 p.m. Central Standard Time. It arrived in Los Angeles at 6:10 p.m. Central Standard Time. How long did the flight take? What was the Pacific Standard Time when the plane arrived in Los Angeles?

8. **Strategy Practice** Mike's time card for two days at work looked like this:

MONDAY		TUESDAY	
IN	8:05 a.m.	IN	7:50 a.m.
OUT	11:45 a.m.	OUT	12:15 p.m.
IN	12:54 p.m.	IN	1:05 p.m.
OUT	4:47 p.m.	OUT	4:56 p.m.

How much longer did Mike work on Tuesday than on Monday?

Problem-Solving Strategy:
Work Backward

Problems that give data about the final result of a series of operations can be solved most easily by using a strategy called

Work Backward

It often helps to think about a **flowchart** and a **reverse flowchart** to solve the problem.

Try This Nan checked the price of a share of stock on the New York Stock Exchange on January 1. On June 1 its price was $8 higher. By December its price was twice as great as on June 1. The price on December 1 was $46 a share. What was the price on January 1?

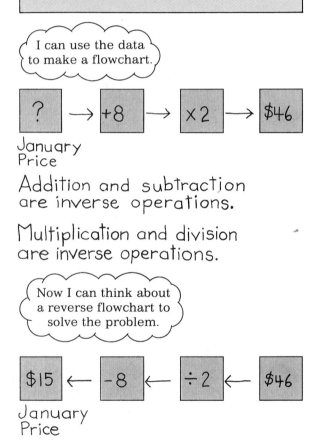

I can use the data to make a flowchart.

| ? | → | +8 | → | ×2 | → | $46 |

January Price

Addition and subtraction are inverse operations.

Multiplication and division are inverse operations.

Now I can think about a reverse flowchart to solve the problem.

| $15 | ← | −8 | ← | ÷2 | ← | $46 |

January Price

The stock was worth $15 on January 1.

Solve.

1. Janet had some tulip bulbs. She gave 8 to her mother and equally divided the ones that were left among herself and 2 friends. Her final share was 12 bulbs. How many did she have at the beginning?

2. Bill bought a belt for $5.75 and a pair of pants that cost 4 times as much as the belt. Then he had $4.24 left. How much money did he have before he bought the belt and pants?

Chapter Review-Test

Give the missing units or numbers.

1. 100 cm = 1 <u>?</u>   **2.** 1 dm = 100 <u>?</u>   **3.** 1,000 m = 1 <u>?</u>   **4.** 1 <u>?</u> = 10 dm

5. 1 m = ▥ mm   **6.** 1 dm = ▥ cm   **7.** 1 cm = ▥ mm   **8.** 1 km = ▥ m

9. Estimate the length of this segment in centimeters. (Use a decimal if you wish.) Then measure the actual length.

Write decimals for these measurements. Use a single unit.

10. 4 m 8 dm   **11.** 6 m 46 cm   **12.** 12 cm 7 mm   **13.** 9 dm 5 cm

Give the missing numbers.

14. 4 m = ▥ dm   **15.** 8 m = ▥ cm   **16.** 2.6 cm = ▥ mm   **17.** 6 km = ▥ m

18. 400 m = ▥ km   **19.** 279 cm = ▥ m   **20.** 2 kL = ▥ L   **21.** 3L = ▥ mL

Choose the best estimate for each.

22. Capacity

250 mL   250 L   250 kL

23. Weight

150 mg   150 g   150 kg

24. Temperature

⁻8°C   8°C   80°C

Give the missing numbers.

25. 4 h = ▥ min   **26.** 5 min = ▥ s   **27.** 3 yr = ▥ mo   **28.** 6 wk = ▥ d

Solve.

29. Jeff worked 8 h 45 min on Monday and 6 h 53 min on Tuesday. How many hours was this in all? How much longer did he work on Monday than on Tuesday?

30. A parking meter showed 2 h 15 min of time left when Mindy parked by it. Her watch showed 3:05 p.m. At what time did the meter need more coins?

Another Look

Length

1 kilometer (km) = 1,000 meters (m)

1 m = 100 centimeters (cm)
          or 10 decimeters (dm)

1 cm = 10 millimeters (mm)

2 m 45 cm = 2.45 m

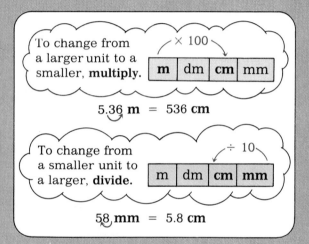

To change from a larger unit to a smaller, **multiply.**

× 100

| m | dm | cm | mm |

5.36 m = 536 cm

To change from a smaller unit to a larger, **divide.**

÷ 10

| m | dm | cm | mm |

58 mm = 5.8 cm

Capacity

1 liter (L) = 1,000 milliliters (mL)
1 kiloliter (kL) = 1,000 L

Weight

1 kilogram (kg) = 1,000 grams (g)
1 g = 1,000 milligrams (mg)

Temperature

Water freezes at 0°C (degrees Celsius).
Water boils at 100°C.

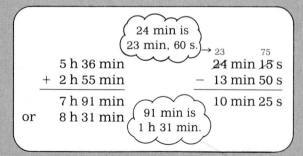

24 min is
23 min, 60 s.

23   75
24 min 1̸5̸ s
− 13 min 50 s

5 h 36 min
+ 2 h 55 min

7 h 91 min
or   8 h 31 min

91 min is
1 h 31 min.

10 min 25 s

Give the missing units.

1. 1 mm = 0.1 ?
2. 1 cm = 10 ?
3. 1 cm = 0.01 ?
4. 1,000 m = 1 ?
5. 1 m = 0.001 ?
6. 10 dm = 1 ?
7. 1 dm = 10 ?
8. 1 m = 100 ?
9. 8 km 435 m = 8.435 ?
10. 5 m 3 dm = 5.3 ?

Give the missing numbers.

11. 1 m − ▦ cm
12. 1,000 m = ▦ km
13. 1 cm = ▦ mm
14. 1 dm = ▦ cm
15. 1 m = ▦ km
16. 1 dm = ▦ m
17. 8 m = ▦ cm
18. 12 cm = ▦ mm
19. 5.46 m = ▦ cm
20. 384 mm = ▦ cm
21. 1,386 m = ▦ km

Give the missing units.

22. 1,000 mL = 1 ▦
23. 1,000 mg = 1 ▦
24. 1,000 L = 1 ▦
25. 1,000 g = 1 ▦
26. Hot day temperature: 38 ▦

Give the missing numbers.

27. 3 L = ▦ mL
28. 2,000 L = ▦ kL
29. 1 kg = ▦ g
30. 1 g = ▦ mg

Add or subtract.

31.   6 h 42 min
      + 8 h 56 min

32.   52 min 12 s
      − 27 min 38 s

33.   17 h 20 min
      −   7 h 45 min

34.   35 min 48 s
      + 19 min 32 s

Enrichment

Estimating Size

Estimate your "size" for each item in the table. Record your estimate. Then measure and record the actual "size." Find the difference between your estimate and the measure. Then find the sum of these differences. The smallest sum wins!

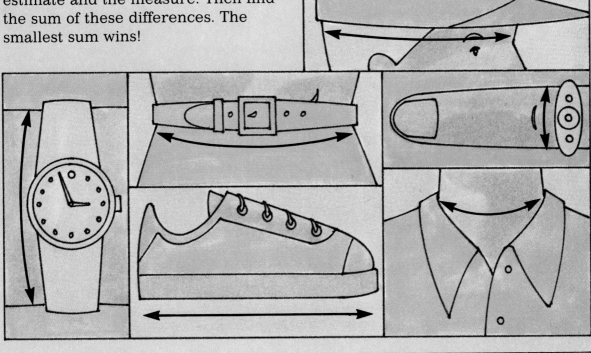

Size	Estimate	Actual measurement	Difference between estimate and actual measure
Ring size	▥ cm	▥ cm	▥ cm
Wristwatch size	▥ cm	▥ cm	▥ cm
Hat size	▥ cm	▥ cm	▥ cm
Collar size	▥ cm	▥ cm	▥ cm
Belt size	▥ cm	▥ cm	▥ cm
Shoe size	▥ cm	▥ cm	▥ cm
		Sum of differences =	▥ cm

Cumulative Review

Multiply or divide.

1. 7 × 60
   - A 42
   - B 420
   - C 4,200
   - D not given

2. 436
   × 9
   - A 39.24
   - B 392.4
   - C 39,240
   - D not given

3. 215
   × 67
   - A 14,405
   - B 16,340
   - C 16,817
   - D not given

4. 505
   × 505
   - A 25,525
   - B 25,502
   - C 25,505
   - D not given

5. 500 × 500
   - A 250,000
   - B 25,000
   - C 2,500
   - D not given

6. 5.72 × 100
   - A 0.572
   - B 57.2
   - C 572
   - D not given

7. 0.333 × 1,000
   - A 3.33
   - B 33.3
   - C 333
   - D not given

8. 9.8
   × 0.2
   - A 1.96
   - B 19.6
   - C 196
   - D not given

9. 5.7
   × 0.07
   - A 0.0399
   - B 0.399
   - C 3.99
   - D not given

10. 7)1.19
    - A 1.7
    - B 0.17
    - C 0.017
    - D not given

11. 52.6 ÷ 100
    - A 526
    - B 5.26
    - C 0.526
    - D not given

12. 3.1)27.9
    - A 9
    - B 0.9
    - C 9.9
    - D not given

13. Marcia put 36 stamps on each of 28 pages. How many stamps did she use?
    - A 1,800
    - B 1,080
    - C 1,008
    - D not given

14. Each of 12 students needs 2.9 m of cloth for a costume. How many meters of cloth are needed in all?
    - A 348 m
    - B 34.8 m
    - C 3.48 m
    - D not given

8

Fractions: Addition and Subtraction

Ricardo always was early for the morning rehearsal. He liked to sit back and watch the other 59 Mozart Music Camp musicians take their places on the pine-tree-bordered stage. Ricardo loved playing with a large group. The City Youth Orchestra he played with at home was only half that size. Ricardo played the cello. The cellos made up one fifth of the orchestra. Ricardo was learning a lot from the other talented cellists.

Although about $\frac{1}{2}$ of the students' time was spent playing music, most of the camp's $8\frac{3}{4}$-square mile area was used for traditional camp activities. There was a volleyball court, a softball field, and a wooded area with hiking trails. There also was a lovely lake, $3\frac{1}{4}$ miles long and $1\frac{1}{2}$ miles across, for swimming and canoeing. Ricardo enjoyed swimming, and he loved the lake. Altogether, he thought, the camp offered a wonderful combination of things he liked to do.

Fractions

We can use **fractions** to name a part of a **region** or a part of a **set**.

Regions

What fraction of the table top is painted dark green?

We think: 3 of the 4 parts of the table top are dark green.

We write: $\frac{3}{4}$ ←Numerator ←Denominator

We say: "**Three fourths** of the table is dark green."

Sets

What fraction of the children are girls?

We think: 2 of the 3 children are girls.

We write: $\frac{2}{3}$ ←Numerator ←Denominator

We say: "**Two thirds** of the children are girls."

Other Examples

32 squares out of 64 squares are red.
$\frac{32}{64}$ of the checkerboard is red.

2 out of 5 paddles are green.
$\frac{2}{5}$ of the paddles are green.

Warm Up   Write the fraction for each picture.

1.

▥ of the balls are footballs.

2.

▥ of the starter's flag is shaded blue.

3.

▥ of the bowling pins are still standing.

194

Practice Write the fraction for each picture.

1.

▧ of the tennis balls are orange.

2.

▧ of the sports blanket is blue.

3.

▧ of the schedule board is filled.

4.

▧ of the circle is yellow.

5.

▧ of the strip is green.

6.

▧ of the stars are blue.

Write the fraction.

7. two fifths

8. four sixths

9. one third

10. seven tenths

11. one half

12. three eighths

Write the word name for each fraction.

13. $\frac{2}{3}$ 14. $\frac{1}{10}$ 15. $\frac{3}{4}$ 16. $\frac{5}{8}$ 17. $\frac{5}{6}$ 18. $\frac{4}{5}$

19. Which region has $\frac{1}{4}$ shaded?

A.   B.   C.   D.

★ 20. Draw a circle and shade $\frac{3}{4}$ of it.

★ 21. Draw a rectangle and shade $\frac{1}{3}$ of it.

Think

Shape Perception

A cube has 6 faces. Study the outlined regions.

Which ones could be folded on the dotted lines to form a cube?

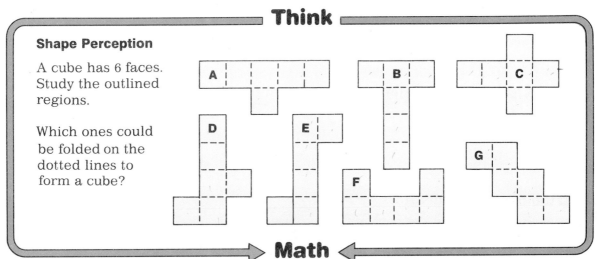

Math

195

Equivalent Fractions

Lupe bought some candles. Some of them were yellow and some were red. What fraction describes the part of the candles that were red?

2 out of **6** candles are red.
$\frac{2}{6}$ of the candles are red.

OR

1 out of **3** pairs have red candles.
$\frac{1}{3}$ of the candles are red.

$\frac{2}{6}$ and $\frac{1}{3}$ are **equivalent fractions.**

$$\frac{2}{6} = \frac{1}{3}$$

> Two fractions that name the same part of a set or the same part of a region are **equivalent fractions.**

We can multiply to find equivalent fractions. Multiply the numerator and denominator by the same number (not zero).

$$\frac{1}{3} = \frac{2}{6}$$

Think: $\frac{1 \;\boxed{\times 2} \rightarrow\; 2}{3 \;\boxed{\times 2} \rightarrow\; 6}$

Other Examples

$$\frac{3}{4} = \frac{15}{20}$$

Think: $\frac{3 \;\boxed{\times 5} \rightarrow\; 15}{4 \;\boxed{\times 5} \rightarrow\; 20}$

$$\frac{2}{5} = \frac{4}{10} \qquad \frac{1}{6} = \frac{6}{36}$$

Warm Up   Find equivalent fractions by multiplying by 3.

1. $\dfrac{1 \times 3}{2 \times 3} = \dfrac{\text{▥}}{\text{▥}}$

2. $\dfrac{3}{5} = \dfrac{\text{▥}}{\text{▥}}$

3. $\dfrac{3}{8} = \dfrac{\text{▥}}{\text{▥}}$

4. $\dfrac{2}{3} = \dfrac{\text{▥}}{\text{▥}}$

Find the missing numerators.

5. $\dfrac{1}{3} = \dfrac{\text{▥}}{12}$

6. $\dfrac{5}{6} = \dfrac{\text{▥}}{18}$

7. $\dfrac{3}{10} = \dfrac{\text{▥}}{50}$

8. $\dfrac{1}{4} = \dfrac{\text{▥}}{12}$

Practice Write two equivalent fractions for the red part.

1.

2.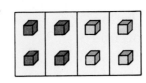

3.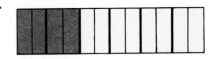

Write an equivalent fraction by multiplying by 2.

4. $\dfrac{1}{2} = \dfrac{\text{▥}}{\text{▥}}$

5. $\dfrac{7}{10} = \dfrac{\text{▥}}{\text{▥}}$

6. $\dfrac{5}{8} = \dfrac{\text{▥}}{\text{▥}}$

7. $\dfrac{1}{6} = \dfrac{\text{▥}}{\text{▥}}$

8. $\dfrac{2}{3} = \dfrac{\text{▥}}{\text{▥}}$

Find the missing numerator or denominator.

9. $\dfrac{2}{5} = \dfrac{\text{▥}}{20}$

10. $\dfrac{3}{10} = \dfrac{\text{▥}}{100}$

11. $\dfrac{2}{2} = \dfrac{\text{▥}}{8}$

12. $\dfrac{3}{4} = \dfrac{\text{▥}}{32}$

13. $\dfrac{5}{12} = \dfrac{\text{▥}}{48}$

14. $\dfrac{3}{8} = \dfrac{\text{▥}}{24}$

15. $\dfrac{1}{2} = \dfrac{\text{▥}}{100}$

16. $\dfrac{1}{4} = \dfrac{\text{▥}}{16}$

17. $\dfrac{9}{10} = \dfrac{\text{▥}}{80}$

18. $\dfrac{4}{7} = \dfrac{\text{▥}}{21}$

19. $\dfrac{5}{6} = \dfrac{25}{\text{▥}}$

20. $\dfrac{2}{3} = \dfrac{40}{\text{▥}}$

21. $\dfrac{7}{8} = \dfrac{28}{\text{▥}}$

22. $\dfrac{5}{8} = \dfrac{60}{\text{▥}}$

23. $\dfrac{3}{5} = \dfrac{27}{\text{▥}}$

Write one fraction equivalent to the given fraction.

24. $\dfrac{4}{5}$

25. $\dfrac{7}{8}$

26. $\dfrac{7}{12}$

27. $\dfrac{3}{8}$

28. $\dfrac{5}{6}$

29. $\dfrac{3}{4}$

30. $\dfrac{1}{10}$

31. $\dfrac{5}{12}$

Write the next three equivalent fractions.

32. $\dfrac{1}{5}, \dfrac{2}{10}, \dfrac{3}{15}, \dfrac{\text{▥}}{\text{▥}}, \dfrac{\text{▥}}{\text{▥}}, \dfrac{\text{▥}}{\text{▥}}$

33. $\dfrac{3}{8}, \dfrac{6}{16}, \dfrac{9}{24}, \dfrac{\text{▥}}{\text{▥}}, \dfrac{\text{▥}}{\text{▥}}, \dfrac{\text{▥}}{\text{▥}}$

34. $\dfrac{2}{7}, \dfrac{4}{14}, \dfrac{6}{21}, \dfrac{\text{▥}}{\text{▥}}, \dfrac{\text{▥}}{\text{▥}}, \dfrac{\text{▥}}{\text{▥}}$

Skillkeeper

Give the missing units.

1. 1 m = 100 _?_

2. 1,000 mm = 1 _?_

3. 1 dm = 10 _?_

4. 1 _?_ = 1,000 m

5. 1 kg = 1,000 _?_

6. 1,000 mL = 1 _?_

Give the missing numbers.

7. 2 dm = ▥ cm

8. 1 kL = ▥ L

9. 500 cm = ▥ m

10. 5 kg = ▥ g

11. 4 km = ▥ m

12. 3,000 mm = ▥ m

13. 1 m = ▥ km

14. 50 cm = ▥ m

15. 7 mm = ▥ cm

Greatest Common Factor

The idea of the **greatest common factor (GCF)** of two numbers will help you find lowest-terms fractions in the next lesson. What is the greatest common factor of the numerator and denominator of $\frac{24}{36}$?

$\frac{24}{36}$

List the factors of the two numbers.	→	List the common factors (the numbers that are in both lists).	→	Choose the greatest common factor.

Factors of 24:
1, 2, 3, 4, 6, 8, 12, 24

Factors of 36:
1, 2, 3, 4, 6, 9, 12, 18, 36

1, 2, 3, 4, 6, 12

1 2

Other Examples

16 → 1, 2, 4, 8, 16
24 → 1, 2, 3, 4, 6, 8, 12
Common factors: 1, 2, 4, 8
Greatest common factor: **8**

9 → 1, 3, 9
13 → 1, 13
Common factor: 1
Greatest common factor: **1**

Find the greatest common factor for **24** and **36**.

Shortcut

A List only the factors of the smaller number.

24: 1, 2, 3, 4, 6, 8, 12, 24

B List those that are also factors of the other number (36).

1, 2, 3, 4, 6, 12

C The largest is the greatest common factor.

1 2

Find the greatest common factor for each pair of numbers.

1. $\frac{8}{24}$ 2. $\frac{3}{12}$ 3. $\frac{15}{25}$ 4. $\frac{4}{8}$ 5. $\frac{7}{20}$ 6. $\frac{12}{54}$

7. $\frac{18}{30}$ 8. $\frac{20}{50}$ 9. $\frac{6}{7}$ 10. $\frac{18}{38}$ 11. $\frac{12}{36}$ 12. $\frac{9}{32}$

13. $\frac{42}{36}$ 14. $\frac{100}{50}$ 15. $\frac{15}{45}$ 16. $\frac{14}{63}$ 17. $\frac{21}{60}$ 18. $\frac{45}{72}$

More Practice, page 437, Set D

Lowest-Terms Fractions

In Lettie's class, 6 out of 24 students, or $\frac{6}{24}$ of the class, are in the tumbling club. To show this number more simply, we write $\frac{6}{24}$ as a **lowest-terms fraction.**

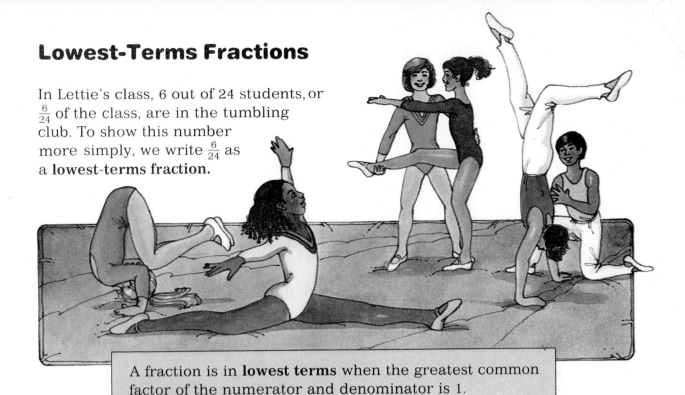

A fraction is in **lowest terms** when the greatest common factor of the numerator and denominator is 1.

To reduce a fraction to lowest terms:
Divide the numerator and the denominator by any common factor and continue to divide until you find the lowest-terms fraction.

$$\frac{6 \div 2}{24 \div 2} = \frac{3}{12} \rightarrow \frac{3 \div 3}{12 \div 3} = \frac{1}{4}$$

OR

Divide the numerator and the denominator by the **greatest common factor** (GCF) to find the lowest-terms fraction.

$$\frac{6 \div 6}{24 \div 6} = \frac{1}{4}$$

6 is the GCF.

1 is the only common factor of 1 and 4.

Other Examples

$$\frac{4}{6} = \frac{2}{3}$$

Think: $\frac{4}{6} \begin{array}{c} \div 2 \\ = \\ \div 2 \end{array} \frac{2}{3}$

$$\frac{8}{36} = \frac{2}{9}$$

$$\frac{50}{100} = \frac{1}{2}$$

Reduce to lowest terms.

1. $\frac{25}{50}$ 2. $\frac{27}{30}$ 3. $\frac{6}{9}$ 4. $\frac{7}{35}$ 5. $\frac{6}{30}$ 6. $\frac{8}{24}$

7. $\frac{5}{20}$ 8. $\frac{8}{16}$ 9. $\frac{20}{25}$ 10. $\frac{4}{28}$ 11. $\frac{6}{18}$ 12. $\frac{18}{24}$

13. $\frac{30}{100}$ 14. $\frac{18}{27}$ 15. $\frac{30}{60}$ 16. $\frac{70}{100}$ 17. $\frac{16}{24}$ 18. $\frac{16}{40}$

19. $\frac{24}{30}$ 20. $\frac{45}{60}$ 21. $\frac{32}{40}$ 22. $\frac{80}{100}$ 23. $\frac{30}{36}$ 24. $\frac{24}{36}$

Improper Fractions to Mixed Numbers

If we have 9 jugs of apple juice, how many cases of juice do we have?

Each jug is $\frac{1}{4}$ of a case, so there are $\frac{9}{4}$ cases of juice. We can also say there are $2\frac{1}{4}$ cases of juice. $\frac{9}{4}$ is an **improper fraction**. $2\frac{1}{4}$ is a **mixed number.**

We can use the idea that $\frac{9}{4}$ means $9 \div 4$ to write $\frac{9}{4}$ as a mixed number.

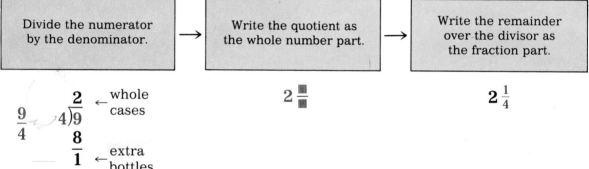

Divide the numerator by the denominator.	→	Write the quotient as the whole number part.	→	Write the remainder over the divisor as the fraction part.

$$\frac{9}{4} \quad 4\overline{)9} \quad \begin{array}{c} 2 \leftarrow \text{whole cases} \\ \underline{8} \\ 1 \leftarrow \text{extra bottles} \end{array}$$

$$2\frac{\text{▦}}{\text{▦}}$$

$$2\frac{1}{4}$$

We have $2\frac{1}{4}$ cases of juice.

Other Examples

$$\frac{23}{5} = 4\frac{3}{5} \quad \begin{array}{c} 4\,R3 \\ 5\overline{)23} \\ \underline{20} \\ 3 \end{array}$$

$$\frac{24}{6} = 4 \quad \begin{array}{c} 4 \\ 6\overline{)24} \\ \underline{24} \\ 0 \end{array}$$

$$\frac{20}{8} = 2\frac{4}{8} = 2\frac{1}{2} \quad \begin{array}{c} 2\,R4 \\ 8\overline{)20} \\ \underline{16} \\ 4 \end{array}$$

Write each improper fraction as a mixed number or whole number.

1. $\frac{27}{5}$ 2. $\frac{9}{2}$ 3. $\frac{15}{4}$ 4. $\frac{23}{10}$ 5. $\frac{32}{8}$ 6. $\frac{7}{3}$

7. $\frac{43}{8}$ 8. $\frac{19}{10}$ 9. $\frac{7}{4}$ 10. $\frac{19}{6}$ 11. $\frac{32}{3}$ 12. $\frac{29}{5}$

13. $\frac{73}{2}$ 14. $\frac{51}{3}$ 15. $\frac{59}{12}$ 16. $\frac{17}{2}$ 17. $\frac{127}{8}$ 18. $\frac{54}{6}$

19. $\frac{719}{100}$ 20. $\frac{84}{20}$ 21. $\frac{200}{25}$ 22. $\frac{130}{40}$ 23. $\frac{150}{50}$ 24. $\frac{28}{10}$

More Practice, page 438, Set B

Mixed Numbers to Improper Fractions

How many orange halves can you get from $5\frac{1}{2}$ oranges?

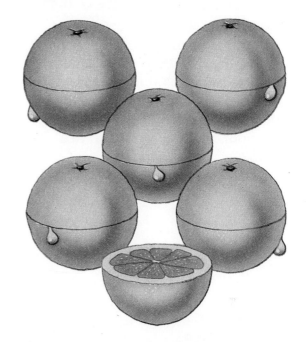

The picture shows 5 whole oranges and $\frac{1}{2}$ of an orange or $5\frac{1}{2}$ oranges. Each whole orange has 2 halves ($\frac{2}{2}$) so we can also say there are $\frac{11}{2}$ oranges.

We can use this method to write $5\frac{1}{2}$ as an improper fraction.

Multiply the whole number by the denominator.	→	Add the numerator to the product.	→	Write the sum over the denominator.

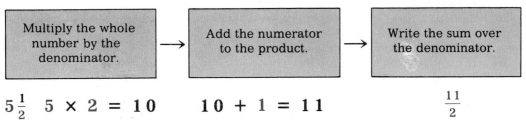

$5\frac{1}{2}$ $5 \times 2 = 10$ $10 + 1 = 11$ $\frac{11}{2}$

Other Examples

$3\frac{2}{5} = \frac{17}{5}$ $6\frac{1}{2} = \frac{13}{2}$ $4\frac{3}{4} = \frac{19}{4}$

$3 \times 5 = 15$ and $6 \times 2 = 12$ and $4 \times 4 = 16$ and
$15 + 2 = 17$ $12 + 1 = 13$ $16 + 3 = 19$

Write each mixed number as an improper fraction.

1. $1\frac{3}{4}$ 2. $2\frac{1}{10}$ 3. $4\frac{1}{2}$ 4. $5\frac{1}{3}$ 5. $4\frac{1}{4}$ 6. $3\frac{1}{6}$

7. $2\frac{3}{5}$ 8. $6\frac{3}{10}$ 9. $3\frac{1}{7}$ 10. $4\frac{3}{8}$ 11. $4\frac{9}{10}$ 12. $2\frac{5}{8}$

13. $6\frac{2}{3}$ 14. $5\frac{5}{8}$ 15. $4\frac{3}{50}$ 16. $9\frac{1}{6}$ 17. $10\frac{1}{8}$ 18. $4\frac{1}{12}$

19. $14\frac{1}{2}$ 20. $8\frac{4}{5}$ 21. $6\frac{17}{100}$ 22. $9\frac{9}{10}$ 23. $12\frac{4}{5}$ 24. $7\frac{5}{6}$

Comparing and Ordering Fractions and Mixed Numbers

Craig and Inez made a map of the neighborhood around their school. They also made a table showing the distance from the school to several important places. Which is closer to the school, the library or the fire station?

School to	police station	library	park	fire station
Miles	$3\frac{1}{2}$	$\frac{3}{10}$	$3\frac{1}{10}$	$\frac{3}{4}$

Look at the denominators.	$\rightarrow$	Write equivalent fractions with a common denominator.	$\rightarrow$	Compare the numerators.	$\rightarrow$	The fractions compare the same way the numerators compare.

$\dfrac{3}{10}$ *Not the same* $\dfrac{3}{4}$

$\dfrac{3}{10} = \dfrac{6}{20}$

$\dfrac{3}{4} = \dfrac{15}{20}$ *Common denominator (the same)*

$6 < 15$

$\dfrac{6}{20} < \dfrac{15}{20}$

so $\dfrac{3}{10} < \dfrac{3}{4}$

The library is closer to the school.

Other Examples

Since the whole number parts are the same, compare the fractions.

$\left.\begin{array}{l} 3\frac{1}{2} = 3\frac{5}{10} \\ 3\frac{1}{10} = 3\frac{1}{10} \end{array}\right\}$ $3\frac{1}{2} > 3\frac{1}{10}$

$\left.\begin{array}{l} \frac{2}{5} = \frac{16}{40} \\ \frac{3}{8} = \frac{15}{40} \end{array}\right\}$ $\frac{2}{5} > \frac{3}{8}$

Write $>$, $<$, or $=$ for each ▦

1. $\frac{1}{4}$ ▦ $\frac{1}{5}$
2. $\frac{7}{8}$ ▦ $\frac{2}{3}$
3. $\frac{5}{8}$ ▦ $\frac{3}{4}$
4. $\frac{4}{5}$ ▦ $\frac{3}{4}$
5. $\frac{4}{6}$ ▦ $\frac{8}{12}$

6. $\frac{7}{10}$ ▦ $\frac{3}{4}$
7. $\frac{9}{16}$ ▦ $\frac{7}{8}$
8. $\frac{3}{10}$ ▦ $\frac{1}{4}$
9. $4\frac{1}{6}$ ▦ $4\frac{2}{3}$
10. $5\frac{1}{8}$ ▦ $4\frac{2}{7}$

11. $2\frac{5}{8}$ ▦ $2\frac{1}{2}$
12. $9\frac{1}{8}$ ▦ $9\frac{1}{6}$
13. $7\frac{3}{10}$ ▦ $8\frac{3}{10}$
14. $12\frac{1}{2}$ ▦ $12\frac{3}{8}$
15. $1\frac{3}{10}$ ▦ $1\frac{30}{100}$

Compare the fractions or mixed numbers two at a time. Then list them in order from least to greatest.

16. $\frac{1}{3}, \frac{1}{4}, \frac{2}{5}$

17. $5\frac{3}{4}, 6\frac{2}{3}, 5\frac{5}{12}$

18. $1\frac{5}{6}, \frac{5}{8}, 1\frac{1}{3}, 2\frac{1}{4}$

19. $4\frac{1}{2}, 4\frac{1}{3}, 4, 3\frac{4}{5}, 3$

More Practice, page 438, Set D

Problem Solving: Using Data from a Catalog

A store offers special prices on items ordered from their catalog. Use the catalog data shown below to solve the problems.

Clock	Size	Weight	Regular price	Special price
Butcher-block quartz	$11\frac{1}{2}'' \times 11\frac{1}{2}''$	$4\frac{1}{2}$ lb	$31.40	$19.90
Desktop digital	$9\frac{1}{2}'' \times 2\frac{1}{4}''$	$3\frac{1}{3}$ lb	$21.99	$12.99
Cuckoo clock	$9\frac{7}{8}'' \times 7\frac{5}{8}''$	$3\frac{1}{2}$ lb	$61.95	$44.70
Kitchen quartz	$8\frac{1}{2}'' \times 15\frac{1}{2}''$	15 lb	$28.95	$19.90
Round wall clock	14'' diameter	$6\frac{3}{4}$ lb	$39.95	$24.90
World-time quartz	$7\frac{1}{4}'' \times 9\frac{3}{4}''$	$4\frac{1}{4}$ lb	$76.50	$49.94
Electric alarm	$5\frac{3}{4}'' \times 4\frac{2}{4}''$	1 lb	$16.95	$11.89

Solve.

1. There is a space on a kitchen wall that measures $9'' \times 15\frac{3}{8}''$. Will a kitchen quartz clock fit in that wall space?

2. What is the difference in the regular prices of the most expensive clock and the least expensive clock?

3. The mailing charge for a clock is $0.50 per pound. Will it cost more to mail a butcher-block quartz clock or a world-time quartz clock?

4. The butcher-block clock and the world-time clock can be mailed in boxes that are the same weight. When the clocks are boxed for mailing which will be heavier?

5. How much would it cost to mail a kitchen quartz clock, if the mailing charge is $0.50 per pound?

6. A girl bought two electric alarm clocks at the special price. What was the total cost for the clocks not including tax or mailing cost?

7. **DATA BANK** What would be the cost, including sales tax but not mailing charge, of 2 round wall clocks bought at the regular price? (See Data Bank, page 425.)

8. **Strategy Practice** An antique dealer wanted to display 2 of his 5 antique clocks in the store window. How many different choices did the dealer have for the pair of clocks? Hint: Make an organized list.

Adding and Subtracting Fractions and Mixed Numbers: Common Denominators

The Boosters Club at Kirby School volunteered to paint four sections of seats in the local soccer stadium. The first week the club members painted $1\frac{1}{5}$ sections red and $1\frac{3}{5}$ sections blue. How many of the sections did they paint the first week?

Since we want to find the total number of sections painted, we add.

Look at the denominators.	→	Add the fractions. Write the sum of the numerators over the common denominator.	→	Add the whole numbers.

$$1\frac{1}{5}$$
$$+\ 1\frac{3}{5}$$
The same

$$1\frac{1}{5}$$
$$+\ 1\frac{3}{5}$$
$$\overline{\quad\ \frac{4}{5}}$$

$$1\frac{1}{5}$$
$$+\ 1\frac{3}{5}$$
$$\overline{2\frac{4}{5}}$$

The club members painted $2\frac{4}{5}$ sections of the stadium the first week.

Other Examples

$$\begin{array}{r} \frac{2}{3} \\ -\ \frac{1}{3} \\ \hline \frac{1}{3} \end{array}$$

$$\begin{array}{r} \frac{1}{8} \\ +\ \frac{3}{8} \\ \hline \frac{4}{8} = \frac{1}{2} \end{array}$$

$$\begin{array}{r} \frac{5}{6} \\ +\ \frac{2}{6} \\ \hline \frac{7}{6} = 1\frac{1}{6} \end{array}$$

$$\begin{array}{r} 8\frac{1}{4} \\ +\ 3\frac{1}{4} \\ \hline 11\frac{2}{4} = 11\frac{1}{2} \end{array}$$

$$\begin{array}{r} 10\frac{7}{10} \\ -\ \frac{4}{10} \\ \hline 10\frac{3}{10} \end{array}$$

Warm Up   Add or subtract.

1. $\begin{array}{r} \frac{4}{8} \\ +\ \frac{1}{8} \\ \hline \end{array}$

2. $\begin{array}{r} \frac{6}{9} \\ -\ \frac{4}{9} \\ \hline \end{array}$

3. $\begin{array}{r} \frac{4}{7} \\ +\ \frac{1}{7} \\ \hline \end{array}$

4. $\begin{array}{r} \frac{7}{12} \\ -\ \frac{5}{12} \\ \hline \end{array}$

5. $\begin{array}{r} 3\frac{1}{5} \\ +\ 1\frac{2}{5} \\ \hline \end{array}$

6. $\begin{array}{r} 4\frac{3}{8} \\ -\ 2\frac{1}{8} \\ \hline \end{array}$

Practice Add or subtract.

1. $\dfrac{7}{10}$ $-\dfrac{2}{10}$ 2. $\dfrac{3}{4}$ $+\dfrac{3}{4}$ 3. $\dfrac{9}{8}$ $-\dfrac{2}{8}$ 4. $\dfrac{3}{16}$ $+\dfrac{5}{16}$ 5. $\dfrac{1}{6}$ $+\dfrac{5}{6}$ 6. $\dfrac{11}{12}$ $-\dfrac{5}{12}$

7. $\dfrac{9}{10}$ $-\dfrac{7}{10}$ 8. $\dfrac{5}{6}$ $-\dfrac{4}{6}$ 9. $\dfrac{1}{2}$ $+\dfrac{1}{2}$ 10. $\dfrac{3}{5}$ $+\dfrac{4}{5}$ 11. $\dfrac{8}{5}$ $-\dfrac{4}{5}$ 12. $\dfrac{7}{8}$ $+\dfrac{5}{8}$

13. $\dfrac{2}{5}$ $+\dfrac{2}{5}$ 14. $\dfrac{3}{8}$ $+\dfrac{7}{8}$ 15. $\dfrac{7}{8}$ $-\dfrac{4}{8}$ 16. $\dfrac{4}{6}$ $-\dfrac{1}{6}$ 17. $10\dfrac{3}{10}$ $+\ \ 3$ 18. $9\dfrac{4}{5}$ $-\ 3\dfrac{1}{5}$

19. $8\dfrac{7}{12}$ $-\ 8\dfrac{5}{12}$ 20. $7\dfrac{5}{6}$ $-\ 5\dfrac{2}{6}$ 21. $21\dfrac{1}{4}$ $+\ 14$ 22. $19\dfrac{7}{8}$ $-\ 12\dfrac{7}{8}$ 23. $42\dfrac{5}{10}$ $+\ 28\dfrac{3}{10}$ 24. $16\dfrac{1}{12}$ $+\ 37\dfrac{7}{12}$

25. $\dfrac{19}{20} - \dfrac{11}{20}$ 26. $\dfrac{14}{24} + \dfrac{8}{24}$ 27. $2\dfrac{1}{8} + 8\dfrac{4}{8}$ 28. $18\dfrac{1}{5} + 29\dfrac{3}{5}$ 29. $9\dfrac{5}{6} - 5\dfrac{1}{6}$

30. Find the sum of $6\dfrac{1}{6}$ and $3\dfrac{3}{6}$.

31. How much greater is $9\dfrac{7}{8}$ than $\dfrac{5}{8}$?

Mixed Applications

32. The club members used $42\dfrac{3}{4}$ cans of blue paint and $35\dfrac{1}{4}$ cans of red paint to paint the stadium. How much more blue paint than red paint did they use?

33. Write a question you could answer using the data in this story. Then find the answer to your question.

    Joanne earns $6 an hour painting on weekends. She worked $3\dfrac{1}{2}$ h on Saturday and $4\dfrac{1}{2}$ h on Sunday.

Skillkeeper

Add or subtract.

1. $5\text{ h }21\text{ min}$ $+\ 3\text{ h }44\text{ min}$ 2. $7\text{ min }28\text{ s}$ $+\ 3\text{ min }40\text{ s}$

3. $8\text{ h }\ 9\text{ min}$ $-\ 4\text{ h }20\text{ min}$ 4. $28\text{ min }35\text{ s}$ $-\ 19\text{ min }38\text{ s}$

Divide.

5. $8)\overline{5.000}$ 6. $4)\overline{3.00}$

7. $5)\overline{2.00}$ 8. $2)\overline{7.0}$

Problem Solving: Using Estimation

Eileen Owen owns a fleet of school buses. Solve these problems about her buses.

First **estimate** the answer by rounding each mixed number to the nearest whole number. Then find the **exact** answer. (Remember the rules for rounding mixed numbers!)

<table>
<tr><td colspan="2">**Rules for Rounding Mixed Numbers**</td></tr>
<tr><td>•</td><td>**Round down** if the fraction part is less than $\frac{1}{2}$. $2\frac{1}{3} \rightarrow 2$</td></tr>
<tr><td>•</td><td>**Round up** if the fraction part is greater than or equal to $\frac{1}{2}$.
$2\frac{2}{3} \rightarrow 3$</td></tr>
</table>

Example

Bus route A is $9\frac{7}{10}$ miles. Bus route B is $7\frac{1}{10}$ miles. How much longer is route A than route B?

Estimate

$9\frac{7}{10}$ is about 10.
$7\frac{1}{10}$ is about 7.
$10 - 7 = 3$, so route A is about 3 miles longer.

Exact

$$9\frac{7}{10}$$
$$- 7\frac{1}{10}$$
$$\overline{\rule{2cm}{0.4pt}}$$
$$2\frac{6}{10} = 2\frac{3}{5}$$

Route A is $2\frac{3}{5}$ miles longer.

1. Bus 26 travels $5\frac{3}{4}$ miles on its morning route and $8\frac{3}{4}$ miles on its afternoon route. What is the total distance Bus 26 travels?

2. In April Bus 16 traveled an average of $5\frac{1}{5}$ miles on each gallon of gasoline. In May Bus 16 traveled an average of $7\frac{4}{5}$ miles per gallon. How much did the average number of miles per gallon increase from April to May?

3. Bus 17 has an oil leak. On Monday the bus needed $2\frac{1}{4}$ quarts of oil. On Tuesday it needed $3\frac{3}{4}$ quarts of oil. What was the total amount of oil Bus 17 needed on those two days?

4. On the highway Bus 13 averages $9\frac{7}{10}$ miles per gallon of gas. In the city the average is only $5\frac{3}{10}$ miles per gallon. How many more miles per gallon is the highway than the city average?

5. Bus 17 needed $34\frac{9}{10}$ gallons of gas to be filled last week. This week it only needed $25\frac{3}{10}$ gallons. How much less gasoline did it need this week?

6. **Strategy Practice** When Rose got on the bus there were already some people on it. At the next stop, 4 people got on. At the next stop, 2 people got off and 3 got on. At the last stop, all 12 people who were still on the bus, including Rose, got off. How many people were on the bus when Rose got on? Hint: Work backward.

Least Common Multiple (Denominator)

To add fractions with unlike denominators, we must first rewrite the fractions with a **common denominator.**

The **least common denominator** of two or more fractions is the **least common multiple** of the denominators.

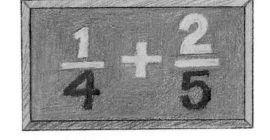

Least Common Multiple	What is the least common multiple of 4 and 5?

A. List some multiples of each number. (Do not include zero.)

$4 \rightarrow$ **4, 8, 12, 16, 20, 24, 28**
$5 \rightarrow$ **5, 10, 15, 20**

B. 20 is the least common multiple of **4** and **5.**

Least Common Denominator	What is the least common denominator of $\frac{1}{4}$ and $\frac{2}{5}$?

A. Find the least common multiple of the denominators.

20 is the least common multiple.

B. 20 is the least common denominator for the fractions $\frac{1}{4}$ and $\frac{2}{5}$.

Other Examples

$\frac{1}{4} \rightarrow$ **4, 8, 1 6**   (multiples of 4)

$\frac{5}{8} \rightarrow$ **8, 1 6**   (multiples of 8)

The least common denominator is **8.**

$\frac{1}{2} \rightarrow$ **2, 4, 6, 8**   (multiples of 2)

$\frac{2}{3} \rightarrow$ **3, 6, 9**   (multiples of 3)

$\frac{5}{6} \rightarrow$ **6, 1 2**   (multiples of 6)

The least common denominator is **6.**

Find the least common denominator of these fractions.

1. $\frac{1}{2}, \frac{3}{4}$ **2.** $\frac{2}{3}, \frac{1}{6}$ **3.** $\frac{1}{3}, \frac{1}{2}$ **4.** $\frac{2}{5}, \frac{7}{10}$ **5.** $\frac{5}{16}, \frac{3}{8}, \frac{3}{4}$

6. $\frac{3}{9}, \frac{2}{3}$ **7.** $\frac{4}{5}, \frac{5}{6}$ **8.** $\frac{1}{3}, \frac{2}{5}$ **9.** $\frac{3}{4}, \frac{2}{3}$ **10.** $\frac{1}{8}, \frac{1}{3}, \frac{1}{2}$

11. $\frac{2}{9}, \frac{5}{8}$ **12.** $\frac{3}{20}, \frac{1}{3}$ **13.** $\frac{5}{10}, \frac{1}{3}$ **14.** $\frac{4}{10}, \frac{5}{8}$ **15.** $\frac{5}{12}, \frac{4}{5}, \frac{5}{6}$

16. $\frac{3}{4}, \frac{1}{9}$ **17.** $\frac{1}{6}, \frac{3}{5}$ **18.** $\frac{2}{3}, \frac{3}{8}$ **19.** $\frac{7}{12}, \frac{1}{5}$ **20.** $\frac{3}{8}, \frac{2}{5}, \frac{3}{4}$

More Practice, page 439, Set B

Adding and Subtracting Fractions: Unlike Denominators

100-Calorie Portions of Foods	
canned apricots	$\frac{1}{2}$ cup
fresh orange juice	$\frac{9}{10}$ cup
canned peaches	$\frac{3}{5}$ cup
lima beans	$\frac{2}{3}$ cup
canned corn	$\frac{3}{4}$ cup

The chart shows 100-calorie portions of selected foods. How much greater is the fraction of a cup of corn than the fraction of a cup of lima beans?

Since we want to compare two amounts, we subtract.

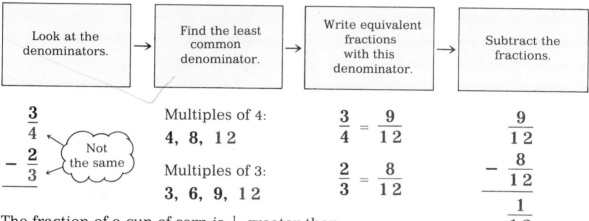

Look at the denominators.	→	Find the least common denominator.	→	Write equivalent fractions with this denominator.	→	Subtract the fractions.

$$\frac{3}{4}$$
$$-\frac{2}{3}$$

Not the same

Multiples of 4:
4, 8, 12

Multiples of 3:
3, 6, 9, 12

$$\frac{3}{4} = \frac{9}{12}$$

$$\frac{2}{3} = \frac{8}{12}$$

$$\frac{9}{12}$$
$$-\frac{8}{12}$$
$$\frac{1}{12}$$

The fraction of a cup of corn is $\frac{1}{12}$ greater than the fraction of a cup of lima beans.

Other Examples

$$\frac{3}{8} = \frac{3}{8}$$
$$+\frac{3}{4} = \frac{6}{8}$$
$$\frac{9}{8} = 1\frac{1}{8}$$

$$\frac{3}{5} = \frac{18}{30}$$
$$+\frac{5}{6} = \frac{25}{30}$$
$$\frac{43}{30} = 1\frac{13}{30}$$

$$\frac{5}{6} = \frac{5}{6}$$
$$-\frac{1}{2} = \frac{3}{6}$$
$$\frac{2}{6} = \frac{1}{3}$$

$$\frac{4}{5} = \frac{8}{10}$$
$$-\frac{1}{2} = \frac{5}{10}$$
$$\frac{3}{10}$$

Warm Up   Add or subtract.

1. $\frac{1}{2}$
$+\frac{3}{4}$

2. $\frac{1}{2}$
$+\frac{1}{3}$

3. $\frac{4}{5}$
$-\frac{7}{10}$

4. $\frac{5}{6}$
$+\frac{3}{4}$

5. $\frac{6}{9}$
$-\frac{2}{3}$

6. $\frac{2}{3}$
$-\frac{1}{4}$

208

Practice   Add or subtract.

1. $\dfrac{3}{10}$
    $+\dfrac{2}{5}$

2. $\dfrac{4}{5}$
    $+\dfrac{1}{2}$

3. $\dfrac{2}{3}$
    $+\dfrac{1}{2}$

4. $\dfrac{5}{6}$
    $+\dfrac{1}{3}$

5. $\dfrac{3}{4}$
    $+\dfrac{3}{8}$

6. $\dfrac{1}{3}$
    $+\dfrac{1}{4}$

7. $\dfrac{3}{8}$
    $+\dfrac{5}{8}$

8. $\dfrac{17}{100}$
    $+\dfrac{3}{10}$

9. $\dfrac{4}{5}$
    $+\dfrac{3}{4}$

10. $\dfrac{13}{16}$
    $+\dfrac{1}{2}$

11. $\dfrac{3}{5}$
    $+\dfrac{2}{3}$

12. $\dfrac{1}{6}$
    $+\dfrac{7}{12}$

13. $\dfrac{9}{10}$
    $-\dfrac{3}{5}$

14. $\dfrac{5}{3}$
    $-\dfrac{1}{2}$

15. $\dfrac{4}{5}$
    $-\dfrac{1}{6}$

16. $\dfrac{3}{2}$
    $-\dfrac{1}{4}$

17. $\dfrac{3}{4}$
    $-\dfrac{3}{8}$

18. $\dfrac{2}{3}$
    $-\dfrac{1}{4}$

19. $\dfrac{5}{8}$
    $-\dfrac{1}{3}$

20. $\dfrac{73}{100}$
    $-\dfrac{7}{10}$

21. $\dfrac{7}{3}$
    $-\dfrac{1}{4}$

22. $\dfrac{11}{12}$
    $-\dfrac{2}{3}$

23. $\dfrac{3}{5}$
    $-\dfrac{1}{3}$

24. $\dfrac{7}{8}$
    $-\dfrac{1}{4}$

25. $\dfrac{1}{2} + \dfrac{1}{3} + \dfrac{1}{4}$

26. $\dfrac{3}{4} + \dfrac{1}{2} + \dfrac{3}{8}$

27. $\dfrac{1}{4} + \dfrac{3}{8} + \dfrac{3}{4}$

28. $\dfrac{3}{4} + \dfrac{1}{6} + \dfrac{1}{3}$

Mixed Applications

Use the chart on page 208 for problems 29 and 30.

29. How much greater is the 100-calorie portion of orange juice than the 100-calorie portion of peaches?

30. The class made a fruit dessert by mixing 100-calorie portions of canned apricots and canned peaches. How many cups of fruit were in the dessert?

31. Write a question that could be answered using the data given below. Then find the answer.

    Irene cooked $\frac{2}{3}$ cup of oatmeal, $\frac{1}{2}$ cup of rice, and $\frac{1}{4}$ cup of granola.

Think

Estimation of Fractions

Use any pair of odd digits 1-9 to write a fraction to match each description.

1. close to 0

2. a little less than $\frac{1}{2}$

3. a little more than $\frac{1}{2}$

4. a little less than 1

Math

Adding Mixed Numbers: Unlike Denominators

The highway department was building a road. The first day they leveled $2\frac{4}{5}$ miles of roadbed. The second day they leveled $2\frac{7}{10}$ miles of roadbed. What was the total number of miles of roadbed leveled in the first two days?

Since we want to find the total distance, we add.

Look at the denominators.	Write equivalent fractions with a common denominator.	Add the fractions.	Add the whole numbers.

$$2\frac{4}{5}$$
$$+\ 2\frac{7}{10}$$

Not the same

$$2\frac{4}{5} = 2\frac{8}{10}$$
$$+\ 2\frac{7}{10} = 2\frac{7}{10}$$

$$2\frac{8}{10}$$
$$+\ 2\frac{7}{10}$$
$$\frac{15}{10}$$

$$2\frac{8}{10}$$
$$+\ 2\frac{7}{10}$$
$$4\frac{15}{10} = 5\frac{5}{10} = 5\frac{1}{2}$$

$$4 + \frac{15}{10} \text{ or } 4 + 1\frac{5}{10}$$

A total of $5\frac{1}{2}$ miles of roadbed were leveled in the first two days.

Other Examples

$$1\frac{1}{2} = 1\frac{3}{6}$$
$$+\ 4\frac{2}{3} = 4\frac{4}{6}$$
$$5\frac{7}{6} = 6\frac{1}{6}$$

$$6\frac{7}{8}$$
$$+\ 3\frac{7}{8}$$
$$9\frac{14}{8} = 10\frac{6}{8} = 10\frac{3}{4}$$

$$2\frac{1}{4} = 2\frac{3}{12}$$
$$3\frac{1}{2} = 3\frac{6}{12}$$
$$+\ 1\frac{5}{6} = 1\frac{10}{12}$$
$$6\frac{19}{12} = 7\frac{7}{12}$$

Warm Up Add.

1. $2\frac{1}{2}$
    $+\ 4\frac{3}{4}$

2. $7\frac{9}{10}$
    $+\ 4\frac{1}{2}$

3. $6\frac{2}{5}$
    $+\ 4\frac{3}{5}$

4. $2\frac{2}{3}$
    $+\ 12\frac{1}{2}$

5. $6\frac{1}{3}$
    $9\frac{1}{2}$
    $+\ 2\frac{5}{6}$

Practice Find the sums.

1. $2\frac{3}{8}$
   $+ 4\frac{3}{4}$

2. $3\frac{3}{4}$
   $+ 5\frac{1}{2}$

3. $7\frac{1}{4}$
   $+ 2\frac{1}{6}$

4. $6\frac{3}{5}$
   $+ 5\frac{4}{5}$

5. $4\frac{7}{8}$
   $+ 1\frac{1}{2}$

6. $6\frac{5}{8}$
   $+ 7\frac{3}{4}$

7. $9\frac{7}{10}$
   $+ 11\frac{3}{10}$

8. $3\frac{5}{6}$
   $+ 8\frac{1}{2}$

9. $61\frac{1}{2}$
   $+ 91\frac{1}{8}$

10. $46\frac{7}{10}$
    $+ 23\frac{1}{2}$

11. $3\frac{1}{2}$
    $7\frac{1}{4}$
    $+ 6\frac{1}{8}$

12. $7\frac{1}{2}$
    $9\frac{1}{3}$
    $+ 6\frac{1}{4}$

13. $19\frac{4}{5}$
    $26\frac{1}{10}$
    $+ 35\frac{1}{4}$

14. $14\frac{1}{4}$
    $12\frac{3}{8}$
    $+ 16\frac{1}{2}$

15. $22\frac{5}{6}$
    $9\frac{1}{2}$
    $+ 11\frac{2}{3}$

16. $15\frac{7}{8} + 22\frac{5}{6}$

17. $4\frac{1}{6} + 2\frac{1}{3} + 8\frac{2}{3}$

18. $16\frac{1}{4} + 7\frac{1}{5} + 9\frac{7}{10}$

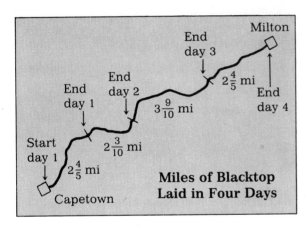

End day 3

Milton

$2\frac{4}{5}$ mi

End day 2

$3\frac{9}{10}$ mi

End day 4

End day 1

Start day 1

$2\frac{3}{10}$ mi

$2\frac{4}{5}$ mi

Miles of Blacktop Laid in Four Days

Capetown

19. Estimate, then find: $7\frac{1}{8} + 6\frac{3}{4}$

Mixed Applications

20. How many more miles of blacktop were laid on day 3 than on day 2?

21. How many miles of blacktop were laid altogether on days 3 and 4?

★ 22. What is the total length of the new road?

Think

Patterns and Fractions

Find the pattern and write the missing fractions or mixed numbers. Be sure the last number fits your pattern.

1. $0, \frac{2}{3}, \frac{4}{3}, \frac{6}{3}, ?, ?, ?, ?, \frac{16}{3}$

2. $2\frac{4}{5}, 4\frac{1}{5}, 5\frac{3}{5}, ?, ?, ?, ?, 12\frac{3}{5}$

3. $12, 10\frac{1}{2}, 9, 7\frac{1}{2}, ?, ?, ?, ?, 0$

Math

Subtracting Mixed Numbers: Unlike Denominators

The Carlsons are putting new wood siding on their house. The width of siding that is not covered by overlapping siding is called the **exposed surface.** The Carlsons are using siding with a total width of $3\frac{3}{4}$ in. and an exposed surface of $2\frac{1}{2}$ in. How much greater is the total width than the exposed surface?

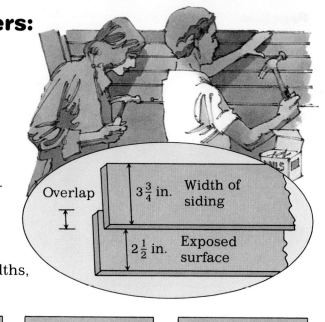

Since we want to compare the two widths, we subtract.

| Look at the denominators. | → | Write equivalent fractions with a common denominator. | → | Subtract the fractions. | → | Subtract the whole numbers. |

$$3\frac{3}{4}$$ Not the same
$$-\ 2\frac{1}{2}$$

$$3\frac{3}{4} = 3\frac{3}{4}$$
$$-\ 2\frac{1}{2} = 2\frac{2}{4}$$

$$3\frac{3}{4}$$
$$-\ 2\frac{2}{4}$$
$$\overline{\ \ \frac{1}{4}}$$

$$3\frac{3}{4}$$
$$-\ 2\frac{2}{4}$$
$$\overline{1\frac{1}{4}}$$

The total width is $1\frac{1}{4}$ in. greater than the exposed surface.

Other Examples

$$12\frac{2}{3} = 12\frac{4}{6}$$
$$-\ \ 4\frac{1}{6} = \ \ 4\frac{1}{6}$$
$$\overline{\qquad\qquad 8\frac{3}{6} = 8\frac{1}{2}}$$

$$7\frac{5}{8}$$
$$-\ 4\phantom{\frac{5}{8}}$$
$$\overline{3\frac{5}{8}}$$

$$2\frac{4}{5} = 2\frac{24}{30}$$
$$-\ \ \frac{1}{6} = \ \ \frac{5}{30}$$
$$\overline{\qquad\quad 2\frac{19}{30}}$$

Warm Up   Subtract.

1. $7\frac{1}{2}$
    $-\ 5\frac{1}{4}$

2. $16\frac{1}{2}$
    $-\ \ 8\frac{4}{9}$

3. $14\frac{5}{8}$
    $-\ 10$

4. $8\frac{2}{3}$
    $-\ 1\frac{1}{2}$

5. $10\frac{1}{2}$
    $-\ \ \frac{1}{5}$

Practice Subtract.

1. $5\frac{7}{10}$
   $- 2\frac{3}{5}$

2. $6\frac{1}{2}$
   $- 5\frac{1}{3}$

3. $9\frac{5}{9}$
   $- 7\frac{2}{9}$

4. $4\frac{1}{3}$
   $- 4\frac{2}{9}$

5. $7\frac{7}{8}$
   $- 3\frac{1}{4}$

6. $8\frac{3}{4}$
   $- \frac{1}{5}$

7. $3\frac{7}{10}$
   $- 1\frac{1}{5}$

8. $21\frac{1}{2}$
   $- 3\frac{1}{8}$

9. $14\frac{4}{5}$
   $- 6$

10. $13\frac{2}{3}$
    $- 4\frac{2}{5}$

11. $7\frac{5}{6}$
    $- 4\frac{1}{6}$

12. $45\frac{5}{6}$
    $- 33\frac{1}{4}$

13. $12\frac{3}{5}$
    $- 10\frac{1}{10}$

14. $67\frac{7}{10}$
    $- 45\frac{45}{100}$

15. $38\frac{5}{9}$
    $- 20\frac{1}{6}$

16. $9\frac{2}{3} - 7\frac{1}{12}$

17. $4\frac{3}{4} - 2\frac{3}{8}$

18. $9\frac{5}{6} - 6\frac{3}{8}$

19. $7\frac{1}{2} - 3\frac{5}{12}$

20. Estimate, then find: $11\frac{5}{6} - 4\frac{3}{4}$

21. Estimate, then find: $5\frac{1}{8} - 2\frac{3}{4}$

Mixed Applications

22. The suggested amount of exposed surface for a siding is $4\frac{3}{4}$ in. When the carpenter finished putting on the siding, it had $\frac{3}{8}$ in. less exposed surface than that. How much of the siding was exposed?

23. The exposed surface for a siding is $3\frac{5}{8}$ in. Another $\frac{1}{2}$ in. is covered by overlapping pieces. What is the total width of this siding?

Think

Fraction Comparison with Cross Products

We can compare fractions by comparing their **cross products.**

First cross product → $5 \times 7 = 35$

Second cross product → $4 \times 9 = 36$

$\frac{4}{5} > \frac{7}{9}$

Since the first cross product is greater, the first fraction is greater than the second fraction.

Which fraction in each pair is greater?

1. $\frac{11}{12}, \frac{15}{16}$

2. $\frac{14}{25}, \frac{5}{12}$

3. $\frac{162}{220}, \frac{215}{300}$

4. $\frac{200}{325}, \frac{300}{475}$

Math

More Practice, page 440, Set B

More Subtracting Mixed Numbers

The speed of a tape recorder is measured in inches per second (ips). Two of the most common speeds for a reel-to-reel recorder are $7\frac{1}{2}$ ips and $3\frac{3}{4}$ ips. What is the difference in the two speeds?

Since we want to compare the two speeds, we should subtract.

| Look at the denominators. | → | Write equivalent fractions with a common denominator. | → | Rename if necessary. Subtract the fractions. | → | Subtract the whole numbers. |

$$7\frac{1}{2}$$
Not the same
$$-\ 3\frac{3}{4}$$

$$7\frac{1}{2} = 7\frac{2}{4}$$
$$-\ 3\frac{3}{4} = 3\frac{3}{4}$$

$6 + 1\frac{2}{4}$ or $6 + \frac{6}{4}$

$$7\frac{2}{4} = 6\frac{6}{4}$$
$$-\ 3\frac{3}{4} = 3\frac{3}{4}$$
$$\frac{3}{4}$$

$$6\frac{6}{4}$$
$$-\ 3\frac{3}{4}$$
$$3\frac{3}{4}$$

The difference in the two recording speeds is $3\frac{3}{4}$ ips.

Other Examples

$$9\frac{1}{6} = 8\frac{7}{6}$$
$$-\ 4\frac{5}{6} = 4\frac{5}{6}$$
$$4\frac{2}{6} = 4\frac{1}{3}$$

$$5\ = 4\frac{3}{3}$$
$$-\ 3\frac{1}{3} = 3\frac{1}{3}$$
$$1\frac{2}{3}$$

$$8\frac{1}{3} = 8\frac{2}{6} = 7\frac{8}{6}$$
$$-\ 4\frac{1}{2} = 4\frac{3}{6} = 4\frac{3}{6}$$
$$3\frac{5}{6}$$

Warm Up   Subtract.

1. $4\frac{1}{3}$
$-\ 1\frac{5}{6}$

2. $9\frac{3}{5}$
$-\ 3\frac{7}{10}$

3. $14\frac{3}{4}$
$-\ 5\frac{3}{8}$

4. 12
$-\ 4\frac{1}{6}$

5. $26\frac{1}{6}$
$-\ 9\frac{7}{12}$

Practice Subtract.

1. $7\frac{1}{5}$
    $-\ 4\frac{5}{10}$

2. $6\frac{1}{4}$
    $-\ 3\frac{3}{4}$

3. $12\frac{1}{2}$
    $-\ 3\frac{3}{4}$

4. 8
    $-\ 5\frac{3}{4}$

5. $9\frac{3}{4}$
    $-\ 2\frac{7}{8}$

6. $7\frac{1}{4}$
    $-\ 6\frac{5}{6}$

7. $8\frac{1}{8}$
    $-\ 1\frac{3}{4}$

8. $12\frac{3}{5}$
    $-\ 7\frac{9}{10}$

9. $24\frac{5}{8}$
    $-\ 8\frac{1}{2}$

10. $15\frac{5}{12}$
    $-\ 11\frac{7}{12}$

11. 14
    $-\ 9\frac{7}{10}$

12. $4\frac{7}{10}$
    $-\ 2\frac{11}{15}$

13. $6\frac{2}{3}$
    $-\ 1\frac{7}{12}$

14. $8\frac{7}{9}$
    $-\ 5\frac{5}{6}$

15. $13\frac{1}{5}$
    $-\ 4\frac{7}{10}$

16. $79\frac{23}{100}$
    $-\ 64\frac{7}{10}$

17. $49\frac{1}{2}$
    $-\ 26\frac{3}{5}$

18. $78\frac{3}{4}$
    $-\ 69\frac{7}{8}$

19. $67\frac{1}{2}$
    $-\ 18\frac{1}{4}$

20. $34\frac{1}{8}$
    $-\ 11\frac{3}{4}$

21. How much greater is $83\frac{2}{3}$ than $15\frac{3}{4}$?

22. Estimate, then subtract: $17\frac{1}{5} - 9\frac{9}{10}$

Mixed Applications

23. Tape cartridges play at only one speed, $3\frac{3}{4}$ ips. Cassettes also play at only one speed, $1\frac{7}{8}$ ips. What is the difference in these speeds?

24. The Kleins' recorder has 2 speeds. The slow speed is $6\frac{5}{8}$ ips. The faster speed is $1\frac{3}{8}$ ips more. What is the faster speed?

25. **DATA HUNT** Record turntables usually have three speeds at which they can be played. Find the difference between the fastest and the slowest.

Think

Logical Reasoning

How many different ways can 4 postage stamps be attached to each other on at least one edge? Draw a picture to show each way.

Math

Practice: Adding and Subtracting Fractions

Add or subtract. Give answers in lowest terms.

1. $\dfrac{1}{3}$ $+\ \dfrac{1}{3}$

2. $\dfrac{4}{5}$ $-\ \dfrac{2}{5}$

3. $\dfrac{1}{4}$ $+\ \dfrac{1}{2}$

4. $\dfrac{1}{3}$ $+\ \dfrac{1}{6}$

5. $\dfrac{5}{8}$ $+\ \dfrac{1}{4}$

6. $\dfrac{11}{12}$ $-\ \dfrac{5}{6}$

7. $\dfrac{3}{4}$ $-\ \dfrac{1}{3}$

8. $\dfrac{2}{3}$ $+\ \dfrac{5}{6}$

9. $\dfrac{1}{4}$ $+\ \dfrac{1}{6}$

10. $\dfrac{4}{5}$ $-\ \dfrac{2}{3}$

11. $\dfrac{3}{8}$ $+\ \dfrac{3}{4}$

12. $\dfrac{2}{3}$ $-\ \dfrac{1}{6}$

13. $\dfrac{5}{6}$ $+\ \dfrac{1}{4}$

14. $\dfrac{5}{16}$ $+\ \dfrac{7}{8}$

15. $\dfrac{2}{3}$ $-\ \dfrac{1}{4}$

16. $\dfrac{1}{4}$ $-\ \dfrac{1}{5}$

17. $\dfrac{6}{7}$ $+\ \dfrac{2}{3}$

18. $\dfrac{1}{3}$ $-\ \dfrac{1}{8}$

19. $2\dfrac{1}{4}$ $+\ 5\dfrac{1}{4}$

20. $7\dfrac{3}{8}$ $-\ 5$

21. $3\dfrac{4}{5}$ $+\ 5\dfrac{1}{5}$

22. $4\dfrac{1}{2}$ $+\ 6$

23. $10\dfrac{5}{6}$ $-\ 5\dfrac{1}{3}$

24. $16\dfrac{3}{4}$ $-\ 9\dfrac{1}{3}$

25. $13\dfrac{5}{6}$ $-\ 8\dfrac{3}{4}$

26. $9\dfrac{1}{8}$ $+\ 7\dfrac{3}{4}$

27. $15\dfrac{1}{2}$ $-\ 6\dfrac{1}{3}$

28. $12\dfrac{1}{4}$ $-\ 5\dfrac{3}{4}$

29. $7\dfrac{3}{8}$ $+\ 6\dfrac{7}{8}$

30. $14\dfrac{1}{2}$ $+\ 4\dfrac{5}{6}$

31. $8\dfrac{2}{5}$ $+\ 5\dfrac{2}{3}$

32. 16 $-\ 7\dfrac{3}{8}$

33. $27\dfrac{1}{8}$ $-\ 14\dfrac{3}{4}$

34. $17\dfrac{7}{8}$ $+\ 12\dfrac{1}{2}$

35. $23\dfrac{1}{4}$ $+\ 8\dfrac{5}{6}$

36. $32\dfrac{2}{5}$ $-\ 19\dfrac{2}{3}$

37. $46\dfrac{5}{6}$ $-\ 26\dfrac{11}{12}$

38. $51\dfrac{3}{8}$ $-\ 38\dfrac{2}{3}$

39. $60\dfrac{7}{12}$ $+\ 29\dfrac{5}{8}$

40. $40\dfrac{1}{2}$ $-\ 17\dfrac{9}{16}$

41. $19\dfrac{4}{5}$ $+\ 18\dfrac{1}{3}$

42. $24\dfrac{7}{10}$ $+\ 35\dfrac{3}{4}$

Problem Solving:
Choosing the Operations

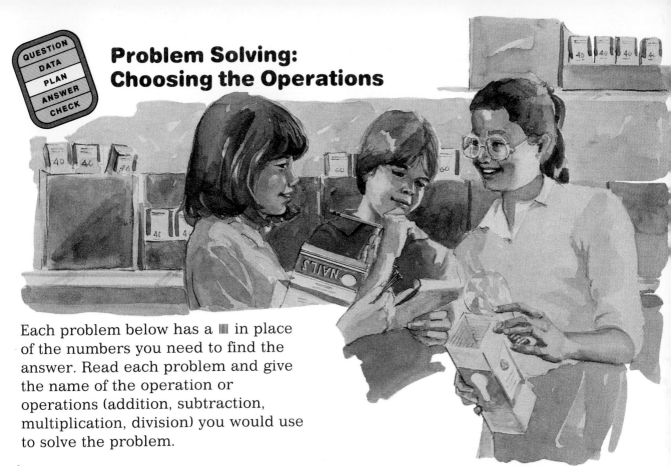

Each problem below has a ▥ in place of the numbers you need to find the answer. Read each problem and give the name of the operation or operations (addition, subtraction, multiplication, division) you would use to solve the problem.

1. A 500-ft length of rope costs $▥. A 1,200-ft length of the same rope costs $▥. How much more does the 1,200-ft length cost?

2. A 2-pound box of nails costs $▥. What is the cost of ▥ boxes?

3. A spool of electrical wire has ▥ ft of wire on it. How many ▥-ft pieces can be cut from one spool?

4. A jigsaw blade costs $▥. A drill bit costs $▥. How much would you pay if you bought ▥ jigsaw blades and ▥ drill bits?

5. A painter bought ▥ gallons of paint. Each gallon regularly costs $▥, but there was $▥ off the regular price for each gallon. What was the total cost for the ▥ gallons?

6. Plywood was on sale for $▥. The regular price is $▥ more. How much money do you save buying ▥ pieces of plywood on sale?

7. A bag of cement costs $▥. A bag of grass seed costs $▥. What is the total cost for ▥ bags of cement and ▥ bags of grass seed?

8. A boy bought two rolls of tape and a paint brush. The total cost was $▥. If a roll of tape costs $▥ what was the cost of the paint brush?

9. **Strategy Practice** Out of every 5 light bulbs in a carton, 1 bulb was broken. There were 20 bulbs in the carton that were not broken. How many bulbs were broken? Hint: Make a table.

Mixed Skills Practice

Computation

Find the answers.

1. $37{,}489 + 86{,}938$

2. $54{,}305 - 8{,}578$

3. $65.256 + 89.68$

4. $\$906.46 - 567.80$

5. 807×275

6. 9.38×6.4

7. $8\overline{)189.6}$

8. $\frac{4}{5} + \frac{3}{4}$

9. $\$7.69 \times 0.08$

10. 4.567×0.035

11. $6\frac{5}{8} + 5\frac{5}{6}$

12. $8\frac{1}{4} - \frac{5}{6}$

13. $36.269 \quad 5.047 + 0.783$

14. $\$3.75 \times 56$

15. $25 - 17\frac{3}{8}$

16. $35.415 - 8.78$

17. 674×59

18. $7.6\overline{)9.3936}$

19. $0.05\overline{)24.75}$

20. $86\overline{)26{,}144}$

Mental Math

Write only the answers.

21. $800 + 300$

22. $1{,}400 - 500$

23. 7×600

24. 800×60

25. 400×900

26. $4{,}500 \div 50$

27. $6{,}300 \div 700$

28. $25{,}000 \div 5{,}000$

29. $234 + 345$

30. $123 + 9$

31. $600 - 499$

32. 4×12

33. 3.2×10

34. $5\frac{3}{4} + 6\frac{1}{4}$

35. 4.25×100

36. $5 - \frac{1}{4}$

Estimation

Estimate.

37. $8{,}379 + 5{,}386$

38. $14{,}466 - 6{,}776$

39. $3{,}587 \times 2{,}859$

40. $44{,}578 \div 9{,}084$

41. $576 \div 8$

42. $647 \div 9$

43. $234 \div 6$

44. $3{,}462 \div 5$

45. $546 + 287 + 743$

46. $893 + 612 + 923$

47. $343 + 918 + 464 + 782$

48. $525 + 498 + 519 + 474$

49. $741 + 658 + 684 + 713 + 695$

50. $8{,}759 + 9{,}238 + 8{,}936$

Applied Problem Solving

Your scout troop is planning a backpacking trip to Lost Lake and back. Blazer Trail and Snowman Trail both go to the lake. Which trail will you take?

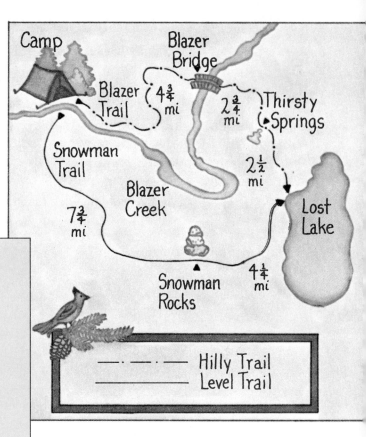

Camp
Blazer Bridge
Blazer Trail $4\frac{3}{4}$ mi
$2\frac{3}{4}$ mi
Thirsty Springs
Snowman Trail
Blazer Creek
$7\frac{3}{4}$ mi
$2\frac{1}{2}$ mi
Lost Lake
Snowman Rocks
$4\frac{1}{4}$ mi

— · — · — Hilly Trail
————— Level Trail

Some Things to Consider

- You will hike no more than 6 hours in 1 day. In 1 hour you can hike 3 mi on level trails or 2 mi on hilly trails.

- The total weight each scout will carry should be no more than 30 lb.

- Each scout will carry the following:
  — backpack, $3\frac{1}{2}$ lb
  — sleeping bag, $4\frac{1}{4}$ lb
  — food, 2 lb for each day plus 2 lb extra
  — water, 3 lb for Snowman (none needed for Blazer)
  — other supplies and clothing, 8 lb

- You will spend 1 whole day at Lost Lake.

Some Questions to Answer

1. How long is each trail?

2. About how long will it take to hike to the lake on each trail?

3. How many days will the round trip take for each trail, including the day at the lake?

4. What is the total weight you will carry for each trail?

What Is Your Decision?

Which trail will you take to Lost Lake?

Problem-Solving Strategy: Solve a Simpler Problem

When a problem has large numbers, you can sometimes find out how to solve it by solving the same problem but with smaller numbers. This strategy is called

Solve a Simpler Problem

Try This There are 20 people in a table tennis tournament. Two people play in each match. Each person plays until she or he loses. How many matches are needed to find a tournament champion?

> How many matches are needed if there are 3 people?

A plays B Winner A-B plays C For 3 people, 2 matches are needed.

> How many matches are needed if there are 4 people?

A plays B Winner A-B For 4 people,
C plays D plays winner 3 matches
C-D are needed.

> I see! You need to play one less match than there are people!

You need 19 matches to find a champion.

Solve.

1. There were 10 girls and 10 boys at a party. Each girl shook hands with each boy one time. How many handshakes were there?

2. Carlton Careless had 12 black socks and 18 blue socks mixed together in a dresser drawer. How many socks would he have to pull out of the drawer to be sure that he got a pair that matched?

Chapter Review-Test

Write a fraction for each ▥.

1.

▥ of the circle is red.

2.

▥ of the stars are red.

3.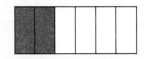

▥ of the strip is red.

Find the missing numerator or denominator.

4. $\dfrac{2}{3} = \dfrac{▥}{12}$ **5.** $\dfrac{5}{8} = \dfrac{▥}{24}$ **6.** $\dfrac{1}{4} = \dfrac{3}{▥}$ **7.** $\dfrac{2}{3} = \dfrac{▥}{9}$ **8.** $\dfrac{4}{5} = \dfrac{12}{▥}$

Give the next two equivalent fractions.

9. $\dfrac{1}{3}, \dfrac{▥}{▥}, \dfrac{▥}{▥}$ **10.** $\dfrac{1}{5}, \dfrac{▥}{▥}, \dfrac{▥}{▥}$ **11.** $\dfrac{3}{4}, \dfrac{▥}{▥}, \dfrac{▥}{▥}$ **12.** $\dfrac{1}{6}, \dfrac{▥}{▥}, \dfrac{▥}{▥}$ **13.** $\dfrac{3}{8}, \dfrac{▥}{▥}, \dfrac{▥}{▥}$

Reduce each fraction to lowest terms.

14. $\dfrac{6}{8}$ **15.** $\dfrac{8}{12}$ **16.** $\dfrac{8}{16}$ **17.** $\dfrac{3}{9}$ **18.** $\dfrac{4}{10}$ **19.** $\dfrac{9}{12}$ **20.** $\dfrac{5}{50}$

Write >, <, or = for each ▥

21. $\dfrac{4}{5} \; ▥ \; \dfrac{4}{7}$ **22.** $\dfrac{5}{8} \; ▥ \; \dfrac{7}{16}$ **23.** $\dfrac{2}{6} \; ▥ \; \dfrac{7}{21}$ **24.** $\dfrac{8}{15} \; ▥ \; \dfrac{3}{5}$ **25.** $\dfrac{7}{8} \; ▥ \; \dfrac{13}{16}$

Add or subtract. Give answers in lowest terms.

26. $\begin{array}{r} \frac{3}{8} \\ + \frac{3}{8} \\ \hline \end{array}$ **27.** $\begin{array}{r} \frac{5}{6} \\ - \frac{1}{6} \\ \hline \end{array}$ **28.** $\begin{array}{r} \frac{7}{8} \\ - \frac{5}{8} \\ \hline \end{array}$ **29.** $\begin{array}{r} 1\frac{1}{5} \\ + 3\frac{2}{5} \\ \hline \end{array}$ **30.** $\begin{array}{r} 11\frac{7}{12} \\ - 3\frac{5}{12} \\ \hline \end{array}$ **31.** $\begin{array}{r} 4\frac{1}{6} \\ + 3\frac{5}{6} \\ \hline \end{array}$

32. $\begin{array}{r} \frac{7}{8} \\ - \frac{1}{2} \\ \hline \end{array}$ **33.** $\begin{array}{r} \frac{4}{5} \\ + \frac{3}{10} \\ \hline \end{array}$ **34.** $\begin{array}{r} 6\frac{3}{4} \\ - 2\frac{1}{3} \\ \hline \end{array}$ **35.** $\begin{array}{r} 12\frac{3}{8} \\ - 9\frac{3}{4} \\ \hline \end{array}$ **36.** $\begin{array}{r} 7\frac{1}{4} \\ + 2\frac{5}{6} \\ \hline \end{array}$ **37.** $\begin{array}{r} 16\frac{2}{3} \\ - 5\frac{8}{9} \\ \hline \end{array}$

Solve.

38. Marlene worked $12\frac{1}{2}$ h last week. This week she worked $15\frac{1}{4}$ h. How many hours in all did Marlene work in the last two weeks?

39. Marlene received 20 cases of juice on Monday. By the end of the week only $2\frac{1}{2}$ cases were left. How many cases of juice were used?

221

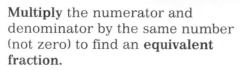

Another Look

Multiply the numerator and denominator by the same number (not zero) to find an **equivalent fraction.**

$$1 \xrightarrow{\times 3} 3 \qquad 3 \xrightarrow{\times 4} 12$$
$$\frac{\ }{\ } = \frac{\ }{\ } \qquad \frac{\ }{\ } = \frac{\ }{\ }$$
$$2 \xrightarrow{\times 3} 6 \qquad 5 \xrightarrow{\times 4} 20$$

Divide the numerator and denominator by common factors to get a fraction in **lowest terms.**

$$\frac{6}{18} \longrightarrow \frac{6 \div 2}{18 \div 2} = \frac{3}{9} \longrightarrow \frac{3 \div 3}{9 \div 3} = \frac{1}{3}$$

Two fractions with unlike denominators

Multiples of 2: 2, 4, 6, 8, . . .

Multiples of 3: 3, 6, 9, . . .

6 is the least common denominator.

$$\frac{1}{2} = \frac{3}{6}$$
$$+ \frac{2}{3} = \frac{4}{6}$$
$$\overline{\qquad} \quad \frac{7}{6} = 1\frac{1}{6}$$

$$\frac{7}{6} = \frac{6}{6} + \frac{1}{6}$$

Rename:
$$4\frac{2}{6} = 3 + 1 + \frac{2}{6} = 3 + \frac{6}{6} + \frac{2}{6}$$

$$4\frac{1}{3} = 4\frac{2}{6} = 3\frac{8}{6}$$
$$- 1\frac{1}{2} = 1\frac{3}{6} = 1\frac{3}{6}$$
$$\overline{\qquad\qquad\qquad} \quad 2\frac{5}{6}$$

$$7\frac{7}{8}$$
$$+ 4\frac{5}{8} \qquad (11 + 1\frac{4}{8})$$
$$\overline{\qquad\qquad\qquad}$$
$$11\frac{12}{8} = 12\frac{4}{8} = 12\frac{1}{2}$$

Find the missing numerator or denominator.

1. $\frac{1}{3} = \frac{\blacksquare}{12}$ 2. $\frac{3}{8} = \frac{\blacksquare}{24}$ 3. $\frac{7}{10} = \frac{\blacksquare}{100}$

4. $\frac{5}{6} = \frac{30}{\blacksquare}$ 5. $\frac{3}{4} = \frac{15}{\blacksquare}$ 6. $\frac{2}{3} = \frac{\blacksquare}{6}$

Give the next two equivalent fractions.

7. $\frac{1}{2}, \frac{\blacksquare}{\blacksquare}, \frac{\blacksquare}{\blacksquare}$ 8. $\frac{1}{3}, \frac{\blacksquare}{\blacksquare}, \frac{\blacksquare}{\blacksquare}$ 9. $\frac{3}{4}, \frac{\blacksquare}{\blacksquare}, \frac{\blacksquare}{\blacksquare}$

Reduce each fraction to lowest terms.

10. $\frac{3}{12}$ 11. $\frac{6}{8}$ 12. $\frac{8}{24}$ 13. $\frac{9}{27}$

14. $\frac{12}{24}$ 15. $\frac{10}{12}$ 16. $\frac{20}{100}$ 17. $\frac{35}{70}$

Add or subtract.

18. $\frac{3}{4}$ 19. $\frac{1}{2}$ 20. $\frac{3}{5}$ 21. $\frac{1}{6}$
   $+ \frac{3}{4}$ $+ \frac{3}{8}$ $+ \frac{7}{10}$ $+ \frac{5}{9}$

22. $\frac{3}{8}$ 23. $\frac{5}{6}$ 24. $\frac{1}{2}$ 25. $\frac{5}{6}$
   $- \frac{1}{4}$ $- \frac{1}{4}$ $- \frac{1}{5}$ $- \frac{3}{8}$

Add or subtract.

26. $9\frac{3}{5}$ 27. $10\frac{2}{3}$ 28. $20\frac{4}{5}$
   $+ 6\frac{4}{5}$ $+ 8\frac{5}{6}$ $+ 32\frac{3}{4}$

29. $5\frac{3}{4}$ 30. $14\frac{1}{3}$ 31. $64\frac{1}{4}$
   $- 2\frac{5}{8}$ $- 5\frac{5}{6}$ $- 45\frac{5}{7}$

Space Perception

Each of the twelve figures below is made with five squares. They are called **pentominoes**. Figure G can be folded on the dotted lines to make an open-top box as shown.

1. Which other pentominoes can be folded to make an open-top box?

2. A hexomino is made of 6 squares. Show on graph paper 5 hexominoes that can be folded to make a closed box.

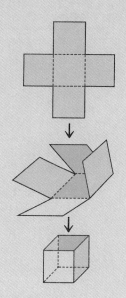

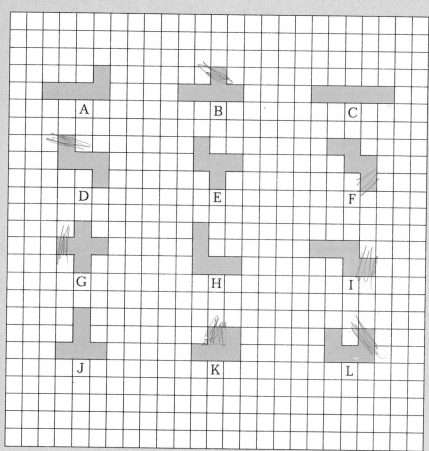

Cumulative Review

Add, subtract, or divide.

1. 9)685
   - **A** 76
   - **B** 76 R1
   - **C** 76 R8
   - **D** not given

2. 8)18,240
   - **A** 228
   - **B** 2,228
   - **C** 2,280
   - **D** not given

3. 27)1,323
   - **A** 4.9
   - **B** 49
   - **C** 490
   - **D** not given

4. 30)137,010
   - **A** 4,765
   - **B** 4,567
   - **C** 4,657
   - **D** not given

Give the missing units.

5. 8 m = 800 ?
   - **A** dm
   - **B** cm
   - **C** mm
   - **D** not given

6. 476 mm = 0.476 ?
   - **A** cm
   - **B** dm
   - **C** m
   - **D** not given

7. 10 km = 10,000 ?
   - **A** m
   - **B** dm
   - **C** cm
   - **D** not given

Give the missing numbers.

8. 3 L = ▥ kL
   - **A** 0.3
   - **B** 30
   - **C** 0.03
   - **D** not given

9. 2 kg = ▥ g
   - **A** 20
   - **B** 200
   - **C** 2,000
   - **D** not given

10. 5 h 32 min
    + 2 h 15 min
    - **A** 7 h 47 min
    - **B** 5 h 47 min
    - **C** 3 h 17 min
    - **D** not given

11. 51 min 12 s
    − 22 min 20 s
    - **A** 73 min 32 s
    - **B** 28 min 52 s
    - **C** 28 min 52 s
    - **D** not given

12. 5 min 12 s
    + 3 min 15 s
    - **A** 9 min 57 s
    - **B** 8 min 47 s
    - **C** 2 min 27 s
    - **D** not given

13. 416 people are going on a bus trip. If each bus can carry 52 people, how many buses are needed?
    - **A** 7
    - **B** 8
    - **C** 9
    - **D** not given

14. If a plane can carry 188 people, how many planes are needed for 1,620 people?
    - **A** 12
    - **B** 9
    - **C** 8
    - **D** not given

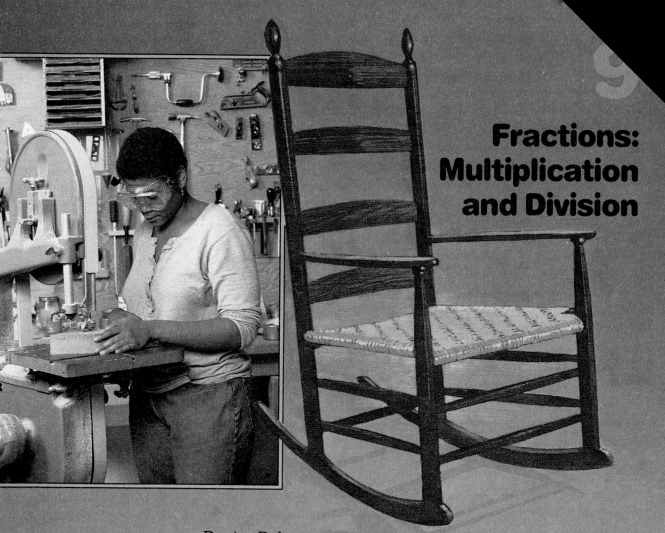

Fractions: Multiplication and Division

Denise Dobson put great care and effort into every piece of furniture she made. The rocking chair she was working on now, though, called for even more care. She wanted to be sure that this wedding gift for her sister would be the finest piece of furniture she had ever made.

She again studied the plans she had drawn. She would need 6 slats of oak $22\frac{1}{2}$ inches long and $\frac{1}{4}$ inch wide. The top 4 rungs beneath the seat would be $14\frac{1}{4}$ inches long, while the lower 4 rungs would be $16\frac{1}{8}$ inches long. Even as she reviewed her plans, Denise continued to worry about the kind of finish she should use on the chair. Which would look best in her sister's new home—a light, natural finish or a hard, glossy finish? She was used to having her customers decide on the type of finish she should use on the pieces of furniture they ordered. Finally she decided that her sister's choice would be the same as her own—a soft, waxed finish that would hide none of the natural beauty of the wood's grain and texture.

Fraction of a Number: Mental Math

Janet's coin collection
4 dimes. On one full page
s are Liberty Heads.
re Liberty Heads?

$\frac{1}{3}$ of 24 is 8.

We write: $\frac{1}{3} \times 24 = 8$

> To find $\frac{1}{3}$ of a number, divide the number by 3. Think: $24 \div 3 = 8$

8 of the 24 dimes are Liberty Head dimes.

The remaining $\frac{2}{3}$ of the dimes on the page in Janet's book are Roosevelt dimes. How many are Roosevelt dimes?

$\frac{2}{3}$ of 24 is 16.   We write: $\frac{2}{3} \times 24 = 16$

> To find $\frac{2}{3}$ of a number, divide by 3 and multiply the result by 2. Think: $24 \div 3 = 8$, $8 \times 2 = 16$

16 of the dimes are Roosevelt dimes.

Other Examples

1 hour = 60 minutes

$\frac{1}{2}$ of 60 is 30.

$\frac{1}{2} \times 60 = 30$

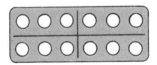

1 dozen = 12

$\frac{3}{4}$ of 12 is 9.

$\frac{3}{4} \times 12 = 9$

1 foot = 12 inches

$\frac{1}{4}$ of 12 is 3.

$\frac{1}{4} \times 12 = 3$

Warm Up   Use mental math to find the fraction of the number.

1. $\frac{1}{3} \times 18$

2. $\frac{2}{3} \times 18$

3. $\frac{1}{4} \times 24$

4. $\frac{3}{4} \times 24$

5. $\frac{1}{2} \times 10$

6. $\frac{1}{5} \times 25$

7. $\frac{3}{5} \times 25$

8. $\frac{4}{5} \times 25$

9. $\frac{1}{2} \times 16$

10. $\frac{1}{4} \times 16$

11. $\frac{3}{10} \times 50$

12. $\frac{7}{8} \times 24$

Practice Find the fraction of the number.

1.
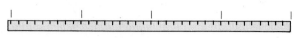
yardstick

1 yard = 36 inches

$\frac{1}{4} \times 36 = $ ▓

2.

1 qt 1 qt 1 qt 1 qt 1 gallon

4 qt (quarts) = 1 gallon

$\frac{3}{4} \times 4 = $ ▓

3. $\frac{1}{2} \times 20$

4. $\frac{3}{4} \times 36$

5. $\frac{1}{3} \times 12$

6. $\frac{2}{3} \times 9$

7. $\frac{1}{8} \times 32$

8. $\frac{3}{8} \times 32$

9. $\frac{1}{10} \times 40$

10. $\frac{2}{5} \times 25$

11. $\frac{3}{10} \times 60$

12. $\frac{1}{7} \times 28$

13. $\frac{5}{6} \times 30$

14. $\frac{4}{5} \times 40$

15. $\frac{7}{8} \times 24$

16. $\frac{1}{4} \times 100$

17. $\frac{1}{5} \times 100$

18. $\frac{5}{8} \times 40$

19. $\frac{2}{3} \times 12$

20. $\frac{5}{6} \times 18$

21. $\frac{1}{6} \times 18$

22. $\frac{9}{10} \times 50$

23. $\frac{1}{3} \times 27$

24. $\frac{7}{10} \times 100$

25. $\frac{2}{7} \times 35$

26. $\frac{3}{5} \times 100$

Mixed Applications

27. On one page of a coin collection book $\frac{3}{8}$ of the 24 coins are Indian Head pennies. How many Indian Head pennies are on the page?

28. Jeremy's coin collection book has spaces for 24 coins on each of its 8 pages. The book is $\frac{5}{6}$ full. How many coins are in Jeremy's book?

29. Denise has a coin book for nickels with spaces for 30 nickels on each of its 8 pages. She also has a book for dimes. It has spaces for 36 dimes on each of 6 pages. Her nickel book is $\frac{5}{8}$ full and her dime book is $\frac{3}{4}$ full. Does Denise have more nickels or more dimes? How many more?

30. **DATA HUNT** Suppose you have $\frac{1}{4}$ of a **score** of nickels and $\frac{2}{3}$ of a **gross** of dimes. How much money do you have? (Use a dictionary if necessary.)

Think

Estimation

Choose a whole number that is compatible with the fraction, and estimate the following amounts.

Example: Estimate $\frac{1}{3}$ of 25
Think: I can replace 25 with 24 and divide by 3. $\frac{1}{3}$ of 25 is about 24 ÷ 3, or 8.

1. $\frac{1}{2}$ of 19

2. $\frac{1}{3}$ of 22

3. $\frac{1}{4}$ of 18

4. $\frac{1}{5}$ of 32

5. $\frac{1}{6}$ of 50

6. $\frac{1}{8}$ of 39

Math

Multiplying Fractions: Reciprocals

Jeff found $\frac{3}{4}$ of a whole carrot cake on the table.

He saved $\frac{1}{2}$ of it for his sister.

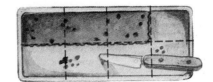

How much of the whole cake did Jeff's sister get?

The picture shows that $\frac{1}{2}$ of $\frac{3}{4}$ of the cake is $\frac{3}{8}$ of the whole cake. This suggests the following way to multiply two fractions.

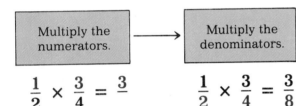

| Multiply the numerators. | → | Multiply the denominators. |

$$\frac{1}{2} \times \frac{3}{4} = \frac{3}{} \qquad \frac{1}{2} \times \frac{3}{4} = \frac{3}{8}$$

Jeff's sister received $\frac{3}{8}$ of the whole cake.

Other Examples

$$\frac{2}{3} \times \frac{7}{4} = \frac{14}{12} = 1\frac{2}{12} = 1\frac{1}{6} \qquad 12 \times \frac{2}{3} = \frac{12}{1} \times \frac{2}{3} = \frac{24}{3} = 8 \qquad \frac{3}{5} \times \frac{5}{3} = \frac{15}{15} = 1$$

> Two numbers whose product is 1 are **reciprocals** of each other.

Warm Up   Multiply.

1. $\frac{1}{2} \times \frac{1}{3}$
2. $\frac{2}{5} \times \frac{2}{3}$
3. $\frac{3}{4} \times \frac{5}{3}$
4. $\frac{5}{8} \times \frac{8}{5}$
5. $\frac{4}{5} \times \frac{1}{4}$

6. $12 \times \frac{2}{3}$
7. $3 \times \frac{1}{3}$
8. $\frac{9}{10} \times \frac{3}{10}$
9. $\frac{4}{3} \times 9$
10. $3 \times \frac{2}{3}$

11. Which of exercises 1–10 show numbers that are reciprocals of each other?

Give the reciprocal of each number.

12. $\frac{2}{3}$
13. $\frac{5}{4}$
14. 3
15. $\frac{3}{8}$
16. $\frac{7}{5}$
17. 6
18. $\frac{12}{3}$

Practice Multiply. Reduce to lowest terms.

1. $\frac{2}{5} \times \frac{1}{3}$
2. $\frac{1}{2} \times \frac{1}{4}$
3. $\frac{3}{4} \times \frac{7}{8}$
4. $\frac{2}{3} \times 9$
5. $\frac{5}{6} \times \frac{2}{3}$

6. $\frac{2}{3} \times 36$
7. $\frac{2}{3} \times \frac{3}{5}$
8. $\frac{7}{4} \times \frac{3}{2}$
9. $\frac{4}{5} \times \frac{5}{4}$
10. $\frac{3}{4} \times \frac{1}{3}$

11. $4 \times \frac{3}{5}$
12. $\frac{3}{5} \times \frac{7}{10}$
13. $\frac{3}{4} \times 32$
14. $\frac{3}{8} \times \frac{4}{5}$
15. $\frac{1}{6} \times \frac{6}{7}$

16. $\frac{1}{10} \times \frac{9}{10}$
17. $\frac{7}{3} \times \frac{1}{2}$
18. $\frac{1}{4} \times 48$
19. $\frac{4}{3} \times \frac{5}{2}$
20. $20 \times \frac{2}{5}$

21. $\frac{3}{8} \times \frac{8}{3}$
22. $\frac{5}{6} \times \frac{3}{4}$
23. $\frac{5}{8} \times \frac{2}{3}$
24. $6 \times \frac{1}{6}$
25. $\frac{7}{8} \times 4$

26. $\frac{2}{5} \times \frac{3}{4}$
27. $\frac{5}{8} \times 4$
28. $\frac{1}{3} \times \frac{3}{5}$
29. $6 \times \frac{2}{3}$
30. $\frac{5}{6} \times \frac{3}{10}$

31. Which of exercises 1–30 show numbers that are reciprocals of each other?

Give the reciprocal of each number.

32. $\frac{2}{3}$
33. $\frac{1}{2}$
34. 4
35. $\frac{7}{5}$
36. 5
37. $\frac{3}{4}$
38. 8

Mixed Applications

39. Vicky's recipe called for $\frac{3}{4}$ cup of flour. How much flour should she use to make $\frac{1}{2}$ of the recipe?

40. Chano worked in the bakery 7 hours Friday and $\frac{3}{5}$ that long Saturday. How many hours did he work in all?

41. Tell what data in this problem is not needed. Then solve.
Whole wheat bread takes $\frac{2}{3}$ hour to bake. It takes gingerbread $\frac{3}{4}$ as long. Blueberry muffins take $\frac{5}{8}$ as long. How long does it take gingerbread to bake?

Skillkeeper

Add or subtract.

1. $\frac{5}{6}$
$+ \frac{5}{6}$

2. $\frac{3}{4}$
$+ \frac{1}{12}$

3. $\frac{5}{8}$
$- \frac{1}{2}$

4. $\frac{2}{3}$
$- \frac{1}{4}$

5. $\frac{5}{6}$
$+ \frac{1}{4}$

6. $6\frac{1}{4}$
$+ 3\frac{1}{4}$

7. $7\frac{2}{3}$
$+ 4\frac{1}{9}$

8. $11\frac{3}{5}$
$- 6\frac{1}{2}$

9. $13\frac{1}{3}$
$- 7\frac{4}{5}$

10. $8\frac{2}{5}$
$+ 9\frac{3}{4}$

Multiplying Fractions: A Shortcut

Jan had $\frac{7}{8}$ of a yard of ribbon. She cut off $\frac{4}{5}$ of it. How much ribbon was cut off? Here are two ways to find the product.

We can multiply the fractions and then divide the numerator and the denominator by 4.

$$\overset{28 \div 4}{\frac{4}{5} \times \frac{7}{8} = \frac{28}{40} = \frac{7}{10}}$$
$$40 \div 4$$

OR

Shortcut

We can divide a numerator and a denominator by 4 and then multiply the fractions.

$$4 \div 4$$
$$\frac{\overset{1}{\cancel{4}}}{5} \times \frac{7}{\underset{2}{\cancel{8}}} = \frac{7}{10}$$
$$8 \div 4$$

The product is the same either way. Jan cut off $\frac{7}{10}$ of a yard of ribbon.

Other Examples

$$\frac{\overset{1}{\cancel{2}}}{\underset{1}{\cancel{3}}} \times \frac{\overset{3}{\cancel{9}}}{\underset{2}{\cancel{4}}} = \frac{3}{2} \qquad \text{Here we use the shortcut twice!} \qquad \frac{3}{\underset{1}{\cancel{4}}} \times \overset{6}{\cancel{24}} = 18$$

Warm Up   Find the products. Use the shortcut when possible.

1. $\frac{2}{3} \times \frac{5}{8}$ **2.** $\frac{3}{5} \times \frac{7}{12}$ **3.** $\frac{3}{8} \times \frac{4}{9}$ **4.** $\frac{3}{4} \times \frac{5}{6}$ **5.** $\frac{5}{9} \times \frac{3}{10}$

6. $\frac{5}{8} \times \frac{4}{15}$ **7.** $\frac{7}{10} \times 80$ **8.** $\frac{8}{5} \times \frac{9}{12}$ **9.** $\frac{3}{5} \times 20$ **10.** $\frac{3}{8} \times \frac{8}{9}$

230

Practice Find the product in lowest terms. Use the shortcut when possible.

1. $\frac{3}{4} \times \frac{4}{5}$

2. $\frac{3}{5} \times \frac{5}{6}$

3. $\frac{4}{3} \times \frac{3}{4}$

4. $\frac{1}{2} \times 10$

5. $\frac{5}{12} \times \frac{9}{10}$

6. $\frac{5}{6} \times \frac{12}{25}$

7. $\frac{5}{9} \times \frac{3}{8}$

8. $\frac{8}{9} \times \frac{21}{12}$

9. $\frac{8}{3} \times \frac{7}{24}$

10. $6 \times \frac{2}{3}$

11. $\frac{1}{3} \times 15$

12. $\frac{7}{5} \times \frac{5}{14}$

13. $\frac{2}{3} \times 27$

14. $\frac{3}{4} \times \frac{8}{9}$

15. $28 \times \frac{3}{7}$

16. $\frac{3}{5} \times \frac{5}{12}$

17. $\frac{5}{6} \times \frac{18}{25}$

18. $\frac{4}{3} \times \frac{3}{8}$

19. $\frac{2}{3} \times 18$

20. $\frac{7}{10} \times 5$

21. $\frac{6}{5} \times \frac{5}{14}$

22. $\frac{7}{6} \times \frac{6}{21}$

23. $\frac{1}{6} \times \frac{9}{4}$

24. $\frac{5}{8} \times \frac{8}{15}$

25. $\frac{5}{16} \times \frac{4}{15}$

26. $24 \times \frac{3}{8}$

27. $\frac{3}{8} \times \frac{8}{3}$

28. $6 \times \frac{1}{6}$

29. $100 \times \frac{7}{10}$

30. $\frac{5}{9} \times 27$

31. $\frac{5}{8} \times 16$

32. $\frac{5}{12} \times \frac{7}{10}$

33. $21 \times \frac{2}{3}$

34. $\frac{5}{33} \times 11$

35. $\frac{6}{11} \times \frac{33}{42}$

Mixed Applications

36. Janella used $\frac{1}{3}$ of a piece of ribbon that was $\frac{3}{4}$ yd long. What part of a yard of ribbon was the piece that she used?

37. Kerry bought 18 yd of blue ribbon and 10 yd of silver ribbon to wrap some presents. She used $\frac{5}{6}$ of the blue ribbon and $\frac{2}{3}$ of the silver ribbon. What was the total number of yards of ribbon used?

38. Write a question for this data, then solve the problem.

    Ted needed 24 pieces of ribbon for party decorations. Each piece had to be $\frac{3}{4}$ yd long.

★ Find the reciprocal by finding the number for n.

39. $\frac{2}{3} \times n = 1$

40. $n \times \frac{5}{6} = 1$

41. $4 \times n = 1$

42. $\frac{4}{5} \times n = 1$

43. $n \times \frac{1}{3} = 1$

44. $n \times 5 = 1$

45. $\frac{7}{4} \times n = 1$

46. $n \times \frac{8}{7} = 1$

More Practice, page 441, Set A

Think

Guess and Check

$$\boxed{} \times \boxed{} = 1$$

Two numbers are reciprocals of each other. One of them is 4 times as large as the other. What are the two numbers?

Math

Multiplying Mixed Numbers

Space Fact

Each planet in our solar system pulls objects toward it with a different amount of force. Since the force is less on a smaller planet, you could jump higher there. For example, a person might jump $2\frac{1}{2}$ times as high on Mars as on Earth!

Dennis can high jump $3\frac{2}{3}$ ft (3 ft 8 in.). How high could he jump on the planet Mars?

Since we want to find $2\frac{1}{2}$ times the given height, we multiply.

Write the mixed numbers as improper fractions.	→	Multiply the fractions.

$$2\frac{1}{2} \times 3\frac{2}{3} = \frac{5}{2} \times \frac{11}{3} \qquad \frac{5}{2} \times \frac{11}{3} = \frac{55}{6} = 9\frac{1}{6}$$

Dennis could jump $9\frac{1}{6}$ ft (9 ft 2 in.) on Mars.

Other Examples

$$3\frac{3}{4} \times 2\frac{4}{5} = \frac{\cancel{15}^{3}}{\cancel{4}_{2}} \times \frac{\cancel{14}^{7}}{\cancel{5}_{1}} = \frac{21}{2} = 10\frac{1}{2} \qquad 6 \times 4\frac{3}{8} = \frac{\cancel{6}^{3}}{1} \times \frac{35}{\cancel{8}_{4}} = \frac{105}{4} = 26\frac{1}{4}$$

Warm Up   Multiply. Use the shortcut when possible.

1. $1\frac{1}{3} \times 2\frac{1}{2}$

2. $2\frac{1}{5} \times 1\frac{1}{4}$

3. $3\frac{1}{2} \times \frac{1}{2}$

4. $9 \times 1\frac{2}{3}$

5. $3\frac{3}{4} \times 2\frac{2}{3}$

6. $1\frac{3}{8} \times 2\frac{1}{3}$

7. $8 \times 4\frac{3}{4}$

8. $2\frac{2}{5} \times 6\frac{1}{2}$

9. $2\frac{1}{10} \times 5$

10. $\frac{3}{4} \times 16$

11. $\frac{3}{4} \times 2\frac{5}{8}$

12. $4\frac{1}{2} \times 3\frac{1}{3}$

Practice Find the product in lowest terms.

1. $2\frac{2}{3} \times 1\frac{1}{4}$ **2.** $1\frac{3}{5} \times \frac{3}{5}$ **3.** $1\frac{1}{2} \times 2\frac{2}{3}$ **4.** $2\frac{1}{4} \times 5\frac{1}{3}$

5. $1\frac{3}{4} \times 1\frac{1}{2}$ **6.** $2\frac{2}{5} \times 4\frac{5}{6}$ **7.** $6 \times 3\frac{3}{4}$ **8.** $4\frac{5}{6} \times 3\frac{3}{4}$

9. $\frac{9}{10} \times 3\frac{1}{3}$ **10.** $2\frac{1}{4} \times 20$ **11.** $2\frac{3}{4} \times 1\frac{1}{10}$ **12.** $4\frac{1}{3} \times 5\frac{1}{2}$

13. $15 \times 4\frac{1}{6}$ **14.** $3\frac{1}{4} \times 2\frac{2}{3}$ **15.** $\frac{4}{5} \times 3\frac{3}{8}$ **16.** $\frac{3}{4} \times 16$

17. $15 \times 3\frac{1}{10}$ **18.** $4 \times 5\frac{3}{8}$ **19.** $3\frac{1}{5} \times 4\frac{2}{3}$ **20.** $3\frac{1}{4} \times 3\frac{1}{4}$

21. $18 \times 2\frac{2}{3}$ **22.** $3\frac{1}{7} \times 2\frac{1}{2}$ **23.** $8 \times 1\frac{3}{4}$ **24.** $1\frac{7}{10} \times 2\frac{3}{10}$

25. $5\frac{1}{3} \times 3\frac{3}{4}$ **26.** $6\frac{1}{4} \times 2\frac{2}{5}$

27. What is the product when 9 is multiplied by $4\frac{1}{3}$?

Mixed Applications

28. The world's record for the high jump in a recent year was about $7\frac{3}{4}$ ft. On Mars this jump would be $2\frac{1}{2}$ times as high. How high would that be?

29. Suppose you can high jump $4\frac{1}{6}$ ft (4 ft 2 in.) on Earth. You could jump only $3\frac{1}{2}$ ft on Saturn. How much higher can you jump on Earth?

30. You could jump $6\frac{1}{4}$ times as high on the moon as on Earth. Jack can jump $5\frac{7}{12}$ ft high on Earth. How high could he jump on the moon? Estimate which of these answers is reasonable.

   A $7\frac{3}{20}$ ft   **B** 35 ft   **C** 30 ft   **D** $3\frac{1}{2}$ ft

31. **DATA HUNT** Find the latest women's and men's world records for the high jump. How high would each of these jumps be on Mars?

Think

Mental Math

You can use the multiplication-addition property (page 5) to multiply mixed numbers mentally.

$4 \times 3\frac{1}{2}$

> $4 \times 3 = 12$
> $4 \times \frac{1}{2} = 2$
> so $4 \times 3\frac{1}{2} = 14$

Try these!

1. $6 \times 2\frac{1}{3}$ **2.** $9 \times 5\frac{1}{3}$

3. $20 \times 2\frac{1}{4}$ **4.** $12 \times 2\frac{2}{3}$

5. $24 \times 2\frac{3}{4}$ **6.** $15 \times 3\frac{4}{5}$

Math

Problem Solving: Using Data from a Plan Sheet

Kay and Scott's parents agreed to help them build a tree house. They used a plan they found in a magazine. Here are some problems they needed to solve. Use the data from the drawings as needed to solve the problems.

1. They used 18 of the 1 by 6 boards side by side to make the floor. How many inches wide was the floor?

$5\frac{1}{2} \times 18$

2. The 1 by 6 boards must be $8\frac{1}{4}$ ft long to make the floor a square. How many total feet of board will actually be needed if 18 boards are used? $18 \times 8\frac{1}{4} =$

3. The 1 by 6 boards cost $0.29 per foot of length. If there were no waste, what would be the cost for the floor? (Use the answer from problem 2.)

$\times .29$

4. What size nail should you use if you want to nail three 1 by 6 boards together as shown and have the nail go $\frac{1}{2}$ in. into the third board?

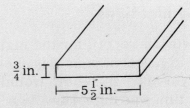

Plan Sheet A

Use 1 by 6 boards for the floor.

Note that 1 by 6 boards have the dimensions shown.

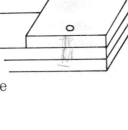

$\frac{3}{4}$ in.

$5\frac{1}{2}$ in.

These boards are available in 6, 8, 10, 12, 14, 16, 18, and 20 foot lengths.

Information About Nails

With each 1 "penny" increase, the length of the nail increases $\frac{1}{4}$ in.

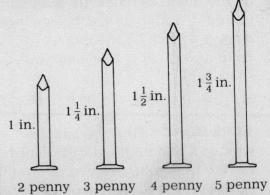

1 in. $1\frac{1}{4}$ in. $1\frac{1}{2}$ in. $1\frac{3}{4}$ in.

2 penny   3 penny   4 penny   5 penny

Plan Sheet B

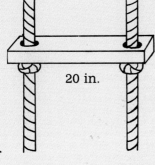

Make a rope ladder for the tree house. Use $\frac{3}{8}$-in. rope.

20 in.

$4\frac{3}{4}$ in. of rope are needed for each knot.

5. They will need to tie 20 knots to make the rope ladder. How many extra inches of rope must they include for the knots?

6. To make the ladder, ten 2 by 2 boards, each 20 in. long, are needed. How many inches of these boards do they need? How many feet? (1 foot = 12 inches. Round to the nearest foot.) If these boards cost 13.7¢ per foot, what would the total cost for ladder boards?

Plan Sheet C

Use three 2 by 4 boards for each side of a low wall around the tree house. Note that 2 by 4 boards have the dimensions shown:

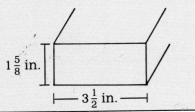

$1\frac{5}{8}$ in.

$3\frac{1}{2}$ in.

7. How high would a wall made with three 2 by 4 boards be?

8. How high is a stack of four 2 by 4 boards?

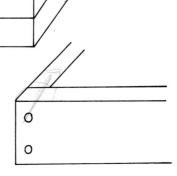

9. How long a nail should you use if you want to nail 2 by 4 boards like this and have the nail go $\frac{3}{4}$ in. into the second board?

10. **Strategy Practice** Scott wanted to cut a long board into 20 pieces. How many cuts are needed to do this? Hint: Solve a simpler problem.

Fractions and Decimals

Work with a group. You will need graph paper and marking pens and number cubes.

Part 1

You can use graph paper to explore how fractions and decimals are related. Cut several 10-by-10 grids from graph paper.

1. Fractions such as $\frac{1}{2}$, $\frac{1}{3}$, and $\frac{1}{4}$, with a numerator of 1, are called **unit fractions.** On each 10-by-10 grid, color only whole small squares to show a unit fraction.

   • Label each grid with its unit fraction.
   • Can you show $\frac{1}{8}$ if you can also color half of a small square? Try it.
   • Share your work with another group. Compare results and discuss any differences.

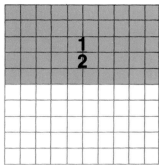

2. Discuss how you can show fractions with numerators other than 1.
   • Each person colors at least two examples and labels them with the fractions they represent.
   • Compare your examples with those of other groups.

3. Look at each grid and determine a decimal that represents the colored part. Make a table and record a decimal for each fraction you showed.

Part 2

Use what you have learned to find decimals for other fractions.

4. Talk about how to estimate the location of these fractions on the number line: $\frac{1}{2}$, $\frac{1}{4}$, $\frac{3}{4}$, $\frac{1}{8}$, $\frac{3}{8}$, $\frac{5}{8}$, and $\frac{7}{8}$.

   • Which are "halfway between" which others? Explain.
   • Show the fractions on the number line.
   • Discuss how thinking about the locations on the number line can help you use the decimal for $\frac{1}{2}$ to find decimals for the other fractions.

More Practice, page 441, Set C

- How could you use the location and the decimal for $\frac{1}{8}$ to find the decimals for other fractions shown on your number line?
- How could you use the decimal for $\frac{1}{5}$ to find the decimals for $\frac{2}{5}$, $\frac{3}{5}$, and $\frac{4}{5}$? To find the decimal for $\frac{1}{10}$?

5. Add to your table the fractions in exercise 4 and the decimals you have found for them.
   - Look at the fractions and decimals in your table. How might you use a calculator to help you find the decimals for the fractions? Experiment with your calculator and write a description of the method you discovered.
   - Use your method to find decimals for the fractions $\frac{1}{3}$ and $\frac{1}{6}$.

     How are they different from the other decimals you have found? Explain.
   - How might you use the decimals for $\frac{1}{3}$ and $\frac{1}{6}$ to find the decimals for $\frac{2}{3}$ and $\frac{5}{6}$?
   - Include in your table the new fractions and decimals you have found.

Part 3

Use what you have learned to play "Gridlock." The object of the game is to avoid becoming gridlocked. You are gridlocked when you cannot make a fraction or decimal as described in the rules below. Take turns. Each player begins the game with 0.

With these numbers, I can make $\frac{1}{3}$, $\frac{1}{5}$, $\frac{3}{5}$, .11, .13, .15, .51, .35, .51, .53.

Rules
- On your turn, roll four number cubes.
- Use any two of the numbers you roll to make a fraction or decimal larger than your last number and less than 1.
- Record your fraction or decimal for each turn. For each fraction, also record its decimal to the nearest hundredth.
- When a player is gridlocked, he or she is out of the game. The last remaining player wins.

Jill's Record
0
0.16
$\frac{1}{5}$ (0.20)
0.44
0.65
$\frac{4}{6}$ (0.67)
$\frac{3}{4}$ (0.75)

6. Discuss your strategies for playing the game.

More Practice, page 441, Set D

Writing Fractions as Mixed Decimals

The area of Africa is about $\frac{2}{3}$ the area of Asia.

What decimal can be used for this fraction?

You can find a **mixed decimal** for $\frac{2}{3}$ by dividing to two places and writing a fraction using the remainder and the divisor.

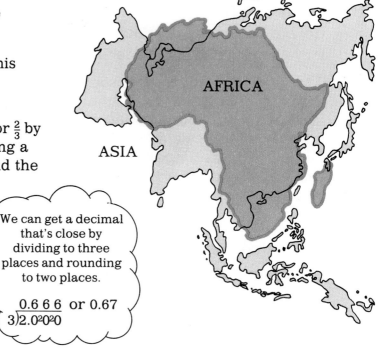

ASIA

AFRICA

$$
\begin{array}{r}
0.6\,6\,\frac{2}{3} \\
3\overline{)2.0\,0} \\
1\,8 \\
\hline
2\,0 \\
1\,8 \\
\hline
2
\end{array}
$$

$0.66\frac{2}{3}$ is a mixed decimal.

We can get a decimal that's close by dividing to three places and rounding to two places.

$$
\begin{array}{r}
0.6\,6\,6 \text{ or } 0.67 \\
3\overline{)2.0^{2}0^{2}0}
\end{array}
$$

The area of Africa is about $0.66\frac{2}{3}$ or 0.67 of the area of Asia.

Other Examples

$$
\frac{5}{6} \rightarrow
\begin{array}{r}
0.8\,3 \\
6\overline{)5.0\,0} \\
4\,8 \\
\hline
2\,0 \\
1\,8 \\
\hline
2
\end{array}
\rightarrow 0.8\,3\,\frac{2}{6} \text{ or } 0.8\,3\,\frac{1}{3}
$$

$$
\frac{9}{8} \rightarrow
\begin{array}{r}
1.1\,2 \\
8\overline{)9.0\,0} \\
8 \\
\hline
1\,0 \\
8 \\
\hline
2\,0 \\
1\,6 \\
\hline
4
\end{array}
\rightarrow 1.1\,2\,\frac{4}{8} \text{ or } 1.1\,2\,\frac{1}{2}
$$

Write a mixed decimal for each fraction.

1. $\frac{1}{8}$ 2. $\frac{5}{6}$ 3. $\frac{1}{3}$ 4. $\frac{5}{8}$ 5. $\frac{5}{3}$ 6. $\frac{7}{16}$

7. $\frac{1}{6}$ 8. $\frac{7}{12}$ 9. $\frac{7}{6}$ 10. $\frac{5}{16}$ 11. $\frac{5}{9}$ 12. $\frac{4}{15}$

Write a decimal rounded to the nearest hundredth for each fraction.

13. $\frac{7}{8}$ 14. $\frac{7}{3}$ 15. $\frac{11}{6}$ 16. $\frac{5}{16}$ 17. $\frac{3}{8}$ 18. $\frac{5}{12}$

Getting Ready to Divide Fractions

The exercises below will help you get ready to divide fractions. Use the pictures to answer the questions.

By counting, we see there are six $\frac{1}{2}$s in 3 oranges.

We count the number of $\frac{1}{4}$ pieces in the $\frac{5}{2}$ pizzas!

1. How many $\frac{1}{2}$s are in 3?

2. How many $\frac{1}{4}$s are in $\frac{5}{2}$?

3.

How many $\frac{1}{6}$s are in $\frac{2}{3}$?

4.
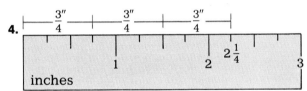

How many $\frac{3}{4}$s are in $2\frac{1}{4}$?

5.
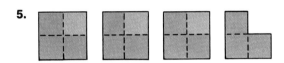

How many $\frac{3}{4}$s are in $3\frac{3}{4}$?

6.

How many $\frac{1}{8}$s are in $\frac{3}{4}$?

Use the pictures to help you solve the equations.
Check each division by multiplying.

7.

How many $\frac{1}{4}$s are in 2?

$$2 \div \frac{1}{4} = n$$

8.
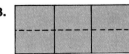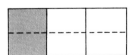

How many $\frac{1}{6}$s are in $\frac{4}{3}$?

$$\frac{4}{3} \div \frac{1}{6} = n$$

239

Dividing Fractions

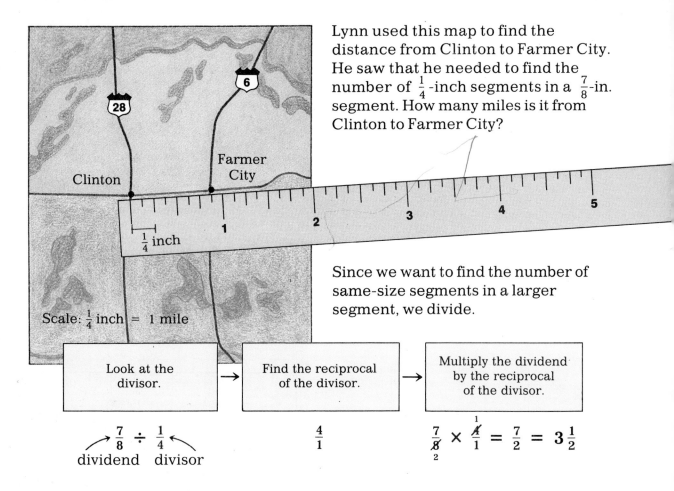

Lynn used this map to find the distance from Clinton to Farmer City. He saw that he needed to find the number of $\frac{1}{4}$-inch segments in a $\frac{7}{8}$-in. segment. How many miles is it from Clinton to Farmer City?

Since we want to find the number of same-size segments in a larger segment, we divide.

Look at the divisor.	→	Find the reciprocal of the divisor.	→	Multiply the dividend by the reciprocal of the divisor.

$$\overset{\nearrow\quad\nwarrow}{\frac{7}{8} \div \frac{1}{4}}$$
dividend divisor

$$\frac{4}{1}$$

$$\frac{7}{\cancel{8}_{2}} \times \frac{\cancel{4}^{1}}{1} = \frac{7}{2} = 3\frac{1}{2}$$

The distance from Clinton to Farmer City is $3\frac{1}{2}$ mi.

Other Examples

$$\frac{3}{5} \div \frac{2}{3} = \frac{3}{5} \times \frac{3}{2} = \frac{9}{10} \qquad 6 \div \frac{3}{4} = \frac{\cancel{6}^{2}}{1} \times \frac{4}{\cancel{3}_{1}} = 8 \qquad 6 \div 9 = \frac{\cancel{6}^{2}}{1} \times \frac{1}{\cancel{9}_{3}} = \frac{2}{3}$$

Check: $\dfrac{\cancel{9}^{3}}{\cancel{10}_{5}} \times \dfrac{\cancel{2}^{1}}{\cancel{3}_{1}} = \dfrac{3}{5}$

Warm Up   Find the quotients. Check by multiplying.

1. $\frac{2}{3} \div \frac{1}{4}$ 2. $\frac{1}{2} \div \frac{2}{5}$ 3. $\frac{3}{4} \div \frac{1}{10}$ 4. $4 \div \frac{3}{8}$ 5. $\frac{2}{5} \div \frac{1}{2}$

6. $\frac{2}{3} \div 5$ 7. $3 \div 5$ 8. $\frac{9}{10} \div \frac{1}{5}$ 9. $\frac{5}{6} \div \frac{2}{3}$ 10. $\frac{3}{4} \div \frac{7}{8}$

Practice Find the quotients. Check by multiplying.

1. $\frac{1}{2} \div \frac{4}{5}$ 2. $\frac{3}{4} \div \frac{3}{5}$ 3. $\frac{2}{3} \div \frac{3}{4}$ 4. $\frac{1}{2} \div \frac{1}{4}$ 5. $\frac{7}{8} \div \frac{7}{8}$

6. $5 \div \frac{2}{5}$ 7. $\frac{5}{6} \div 10$ 8. $3 \div 8$ 9. $\frac{1}{2} \div \frac{5}{8}$ 10. $\frac{9}{14} \div \frac{3}{7}$

11. $\frac{7}{8} \div \frac{3}{4}$ 12. $\frac{1}{3} \div \frac{2}{3}$ 13. $\frac{3}{10} \div \frac{3}{4}$ 14. $\frac{4}{5} \div \frac{2}{3}$ 15. $\frac{1}{2} \div \frac{7}{10}$

16. $7 \div \frac{2}{3}$ 17. $\frac{9}{10} \div 3$ 18. $4 \div 12$ 19. $\frac{1}{10} \div \frac{3}{10}$ 20. $\frac{3}{5} \div \frac{2}{3}$

21. $\frac{3}{8} \div \frac{3}{4}$ 22. $\frac{2}{5} \div \frac{3}{2}$ 23. $\frac{5}{6} \div \frac{2}{3}$ 24. $\frac{3}{8} \div \frac{4}{3}$ 25. $4 \div \frac{1}{8}$

26. $8 \div \frac{2}{5}$ 27. $\frac{5}{8} \div \frac{1}{3}$ 28. $\frac{4}{5} \div \frac{1}{6}$ 29. $\frac{5}{2} \div \frac{3}{4}$ 30. $\frac{5}{12} \div \frac{1}{6}$

Mixed Applications

31. Each $\frac{1}{2}$ in. on a certain map represents a mile on the road. It is $\frac{3}{4}$ in. between two cities on the map. How many miles is it between the two cities?

32. Use the data given on the map to find the actual distance from Perry to Milton.

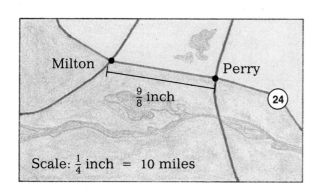

33. **DATA BANK** How many miles farther is it from Orlando to Ocala than it is from Sanford to DeLand? (See page 425.)

More Practice, page 442, Set A

Think

Understanding Fractions

You can find a fraction between any two fractions by finding the average of those fractions. Find a fraction between $\frac{2}{3}$ and $\frac{3}{4}$ by dividing the sum of these fractions by 2. Use the symbol < to show that your fraction is greater than $\frac{2}{3}$ but less than $\frac{3}{4}$.

Math

Dividing with Mixed Numbers

Gwen Strothers is putting new tiles around her kitchen sink. She needs to glue $4\frac{1}{4}$-in. square ceramic tiles on a wall $27\frac{5}{8}$ in. wide. How many tiles will Ms. Strothers need to glue in each row across the wall?

Since we want to find how many same-size tiles, we divide.

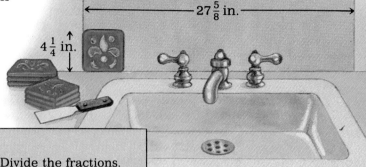

$27\frac{5}{8}$ in.

$4\frac{1}{4}$ in.

Write the mixed numbers or whole numbers as improper fractions.	→	Divide the fractions.

$$27\frac{5}{8} \div 4\frac{1}{4} = \frac{221}{8} \div \frac{17}{4} \qquad \frac{\overset{13}{\cancel{221}}}{\underset{2}{\cancel{8}}} \times \frac{\overset{1}{\cancel{4}}}{\underset{1}{\cancel{17}}} = \frac{13}{2} = 6\frac{1}{2}$$

Ms. Strothers will need to glue $6\frac{1}{2}$ tiles in each row across the wall.

Other Examples

$$2\frac{2}{3} \div \frac{3}{4} = \frac{8}{3} \div \frac{3}{4} = \frac{8}{3} \times \frac{4}{3} = \frac{32}{9} = 3\frac{5}{9}$$

$$8 \div 3\frac{1}{5} = \frac{8}{1} \div \frac{16}{5} = \frac{\overset{1}{\cancel{8}}}{1} \times \frac{5}{\underset{2}{\cancel{16}}} = \frac{5}{2} = 2\frac{1}{2}$$

$$6\frac{3}{8} \div \frac{3}{4} = \frac{51}{8} \div \frac{3}{4} = \frac{\overset{17}{\cancel{51}}}{\underset{2}{\cancel{8}}} \times \frac{\overset{1}{\cancel{4}}}{\underset{1}{\cancel{3}}} = \frac{17}{2} = 8\frac{1}{2}$$

Warm Up   Divide.

1. $2\frac{1}{2} \div 1\frac{1}{3}$ 　　**2.** $3\frac{1}{4} \div \frac{3}{8}$ 　　**3.** $\frac{4}{5} \div 4\frac{3}{4}$ 　　**4.** $5\frac{3}{8} \div 2\frac{1}{2}$ 　　**5.** $1\frac{5}{6} \div 2\frac{1}{3}$

6. $9 \div 1\frac{1}{2}$ 　　**7.** $4\frac{5}{8} \div 6$ 　　**8.** $\frac{9}{10} \div 1\frac{1}{4}$ 　　**9.** $3\frac{1}{2} : 2\frac{1}{4}$ 　　**10.** $8 \div 3\frac{1}{5}$

242

Practice Divide and check.

1. $1\frac{3}{8} \div 4\frac{1}{3}$ 2. $3\frac{2}{3} \div 2$ 3. $5\frac{1}{4} \div 2\frac{1}{2}$ 4. $4 \div 1\frac{1}{3}$ 5. $3\frac{1}{2} \div 2\frac{1}{3}$

6. $8 \div 3\frac{1}{5}$ 7. $8\frac{1}{3} \div 1\frac{1}{6}$ 8. $7 \div 1\frac{1}{7}$ 9. $\frac{1}{6} \div 3\frac{1}{2}$ 10. $\frac{5}{6} \div 1\frac{2}{3}$

11. $2\frac{2}{3} \div 1\frac{1}{4}$ 12. $10 \div 1\frac{1}{4}$ 13. $4\frac{3}{5} \div 2\frac{1}{5}$ 14. $8 \div 3\frac{1}{4}$ 15. $3\frac{3}{8} \div 2\frac{1}{4}$

16. $2\frac{3}{8} \div 4$ 17. $6\frac{1}{4} \div 1\frac{1}{8}$ 18. $2\frac{1}{10} \div 1\frac{1}{5}$ 19. $3\frac{1}{3} \div 1\frac{2}{3}$ 20. $4 \div 1\frac{2}{5}$

21. $6\frac{1}{2} \div 1\frac{1}{4}$ 22. $4\frac{1}{2} \div 2\frac{7}{10}$ 23. $7\frac{1}{4} \div 3$ 24. $1\frac{3}{10} \div 2\frac{4}{5}$ 25. $3\frac{2}{3} \div 2\frac{1}{6}$

26. $\frac{5}{8} \div 4\frac{1}{4}$ 27. $2\frac{4}{5} \div \frac{7}{8}$ 28. $\frac{9}{5} \div 2\frac{1}{3}$ 29. $6\frac{1}{2} \div 4$ 30. $2\frac{1}{8} \div 3\frac{3}{4}$

Round each mixed number to the nearest whole number
and estimate the quotient.

31. $35\frac{3}{4} \div 8\frac{7}{8}$ 32. $16\frac{2}{5} \div 3\frac{7}{8}$ 33. $12\frac{1}{6} \div 5\frac{2}{3}$ 34. $23\frac{4}{5} \div 5\frac{3}{4}$ 35. $17\frac{5}{8} \div 3\frac{4}{9}$

Mixed Applications

36. The tiled area around a sink is $25\frac{1}{2}$ inches high. How many $4\frac{1}{4}$-inch tiles high is this?

37. Write a question for this data. Then solve the problem. A small box of tiles weighs $11\frac{1}{2}$ pounds. A larger box of tiles weighs $17\frac{3}{8}$ pounds.

Skillkeeper

Give the missing numbers.

1. $\frac{1}{4} = \frac{\blacksquare}{16}$ 2. $\frac{2}{5} = \frac{10}{\blacksquare}$ 3. $\frac{2}{3} = \frac{\blacksquare}{24}$ 4. $\frac{5}{9} = \frac{15}{\blacksquare}$ 5. $\frac{3}{4} = \frac{12}{\blacksquare}$

6. $\frac{5}{6} = \frac{15}{\blacksquare}$ 7. $\frac{1}{2} = \frac{\blacksquare}{16}$ 8. $\frac{3}{8} = \frac{12}{\blacksquare}$ 9. $\frac{4}{7} = \frac{\blacksquare}{35}$ 10. $\frac{3}{10} = \frac{\blacksquare}{60}$

Reduce each fraction to lowest terms.

11. $\frac{4}{10}$ 12. $\frac{16}{48}$ 13. $\frac{15}{30}$ 14. $\frac{6}{21}$ 15. $\frac{12}{20}$ 16. $\frac{10}{12}$

17. $\frac{50}{100}$ 18. $\frac{18}{42}$ 19. $\frac{4}{12}$ 20. $\frac{9}{15}$ 21. $\frac{27}{30}$ 22. $\frac{24}{36}$

Problem Solving: Choosing a Calculation Method

Your choice!

Pencil-Paper • Mental Math • Estimation • Calculator

You may use any of these methods to solve the problems, but use each method at least once.

1. During summer vacation, Kim works in Mr. James's flower shop $5\frac{1}{2}$ hours each day. Her salary is $3.50 an hour. How much does she earn each day?

2. Mrs. Carl bought a potted plant for $7.98, some plant food for $3.85, and a small stand for $5.89. If tax is included in the prices, can she pay with a $20 bill?

3. Suzy needs $3\frac{1}{4}$ yd of rope to make a hanger for a plant. How many plants can she hang with $9\frac{3}{4}$ yd of rope?

4. If a 3-lb bag of plant soil costs $2.95, is the cost per pound more than or less than the cost per pound of a 10-lb bag that costs $12.50?

5. Mr. James pays about $\frac{7}{8}$ of his total income for expenses. The rest is profit. His income for one month was $6,400. What was his profit?

6. When mixed with water, $\frac{1}{2}$ teaspoon of a special plant food mixture makes $1\frac{1}{2}$ quarts of plant food. How many teaspoons are needed to make 6 quarts of plant food?

7. Gina's regular pay is $4.37 per hour. She earns one and one-half times her regular hourly pay if she works overtime. One week she worked 2.75 hours overtime each evening for 6 days. How much did she earn for overtime work that week?

8. **Strategy Practice** Mr. James has 6 plant food pellets that look exactly alike, but one is heavier than the others. How can he be sure to find the heavier pellet in just two weighings on the balance scale?

Problem Solving: Using Estimation

First estimate the answer for problems 1 through 7. Then find the exact answer and compare it with the estimate to see whether it is reasonable.

1. Chad helps in his mother's plant store for $3\frac{3}{4}$ h (hours) 5 days a week. How many hours does he work each week?

2. A juice glass holds $5\frac{7}{8}$ oz (ounces). How many glasses can you fill from a pitcher containing 48 oz of juice?

3. A faucet leaks 1 qt (quart) of water every $\frac{3}{4}$ h. How many quarts will it leak in $3\frac{3}{4}$ h?

4. Nan drove 252 miles in $4\frac{2}{3}$ h. What was her average speed in miles per hour?

5. Roland spends $\frac{7}{8}$ of an hour giving a tennis lesson. About how many lessons can he give in 7 hours?

6. A recipe calls for $1\frac{3}{4}$ cups of flour. Kip wants to make $2\frac{1}{2}$ times as much as the recipe. How many cups of flour must he use?

7. It takes $2\frac{7}{8}$ yd (yards) of fabric to make a dress and $\frac{3}{4}$ yd to make a jacket. How many yards of fabric are needed for 3 dress-and-jacket outfits?

8. **Strategy Practice** Jenny lived half her life in New York and one third of her life in Los Angeles. Then she moved to Chicago. If she has lived in Chicago for 4 years, how old is she now?

245

Problem-Solving Strategy: Find a Pattern

QUESTION DATA PLAN ANSWER CHECK

To solve this problem, first try the strategy Make a Table. Then it might help to use a strategy called

Find a Pattern

Try This Jane's uncle offered her a choice of two salary plans for a job that would last 16 days.

PLAN A: $20 a day for each of the 16 days.

PLAN B: 1¢ the first day, 2¢ the second, 4¢ the third, 8¢ the fourth, and so on.

Jane found what her salary would be for the sixteenth day under plan B and made her choice. Which plan do you think she chose?

> First I'll make a table. I'll label it carefully and list the pay for the first 5 days.

Plan B

Day	Pay
1	1¢
2	2¢
3	4¢ = 2 × 2
4	8¢ = 2 × 2 × 2
5	16¢ = 2 × 2 × 2 × 2

> Now I'll look for a pattern. Aha! I use 2 as a factor one less time than the number of days.

Day	Pay
1	1¢
2	2¢
3	4¢ = 2 × 2 (two factors)
4	8¢ = 2 × 2 × 2 (three factors)
5	16¢ = 2 × 2 × 2 × 2 (four factors)

Under plan B Jane's salary just for day 16 would be

$$2 \times 2 \times 2 \times 2 \times 2 \times 2 \times 2 \times 2 \times 2 \times 2 \times 2 \times 2 \times 2 \times 2 \times 2$$

or $327.68. Jane probably chose plan B, since her total plan A salary would be only $320.

Solve.

1. Suppose you catch 1 fish the first day and 2 more fish each day than the day before. How many fish will you catch during a 12-day vacation?

2. Each of 8 friends rides a Ferris wheel once with everyone else in the group (2 friends to a seat). How many rides do they take altogether?

Chapter Review-Test

Give the product in lowest terms.

1. $\frac{1}{3} \times 12$ **2.** $\frac{3}{5} \times \frac{1}{4}$ **3.** $\frac{5}{6} \times \frac{3}{10}$ **4.** $100 \times \frac{4}{5}$ **5.** $\frac{5}{8} \times \frac{3}{5}$

6. $\frac{8}{3} \times \frac{9}{16}$ **7.** $2\frac{1}{3} \times 5\frac{3}{4}$ **8.** $8 \times 3\frac{1}{4}$ **9.** $4\frac{7}{10} \times 5$ **10.** $3\frac{1}{3} \times 2\frac{7}{10}$

Write a lowest-terms fraction for each decimal.

11. 0.375   **12.** 0.5   **13.** 0.25   **14.** 0.125   **15.** 0.35   **16.** 0.60

17. 0.75   **18.** 0.625   **19.** 0.9   **20.** 0.875   **21.** 0.4   **22.** 0.99

Write as a decimal.

23. $\frac{7}{10}$ **24.** $\frac{3}{4}$ **25.** $\frac{2}{5}$ **26.** $\frac{3}{8}$ **27.** $\frac{7}{20}$ **28.** $\frac{4}{25}$

29. $\frac{9}{20}$ **30.** $\frac{3}{10}$ **31.** $\frac{5}{16}$ **32.** $\frac{3}{20}$ **33.** $\frac{1}{10}$ **34.** $\frac{9}{100}$

35. Write $\frac{9}{24}$ as a mixed decimal.   **36.** Write $\frac{30}{45}$ as a mixed decimal.

Give the quotient in lowest terms. Check by multiplying.

37. $4 \div \frac{1}{3}$ **38.** $\frac{3}{4} \div \frac{2}{3}$ **39.** $8 \div \frac{3}{4}$ **40.** $6 \div 8$ **41.** $\frac{5}{6} \div 3\frac{1}{3}$

42. $\frac{3}{8} \div \frac{5}{4}$ **43.** $3\frac{2}{3} \div \frac{5}{6}$ **44.** $12 \div 3\frac{1}{4}$ **45.** $2\frac{3}{4} \div 3\frac{2}{3}$ **46.** $3\frac{1}{2} \div 2\frac{1}{6}$

Solve.

47. Earl bought a $34\frac{1}{2}$-oz bottle of grape juice. He poured all of the juice into some glasses that hold $5\frac{3}{4}$ oz each. How many glasses was he able to fill?

48. For one side of a rope ladder, you need to end up with a 182-in. length of rope that includes 8 knots. If each knot uses up $4\frac{3}{4}$ in. of rope and adds $1\frac{1}{2}$ in. to the length of the rope, how much rope do you need to use?

Another Look

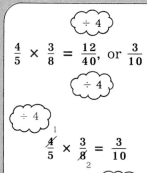

$$\frac{4}{5} \times \frac{3}{8} = \frac{12}{40}, \text{ or } \frac{3}{10}$$

$$\overset{1}{\cancel{4}}{5} \times \frac{3}{\underset{2}{\cancel{8}}} = \frac{3}{10}$$

You can multiply first, then divide, or divide first, then multiply!

To divide by a fraction, multiply by its reciprocal.

$$\frac{2}{3} \div \frac{3}{4} = \frac{2}{3} \times \frac{4}{3} = \frac{8}{9}$$

reciprocal

$$3\frac{1}{2} \quad \times \quad 1\frac{3}{4}$$

$(3 \times 2) + 1$ $(1 \times 4) + 3$

$$\frac{7}{2} \quad \times \quad \frac{7}{4} = \frac{49}{8} \text{ or } 6\frac{1}{8}$$

To multiply or divide mixed numbers, first change them to improper fractions.

Think about place value to write a decimal as a fraction.

$$0.75 = \frac{75}{100} = \frac{3}{4}$$

To write a fraction as a decimal or mixed decimal, divide.

$$\frac{5}{8} \rightarrow \quad 0.6\,2\,5 \rightarrow 0.6\,2\,5 \text{ or } 0.6\,2\frac{1}{2}$$
$$8)\overline{5.0\,0\,0}$$

Give the product in lowest terms.

1. $\frac{3}{5} \times \frac{1}{4}$ 2. $\frac{5}{8} \times \frac{2}{3}$ 3. $\frac{1}{2} \times \frac{2}{5}$

4. $\frac{5}{6} \times \frac{4}{5}$ 5. $\frac{7}{12} \times \frac{3}{14}$ 6. $\frac{3}{4} \times \frac{5}{8}$

7. $\frac{3}{8} \times \frac{4}{9}$ 8. $8 \times \frac{3}{4}$ 9. $\frac{5}{6} \times 2$

Divide.

10. $\frac{1}{4} \div \frac{2}{3}$ 11. $\frac{3}{4} \div \frac{5}{8}$ 12. $\frac{1}{6} \div \frac{1}{2}$

13. $\frac{5}{6} \div \frac{1}{5}$ 14. $\frac{3}{5} \div \frac{3}{8}$ 15. $4 \div \frac{2}{5}$

Multiply or divide.

16. $2\frac{4}{5} \times 1\frac{1}{3}$ 17. $5\frac{3}{8} \times \frac{3}{4}$ 18. $2\frac{1}{6} \div \frac{1}{2}$

19. $3\frac{1}{2} \div \frac{3}{4}$ 20. $5\frac{2}{3} \div 1\frac{5}{6}$ 21. $2\frac{2}{3} \times \frac{3}{8}$

22. $6 \times 3\frac{2}{3}$ 23. $12\frac{1}{2} \div 1\frac{1}{4}$ 24. $4\frac{2}{5} \times 2\frac{1}{2}$

Write a fraction in lowest terms.

25. 0.3   26. 0.85   27. 0.625   28. 0.02

Write a decimal.

29. $\frac{3}{4}$ 30. $\frac{3}{5}$ 31. $\frac{7}{8}$ 32. $\frac{6}{15}$

Enrichment

Patterns in Repeating Decimals

When Tico tried to find a decimal for $\frac{2}{11}$, he saw a pattern in the digits on his calculator. When he divided 2 by 11, he could see that the digits 1 and 8 would continue to repeat.

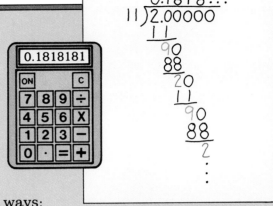

The decimal for $\frac{2}{11}$ is called a repeating decimal. We can write it in either of these ways:

$$\frac{2}{11} = 0.1\,8\,1\,8\,1\,8\,\ldots \quad \text{or} \quad \frac{2}{11} = 0.\overline{18}$$

The dots show that the digits 1 and 8 continue to repeat.

The bar shows that the digits under it continue to repeat.

Let's look at some patterns of repeating decimals.

1. Here is the repeating decimal for $\frac{1}{3}$.

   $\frac{1}{3} = 0.333 \ldots = 0.\overline{3}$

   Give the repeating decimal for $\frac{2}{3}$ without calculating.

   Use a calculator, if you wish, to find repeating decimals for $\frac{1}{6}, \frac{5}{6}$, and $\frac{1}{12}$.

2. Check these repeating decimals by dividing.

   $\frac{1}{11} = 0.\overline{09} \qquad \frac{2}{11} = 0.\overline{18} \qquad \frac{3}{11} = 0.\overline{27}$

   Can you give repeating decimals for the fractions $\frac{4}{11}$ through $\frac{10}{11}$ without calculating?

3. Check these repeating decimals by dividing.

   $\frac{4}{99} = 0.\overline{04} \qquad \frac{12}{99} = 0.\overline{12} \qquad \frac{23}{99} = 0.\overline{23}$

   Can you give the fractions for these repeating decimals?

   $0.\overline{08}, 0.\overline{47}, 0.\overline{65}, 0.\overline{98}$

4. Check these repeating decimals by dividing.

   $\frac{5}{999} = 0.\overline{005} \quad \frac{76}{999} = 0.\overline{076} \quad \frac{345}{999} = 0.\overline{345}$

   Can you give fractions for these repeating decimals?

   $0.\overline{008}, 0.\overline{083}, 0.\overline{694}, 0.\overline{996}, 0.\overline{444}$

249

Cumulative Review

Multiply or divide.

1. 12.483×100

    A 1,248.3   **B** 124.83
    C 0.12483   **D** not given

2. $\begin{array}{r} 1.8 \\ \times\ 0.09 \\ \hline \end{array}$

    A 0.162   **B** 0.972
    C 1.89   **D** not given

3. $\begin{array}{r} 4.3 \\ \times\ 4.3 \\ \hline \end{array}$

    A 184.9   **B** 1.849
    C 12.09   **D** not given

4. $34.8 \div 100$

    A 3,480   **B** 348
    C 3.48   **D** not given

5. $4\overline{)9.64}$

    A 241   **B** 2.41
    C 1.94   **D** not given

6. What is the missing numerator?

$$\frac{5}{8} = \frac{\text{▦}}{40}$$

    A 25   **B** 36   **C** 32   **D** not given

7. What is the missing denominator?

$$\frac{5}{9} = \frac{20}{\text{▦}}$$

    A 45   **B** 36   **C** 18   **D** not given

8. Reduce $\frac{18}{48}$ to lowest terms.

    A $\frac{2}{5}$ **B** $\frac{1}{3}$ **C** $\frac{3}{8}$ **D** not given

Add or subtract.

9. $\begin{array}{r} \frac{2}{5} \\ +\ \frac{3}{10} \\ \hline \end{array}$ **A** $\frac{1}{10}$ **B** $\frac{5}{10}$
    C $\frac{7}{10}$ **D** not given

10. $\begin{array}{r} \frac{8}{9} \\ -\ \frac{1}{3} \\ \hline \end{array}$ **A** $\frac{2}{3}$ **B** $\frac{5}{9}$
    C $\frac{7}{9}$ **D** not given

11. $\begin{array}{r} 6\frac{1}{2} \\ +\ 2\frac{1}{3} \\ \hline \end{array}$ **A** $8\frac{5}{6}$ **B** $9\frac{1}{6}$
    C $4\frac{1}{6}$ **D** not given

12. $\begin{array}{r} 9\frac{1}{4} \\ -\ 3\frac{1}{2} \\ \hline \end{array}$ **A** $12\frac{3}{4}$ **B** $6\frac{3}{4}$
    C $5\frac{1}{4}$ **D** not given

13. A recipe calls for $\frac{1}{4}$ cup of milk and $\frac{1}{2}$ cup of water. What is the total amount of liquid?

    A $\frac{1}{4}$ cup   **B** $\frac{1}{8}$ cup

    C $\frac{3}{4}$ cup   **D** not given

14. A rope 10.5 m long is cut into 7 pieces of equal length. How long is each piece?

    A 15 m   **B** 1.5 m
    C 7 m   **D** not given

The students in Doug's school decided to make banners to decorate the auditorium for the school play. The play was about events that took place in the Middle Ages—a time in history when noble families used banners to display their coats of arms.

The banners Doug designed were made up of a variety of geometric shapes. He worked carefully with a ruler and compass to draw circles, triangles, squares, and rectangles. Then he chose the colors. He knew that colors on coats of arms had special meanings. Green, for example, meant "youth" and "hope." He thought about these meanings as he added color to his designs.

When his work was finished, Doug had the pleasure of seeing his banners hanging on the walls of the auditorium. He looked forward to the day when he would attend art school to prepare for a career as a graphic artist.

Basic Geometric Figures

Many real world objects suggest important geometric ideas and figures.

We see	We think	We write
Pin tip	a **point**	P
Center line of a road	a **line**	ℓ or $\overleftrightarrow{AB}$
File cabinet top	a **line segment** (with **endpoints** C and D) a **plane**	$\overline{CD}$ plane P
Penlight beam	a **ray** (with **endpoint** E)	$\overrightarrow{EF}$
Clock hands	an **angle** (with **vertex** S and **sides** $\overrightarrow{SR}$ and $\overrightarrow{ST}$)	$\angle RST$ or $\angle TSR$ or $\angle S$

Write the name and symbol for each figure.

1.

2.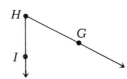

3.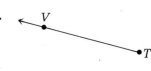

4.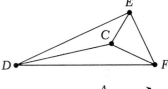

5.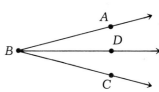

6.

Draw a picture for each symbol.

7. $\overline{DE}$ **8.** $\angle EFG$ **9.** point G **10.** $\overrightarrow{BC}$ **11.** $\overleftrightarrow{MN}$

12. Name 6 different line segments in this figure.

13. Name 3 different rays in this figure.

14. Name 3 different angles in this figure.

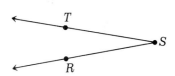

15. Name 2 different rays in this figure.

16. Give 3 different names for this angle.

★ **17.** Name 10 different line segments in this figure.

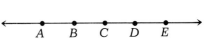

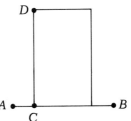

Think

Optical Illusions

Which segment, $\overline{AB}$ or $\overline{CD}$, do you think is longer? Or are they the same length?

First estimate. Then check by measuring to the nearest millimeter.

A Tall Hat!

Math

Measuring Angles

A **protractor** is used for measuring angles. The unit of angle measure is the **degree** (°).

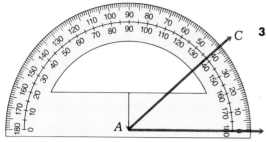

3. Read the measure of the angle.

2. Place the zero edge on one side of the angle.

1. Place the arrow on the vertex of the angle.

The measure of ∠*BAC* is 42°.

Angles are named by their measures.

 90°

Right angle

 less than 90°

Acute angle

 greater than 90°

Obtuse angle

First estimate the measure of each angle. Then measure to check your estimate. Is the angle **right, acute,** or **obtuse?**

1.

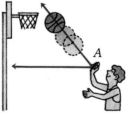

Angle of release when shooting a basketball

2.

Angle of bank for an airplane

3.

8 iron golf club (angle with ground)

4.

3 wood golf club (angle with shaft)

5.

Angle between due North and due East on a compass

Estimating Angle Measure

Follow the steps below to draw ∠ABC with measure 25°.

Step 1

Draw $\overrightarrow{AB}$.

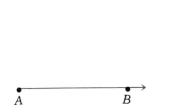

Step 2

Place the protractor arrow on A and mark point C at 25°.

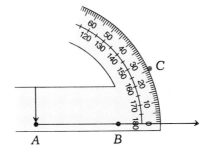

Step 3

Remove the protractor and draw $\overrightarrow{AC}$.

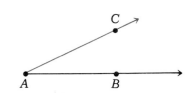

The measure of ∠CAB is 25°.

Draw angles (without using a protractor) which you estimate to have the measures given below. Then measure each angle to check your estimate.

1. 35°   **2.** 50°   **3.** 95°   **4.** 120°   **5.** 145°   **6.** 175°

7. 20°   **8.** 45°   **9.** 80°   **10.** 110°   **11.** 150°   **12.** 170°

★ **13.** The measure of ∠B is twice the measure of ∠A.
The sum of the measures of ∠A and ∠B is 90°.
Draw ∠A and ∠B.

Skillkeeper

Estimate the sum or difference by rounding to the nearest hundred.

1.	**2.**	**3.**	**4.**	**5.**
672	358	792	919	638
+ 415	+ 240	− 483	− 174	+ 768

Estimate the sum or difference by rounding to the nearest dollar.

6.	**7.**	**8.**	**9.**	**10.**
$8.43	$15.88	$9.75	$7.29	$17.62
+ 6.72	− 2.17	− 3.58	+ 8.80	− 12.70

Perpendicular Lines

We see	We think	We write
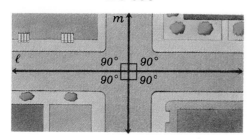	**Perpendicular lines** (lines that intersect at right angles)	$\ell \perp m$ (We say: "Line ℓ is perpendicular to line m.")

An intersection of two streets

Here are two ways to draw perpendicular lines.

Method 1: Using a Protractor

Draw a line ℓ. Mark points P and Q.

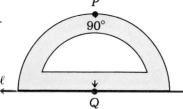

Draw line m through P and Q. $m \perp \ell$

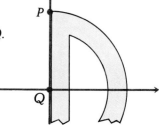

Method 2: Using a Compass and Ruler

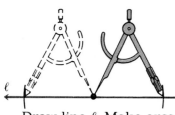

Draw line ℓ. Make arcs with your compass.

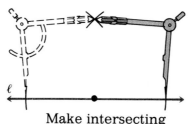

Make intersecting arcs above the line.

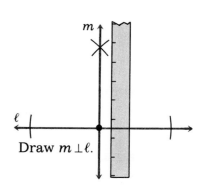

Draw $m \perp \ell$.

1. Use method 1 to draw a pair of perpendicular lines.

2. Use method 2 to draw a pair of perpendicular lines.

3. Line r is perpendicular to line s. The angles formed are named by the numerals. Give the measure of $\angle 1$, $\angle 2$, $\angle 3$, and $\angle 4$.

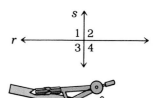

★ 4. Draw a segment AB. Without measuring, draw a line that goes through a point midway between A and B.

Parallel Lines

We see	We think	We write

Railroad tracks

Parallel lines (lines that do not intersect)

$\ell \parallel m$ (We say: "Line ℓ is parallel to line m.")

Here are two ways to draw parallel lines.

Method 1: Using a Ruler

Draw a line on each side of your ruler.

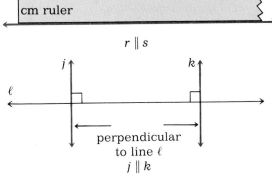

$r \parallel s$

Method 2: Using Perpendicular Lines

Draw line ℓ. Then use a protractor or compass and ruler to draw 2 other lines, each perpendicular to ℓ.

perpendicular to line ℓ
$j \parallel k$

1. Use method 1 to draw a pair of parallel lines.

2. Use method 2 to draw a pair of parallel lines with a protractor.

3. Use method 2 to draw a pair of parallel lines with a compass and ruler.

4. In this figure, $k \parallel \ell$. The angles formed are named by the numerals. Which angles do you think have the same measure?

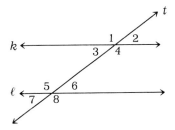

Triangles

Here are some important kinds of triangles.

We see	We think	We write
Scrap of lumber	**Scalene triangle** (All 3 sides have different lengths.)	$\triangle ABC$
Pennant	**Isosceles triangle** (At least 2 sides have the same length.)	$\triangle DEF$
"Yield" sign	**Equilateral triangle** (All 3 sides have the same length.)	$\triangle GHI$

Triangles are also named according to the size of their angles.

Acute triangle

All angles measure less than 90°.

Right triangle

One angle measures 90°.

Obtuse triangle

One angle measures greater than 90°.

Here is an important fact about the angles of a triangle.

- The sum of the angles of a triangle is 180°.

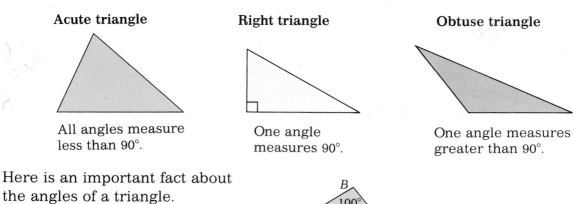

$30° + 100° + 50° = 180°$

Use letters to name each triangle. Tell whether the triangle is **scalene**, **isosceles**, or **equilateral**.

1.
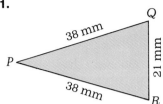
38 mm
21 mm
38 mm
P Q R

2.
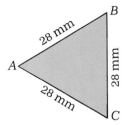
28 mm
28 mm
28 mm
A B C

3.
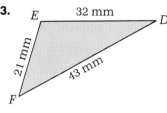
32 mm
21 mm
43 mm
E D F

Tell whether the triangle is **acute**, **right**, or **obtuse**.

4.
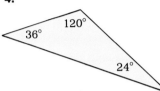
120°
36°
24°

5.
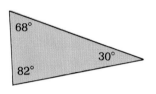
68°
82°
30°

6.
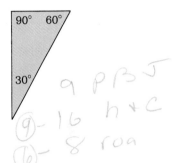
90° 60°
30°

Give all possible names for each triangle (for example, **acute** and **scalene**).

7.
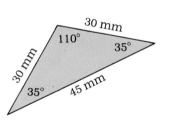
30 mm
110°
35°
30 mm
35°
45 mm

8.
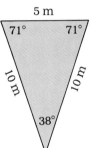
5 m
71° 71°
10 m
10 m
38°

9.
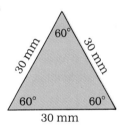
60°
30 mm
30 mm
60° 60°
30 mm

In each triangle find the angle measures that are not given.

10.
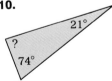
21°
?
74°

11.
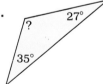
27°
?
35°

★ **12.**
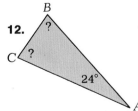
B
?
C ?
24°
A

Isosceles (∠C and ∠B have the same measure.)

★ **13.**

?
? ?

Equilateral (All angles have the same measure.)

Think

Triangle Puzzle

Count the number of different triangles. There are 27 in all! How many can you find?

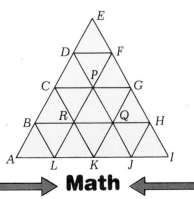

Math

259

Quadrilaterals

A **quadrilateral** is a closed figure with 4 sides. Some information about different types of quadrilaterals is given below. For each picture give the letter of the description that fits it best.

Pictures

Descriptions

1.

A. A **parallelogram** has two pairs of parallel sides. It also has two pairs of sides that have the same length.

2.
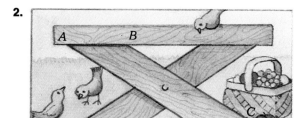

B. A **square** has all sides the same length. All angles are right angles.

3.

C. A **trapezoid** has exactly one pair of parallel sides.

4.
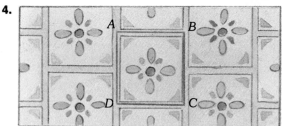

D. A **rhombus** has all sides the same length and two pairs of parallel sides.

5.

E. A **rectangle** has two pairs of sides the same length and four right angles.

Solve these problems about quadrilaterals.

1. Any figure with two pairs of parallel sides can be called a parallelogram. Which of these figures can also be called a parallelogram?

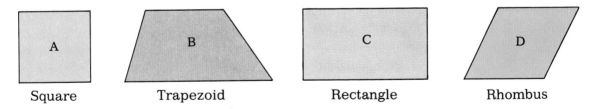

A
Square

B
Trapezoid

C
Rectangle

D
Rhombus

2. Any figure with four right angles can be called a rectangle. Which figure above (other than C) can also be called a rectangle?

Find the sum of the angles of each quadrilateral below. Then complete the statement in exercise 7.

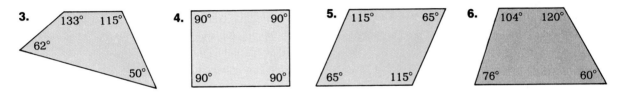

3. 133° 115° 62° 50°

4. 90° 90° 90° 90°

5. 115° 65° 65° 115°

6. 104° 120° 76° 60°

7. The sum of the angles of any quadrilateral is __?__°.

8. Find the measure of ∠A without using a protractor.

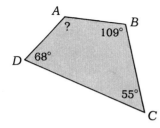

A ? B 109°
D 68°
55°
C

9. Which quadrilateral has four sides of equal length but is not a square?

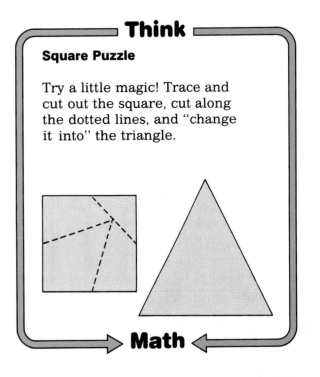

Other Polygons

A **polygon** is a simple closed figure formed by line segments. Triangles and quadrilaterals are polygons. The pictures below suggest some other polygons.

Shape on soccer ball | Commonly used nut | Rug design | Costume jewelry

 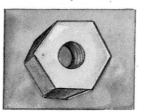 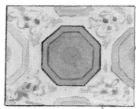 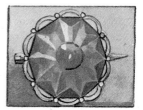

Pentagon–5 sides | Hexagon–6 sides | Octagon–8 sides | Decagon–10 sides

Name each of these polygons.

1.   **2.**   **3.**   **4.**

Regular polygons have all sides the same length and all angles the same measure.

Are the figures below regular polygons? If not, why not?

5.   **6.** 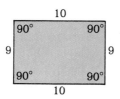 **7.**   **8.**

Polygons are sometimes named by the number of sides they have. For example, a pentagon may be called a **5-gon**. Use this idea to name these two figures.

9.   **10.**

11. A **diagonal** is a segment (not a side) connecting two vertices of a polygon. How many diagonals does a hexagon have?

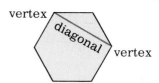

vertex / diagonal / vertex

Circles

A Ferris wheel suggests a **circle.** All the points on a circle are the same distance from the **center** (O).

Here are some more ideas about circles.

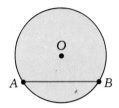

A **chord** is a segment with endpoints on the circle.

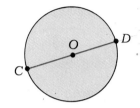

A **diameter** is a chord that contains the center.

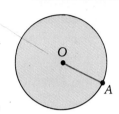

A **radius** is a segment with the center and a point on the circle as endpoints. It is half the length of the diameter.

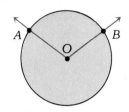

A **central angle** of a circle has the center as its vertex.

You can draw a circle using a compass.

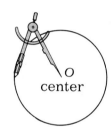

Give the length of the radius or diameter of each circle.

1.

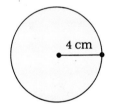

4 cm

Diameter: ▦

2.

3.5 m

Diameter: ▦

3.

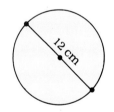

12 cm

Radius: ▦

4.

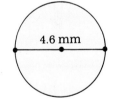

4.6 mm

Radius: ▦

Draw a circle with the given radius or diameter.

5. radius 4.5 cm   **6.** diameter 10 cm   **7.** radius 6 cm

Draw a circle with a central angle having the given measure.

8. 90°   **9.** 35°   **10.** 165°

11. Draw a 4-cm chord of a circle with a 3-cm radius.

263

Congruent Figures

A figure and a copy of the figure that is the same size and shape as the original suggest the idea of **congruent figures.**

Two geometric figures are congruent to each other if they have the same size and shape.

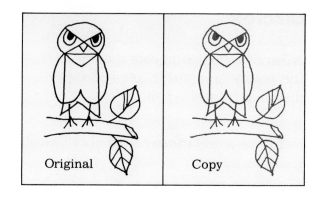

Original   Copy

Two segments are congruent if they have the same length.

We write: $\overline{AB} \cong \overline{CD}$

We say: "Segment *AB* **is congruent to** segment *CD*."

Two angles are congruent if they have the same measure.

We write: $\angle DEF \cong \angle GHI$

We say: "Angle *DEF* **is congruent to angle** *GHI*."

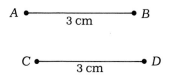

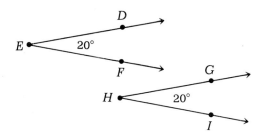

Two polygons are congruent if you can slide, flip, or turn one to make it fit exactly on the other. A tracing of one congruent figure will fit exactly on the figure congruent to it.

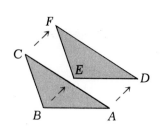

Slide
$\triangle ABC \cong \triangle DEF$

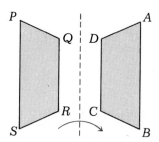

Flip
trapezoid *PQRS* $\cong$ trapezoid *ADCB*

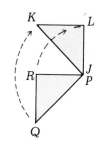

Turn
$\triangle JKL \cong \triangle PQR$

Two congruent polygons, such as $\triangle ABC$ and $\triangle DEF$, **have matching angles congruent and matching sides congruent.**
($\angle C \cong \angle F$, $\angle B \cong \angle E$, $\angle A \cong \angle D$ and $\overline{BC} \cong \overline{EF}$, $\overline{AB} \cong \overline{DE}$, $\overline{CA} \cong \overline{FD}$.)

1. Which pairs of segments are congruent? Measure or use a tracing to make sure.

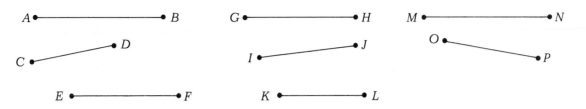

2. Which pairs of angles are congruent? Use your protractor or a tracing.

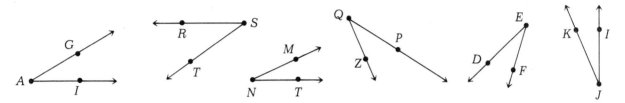

Make a tracing of one of each pair of figures and slide, turn, or flip it to try to make it fit on the other figure. Are the pairs of figures congruent? (Write **yes** or **no**.) Which motion did you use? (Write **slide**, **turn**, or **flip**.)

3.   4.   5.   6.

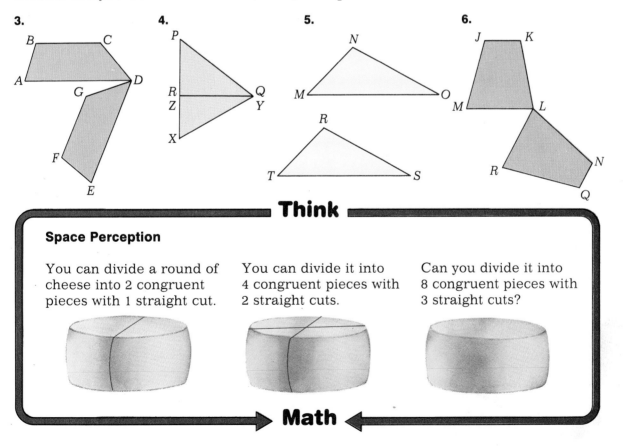

Think

Space Perception

You can divide a round of cheese into 2 congruent pieces with 1 straight cut.

You can divide it into 4 congruent pieces with 2 straight cuts.

Can you divide it into 8 congruent pieces with 3 straight cuts?

Math

Symmetric Figures

The picture on this greeting card suggests the idea of a **symmetric figure.** When the card is closed, the two halves of the figure fit exactly on each other. The fold line of the card is the **line of symmetry** of the figure.

Here are three familiar types of triangles and their lines of symmetry.

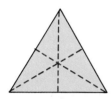

Equilateral triangle
3 lines of symmetry

Isosceles triangle
1 line of symmetry

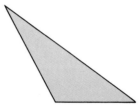

Scalene triangle
0 lines of symmetry

Is the dotted line a line of symmetry of the figure?
Write **yes** or **no.**

1.

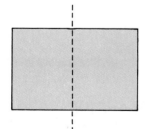

2.

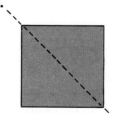

3.

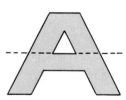

4.

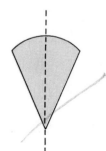

5.

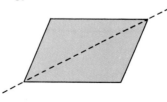

6.

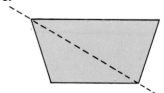

Give the numbers of lines of symmetry for each quadrilateral. Trace the figures, fold, and draw the lines if necessary.

1.

Rectangle

2.

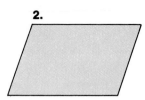

Parallelogram

3.

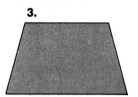

Isosceles trapezoid

4.

Square

5.

Kite-shaped quadrilateral

6.

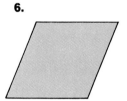

Rhombus

7. Which capital letters have just 1 line of symmetry? 2 lines of symmetry? more than 2 lines of symmetry?

8. Fold a square sheet of paper once and make a cut so that the unfolded piece is
   A a heart   **B** a tree   **C** a pumpkin
   D the letter x   **E** another figure of your choice

★ **9.** Fold a square sheet of paper two times and cut off a corner. Unfold. How many lines of symmetry does the cut-out figure have? Experiment with a piece folded three times.

Skillkeeper

Give the next three equivalent fractions.

1. $\frac{1}{8}, \frac{2}{16}, \frac{\blacksquare}{\blacksquare}, \frac{\blacksquare}{\blacksquare}, \frac{\blacksquare}{\blacksquare}$

2. $\frac{2}{3}, \frac{4}{6}, \frac{\blacksquare}{\blacksquare}, \frac{\blacksquare}{\blacksquare}, \frac{\blacksquare}{\blacksquare}$

3. $\frac{1}{2}, \frac{2}{4}, \frac{\blacksquare}{\blacksquare}, \frac{\blacksquare}{\blacksquare}, \frac{\blacksquare}{\blacksquare}$

4. $\frac{2}{5}, \frac{4}{10}, \frac{\blacksquare}{\blacksquare}, \frac{\blacksquare}{\blacksquare}, \frac{\blacksquare}{\blacksquare}$

5. $\frac{3}{4}, \frac{6}{8}, \frac{\blacksquare}{\blacksquare}, \frac{\blacksquare}{\blacksquare}, \frac{\blacksquare}{\blacksquare}$

6. $\frac{1}{10}, \frac{2}{20}, \frac{\blacksquare}{\blacksquare}, \frac{\blacksquare}{\blacksquare}, \frac{\blacksquare}{\blacksquare}$

7. $\frac{3}{8}, \frac{6}{16}, \frac{\blacksquare}{\blacksquare}, \frac{\blacksquare}{\blacksquare}, \frac{\blacksquare}{\blacksquare}$

8. $\frac{5}{6}, \frac{10}{12}, \frac{\blacksquare}{\blacksquare}, \frac{\blacksquare}{\blacksquare}, \frac{\blacksquare}{\blacksquare}$

9. $\frac{4}{5}, \frac{8}{10}, \frac{\blacksquare}{\blacksquare}, \frac{\blacksquare}{\blacksquare}, \frac{\blacksquare}{\blacksquare}$

10. $\frac{2}{7}, \frac{4}{14}, \frac{6}{21}, \frac{\blacksquare}{\blacksquare}, \frac{\blacksquare}{\blacksquare}, \frac{\blacksquare}{\blacksquare}$

11. $\frac{1}{6}, \frac{2}{12}, \frac{3}{18}, \frac{\blacksquare}{\blacksquare}, \frac{\blacksquare}{\blacksquare}, \frac{\blacksquare}{\blacksquare}$

12. $\frac{5}{9}, \frac{10}{18}, \frac{15}{27}, \frac{\blacksquare}{\blacksquare}, \frac{\blacksquare}{\blacksquare}, \frac{\blacksquare}{\blacksquare}$

Graphing Geometric Figures

Graphing a Figure

You can graph a figure by graphing points and connecting them in order. The number pairs that tell us the location of a point on the graph are called **coordinates.** The graph of a common geometric figure is started for you. The figure is graphed by using these coordinates:

(3,5), (5,3), (5,0), (0,5), (3,5).

Show the complete figure on your graph.

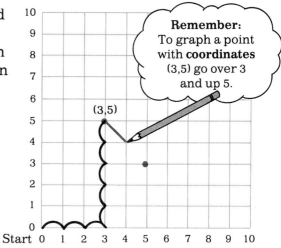

Graphing Congruent Figures

You can find coordinates of a square congruent to the square shown by adding the same number to each of its coordinates. For example, try adding 4.

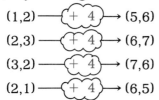

(1,2) —(+ 4)→ (5,6)
(2,3) —(+ 4)→ (6,7)
(3,2) —(+ 4)→ (7,6)
(2,1) —(+ 4)→ (6,5)

Graph the new coordinates on your paper to show the congruent square.

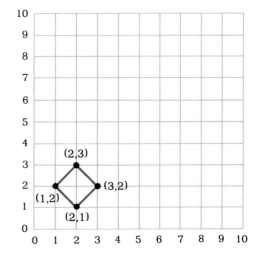

Graphing Similar Figures

You can find the coordinates of a triangle similar to the triangle shown by multiplying each of its coordinates by the same number. For example, try multiplying by 3.

(1,3) —(× 3)→ (3,9)
(2,1) —(× 3)→ (6,3)
(1,1) —(× 3)→ (3,3)

Graph the new coordinates on your paper to show the similar triangle.

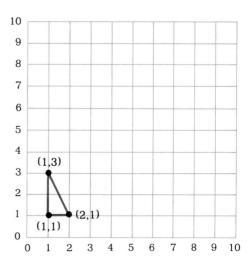

268

Graph each of these figures.

1. (1,1), (3,6), (6,3), (1,1)

2. (2,2), (2,6), (8,6), (8,2), (2,2)

3. (6,1), (4,3), (4,7), (6,9), (8,7), (8,3), (6,1)

Graph the figure for the coordinates given. Then graph a congruent figure by adding the number given to each of the coordinates.

4. (1,1), (3,3), (3,1), (1,1) + 3

5. (1,1), (2,5), (2,1), (1,1) + 2

6. (1,4), (1,6), (3,6), (3,4), (2,3), (1,4) + 4

7. (1,2), (3,4), (7,4), (5,2), (1,2) + 3

Graph the figure for the coordinates given. Then graph a similar figure by multiplying each of the coordinates by the number given.

8. (2,2), (1,3), (4,2), (2,2) × 2

9. (1,1), (2,2), (2,1), (1,1) × 3

10. (2,4), (6,6), (8,2), (4,0), (2,4) × $\frac{1}{2}$

11. (3,3), (3,6), (9,6), (9,3), (3,3) × $\frac{1}{3}$

12. Trace a favorite cartoon character on graph paper.

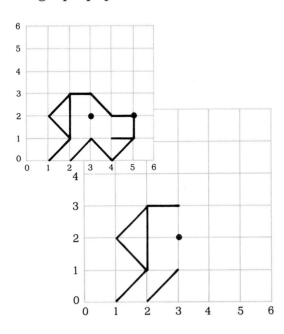

Use graph paper with larger squares or use a larger scale to make a similar but larger figure.

Think

Maze Puzzle

Give the shortest path along the blue lines to point C in the maze by writing, in order, the coordinates of the points where you turn.

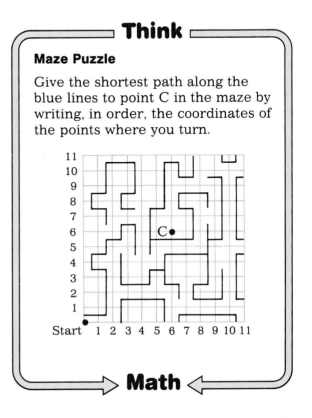

Math

269

Space Figures

Work with a group to build space figures and explore their relationships. You will need pattern blocks, construction paper, scissors, and tape.

Part 1

1. Everyone in your group should build at least one three-dimensional space figure. Trace some polygons on construction paper and cut out four or five of them. Tape some of these polygons together so that the edges align and the corners fit closely together. Try different combinations such as triangles with squares, or squares and rectangles with pentagons, or all triangles.

Some space figures have **faces, vertices,** and **edges.** Space figures whose faces are polygons are called **polyhedrons.**

Edge

Face

Vertex

Part 2

Prisms and pyramids are two kinds of polyhedrons.

Prisms	**Pyramids**

Hexagonal
prism

Pentagonal
Pyramid

Triangular
prism

Rectangular
prism

Triangular
pyramid

Rectangular
pyramid

Find all the prisms and pyramids that your group made. If you have none, make one of each. Write a description of how prisms and pyramids are alike and how they are different.

Part 3

Use all the polyhedrons your group made.

2. Copy this chart on your paper. Count the number of faces, vertices, and edges on each polyhedron. Record the numbers for each figure on the chart.

Polyhedron	Number of Faces (F)	Number of Vertices (V)	Number of Edges (E)
Triangular prism			
Cube			

3. A relationship exists between the number of edges and the sum of the faces (F) and the vertices (V). Use your chart to find this relationship. State it as a formula.

4. Do you think that the formula will work for prisms and pyramids? For other polyhedrons? Test your answer.

5. Suppose you sliced off each corner of a block of cheese. Would the new figure be a polyhedron? Explain your answer. Check to see if the formula works.

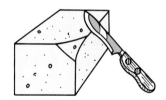

Problem Solving: Using the Strategies

Choose one or more of the strategies listed to help you solve each problem.

Choose the Operations
Guess and Check
Draw a Picture
Make a Table
Make an Organized List
Use Logical Reasoning
Work Backward
Solve a Simpler Problem
Find a Pattern

QUESTION
DATA
PLAN
ANSWER
CHECK

1. Arlene is building a fence around a rectangular garden 30 m long and 20 m wide. If she sets the posts 5 m apart, how many posts will she need for the fence?

2. The houses on one side of Gregory Street all have odd numbers. The first house number is 3, the second is 5, the third is 7, and so on. What is the fifteenth house number?

3. Jon now has 3 times as many records as Lou. If each of them gets 4 more records, Jon will have only twice as many as Lou. How many records does each have now?

4. Some of Graciela's friends went to a movie. After the movie, half of them went to a restaurant. Of those who did not go to the restaurant, half went for a walk and 4 went home. This left 5 to play miniature golf. How many went to the movie?

Give the name and symbol for each figure.

1.

2.

3.

4.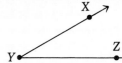

Give the measure of each angle and tell whether it is **acute**, **right**, or **obtuse**.

5.

6.

7.

Use the figure on the right for items 8 and 9.

8. Use a symbol to name a pair of parallel lines.

9. Use a symbol to name a pair of perpendicular lines.

Give the name that best describes each polygon.

10.
11.
12.
13.
14.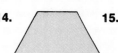
15.

16. Which segment in circle O is a radius?

17. Which segment is a chord that is not a diameter?

Use the figures in the graph for items 18–20.

18. Give the coordinates of the figure that is similar but not congruent to the figure whose coordinates are (0,0), (2,0), (2,2).

19. Name the figure that is congruent to figure D.

20. How many lines of symmetry has figure G?

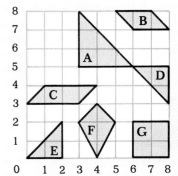

Use the figures at the right for items 21 and 22.

21. Give the name of each polyhedron.

22. Figure A has ▦ faces, ▦ edges, and ▦ vertices.

A   B

Another Look

Triangles

No sides ≅	At least 2 sides ≅	All sides ≅
Scalene	Isosceles	Equilateral

All angles < 90°	A 90° angle	An angle > 90°
Acute	Right	Obtuse

The sum of the angles of a triangle is 180°.

Quadrilaterals and Other Polygons

Trapezoid   Parallelogram

Rhombus   Rectangle

Square

Pentagon: 5 sides
Hexagon: 6 sides
Octagon: 8 sides

Circles

$\overline{RS}$ —Chord

$\overline{AB}$ —Diameter

$\overline{OB}$ —Radius

$\angle BOE$ —Central angle

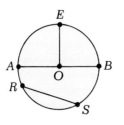

Write the words that best describe each triangle.

1.    2.

3. 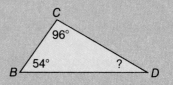   4.

5. What is the measure of ∠D?

Give the name of each polygon.

6.   7.   8.

9.   10.   11.

Complete each statement.

12. $\overline{PQ}$ is a __?__ of the circle.

13. $\overline{OR}$ is a __?__ of the circle.

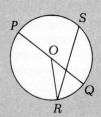

14. $\overline{RS}$ is a __?__ of the circle.

15. ∠QOR is a __?__ .

274

Enrichment

Geometric Constructions

To **construct** geometric figures, you use only a compass and the edge of a ruler. You do not use the ruler for measuring.

Compass

unmarked straight edge

Here are some simple construction methods.

Copying a Segment

Step 1

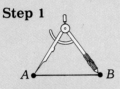

Given segment

Open your compass the length of the given segment.

Step 2

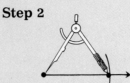

Draw a ray longer than the given segment. Use the opened compass to mark a copy of the segment on the ray.

Copying an Angle

Step 1

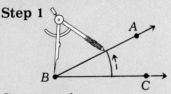

Given angle

Make an arc on the given angle.

Step 2

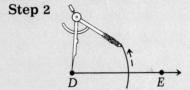

Draw a ray and draw an arc with the same radius on it.

Step 3

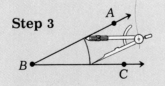

Measure the angle opening.

Step 4

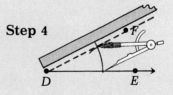

Mark the opening and draw the other side of the angle.

1. Use the idea of copying a segment to help you construct a triangle congruent to $\triangle RST$.

2. Use the idea of copying an angle to help you start with this side and construct a triangle similar to $\triangle RST$. (Remember: the angles of similar triangles are congruent.)

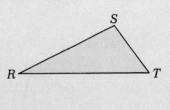

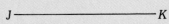

275

Cumulative Review

Give the missing units.

1. 400 cm = 4 __?__

   A mm   B dm

   C m   D not given

2. 700 mL = 0.7 __?__

   A kg   B l

   C kl   D not given

3. Write a fraction for 0.25.

   A $\frac{2}{5}$ B $\frac{1}{4}$

   C $\frac{3}{4}$ D not given

4. Write a decimal for $\frac{4}{5}$.

   A 0.45   B 0.75

   C 0.8   D not given

5. Write a mixed decimal for $\frac{3}{8}$.

   A $0.37\frac{1}{2}$ B $0.62\frac{1}{2}$

   C $0.24\frac{1}{2}$ D not given

Multiply or divide.

6. $\frac{2}{5} \times \frac{3}{4}$

   A $\frac{5}{9}$ B $\frac{6}{9}$

   C $\frac{3}{20}$ D not given

7. $7 \times \frac{5}{14}$

   A $\frac{12}{14}$ B $5\frac{1}{2}$

   C $\frac{35}{98}$ D not given

8. $1\frac{1}{2} \times 1\frac{1}{2}$

   A 3   B $2\frac{1}{4}$

   C $1\frac{1}{4}$ D not given

9. $\frac{4}{9} \div \frac{4}{6}$

   A $\frac{8}{15}$ B $\frac{1}{3}$

   C $\frac{2}{3}$ D not given

10. $\frac{5}{9} \div 10$

    A 18   B $5\frac{5}{9}$

    C $\frac{1}{18}$ D not given

11. $6\frac{1}{4} \div \frac{5}{8}$

    A $\frac{32}{35}$ B 10

    C 18   D not given

12. Bud traveled for 4 h 16 min one day and 3 h 35 min the next day. What was his total traveling time?

    A 7 h 51 min   B 7 h 15 min

    C 8 h 1 min   D not given

13. Shelly wants to make 8 dog collars. She needs a piece of leather $\frac{3}{8}$ m long for each collar. How much leather does she need?

    A 3 m   B $3\frac{3}{8}$ m

    C $2\frac{3}{8}$ m   D not given

11

Ratio and Proportion

Tina checked her map and compass and jogged northwest toward the next control point in the orienteering race. She picked her way through the bushes until she spotted the red and white control marker hanging from a tree. Quickly she stamped the symbol for that marker on her card, to prove she had been there. Now she had only one more marker to find before heading for the finish line. Tina decided to jog on dirt roads rather than to take the more direct route through thick woodlands. On the road she could cover 300 meters in 2 minutes, but through the woods it would take her 8 minutes to travel 300 meters.

So far Tina knew she had made good time in finding the control markers along the $4\frac{1}{2}$-kilometer route marked on her map. She realized she was just one of 17 people (9 girls and 8 boys) entered in the race. Still, she felt, her chances of winning were very good!

Ratio

A **ratio** is used to compare two quantities. In the long-distance bike race, 3 of the bikes are blue and 4 of the bikes are red.

The ratio of blue bikes to red bikes is

3 to 4

We show this ratio by writing $3:4$ or $\frac{3}{4}$.

Here are some other examples of how ratios are used. Write each ratio as a fraction.

1. In the long-distance bike race 3 out of every 5 riders are less than 18 years old. What is the ratio of **riders less than 18 to all riders?**

2. When the pedal on a bike has turned 3 times in fourth gear, the rear wheel has turned 7 times. What is the ratio of **pedal turns to wheel turns?**

3. Isabel bought 2 tickets for seats in the grandstand for $7. What is the ratio of **tickets to dollars?**

4. A map showing the race course compares centimeters on the map to kilometers on the course by using the scale $1:5$. What is the ratio of **centimeters to kilometers?**

5. Kyle traveled an average of 20 km for every hour while bike riding. This average speed is written 20 km/h. What is the ratio of **kilometers to hours?**

6. The refreshment stand sold 10 cases of beverages in 3 hours. What is the ratio of **cases to hours?**

Use the Bike Race Facts Sheet. Give each ratio as a fraction.

Bike Race Facts Sheet

Number of riders entered		36
Girls	15	
Boys	12	
Women	4	
Men	5	
Number of riders finishing		32
Total kilometers		75
Uphill	20	
Downhill	15	
Last year's winning time		3 h 20 min
This year's winning time		3 h 15 min

1. number of riders finishing to number entered

2. number of women entered to number of girls entered

3. number of girls entered to number of women entered

4. number of females entered to number of males entered

5. number of uphill kilometers to total number of kilometers

6. This year's winning time in minutes to last year's winning time in minutes.

Write these ratios as fractions.

7. Bike flags: 2 for $5. What is the ratio of flags to dollars?

8. Arturo rode 47 km in 2 h. What is the ratio of kilometers to hours?

9. Out of every 8 bikes in the race, 7 were 10-speed bikes. What is the ratio of all bikes to 10-speed bikes?

10. A bike travels 29 m for every 14 times the wheel turns. What is the ratio of meters to wheel turns?

11. 4 to 5

12. 7:10

13. 3 out of 7

14. 3 for every 2

15. 2 for 3

16. 1 of every 5

Think

Discovering a Pattern

Find the patterns in these ratios and give the next three ratios.

$$\frac{1}{2}, \frac{3}{1}, \frac{4}{3}, \frac{7}{4}, \blacksquare, \blacksquare, \blacksquare$$

$$\frac{3}{2}, \frac{7}{5}, \frac{17}{12}, \frac{41}{29}, \blacksquare, \blacksquare, \blacksquare$$

Math

Equal Ratios: Cross Products

At Madison School the ratio of students who walk to school to students who ride to school is $\frac{5}{6}$. In Sylvia's class the ratio is $\frac{10}{12}$. Are these ratios equal?

We can use either of these methods to decide.

Method 1
Thinking About Equivalent Fractions

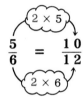

$$\frac{5}{6} = \frac{10}{12}$$

Since the fractions are equivalent, the ratios are equal.

We can find equal ratios the same way we find equivalent fractions.

Method 2
Using Cross Products

$$\frac{5}{6} \times \frac{10}{12} \rightarrow \begin{matrix} 60 \\ 60 \end{matrix}$$

Since these cross products are equal, the ratios are equal. When the cross products are not equal, the ratios are not equal.

$$\frac{5}{6} = \frac{10}{12} = \frac{15}{18} = \frac{20}{24} = \frac{25}{30}$$

(2 × 5) (3 × 5) (4 × 5) (5 × 5)
(2 × 6) (3 × 6) (4 × 6) (5 × 6)

Warm Up

1. Write four ratios equal to $\frac{2}{3}$.

2. Use equivalent fractions to decide whether or not these ratios are equal: $\frac{3}{5}, \frac{12}{20}$

3. Use the cross-products method to decide whether or not these ratios are equal: $\frac{4}{5}, \frac{7}{8}$

Practice Write four ratios in fraction form equal to each ratio given.

1. $\frac{1}{2}$
2. $\frac{3}{4}$
3. $\frac{5}{2}$
4. $\frac{10}{3}$
5. $\frac{3}{8}$

Think about equivalent fractions to decide whether the ratios are equal. Write **equal** or **not equal**.

6. $\frac{4}{5}, \frac{8}{10}$
7. $\frac{2}{5}, \frac{4}{9}$
8. $\frac{3}{2}, \frac{6}{4}$
9. $\frac{1}{3}, \frac{3}{9}$

Use cross products to decide whether the ratios are equal.

10. $\frac{3}{4}, \frac{5}{7}$
11. $\frac{2}{3}, \frac{6}{9}$
12. $\frac{1}{4}, \frac{5}{20}$
13. $\frac{2}{3}, \frac{7}{10}$

14. $\frac{5}{3}, \frac{7}{4}$
15. $\frac{3}{8}, \frac{12}{32}$
16. $\frac{8}{20}, \frac{6}{15}$
17. $\frac{3}{9}, \frac{5}{15}$

18. $\frac{6}{4}, \frac{7}{5}$
19. $\frac{8}{12}, \frac{6}{9}$
20. $\frac{7}{8}, \frac{4}{5}$
21. $\frac{5}{7}, \frac{4}{6}$

Mixed Applications

22. At Carver School 2 out of every 5 students walk to school. Is this ratio equal to 12 out of 30?

23. **DATA HUNT** Find the ratio of students in your school who take a bus to school to all students in your school. Is this ratio equal to the ratio for your class?

Skillkeeper

Give each product in lowest terms.

1. $\frac{3}{4} \times \frac{1}{2}$
2. $\frac{5}{6} \times \frac{2}{3}$
3. $\frac{3}{8} \times \frac{1}{4}$
4. $\frac{4}{9} \times \frac{2}{3}$
5. $\frac{1}{3} \times \frac{3}{10}$

6. $\frac{2}{5} \times \frac{2}{5}$
7. $\frac{4}{5} \times 15$
8. $\frac{9}{10} \times 2$
9. $1\frac{1}{2} \times 3$
10. $2\frac{1}{4} \times 1\frac{1}{3}$

Give each quotient in lowest terms.

11. $3 \div \frac{1}{2}$
12. $\frac{3}{4} \div \frac{3}{8}$
13. $\frac{2}{5} \div \frac{4}{9}$
14. $\frac{5}{12} \div 2$
15. $\frac{5}{6} \div \frac{1}{3}$

16. $15 \div \frac{2}{3}$
17. $\frac{7}{8} \div \frac{1}{4}$
18. $\frac{2}{5} \div 4$
19. $2\frac{1}{2} \div 1\frac{1}{3}$
20. $1\frac{1}{4} \div 1\frac{1}{2}$

Solving Proportions

A bakery uses 2 eggs for each 3 dozen rolls. How many eggs does the bakery need for 42 dozen rolls?

The ratio of eggs to dozens of rolls is 2 to 3. If we let the letter n represent the number of eggs for 42 dozen, we can write a ratio equal to $\frac{2}{3}$.

$$\frac{2}{3} = \frac{n}{42}$$

A statement that two ratios are equal is called a **proportion.**

| Write a proportion. | → | Write the cross-product equation. | → | Solve the equation. |

$$\begin{array}{c} \text{eggs} \rightarrow \\ \text{dozens} \rightarrow \\ \text{of rolls} \end{array} \frac{2}{3} = \frac{n}{42}$$

$$3 \times n = 2 \times 42$$

$$3 \times n = 84$$
$$n = 84 \div 3$$
$$n = 28$$

Check:

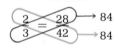
$$\frac{2}{3} = \frac{28}{42} \quad \begin{array}{l} \rightarrow 84 \\ \rightarrow 84 \end{array}$$

Since the cross products are equal, the ratios are equal when $n = 28$.

The bakery needs 28 eggs for 42 dozen rolls.

Other Examples

$$\frac{3}{4} = \frac{n}{52}$$

$4 \times n = 3 \times 52$
$4 \times n = 156$
$\qquad n = 156 \div 4,$ or 39

$$\frac{3}{5} = \frac{42}{n}$$

$3 \times n = 5 \times 42$
$3 \times n = 210$
$\qquad n = 210 \div 3,$ or 70

$$\frac{24}{n} = \frac{4}{3}$$

$4 \times n = 24 \times 3$
$4 \times n = 72$
$\qquad n = 72 \div 4,$ or 18

Warm Up Solve the proportions.

1. $\frac{1}{2} = \frac{n}{34}$

2. $\frac{5}{4} = \frac{20}{n}$

3. $\frac{3}{4} = \frac{48}{n}$

4. $\frac{n}{64} = \frac{3}{4}$

Practice Solve the proportions.

1. $\frac{1}{4} = \frac{n}{48}$

2. $\frac{4}{5} = \frac{n}{60}$

3. $\frac{3}{8} = \frac{n}{96}$

4. $\frac{2}{3} = \frac{n}{45}$

5. $\frac{4}{7} = \frac{n}{28}$

6. $\frac{3}{4} = \frac{24}{n}$

7. $\frac{1}{3} = \frac{16}{n}$

8. $\frac{3}{10} = \frac{30}{n}$

9. $\frac{5}{6} = \frac{75}{n}$

10. $\frac{6}{5} = \frac{72}{n}$

11. $\frac{n}{42} = \frac{15}{18}$

12. $\frac{n}{36} = \frac{45}{60}$

13. $\frac{n}{35} = \frac{96}{60}$

14. $\frac{n}{24} = \frac{65}{78}$

15. $\frac{n}{7} = \frac{33}{21}$

16. $\frac{16}{n} = \frac{24}{36}$

17. $\frac{27}{n} = \frac{51}{34}$

18. $\frac{18}{n} = \frac{21}{35}$

19. $\frac{45}{n} = \frac{20}{36}$

20. $\frac{57}{n} = \frac{19}{9}$

21. $\frac{8}{15} = \frac{n}{75}$

22. $\frac{11}{n} = \frac{110}{70}$

23. $\frac{n}{13} = \frac{30}{78}$

24. $\frac{7}{20} = \frac{56}{n}$

25. $\frac{14}{n} = \frac{70}{85}$

26. $\frac{42}{18} = \frac{7}{n}$

27. $\frac{n}{51} = \frac{2}{3}$

28. $\frac{5}{14} = \frac{n}{56}$

29. $\frac{33}{n} = \frac{11}{3}$

30. $\frac{12}{13} = \frac{84}{n}$

Mixed Applications

31. The bakery uses 3 apples for every 4 pieces of apple crisp. A club needs 72 pieces of apple crisp for a dinner party. How many apples will the bakery need to use?

32. The bakery uses 5 cups of flour for every 2 loaves of bread. How much flour is needed for 3 dozen loaves of bread? (Be careful!)

33. The ratio of the amount of wheat produced in China to the amount of wheat produced in the United States in a recent year was 3 to 4. If the United States produced 58,304 thousand tons that year, how many thousand tons were produced in China?

Think

Estimation

About how long would it take you to read a 400-page book? (Hint: Estimate the number of words you can read in 1 minute and the number of words on an average page.)

Math

Problem Solving: Using Data from a Story

QUESTION
DATA
PLAN
ANSWER
CHECK

Try these problems about story characters that either change sizes or are different size than usual!

Adapted from

Alice's Adventures in Wonderland

by Lewis Carroll

Alice came suddenly upon an open place, with a little house in it 4 feet high. "Whoever lives there," thought Alice, "it'll never do to come upon them in my normal size. Why, I should frighten them out of their wits!" So she began nibbling at the right-hand bit of wheatcake again and did not go near the house till she had brought herself down to 9 inches high.

1. What is Alice's reduced height in the story?

2. What is the height of the little house in inches?

3. What is the lowest-terms fraction for the ratio of Alice's reduced height to the height of the little house? (Use the answers to problems 1 and 2.)

For problems 4–6, suppose that Alice's normal height is 4 feet 6 inches.

4. What is the lowest-terms fraction for the ratio of Alice's reduced height to her normal height?

5. When Alice ate a small wheatcake from her left hand, she grew from her normal height to a height of 9 feet. If her normal shoe length was 6 inches and her shoes grew at the same rate as her height, how long would they be?

6. Suppose the little house suddenly grew so that the ratio of its new height to Alice's normal height was equal to the ratio of its old height to Alice's reduced height. How many inches high would the house be?

Adapted from

Gulliver's Travels

by Jonathan Swift

(Gulliver explains why he felt like a giant in the kingdom of the tiny Lilliputians!)

Two hundred seamstresses were employed to make me shirts. Their linen is usually 3 inches wide, while ours is 3 feet wide.

The seamstresses took my measure as I lay on the ground, with an inch-long ruler. Then they measured my thumb, and desired no more; for by a mathematical computation, twice round the thumb is once round the wrist.

7. Suppose the ratio of the width of Lilliputian linen to the width of our linen is equal to the ratio of a Lilliputian's height to a normal person's height. What is a Lilliputian's height? (Use 6 feet as "normal height.")

8. What is the ratio of the length of the Lilliputian ruler to the length of our customary foot ruler? Is this the same as the ratio of Lilliputian height to normal height? (Use data from problem 7.)

9. The Lilliputian horses were $4\frac{1}{2}$ inches high. How high would a comparable normal horse be? (Use a 1 to 12 ratio.)

10. DATA HUNT By how much does twice the distance around the base of your thumb differ from the distance around your wrist?

11. Strategy Practice One morning a Lilliputian starts out to climb a steep mountain. The distance to the top is 10 yards. Each day he climbs 2 yards. Each night he slips back 1 yard. On what day—the eighth, the ninth, or the tenth—does he reach the top?

Similar Figures

Original

Copy (enlarged)

A figure and a copy of the figure that is the same shape as the original suggest the idea of **similar figures.** One similar figure may be larger or smaller than the other, or it may be the same size.

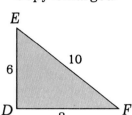

We write: $\triangle ABC \sim \triangle DEF$

We say: "$\triangle ABC$ is similar to $\triangle DEF$."

When triangles are similar:

- Matching angles are congruent. $\angle A \cong \angle D,\ \angle B \cong \angle E,\ \angle C \cong \angle F$
- The lengths of matching sides have equal ratios:

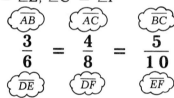

$$\frac{3}{6} = \frac{4}{8} = \frac{5}{10}$$

Warm Up

Are the pairs of figures similar? Write **yes** or **no.**

1.

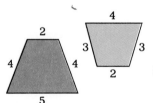

2.

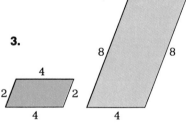

3.

4. Which triangle is similar to $\triangle PQR$? Write proportions showing that matching sides have equal ratios.

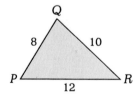

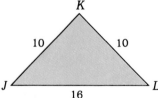

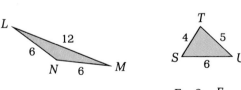

5. These two quadrilaterals are similar. Write proportions showing that matching sides have equal ratios. Include the length of the missing side.

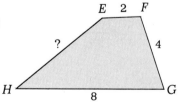

286

Practice Are the pairs of figures similar? Write **yes** or **no**.

1.
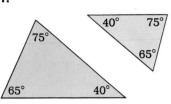

2.
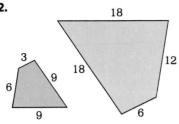

3.

The figures in each exercise are similar. Write
proportions showing that matching sides have equal ratios.
Include the missing side length.

4.
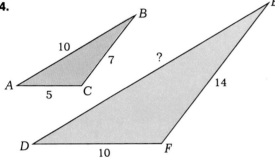

5.
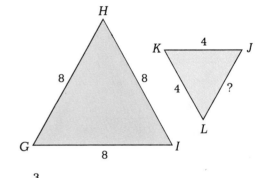

6.
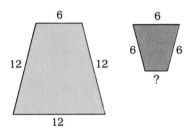

7.
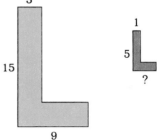

★ **8.** Copy this figure on a sheet of graph
paper. Then draw a similar figure
with sides twice as long on the
graph paper.

Using Proportions

How tall would George Washington be at Mount Rushmore if his whole body were carved in the rock? How long is the Statue of Liberty's hand? You can find out by solving proportions using your own body measurements.

Work with a group. You will need a meter stick or tape measure.

Part 1

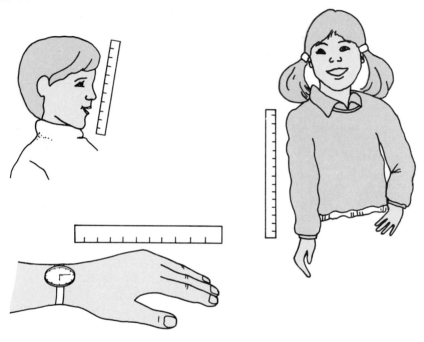

1. Measure the height of your head vertically from your chin to the top of your head. Then measure your height from head to toe. Write these measurements as a ratio.

2. The height of Washington's head at Mount Rushmore is 18 meters. Write a proportion using the ratio of your measurements to find out how tall Washington would be. Compare your results with those in your group. Why might your answers be different?

3. The height of the Statue of Liberty is 33.8 meters. Use the ratio of your measurements to find the height of her head. What would happen if you used the ratio of Washington's measurements? Why? Try it.

4. Complete the chart below with your own body measurements. Then use them to set up proportions and find the missing measurements for the Statue of Liberty. Work in a group to decide which measurements to compare for each ratio. For example, to find the length of her hand, would you compare her hand with her height or with the length of her head, finger, arm, or nose? Does it make a difference which measurements you compare?

Measurement	Me	Statue of Liberty
Head		
Height		33.8 meters
Length of index finger		2.4 meters
Length of hand		
Length of arm		
Distance across eye	0.032 meters	0.8 meters
Length of nose		

5. Talk about how you solved each proportion and whether the results seem reasonable. Which proportions were the most difficult to solve and which were the easiest? Why?

6. How could you determine how much taller the Statue of Liberty is than you are? Try to find out using several ratios.

Part 2

Experiment with measuring objects outdoors. Use the height of one member of your group and the length of his or her shadow to set up a ratio. Use this ratio to set up a proportion.

7. Find the height of trees, telephone poles, the school building, or other things by measuring the shadows these objects cast and solving proportions. Compare your group's proportions with those of another group. Explain how you solved them. What other things could you measure using proportions.

8. How does the time of day affect your proportions? Choose another time of day and describe how your proportions might be different if you had measured the shadows then. What do you think would be the best time of day for taking these measurements?

Making Scale Drawings

Suppose you wanted to rearrange the furniture in your classroom. How would you plan where to put each piece?

Interior decorators often start by making a floor plan. In a floor plan, everything is drawn to scale. The scale tells how many floor-plan units represent a number of actual units.

In this lesson, your group will make a floor plan of your classroom. On the floor plan, you can try different arrangements of furniture.

Work with a group. You will need rulers, graph paper, scissors, and tape.

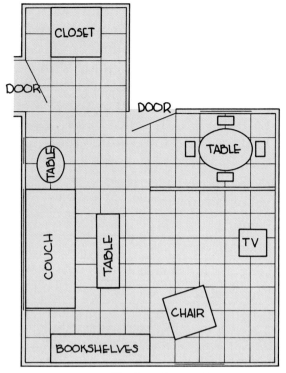

Scale 3 in : 20 ft

> 3 inches on the floor plan represents 20 feet in the room.

1. In your group, talk about how you will make your floor plan. List some scales you might use. Here are some things to consider:
   - What units of measure might you use in your scale?
   - About how large will your floor plan be for each scale you listed? Will the floor plan fit on one sheet of graph paper, or will you need to tape several sheets together?
   - How large would a desk be on each scale floor plan?

2. Based on your explorations, select a scale appropriate for planning the furniture arrangement.
   - Record your scale as a ratio of floor-plan units to actual units.
   - Measure the floor and the furniture in your classroom, and organize the measurements on a record sheet.

3. As a group, find the floor-plan measurement for each actual measurement on your record sheet.
   - Write these figures next to the corresponding actual measurements on your record sheet.
   - Discuss how you found the floor-plan measurements.

4. Use your record sheet to help you draw the floor plan on graph paper. How will you decide where to mark the doors and windows?

5. Decide with your group how to arrange each piece of furniture on the floor plan. Cut to scale, shade, and label a piece of paper to represent each piece of furniture.

6. Compare floor plans with other groups. Talk about the scales and the sizes of the plans.
   - What patterns do you notice?
   - Could you predict the size of a floor plan of your classroom if you knew only the scale?

7. Suppose you wanted to know the actual distance between the middle of a doorway and the farthest corner of the classroom. How could you use your floor plan to find this distance?
   - After each group finds a way, compare results.
   - Which group's results are closest to the actual distance? Discuss why this might be so.

8. Evaluate the advantages and disadvantages of the furniture arrangements on the different floor plans. Does the spacing of the furniture seem reasonable? Why or why not?

9. Imagine showing your math book to scale on each of the floor plans. Could you do it? If so, what size would it be?

10. What items in your classroom would be too small to show to scale on any of the floor plans? What items could you show on some floor plans but not on others? Explain your reasoning.

Map Scale to Estimate Distances

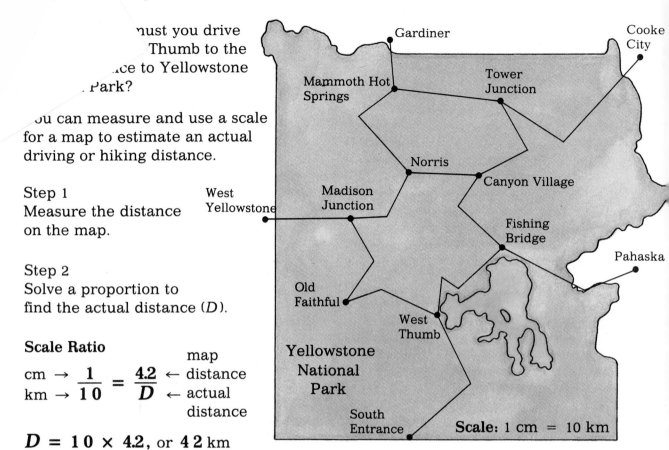

...ust you drive
...Thumb to the
...ce to Yellowstone
...Park?

...ou can measure and use a scale
for a map to estimate an actual
driving or hiking distance.

Step 1
Measure the distance
on the map.

Step 2
Solve a proportion to
find the actual distance (*D*).

Scale Ratio

cm → $\dfrac{1}{10}$ = $\dfrac{4.2}{D}$ ← map distance
km →   ← actual distance

$D = 10 \times 4.2$, or 42 km

Estimate these actual distances in Yellowstone National Park.
Measure to the nearest tenth of a centimeter.

1. Cooke City to Tower Junction

2. Pahaska through Fishing Bridge to Canyon Village

3. Mammoth Hot Springs through Madison Junction to Old
   Faithful

4. Fishing Bridge through West Thumb to Old Faithful

5. South Entrance through Old Faithful to West Yellowstone

6. The shortest route from Gardiner through Canyon
   Village to Fishing Bridge

★ 7. The shortest route from West Yellowstone through the
   park to Pahaska

QUESTION
DATA
PLAN
ANSWER
CHECK

Problem Solving: Mixed Practice

Solve.

1. A group of backpackers in Yellowstone hiked 402 km in 34 days. What was the average number of kilometers they hiked per day, to the nearest tenth of a kilometer?

2. The group started at Gardiner and hiked first to Old Faithful. They hiked 28 km farther than they would have if they had followed the road. Estimate how far they hiked. (Use the map and scale on page 292.)

3. One hiker weighed 56 kg. Her backpack weighed $\frac{1}{4}$ as much as she did. What was the total weight of the hiker and the backpack?

4. Yellowstone National Park has $\frac{3}{4}$ million hectares of land. Forest covers $\frac{4}{5}$ of this land. How many million hectares is covered by forest?

5. Yellowstone Lake is 2,357 m above sea level. Mt. Holmes is 3,162 m above sea level. How much higher than the lake must a hiker climb to reach the top of the mountain?

6. It is estimated that if you travel through Yellowstone by car, you see only 0.05 of the park. The park has an area of 8,983 km². How much of this area do you see if you travel by car?

7. The hikers saw 3 bison and 8 elk. They had heard that there were about 600 bison in the park. If the animals they saw represent the ratio of bison to elk, how many elk would you expect to be in the park?

8. **Strategy Practice** Suppose you can run 8 m/s (meters per second) and a grizzly bear can run 16 m/s. You are 50 m ahead of the bear when it begins to chase you. It will take you 6 s to reach your cabin. Can you get to your cabin before the bear catches up to you?

Problem Solving: Using the Strategies

QUESTION
DATA
PLAN
ANSWER
CHECK

Choose one or more of the strategies listed to help you solve each problem below.

Choose the Operations
Guess and Check
Draw a Picture
Make a Table
Make an Organized List
Use Logical Reasoning
Work Backward
Solve a Simpler Problem
Find a Pattern

1. Andy, Bea, Cathy, and Dino are having a 1-km bike race. If there are no ties, how many different orders of finish for their bike race are possible? (One possible order is Andy first, Bea second, Cathy third, and Dino fourth.)

2. Jack, Kris, Lacey, and Milt each play one of these musical instruments: clarinet, flute, trumpet, guitar. Neither Kris nor Lacey has ever played the guitar. Milt plays the trumpet. Kris played the flute but no longer does. Who plays which instrument?

3. Mrs. Doyle gave a test. The test had 15 questions worth 3 points each and 15 questions worth 5 points each. Lara answered 22 questions correctly and scored 86 points. How many of each type questions did Lara answer correctly?

4. A clown fell 16 m from a trapeze onto a special net. He bounced up $\frac{1}{2}$ as high as he fell each time until he bounced 1 m high and landed on the shoulders of another clown. Find the total distance the clown traveled.

Write these ratios as fractions.

1. 3 to 4　　**2.** 9:10　　**3.** 2 out of 5　　**4.** 7 for 5　　**5.** 9 of every 10

Copy and complete to make equal ratios.

6. $\frac{2}{3} = \frac{4}{\text{▓}} = \frac{6}{\text{▓}} = \frac{8}{\text{▓}} = \frac{10}{\text{▓}}$　　**7.** $\frac{5}{8} = \frac{\text{▓}}{16} = \frac{\text{▓}}{24} = \frac{\text{▓}}{32} = \frac{\text{▓}}{40}$　　**8.** $\frac{5}{4} = \frac{10}{\text{▓}} = \frac{15}{\text{▓}} = \frac{20}{\text{▓}} = \frac{25}{\text{▓}}$

Use cross products to decide whether the ratios are equal.
Write **equal** or **not equal**.

9. $\frac{5}{12}, \frac{3}{8}$　　**10.** $\frac{9}{12}, \frac{6}{8}$　　**11.** $\frac{7}{21}, \frac{3}{9}$　　**12.** $\frac{4}{5}, \frac{12}{20}$　　**13.** $\frac{5}{3}, \frac{25}{15}$　　**14.** $\frac{3}{16}, \frac{9}{48}$

Solve these proportions.

15. $\frac{3}{4} = \frac{n}{36}$　　**16.** $\frac{4}{5} = \frac{32}{n}$　　**17.** $\frac{n}{28} = \frac{15}{35}$　　**18.** $\frac{7}{n} = \frac{42}{60}$　　**19.** $\frac{27}{n} = \frac{15}{5}$

20. Write a proportion and solve it to find the height of the tower.

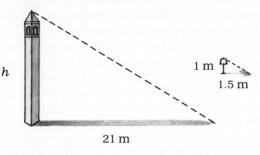

h

1 m

1.5 m

21 m

21. Measure the length of the picture. Then find the actual length of the camptosaurus.

Camptosaurus

Scale
5 cm : 3 m

22. Use the map scale and measurement to estimate the actual distance from Big Horn to Lead.

23. In a recent year there were 3 grizzly bears for every 8 black bears in Yellowstone National Park. There were about 400 black bears in the park. About how many grizzly bears were there?

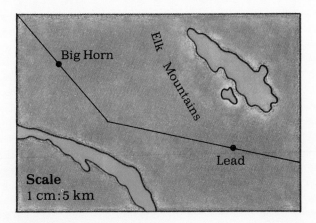

Big Horn

Elk Mountains

Lead

Scale
1 cm : 5 km

Another Look

Ratios compare quantities.

The ratio of saxophones to trombones is

2 to 3

We write: 2:3 or $\frac{2}{3}$

Equal ratios can be found by multiplying both numbers in the ratio by the same factor.

erasers
$$\frac{3}{10} \overset{\times 2}{=} \frac{6}{20} \overset{\times 3}{=} \frac{9}{30} \overset{\times 4}{=} \frac{12}{40}$$
cents

You can solve proportions by multiplying or dividing.

$$\frac{3}{4} \overset{\times 5}{=} \frac{n}{20} \qquad \frac{24}{32} \overset{\div 8}{=} \frac{3}{n}$$

$n = 15 \qquad n = 4$

OR you can use **cross products.**

$\frac{2}{3} = \frac{n}{36}$ ← These products are equal

$3 \times n = 2 \times 36$

$3 \times n = 72$

$n = 72 \div 3$, or 24

Write each ratio as a fraction.

1. The ratio of tubas to drums is 1 to 4.

2. A map used the scale 2 cm = 5 m.

3. At the meeting, 3 out of 4 people were adults.

4. You can buy 3 tickets for $5.

5. A dinosaur traveled 3 km in 1 hour.

6. Allison painted 4 chairs in 3 hours.

7. The ratio of cats to dogs is 3:8.

Copy and complete to make equal ratios.

8. $\frac{3}{8} = \frac{6}{\blacksquare} = \frac{9}{\blacksquare} = \frac{12}{\blacksquare} = \frac{15}{\blacksquare}$

9. $\frac{7}{10} = \frac{\blacksquare}{20} = \frac{\blacksquare}{30} = \frac{\blacksquare}{40} = \frac{\blacksquare}{50}$

10. $\frac{1}{4} = \frac{\blacksquare}{8} = \frac{2}{\blacksquare} = \frac{\blacksquare}{16} = \frac{4}{\blacksquare}$

11. $\frac{5}{6} = \frac{10}{\blacksquare} = \frac{\blacksquare}{18} = \frac{20}{\blacksquare} = \frac{\blacksquare}{30}$

Solve the proportions.

12. $\frac{n}{5} = \frac{8}{20}$

13. $\frac{10}{4} = \frac{5}{n}$

14. $\frac{15}{16} = \frac{n}{32}$

15. $\frac{3}{25} = \frac{9}{n}$

16. $\frac{45}{50} = \frac{n}{10}$

17. $\frac{16}{n} = \frac{24}{30}$

18. $\frac{1.5}{4.5} = \frac{n}{15}$

19. $\frac{12}{5} = \frac{4.8}{n}$

20. $\frac{n}{4} = \frac{6}{5}$

21. $\frac{7}{n} = \frac{3.5}{14}$

Enrichment

The Number π—An Important Ratio

The **circumference** (**C**) of a circle is the distance around the circle. The **diameter** (**d**) of a circle is the distance across the circle (through the center).

The **ratio of C to d** $\left(\dfrac{C}{d}\right)$ is a very important ratio!

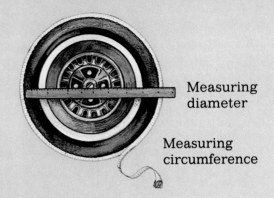

Measuring diameter

Measuring circumference

The circumference of each circle is given. Measure the diameter to the nearest centimeter and find $\dfrac{C}{d}$ as a decimal to the nearest hundredth.

1.

$C = 3.14$ cm

2.

$C = 9.42$ cm

3.

$C = 12.56$ cm

4.

$C = 15.7$ cm

5.

$C = 6.28$ cm

$$\frac{C}{d} = \pi \qquad \text{(the Greek letter pi, pronounced ``pie'')}$$

The decimal for the number π has been computed to over 500,000 decimal places.

$$\pi = 3.141592653589 \ldots$$

6. Using string or a tape measure to find the circumference and diameter of several circular objects (food or drink containers, auto or bike tires, records, bracelet, pots or pans, and the like). Find the ratio $\dfrac{C}{d}$ as a decimal to the nearest hundredth. Is $\dfrac{C}{d}$ for your measurements close to π?

Cumulative Review

Add or subtract.

1. $\frac{3}{8}$
$+\frac{3}{4}$
   A $1\frac{1}{4}$ **C** $\frac{3}{8}$
   B $1\frac{1}{8}$ **D** not given

2. $\frac{5}{9}$
$-\frac{1}{3}$
   A $\frac{2}{9}$ **C** $\frac{4}{9}$
   B $\frac{4}{6}$ **D** not given

3. $3\frac{1}{2}$
$+4\frac{5}{6}$
   A $7\frac{3}{4}$ **C** $8\frac{5}{6}$
   B $8\frac{1}{3}$ **D** not given

4. $6\frac{1}{10}$
$-4\frac{1}{2}$
   A $2\frac{3}{5}$ **C** $2\frac{1}{8}$
   B $1\frac{3}{5}$ **D** not given

What kind of triangle is it?

5.
   A scalene
   B isosceles
   C equilateral
   D not given

6.
   A acute
   B right
   C obtuse
   D not given

7. What is the measure of ∠C?
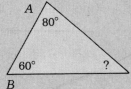
   A 90°
   B 50°
   C 40°
   D not given

8. Name the polygon.
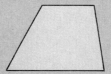
   A parallelogram
   B square
   C rhombus
   D not given

9. Name a diameter of circle O.

   A $\overline{DE}$
   B $\overline{OC}$
   C $\overline{AB}$
   D not given

10. Name a chord of circle O.
   A DE **B** OC
   C AO **D** not given

11. Name the space figure.

   A cone
   B cylinder
   C sphere
   D not given

12. Give the number of faces.

   A 4
   B 5
   C 6
   D not given

13. A recipe calls for $2\frac{1}{2}$ cups of apple juice and $1\frac{3}{4}$ cups of pineapple juice. What is the total amount of juice?
   A $4\frac{1}{4}$ cups   **B** $\frac{3}{4}$ cups
   C $3\frac{1}{4}$ cups   **D** not given

14. Ron has run $3\frac{4}{5}$ km. He wants to run a total of $6\frac{1}{2}$ km. How much farther must he run?
   A $2\frac{7}{10}$ km   **B** $10\frac{3}{10}$ km
   C $3\frac{3}{10}$ km   **D** not given

12

Percent

Justin stood quietly beside his grandmother and watched the giant combine cutting and threshing the wheat on his family's farm. He thought about the stories he had heard and the facts he had read about the ways farming had changed since his great grandfather began growing crops on the same fields many years ago. He found it hard to believe that a hundred years ago farmers had to work at least 64 hours for each acre of wheat they grew. Now they had to work only 5% as many hours to grow an acre of wheat! Justin wondered if such progress could continue in the future. Could future wheat production be increased by 25%? By 50%? Would such increases be needed to meet the needs of the world's growing population?

Percent

Work with a group. You will need 10-by-10 grids and a calculator.

Part 1

You can find percents in many situations, such as opinion polls, test scores, advertisements, and weather reports. How is your sense of percent?

1. With your group, estimate the following percents for your class. Approximately where would they fall on the number line?

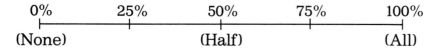

- Percent of students who are in the third grade
- Percent of students who walk to school
- Percent of students under 6 feet tall
- Percent of girls
- Percent of boys
- Percent of students who are in the sixth grade

2. Estimate each of the percents above for your school. Approximately where would they fall on the number line? How do they compare with the estimates for your class?

Part 2

Now take a look at some facts. These facts are not written as percents.

> **A** At Freeman School, 1 of 1,542 students $\left(\text{or } \frac{1}{1,542}\right)$ is from France.
>
> **B** On Tuesday, 163 of 652 students at Bay School $\left(\text{or } \frac{163}{652}\right)$ bought their lunches.
>
> **C** 77 of 3,850 students $\left(\text{or } \frac{77}{3,850}\right)$ are redheads.
>
> **D** 38 of 40 sixth-graders at Carmel School $\left(\text{or } \frac{38}{40}\right)$ take physical education.

3. Which of these facts are easy to picture in your mind? Which are hard to picture? Does everyone in your group agree? Sometimes writing a fraction as a percent makes a fact easier to understand. With your group, explore some ways to change fractions to percents.

4. You can use a grid to find the decimal and the percent for the first four fractions in the table.
   - Talk about how decimals and percents are related. Do you see why percent means "per one hundred"? Explain.
   - Compare your method for using the grid with other groups' methods.

Fraction	Decimal	Percent
$\frac{1}{4}$	0.25	25%
$\frac{1}{2}$		
$\frac{1}{5}$		
$\frac{1}{10}$		
$\frac{3}{4}$		
$\frac{2}{5}$		
$\frac{3}{20}$		

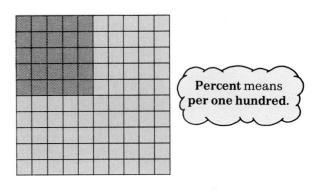

Percent means per one hundred.

5. Consider these questions as you complete the table.
   - What methods, other than the grid, could you use to change a fraction to a decimal and to a percent?
   - How might a calculator help? Experiment with the fractions in the table to see.

6. Do you think your method for using the calculator will work for any fraction?
   - Try $\frac{4}{7}$. What would you write for the decimal? For the percent? Discuss the different possibilities in your group.
   - Make up three fractions. Change them to decimals and percents and add them to the table.

7. Look again at the facts at the beginning of Part 2. Find the ones that were hard to picture.
   - Change these fractions to percents.
   - Are the facts easier to picture now? What would the percents look like on the grid?

Part 3

8. With your group, plan and take a poll.
   - Decide on a question that has a yes or no answer.
   - Predict the percent of yes answers.
   - Survey the people in your group or in your class.
   - Give the results of the poll as a fraction and as a percent.

Percents, Fractions, and Decimals

A recent survey gave this data about breakfast habits of persons in the United States.

Write the decimal and the fraction as percents.

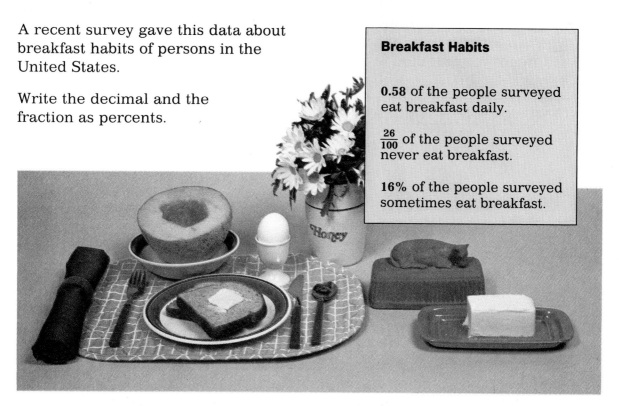

Breakfast Habits

0.58 of the people surveyed eat breakfast daily.

$\frac{26}{100}$ of the people surveyed never eat breakfast.

16% of the people surveyed sometimes eat breakfast.

Decimal   **0.58**
↓
Percent   **58**%

> Think 58 **hundredths.**

Fraction $\frac{26}{100}$
↓
Percent   **26**%

> % means **hundredths.**

Write the percent in the box as a decimal and as a fraction.

Percent   **16**%
↓
Decimal   **0.16**

> Think 16 **hundredths.**

Percent   **16**%
↓
Fraction $\frac{16}{100}$

> % means **hundredths.**

or $\frac{4}{25}$, reduced to lowest terms.

Warm Up   Write each decimal or fraction as a percent.

1. 0.35   **2.** $\frac{15}{100}$ **3.** $\frac{68}{100}$ **4.** 0.06   **5.** $\frac{2}{100}$

Write as lowest-terms fractions.   Write as decimals.

6. 25%   **7.** 75%   **8.** 6%   **9.** 35%   **10.** 100%   **11.** 50%

Practice Write each decimal as a percent.

1. 0.25   **2.** 0.67   **3.** 0.40   **4.** 0.12   **5.** 0.10   **6.** 0.09

7. 0.76   **8.** 0.50   **9.** 0.38   **10.** 0.19   **11.** 0.05   **12.** 0.98

Write each fraction as a percent.

13. $\frac{24}{100}$ **14.** $\frac{50}{100}$ **15.** $\frac{10}{100}$ **16.** $\frac{8}{100}$ **17.** $\frac{1}{100}$ **18.** $\frac{100}{100}$

Write each percent as a decimal.

19. 43%   **20.** 26%   **21.** 17%   **22.** 8%   **23.** 40%   **24.** 2%

25. 50%   **26.** 35%   **27.** 76%   **28.** 87%   **29.** 94%   **30.** 16%

Write each percent as a fraction in lowest terms.

31. 25%   **32.** 35%   **33.** 40%   **34.** 17%   **35.** 110%   **36.** 4%

37. 90%   **38.** 2%   **39.** 45%   **40.** 30%   **41.** 23%   **42.** 65%

Mixed Applications

43. In the survey of breakfast habits only 0.24 of the persons felt they weighed what they should. What percent is this?

45. In a different survey of eating habits, $\frac{4}{5}$ of the persons surveyed said they eat their biggest meal of the day in the evening. What percent of those surveyed eat their biggest meal at some other time?

44. Write each fraction as a percent. Do the fractions add to $\frac{100}{100}$ (100%)?

Eating Habits of People in the United States		
Snack daily	Sometimes snack	Never snack
$\frac{38}{100}$	$\frac{27}{100}$	$\frac{35}{100}$

Skillkeeper

Write each ratio as a fraction.

1. 7 to 9   **2.** 5:11   **3.** 8 out of 12   **4.** 3 for 2   **5.** 3 of 10

6. 5 for every 3   **7.** 6 to 13   **8.** 9:14   **9.** 6 per 4   **10.** 15 to 7

Copy and complete to make equal ratios.

11. $\frac{4}{25} = \frac{\blacksquare}{100}$ **12.** $\frac{13}{50} = \frac{\blacksquare}{100}$ **13.** $\frac{17}{20} = \frac{\blacksquare}{100}$ **14.** $\frac{\blacksquare}{100} = \frac{75}{50}$ **15.** $\frac{\blacksquare}{10} = \frac{70}{100}$

Writing Fractions and Decimals as Percents

Since "pure" gold is 24 karats, 18 karat gold is $\frac{18}{24}$ or $\frac{3}{4}$ pure gold.

What percent of an 18 karat gold ring is gold?

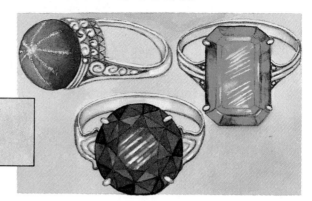

SALE!
18 Karat Gold
Birthstone Rings

Here are two ways to find the percent.

Finding an equivalent fraction with denominator 100

$$\frac{3}{4} = \frac{75}{100}$$

× 25

× 25

Finding a decimal or mixed decimal by dividing

$$
\begin{array}{r}
0.75 \\
4\overline{)3.00} \\
2\,8 \\
\hline
2\,0 \\
2\,0 \\
\hline
0
\end{array}
$$

An 18 karat gold ring is 75% gold.

Other Examples

$\frac{5}{4} = \frac{125}{100} = 125\%$

Sometimes we must first reduce to lowest terms.

$\frac{2}{3} \rightarrow 3\overline{)2.00}\,\,^{0.66\frac{2}{3}} \rightarrow 66\frac{2}{3}\%$

$$
\begin{array}{r}
1\,8 \\
\hline
2\,0 \\
1\,8 \\
\hline
2
\end{array}
$$

$1.35 = 1\frac{35}{100} = \frac{135}{100} = 135\%$

$\frac{6}{8} = \frac{3}{4} = \frac{75}{100} = 75\%$

Warm Up
Find an equivalent fraction with denominator 100. Then write the fraction as a percent.

1. $\frac{1}{2}$ 2. $\frac{1}{4}$ 3. $\frac{3}{5}$ 4. $\frac{7}{10}$ 5. $\frac{5}{4}$ 6. $\frac{13}{20}$

Divide to find a decimal or a mixed decimal for each fraction. Then write the decimal as a percent.

7. $\frac{2}{5}$ 8. $\frac{1}{3}$ 9. $\frac{4}{3}$ 10. $\frac{3}{8}$ 11. $\frac{5}{6}$ 12. $\frac{7}{4}$

Practice Find an equivalent fraction with denominator 100. Then write a percent for each fraction.

1. $\frac{2}{5}$
2. $\frac{3}{10}$
3. $\frac{2}{4}$
4. $\frac{1}{5}$
5. $\frac{9}{20}$
6. $\frac{12}{25}$

7. $\frac{3}{50}$
8. $\frac{19}{20}$
9. $\frac{17}{25}$
10. $\frac{6}{5}$
11. $\frac{24}{20}$
12. $\frac{12}{10}$

Reduce the fraction to lowest terms. Then find an equivalent fraction with denominator 100 and write the percent.

13. $\frac{6}{30}$
14. $\frac{9}{12}$
15. $\frac{8}{16}$
16. $\frac{14}{20}$
17. $\frac{6}{15}$
18. $\frac{15}{12}$

Divide to find a decimal or mixed decimal for each fraction. Then write the decimal as a percent.

19. $\frac{5}{8}$
20. $\frac{3}{5}$
21. $\frac{1}{6}$
22. $\frac{6}{5}$
23. $\frac{7}{8}$
24. $\frac{5}{3}$

25. $\frac{3}{16}$
26. $\frac{7}{12}$
27. $\frac{3}{7}$
28. $\frac{7}{6}$
29. $\frac{7}{5}$
30. $\frac{7}{4}$

Mixed Applications

31. White gold used to make jewelry is often $\frac{4}{5}$ pure gold. What percent of pure gold is this?

32. If pure gold is 24 karats, what percent of a 10-karat ring is pure gold?

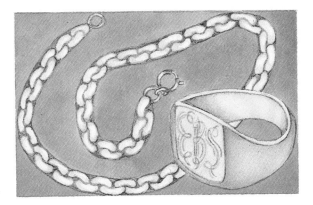

33. Find a percent for each of these fractions. Round to the nearest hundredth.

$\frac{57}{76}, \frac{147}{200}, \frac{51}{85}, \frac{51}{136}, \frac{95}{114}, \frac{347}{689}$

Think

Shape Perception

What percent of the large square is shaded red? How could you show someone that your answer is correct?

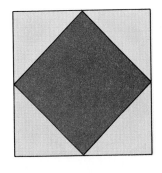

Math

More About Percents, Fractions, and Decimals

A tennis player won $87\frac{1}{2}\%$ of her games during a season. What fraction of the games did she win?

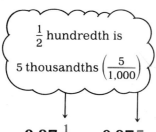

$\frac{1}{2}$ hundredth is 5 thousandths $\left(\frac{5}{1,000}\right)$

$$87\frac{1}{2}\% = 0.87\frac{1}{2} = 0.875$$

$$0.875 = \frac{875}{1,000} = \frac{7}{8}$$

The tennis player won $\frac{7}{8}$ of her games.

Other Examples

$$125\% = \frac{125}{100} = \frac{5}{4} = 1\frac{1}{4}$$

$$125\% = \frac{125}{100} = 1\frac{25}{100} = 1.25$$

$$12\frac{1}{2}\% = 0.12\frac{1}{2} = 0.125 = \frac{125}{1,000} = \frac{1}{8}$$

Practice   Write a decimal and a lowest-terms fraction for each percent.

1. $37\frac{1}{2}\%$	**2.** 150%	**3.** 10%	**4.** 5%	**5.** 120%
6. $27\frac{1}{2}\%$	**7.** 75%	**8.** $62\frac{1}{2}\%$	**9.** 60%	**10.** 110%
11. 175%	**12.** $12\frac{1}{2}\%$	**13.** 8%	**14.** $24\frac{1}{2}\%$	**15.** 30%
16. $22\frac{1}{2}\%$	**17.** 15%	**18.** $87\frac{1}{2}\%$	**19.** 90%	**20.** 145%
21. 55%	**22.** 160%	**23.** 45%	**24.** $112\frac{1}{2}\%$	**25.** 70%

More Practice, page 443, Set B

Problem Solving: Estimation with Percents

The circle graphs show the results of a poll on students' TV preferences. The first graph shows that about $\frac{1}{4}$ of the students named Channel 5 as their favorite. For the problems below, choose the best estimate for the percent described.

Favorite TV Channel

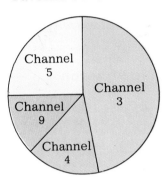

1. About what percent preferred Channel 3?
   A 47%   **B** 55%   **C** 40%

2. About what percent named Channel 4?
   A 15%   **B** $37\frac{1}{2}$%   **C** 25%

3. About what percent of the students liked sports programs best?
   A 25%   **B** 40%   **C** $33\frac{1}{3}$%

Favorite Kind of TV Program

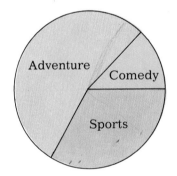

4. About what percent chose adventure?
   A 48%   **B** 55%   **C** 70%

5. About what percent like comedy best?
   A 20%   **B** 5%   **C** $12\frac{1}{2}$%

6. About what percent of the students like watching football best?
   A 15%   **B** 25%   **C** $37\frac{1}{2}$%

7. About what percent prefer watching soccer?
   A 28%   **B** $12\frac{1}{2}$%   **C** 5%

Favorite TV Sports Program

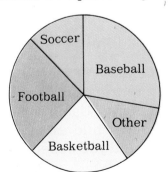

8. What is your estimate of the total percent for basketball and baseball?
   A 50%   **B** 75%   **C** 36%

9. **Strategy Practice**   A TV set was left on 6 hours longer on Monday than on Tuesday. It was on only $\frac{1}{3}$ as long on Tuesday as on Monday. How long was it on each day?

Finding a Percent of a Number

A survey of 32 children showed that 25% of them were afraid of thunder and lightning. How many of the children were afraid of thunder and lightning?

Here are two ways to find a percent of a number.

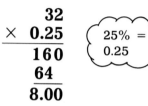

Using a fraction

$$25\% = \frac{25}{100} = \frac{1}{4}$$

$$\frac{1}{4} \times 32 = 8$$

Using a decimal

$$\begin{array}{r} 32 \\ \times\ 0.25 \\ \hline 160 \\ 64 \\ \hline 8.00 \end{array}$$

25% = 0.25

8 of the 32 children were afraid of thunder and lightning.

Practice   Find the percent of each number. Use a fraction.

1. 50% of 120   2. 25% of 20   3. 75% of 40   4. 10% of 150

5. 20% of 35   6. 40% of 45   7. 5% of 80   8. 60% of 500

Find the percent of each number. Use a decimal.

9. 19% of 26   10. 43% of 85   11. 76% of 95   12. $12\frac{1}{2}$% of 72

13. 3% of 32   14. 87% of 24   15. 24% of 36   16. 11% of 20

Find the percent of each number.

17. 31% of 90   18. 78% of 100   19. 25% of 240   20. $12\frac{1}{2}$% of 64

21. 45% of 180   22. 67% of 250   23. 13% of 86   24. $62\frac{1}{2}$% of 720

Mixed Applications

25. Only 8% of a large group of children said they were afraid of heights. Using this percent, how many children in a class of 25 would you expect to be afraid of heights?

26. **DATA BANK**   What is the most common fear among adults in the United States? How many people out of 3,000 have this fear? (See the Data Bank, page 425.)

Percent: Mental Math and Estimation

Mental math can sometimes be used to find a percent of a number.

For example, replacing 25% with the fraction $\frac{1}{4}$ often makes the computation easy.

$$\boxed{\begin{array}{l} \textbf{25\% of 32} \\[6pt] \dfrac{\textbf{1}}{\textbf{4}} \textbf{ of 32, or 8} \end{array}}$$

Other percents that can be replaced by fractions to find compatible numbers for easy computation are: $50\% = \frac{1}{2}$, $33\frac{1}{3}\% = \frac{1}{3}$, $20\% = \frac{1}{5}$, and $10\% = \frac{1}{10}$.

Try these. Use mental math.

1. 20% of 35

2. 10% of 60

3. 25% of 28

4. 50% of 22

5. $33\frac{1}{3}$ % of 24

6. 50% of 48

7. 20% of 25

8. 10% of 40

9. 25% of 36

10. 20% of 15

11. 10% of 30

12. $33\frac{1}{3}$ % of 27

This mental math method can be used to estimate a percent of a number. For example, **26% of 32** can be estimated by finding **25% of 32**.

Estimate.

13. 26% of 28

14. 19% of 25

15. 48% of 82

16. 35% of 21

17. 52% of 18

18. 24% of 44

19. 9% of 70

20. 18% of 45

21. 53% of 120

22. 21% of 55

23. 32% of 69

24. 27% of 48

Skillkeeper

Solve the proportions.

1. $\frac{5}{8} = \frac{15}{n}$

2. $\frac{8}{6} = \frac{n}{3}$

3. $\frac{20}{4} = \frac{n}{1}$

4. $\frac{25}{30} = \frac{5}{n}$

5. $\frac{n}{40} = \frac{7}{4}$

6. $\frac{18}{21} = \frac{n}{7}$

7. $\frac{14}{20} = \frac{7}{n}$

8. $\frac{2}{3} = \frac{n}{30}$

9. $\frac{12}{7} = \frac{24}{n}$

10. $\frac{5}{n} = \frac{35}{21}$

Find the products.

11.	12.	13.	14.	15.
25	80	72	14	5.7
× 0.6	× 0.25	× 0.12	× 1.8	× 0.34

Problem Solving: Finding Interest

Interest is a fee paid for the use of someone's money.

Banks and savings and loan companies pay you interest for using the money you deposit in a savings account.

The interest paid on $125 for 1 year at 8% per year is $10.

Eversafe Savings and Loan Co.

DATE	DEPOSIT (+) WITHDRAWAL (−)	INTEREST	BALANCE
1/1/95	+ $125		
1/1/96		$10.00	$135.00

$$\begin{array}{ccccc}
\text{Rate of} & \times & \text{Amount} & = & \text{Interest} \\
\text{Interest} & & \text{Deposited} & & \\
\downarrow & & \downarrow & & \downarrow \\
8\% & \times & \$125 & = & \$10
\end{array}$$

$$\begin{array}{r}
\$125 \\
\times \; 0.08 \\
\hline
\$10.00
\end{array}$$

You pay interest when you borrow money to buy something.

STEREO—$450

Buy Now!
Pay next year.
Interest rate 12%

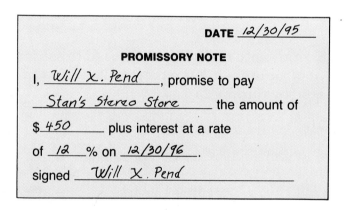

DATE _12/30/95_

PROMISSORY NOTE

I, _Will X. Pend_, promise to pay _Stan's Stereo Store_ the amount of $_450_ plus interest at a rate of _12_ % on _12/30/96_.

signed _Will X. Pend_

$$\begin{array}{ccccc}
\text{Rate of} & \times & \text{Amount} & = & \text{Interest} \\
\text{Interest} & & \text{Borrowed} & & \\
\downarrow & & \downarrow & & \downarrow \\
12\% & & \$450 & = & \$54
\end{array}$$

$$\begin{array}{r}
\$450 \\
\times \; 0.12 \\
\hline
900 \\
450 \\
\hline
\$54.00
\end{array}$$

The interest charge for 1 year on a $450 loan at 12% per year is $54.

Find the interest for 1 year on the following amounts.

1. Amount Deposited: $50
Interest Rate: 10%
Interest:

2. Amount Borrowed: $300
Interest Rate: 15%
Interest:

3. Amount Deposited: $425
Interest Rate: 9%
Interest:

4. Amount Borrowed: $1,500
Interest Rate: 12%
Interest:

Solve these problems about interest on saving and loans.

1. Marcus deposited $50 in a savings account. The rate of interest was 8% per year. How much interest did he receive at the end of a year?

2. The bank paid Joan 10% interest on $280 she deposited in a savings account. How much money did the bank pay Joan for using her money for 1 year?

3. Sam borrowed $500 to buy a TV set. The interest rate was 12%. How much interest must Sam pay at the end of a year?

4. Mr. Cole borrowed $4,000 to help buy a new car. At a 9% rate, how much interest will he pay to borrow this money for 1 year?

5. Esperanza deposited $1000 in a savings account that paid interest at a 7% rate. How much money will be in the account after the interest is paid at the end of 1 year?

6. Joey borrowed $250 at 14% interest. How much interest will he owe at the end of a year? How much will he owe altogether?

7. The Robinsons deposited $2,500 in a savings account that pays interest at the rate of 11%. If they leave the money in the account for a year, what will the total amount in their account be at the end of the year, after the interest has been paid?

8. Ms. Barents borrowed $9,500 to use for home improvements. The interest rate was 12%. How much did she have to pay altogether if she paid back the loan at the end of the year?

9. **DATA HUNT** How much interest would you receive if you deposited $500 in a local bank or savings and loan company for 1 year?

10. **Strategy Practice** Pedro has 6 coins. One third of his coins are dimes. The dimes are $\frac{1}{4}$ of the total value of the coins. What coins does Pedro have?

Problem Solving:
Using Data From an Advertisement

The **discount** is an amount subtracted from the regular price of an item.

The **sale price** is the cost of an item after the discount has been subtracted.

What is the sale price of the Super Group album?

THE SUPER GROUP
Regular Price $6.95
SALE!
20% off *Regular Price*

Step 1. Find the amount of discount (20% of $6.95).

$0.20 \times \$6.95 = \$1.39 \leftarrow$ **discount**

Step 2. Subtract the discount from the regular price.

$\$6.95 - \$1.39 = \$5.56 \leftarrow$ **sale price**

Answer the questions about the ads below.

1. What is the sale price?

CALCULATOR SALE!
20% OFF
Regular Price: $25

2. What is the sale price?

10% discount on all books!
Regular Price $8

3. Which sale price is less? How much less?

$35 watch
Reduced 20%
Bargain Days

$40 watch
Reduced 25%
Special Sale

4. What is the total sale price of the camera and case?

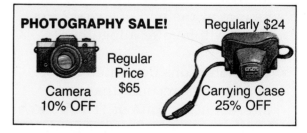

PHOTOGRAPHY SALE!
Regular Price $65
Camera 10% OFF
Regularly $24
Carrying Case 25% OFF

5. Strategy Practice Narissa spent half of her money to buy a record album. Then she spent $4.54 for a record cleaning kit. After that she still had $8.32. With how much money did she start?

Problem Solving: Mixed Practice

Solve these problems about bees and honey.
Use the 5-Point Checklist (page 8).

1. A colony of bees collects 180 kg of nectar a year. The weight of the honey that can be made from this nectar is 25% of the weight of the nectar. How many kilograms of honey is this?

2. The smallest honeybee is only 10 mm long. The largest is 190% as long as the smallest. How long is the largest honeybee?

3. A recipe for honey-nut bread uses $\frac{1}{2}$ cup of honey. How much honey is used to make $2\frac{1}{2}$ times this recipe?

4. There are about 80,000 bees in an average hive. About 2% of these bees are scouts who look for the sources of nectar in the area. How many scouts are in an average hive?

5. An average colony of bees produces about 45 kg of honey a year. The bees eat about 55% of this amount. How many kilograms of honey are left for human use?

6. Some colonies of bees produce as much as 48 kg of honey a year. They fly 70,000 km to collect nectar for 1 kg of honey. How many kilometers do they fly to make an average month's supply of honey?

7. Beekeepers in the United States sell about 93,400,000 kg of honey and beeswax each year. Only 2% of this amount is beeswax. Find how much honey is sold each year.

8. **Strategy Practice** A bee starts at its hive and flies to a flower 100 m away. After each flight it returns to the hive and flies to a new flower half as far away as the one before. How far does it travel if the last flower is 12.5 m away?

Mixed Skills Practice

Computation

Find the answers.

1.
$$\begin{array}{r} 88,975 \\ +\ 9,986 \\ \hline \end{array}$$

2.
$$\begin{array}{r} 27,302 \\ -\ 18,753 \\ \hline \end{array}$$

3. $67\overline{)42,547}$

4.
$$\begin{array}{r} 45.365 \\ +\ 389.46 \\ \hline \end{array}$$

5.
$$\begin{array}{r} 35.23 \\ -\ 29.567 \\ \hline \end{array}$$

6.
$$\begin{array}{r} 57.236 \\ \times\ 8.6 \\ \hline \end{array}$$

7.
$$\begin{array}{r} 6.362 \\ \times\ 0.085 \\ \hline \end{array}$$

8. $7.3\overline{)261.705}$

9.
$$\begin{array}{r} 15\frac{3}{5} \\ +\ 27\frac{5}{6} \\ \hline \end{array}$$

10. $\dfrac{n}{45} = \dfrac{4}{9}$ $n = ?$

11. $3\frac{3}{4} \times 6\frac{2}{3}$

12. 39% of 125

13.
$$\begin{array}{r} 14\frac{2}{3} \\ -\ 11\frac{7}{8} \\ \hline \end{array}$$

14. $\frac{5}{8} \times \frac{7}{12}$

15. $5\frac{1}{4} \div 2\frac{1}{2}$

16.
$$\begin{array}{r} 8,346 \\ \times\ 574 \\ \hline \end{array}$$

17.
$$\begin{array}{r} 57,239 \\ 8,562 \\ +\ 345,948 \\ \hline \end{array}$$

18. $0.08\overline{)0.056}$

19. $\frac{3}{5} \div \frac{2}{3}$

20. $\frac{5}{8} \times 168$

Mental Math

Write only the answers.

21. $9,000 + 8,000$

22. $3,400 - 600$

23. 30×900

24. $5,600 \div 80$

25. $524 + 263$

26. $900 - 598$

27. $9 + 346$

28. 5×35

29. $8 \times 3\frac{1}{4}$

30. 4.78×10

31. 36.074×100

32. $9.251 \times 1,000$

33. $56.4 \div 10$

34. $98.2 \div 100$

35. $9,357.8 \div 1,000$

36. $8.5 + 9.5$

Estimation

Estimate.

37. $8.63 + 5.96$

38. $57.58 - 34.94$

39. 6.87×4.38

40. $47.83 \div 5.98$

41. $532 \div 6$

42. $368 \div 5$

43. 49% of 24

44. 26% of 84

45. $745 + 483 + 856$

46. $5.75 + 6.27 + 3.26$

47. $4.46 + 6.38 + 5.59 + 9.78$

48. $9,827 + 10,078 + 9,605$

49. $5.13 + 4.86 + 4.94 + 5.17$

50. $1,836 + 2,042 + 1,836 + 2,145 + 2,234$

Applied Problem Solving

You are going to start a savings account at the Worthington Federal Bank. Which kind of savings account will you choose?

Super Saver Account
Interest Rate—6% per year

Power Account
Interest Rate—7% per year
$100 minimum balance
(Under $100—5%)

Some Things to Consider

- You have $150 to put in a savings account now.

- You may want to withdraw $60 next week for a pair of skates.

- If you withdraw $60 next week and deposit no more money the rest of the year, the interest is calculated as if you had $90 in the bank all year.

- You get a free blanket if you start a Super-Saver Account and a free calculator if you start a Power Account.

Some Questions to Answer

1. How much interest would you earn if you had $150 in the Power Account for the entire year?

2. How much interest would you earn if you had $150 in the Super-Saver Account for the entire year?

3. How much interest would you earn from each account if you withdrew $60 for skates and did not deposit more money?

What Is Your Decision?

Will you start a Super-Saver Account or a Power Account?

315

Problem Solving: Using the Strategies

Use one or more of the **strategies** listed to solve each problem below.

Choose the Operations
Guess and Check
Draw a Picture
Make a Table
Make an Organized List
Use Logical Reasoning
Work Backward
Solve a Simpler Problem
Find a Pattern

1. Nan found on a map that Bay City and Allenton are 742 km apart. She also noticed that Canton is 459 km from Bay City and Dodge is 217 km from Allenton. All the towns are on the same highway. Dodge is between Allenton and Canton, and Canton is between Dodge and Bay City. How far apart are Dodge and Bay City?

2. Nina bought a tape for $6.98 and a book that cost 3 times as much as the tape. Then she had $7.45 left. How much money did she have before she bought the tape and the book?

3. Mr. Clemens used the letters A, B, C, and D to identify the different sections in an auditorium (for example: AA, AB, and so on). If each section is described by 2 letters, how many different sections can be identified?

4. Jeff had 3 times as many points in a game as Teri. The total of their points was only 4 below the record two-person score of 80 for the game. How many points did each player have?

Chapter Review-Test

Write the ratio, fraction, decimal, and percent to show
how much is shaded.

1. ratio   **2.** fraction   **3.** decimal   **4.** percent

Write each decimal or fraction as a percent.

5. 0.34   **6.** $\frac{74}{100}$ **7.** 0.08   **8.** $\frac{9}{100}$ **9.** $\frac{36}{100}$

Write each percent as a decimal.

10. 43%   **11.** 99%   **12.** 50%   **13.** 5%   **14.** 24%

Write each percent as a fraction in lowest terms.

15. 25%   **16.** 50%   **17.** 75%   **18.** 20%   **19.** 80%

Write a percent for each fraction by finding an equivalent fraction.

20. $\frac{3}{5}$ **21.** $\frac{1}{10}$ **22.** $\frac{7}{4}$ **23.** $\frac{9}{20}$ **24.** $\frac{6}{25}$

Write a percent for each fraction by dividing to find a decimal.

25. $\frac{1}{12}$ **26.** $\frac{3}{16}$ **27.** $\frac{2}{3}$ **28.** $\frac{5}{6}$ **29.** $\frac{3}{8}$

30. Write a decimal and a lowest-terms fraction for $62\frac{1}{2}\%$ and 120%.

Find the percent of each number.

31. 75% of 16   **32.** 23% of 95   **33.** 30% of 200   **34.** 80% of 650

Estimate

35. 49% of 80   **36.** 26% of 28   **37.** 18% of 50

38. How much interest will Tim receive from a deposit of $300 at
a 9% interest rate for 1 year?

39. What is the sale price of a $44-pair of binoculars with a
25% discount?

40. Honey is 20% water. How many kilograms of water are in the
45 kg of honey a colony of bees might produce in a year?

Another Look

Percent means **per hundred**.

$$55\% = \frac{55}{100} = \frac{11}{20}$$

$$\frac{3}{5} = \frac{60}{100} = 60\%$$

$$\frac{5}{8} \rightarrow 8\overline{)5.0\,0\,0}^{\,0.6\,2\,5} \rightarrow 62\tfrac{1}{2}\%$$

$$175\% = \frac{175}{100} = \frac{7}{4} = 1\tfrac{3}{4}$$

Think 72 hundredths

$$72\% = 0.72$$

Think 8 hundredths

$$0.08 = 8\%$$

$\tfrac{1}{2}$ hundredth = 5 thousandths

$$62\tfrac{1}{2}\% = 0.625$$

Finding a percent of a number

1. Using fractions

25% of $48 = \tfrac{1}{4} \times 48$, or 12

2. Using decimals

24% of 48 is 11.52

$$\begin{array}{r} 48 \\ \times\ 0.24 \\ \hline 192 \\ 96 \\ \hline 11.52 \end{array}$$

Write a lowest-terms fraction for each percent.

1. 23%   **2.** 45%   **3.** 50%

4. 17%   **5.** 6%   **6.** 25%

7. 150%   **8.** 75%   **9.** $87\tfrac{1}{2}\%$

Write a percent for each fraction.

10. $\frac{1}{5}$ **11.** $\frac{1}{4}$ **12.** $\frac{2}{5}$

13. $\frac{3}{4}$ **14.** $\frac{5}{8}$ **15.** $\frac{3}{25}$

Write a decimal for each percent.

16. 67%   **17.** 13%   **18.** 8%

19. 125%   **20.** 1%   **21.** $37\tfrac{1}{2}\%$

Write a percent for each decimal.

22. 0.38   **23.** 0.02   **24.** 0.50

25. 0.80   **26.** 1.75   **27.** 0.75

Find the percent of the number.

28. 50% of 50   **32.** 8% of 120

29. 25% of 100   **33.** 75% of 24

30. 10% of 90   **34.** $12\tfrac{1}{2}\%$ of 240

31. 27% of 58   **35.** 125% of 500

Enrichment

Using a Calculator to Explore Number Patterns

A calculator helps you make difficult calculations quickly. It can also help you discover number patterns. Try these. Use your calculator!

---

1. Multiply. List your answers in a column.

$$
\begin{array}{r}
142,857 \\
\times \quad\quad 1 \\
\hline
\end{array}
\qquad
\begin{array}{r}
142,857 \\
\times \quad\quad 2 \\
\hline
\end{array}
\qquad
\begin{array}{r}
142,857 \\
\times \quad\quad 3 \\
\hline
\end{array}
$$

$$
\begin{array}{r}
142,857 \\
\times \quad\quad 4 \\
\hline
\end{array}
\qquad
\begin{array}{r}
142,857 \\
\times \quad\quad 5 \\
\hline
\end{array}
\qquad
\begin{array}{r}
142,857 \\
\times \quad\quad 6 \\
\hline
\end{array}
$$

What did you discover?

---

2. Are these statements true?

$15 \times 15 = (10 \times 20) + 25$
$25 \times 25 = (20 \times 30) + 25$
$35 \times 35 = (30 \times 40) + 25$

Can you discover a pattern and complete these questions?

$45 \times 45 = ?$
$55 \times 55 = ?$
$65 \times 65 = ?$

---

3. Guess the missing numbers. Then check your guesses.

$6 \times 7 = 42$

$66 \times 67 = 4,422$

$666 \times 667 = 444,222$

$6,666 \times 6,667 = n$

$66,666 \times 66,667 = n$

---

4. Look for a pattern. Guess the missing numbers. Then check your guesses.

$74 \times 74 = 5,476 \quad 43 \times 43 = 1,849$
$73 \times 75 = 5,475 \quad 42 \times 44 = 1,848$

$87 \times 87 = 7,569 \quad 68 \times 68 = n$
$86 \times 88 = n \quad\quad\; 67 \times 69 = 4,623$

Try some others like this.

---

5. Guess the missing products. Then check your guesses.

$(15,873 \times 7) \times 1 = 111,111$

$(15,873 \times 7) \times 2 = 222,222$

$(15,873 \times 7) \times 3 = 333,333$

$(15,873 \times 7) \times 4 = n$

$(15,873 \times 7) \times 5 = n$

$(15,873 \times 7) \times 6 = n$

---

6. Find the answers. Is there a pattern?

$(9 - 1) \div 8 = n$
$(98 - 2) \div 8 = n$
$(987 - 3) \div 8 = n$
$(9,876 - 4) \div 8 = n$
$(98,765 - 5) \div 8 = n$
$(987,654 - 6) \div 8 = n$
$(9,876,543 - 7) \div 8 = n$
$(98,765,432 - 8) \div 8 = n$

Cumulative Review

Multiply or divide.

1. $7 \times \frac{5}{8}$

   A $2\frac{1}{2}$ **B** $4\frac{3}{8}$

   C $9\frac{3}{8}$ **D** not given

2. $\frac{2}{3} \times \frac{3}{8}$

   A $\frac{1}{4}$ **B** $\frac{5}{11}$

   C $\frac{5}{24}$ **D** not given

3. $3\frac{3}{4} \times 1\frac{1}{3}$

   A 9 **B** $\frac{1}{5}$

   C $1\frac{1}{4}$ **D** not given

4. $8 \times 2\frac{1}{4}$

   A $10\frac{1}{4}$ **B** $16\frac{1}{4}$

   C 18 **D** not given

5. Write the lowest-terms fraction for 0.05.

   A $\frac{1}{5}$ **B** $\frac{1}{20}$

   C $\frac{5}{10}$ **D** not given

6. Write a decimal for $\frac{4}{25}$.

   A 0.4   **B** 0.25

   C 0.8   **D** not given

7. Write a mixed decimal for $\frac{5}{8}$.

   A $6.2\frac{1}{2}$ **B** $0.62\frac{1}{2}$

   C $0.625\frac{1}{2}$ **D** not given

Divide.

8. $\frac{3}{4} \div \frac{3}{7}$

   A $1\frac{1}{4}$ **B** $1\frac{3}{4}$

   C $\frac{9}{28}$ **D** not given

9. $2\frac{1}{2} \div 7\frac{1}{2}$

   A 3 **B** $18\frac{3}{4}$

   C $\frac{1}{3}$ **D** not given

10. Write the ratio as a fraction: 2 adults to 3 children.

   A $\frac{3}{2}$ **B** $\frac{2}{3}$

   C $\frac{2}{5}$ **D** not given

11. Give the missing number. $\frac{5}{8} = \frac{\rule{1em}{0.5ex}}{40}$

   A 20   **B** 25

   C 32   **D** not given

12. Solve the proportion. $\frac{n}{18} = \frac{5}{6}$

   A $n = 12$ **B** $n = 15$

   C $n = 18$ **D** not given

13. A map scale is 2 cm : 9 km. How many kilometers does 14 cm represent?

   A 28   **B** 23

   C 126   **D** not given

14. $\frac{3}{5}$ of the students in Antonia's class are in the chorus. If there are 25 people in her class, how many are in the chorus?

   A 15   **B** 18

   C 20   **D** not given

Graphing and Probability

When people cut timber, build cities, and put dams across rivers, the homes of wildlife are often destroyed. This is why some species of animals become endangered—that is, in danger of becoming extinct, or dying out. There are now five or six hundred animal species that are endangered.

One of the many kinds of animals that scientists are trying to save from extinction is the whooping crane. In 1941, only 15 of these graceful birds were still living. By 1969, however, the whooping crane population had grown to 55, and by 1983, to about 100.

One of the ways in which scientists are helping these birds is by finding adoptive parents. Usually a female whooping crane lays two eggs. Then there is only one chance in two that both eggs will hatch and the chicks will live to be adult birds. To improve these odds, scientists remove one of the eggs from the nest and put it into the nest of other cranes. This greatly increases the probability that both eggs will hatch into live, healthy chicks.

Bar Graphs

The sixth grade classes at Pond Run School took a vote on where they would like to have their spring picnic. They used a bar graph to show the results of their vote.

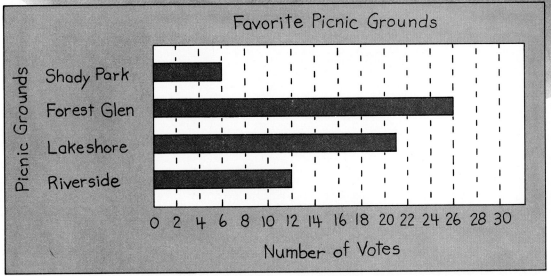

1. What is the title of the bar graph?

2. What do the numbers on the horizontal scale stand for?

3. Which picnic ground received the most votes? How many?

4. How many people voted for Lakeshore?

5. Which were the two least favored picnic grounds? How many students voted for each?

6. How many students voted in all?

The class also voted on which games they wanted to play. They recorded the results of their vote in the table at the right. Copy and complete the bar graph below using the data in the table.

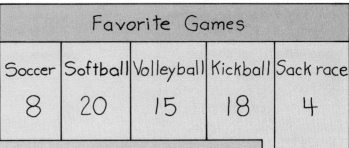

Favorite Games				
Soccer	Softball	Volleyball	Kickball	Sack race
8	20	15	18	4

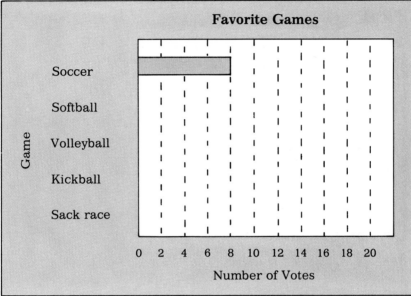

Favorite Games

1. Which game received the most votes?

2. Which bar in your graph is the longest?

3. Which bar in your graph ends between the dotted lines?

4. The class decided to play the two most favored games. Which did they play?

★ 5. Survey your class on one of these ideas. Make a bar graph to show the results of your survey.

    A favorite food

    B favorite drink

    C favorite sport

Think

Graph Estimates

Use the graph to estimate the number of graduates in each year.

1. In 1950?   2. In 1960?

3. In 1970?   4. In 1980?

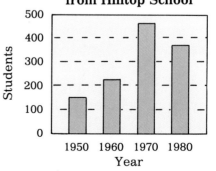

Number of Graduates from Hilltop School

Math

Pictographs

The table shows the populations of the six states with the greatest populations according to the 1980 census. Allan rounded each number to the nearest 1 million and made a **pictograph** to show the data. Use his pictograph to answer the questions below.

State	Exact Population	Rounded Population
California	23,668,562	24,000,000
New York	17,557,288	18,000,000
Texas	14,228,383	14,000,000
Pennsylvania	11,866,728	12,000,000
Illinois	11,418,461	11,000,000
Ohio	10,797,419	11,000,000

Population of the Six Largest States (1980 Census)

California	𝅘𝅥 𝅘𝅥 𝅘𝅥 𝅘𝅥 𝅘𝅥 𝅘𝅥 𝅘𝅥 𝅘𝅥 𝅘𝅥 𝅘𝅥 𝅘𝅥 𝅘𝅥
New York	𝅘𝅥 𝅘𝅥 𝅘𝅥 𝅘𝅥 𝅘𝅥 𝅘𝅥 𝅘𝅥 𝅘𝅥 𝅘𝅥
Texas	𝅘𝅥 𝅘𝅥 𝅘𝅥 𝅘𝅥 𝅘𝅥 𝅘𝅥 𝅘𝅥
Pennsylvania	𝅘𝅥 𝅘𝅥 𝅘𝅥 𝅘𝅥 𝅘𝅥 𝅘𝅥
Illinois	𝅘𝅥 𝅘𝅥 𝅘𝅥 𝅘𝅥 𝅘𝅥 ⌉
Ohio	𝅘𝅥 𝅘𝅥 𝅘𝅥 𝅘𝅥 𝅘𝅥 ⌉

𝅘𝅥 = 2 million people; ⌉ = 1 million people

1. How many people does each 𝅘𝅥 represent?

2. How many people does each ⌉ represent?

3. According to the pictograph, how many more people live in California than in New York?

4. According to the table, exactly how many more people live in California than in New York?

5. In the pictograph, which two states appear to have the same population? According to the exact populations given in the table, do these states actually have the same populations?

6. Suppose a state has a population of 8,248,325. How would you show the state's population in a pictograph like the one above?

Copy the table at the right. Round the population of each city to the nearest million. Then copy and complete the pictograph below the table.

Six Largest United States Cities* (1980 Census)		
City	Exact Population	Rounded Population
New York	9,080,777	9,000,000
Los Angeles	7,445,721	▦
Chicago	7,057,853	▦
Philadelphia	4,700,966	▦
Detroit	4,344,139	▦
San Francisco	3,226,867	▦

*Metropolitan Areas

Six Largest United States Cities* (1980 Census)
New York ☿ ☿ ☿ ☿ ⚲
Los Angeles
Chicago
Philadelphia
Detroit
San Francisco
☿ = 2 million people   ⚲ = 1 million people

*Metropolitan Areas

1. Which city has the greatest population? the least population?

2. According to the pictograph, which cities appear to have the same population? Do these cities actually have the same population?

3. Using data from the graph, what is the total population for all 6 cities?

4. **DATA BANK** About how many more Cherokee than Pueblo Indians are in the United States? (See the Data Bank, page 426.) Round each population to the nearest ten thousand. Make a pictograph to show the data and use your graph to answer the question.

Circle Graphs

Randy made a circle graph to show how he usually spends his time. About how many hours is Randy in school?

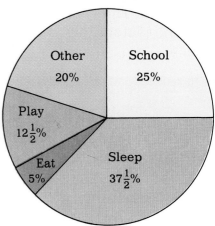

Randy's Activities for One Day (24 h)

Since we want to find how many hours 25% of one day is, we multiply.

Using a Fraction

$$25\% = \frac{25}{100} = \frac{1}{4}$$

$$\frac{1}{4} \times 24 = 6$$

Using a Decimal

$$25\% = 0.25$$

$$\begin{array}{r} 24 \\ \times\ 0.25 \\ \hline 120 \\ 48 \\ \hline 6.00 \end{array}$$

Randy spends about 6 hours in school.

Use the circle graph above to answer these questions.

1. What is the sum of all the percents in the graph?

2. How many hours each day does Randy spend eating?

3. How many hours each day does Randy spend playing?

4. List two activities that could be in the "other" category.

5. Does Randy get more or less than 8 hours of sleep?

6. What percent of the day does he spend sleeping and playing?

7. How many hours of each day is Randy either in school or playing?

Use the circle graph about favorite main dishes for questions 1–4.

1. What is the total number of students in the survey?

2. Which main dish is liked by the most students?

3. How many students prefer chicken?

4. How many prefer spaghetti?

Favorite Main Dishes of 120 Students

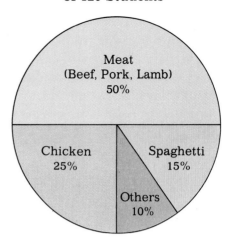

5. Each section in the circle graph shows 10%. Copy and complete the circle graph using the data in the table below. Use the dotted lines as a guide to show the approximate size of each section.

Favorite Kinds of Movies for 100 Students

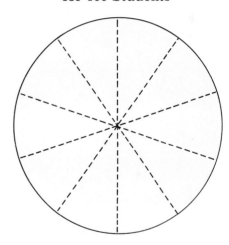

Favorite Kinds of Movies for 100 Students	
Space adventure	45%
Comedy/cartoons	10%
Western	10%
Suspense	15%
Other	20%

Think

Shape Perception

A Fold a piece of paper in half.

B Fold it in half again.

C Cut a shape across the fold.

Draw the shape you think will appear when you unfold the paper. How many lines of symmetry do you think the cut-out shape will have? Unfold the paper and compare the cut-out shape with your drawing.

Math

Line Graphs

All of Dr. Cardona's patients are babies or young children. She keeps records of their changes in height and weight from one visit to the next. The line graph shows how one of her patients grew in height from birth to 12 months of age.

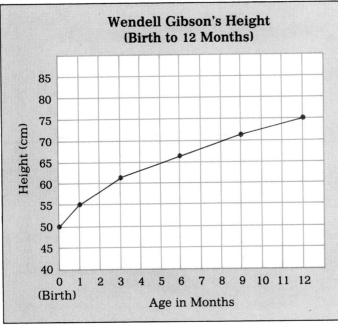

**Wendell Gibson's Height
(Birth to 12 Months)**

Height (cm) vs. Age in Months

Answer these questions about the line graph.

1. What was Wendell's height at birth?

2. How much did Wendell grow from birth to 1 month?

3. During which 3-month period did Wendell grow the fastest: birth to 3 months or 3 months to 6 months?

4. During which two 3-month periods did Wendell grow the same amount?

5. Estimate Wendell's height at 10 months.

Dr. Cardona recorded the weight changes for one of her patients from birth until the baby was 12 months old. Copy and complete the graph using the data about Joanne's weight. Then answer the questions.

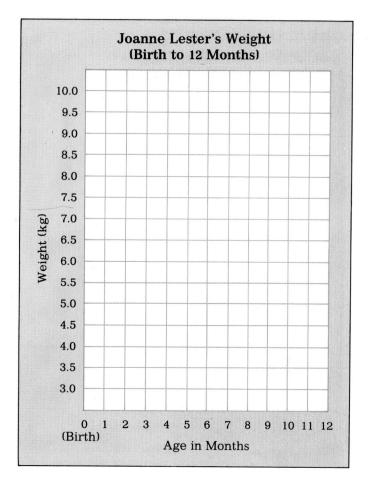

Joanne Lester's Weight

Age	Weight (kg)
Birth	3.5
1 month	4.0
3 months	6.0
6 months	6.8
9 months	8.5
12 months	9.5

1. Did Joanne's weight increase more from 1 to 3 months of age or from 6 to 9 months of age? How much more?

2. About how much do you think Joanne weighed when she was 2 months old?

3. About how much do you think Joanne weighed when she was 13 months old?

★ 4. Use the table below to make a line graph showing Joanne Lester's growth in weight from 2 to 6 years of age.

Age in years	2	3	4	5	6
Weight (kg)	12	14	16	17.5	19.5

Think

Mental Math

Look for a pattern in the products of the first three problems. Use this pattern to find the other products mentally.

1.	15	2.	25	3.	35
	× 15		× 25		× 35
	225		625		1,225

$(1×2)$ $(5×5)$ $(2×3)$ $(5×5)$ $(3×4)$ $(5×5)$

4.	45	5.	55	6.	65
	× 45		55		× 65

Math

Evaluating Graphs

A science class collected data about rainfall during one school year. They recorded their data in a table. Then the class made a bar graph to show the data. Study their table and bar graph. Then answer the questions below.

Monthly Rainfall for One School Year	
Month	Amount (cm)
September	5
October	25
November	20
December	18
January	4
February	7
March	16
April	18
May	10

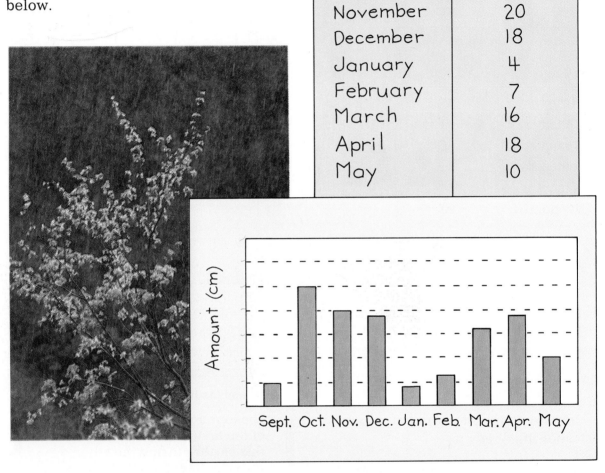

1. All graphs should have a **title.** Write an appropriate title for the bar graph.

2. All parts of a graph should be fully **labeled.** What other label should be on the horizontal scale?

3. Most graphs should have a **number scale.** What numbers should be written on this vertical scale?

4. What other type of graph (line graph, pictograph, or circle graph) could the class have used to show the data?

5. Could the months have been placed on the vertical side and the amount of rainfall on the horizontal side?

The number scale used for a graph may influence the conclusions you reach about the data shown. Study each pair of graphs. Then answer the questions.

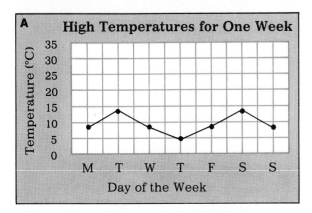

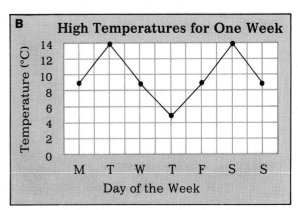

1. Are the temperatures for each day the same on both graphs?

2. How many degrees does each space between horizontal lines represent in graph A? in graph B?

3. Which graph might be more likely to cause you to exclaim, "The daily high temperatures have certainly gone up and down this week!"? Why?

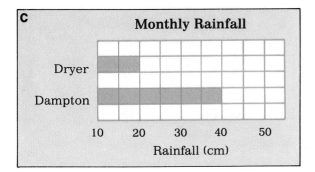

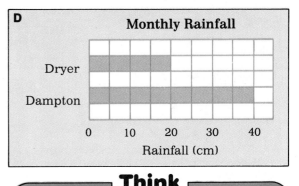

4. Do both graphs show the same total amount of rainfall for each city?

5. Is the length of the bar for Dampton twice as long as the length of the bar for Dryer in both graphs?

6. Which graph, C or D, gives a clearer idea of the relationship between the amounts of rainfall in the two cities?

7. How is the number scale on graph C different from the number scale on graph D?

Mean

Another name for the **average** of a set of numbers is the **mean.** Finding means sometimes involves decimal quotients.

The list shows the number of customers for the 5 students in Mr. Hayden's class who deliver newspapers. What is the mean number of customers for the paper routes?

Neil–156   Justine–148
Carver–138   Miguel–150
Rhonda–154

Find the total number of customers.

```
  1 5 6
  1 3 8
  1 5 4
  1 4 8
+ 1 5 0
-------
  7 4 6
```

The mean number of customers for the paper route is 149.2.

Divide by the number of delivery people.

```
      1 4 9.2
   5)7 4 6.0
     5
     ---
     2 4
     2 0
     ---
       4 6
       4 5
       ---
         1 0
         1 0
         ---
           0
```

Another Example

Find the mean (to the nearest tenth).

84, 39, 46, 52 →

```
   8 4
   3 9
   4 6
 + 5 2
 -----
   2 2 1
```

→

```
      5 5.2 5
   4)2 2 1.0 0
```

→ The mean (rounded to the nearest tenth) is 55.3.

Find the mean. Round to the nearest tenth when necessary.

1. 148, 175, 164, 161

2. 46, 25, 31, 62, 26

3. 318, 262, 178

4. 16.2, 15.7, 15.4, 16.6, 14.8

5. 22, 34, 9, 62, 70, 80

6. 14.22, 17, 8.7, 6.56, 14.27

332

Problem Solving: Using Data from a Double Bar Graph

Estimate the number of customers shown by each bar. Use your estimates to solve the problems below.

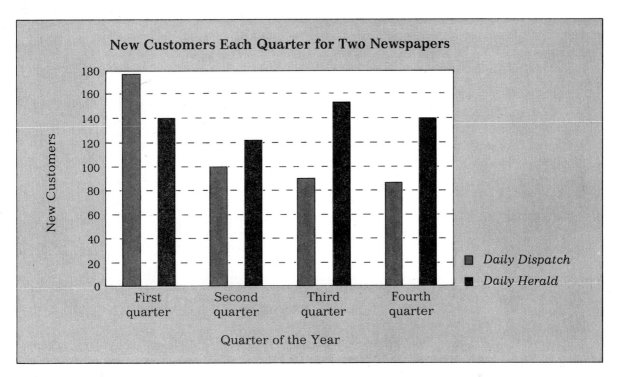

New Customers Each Quarter for Two Newspapers

1. Which paper had the greatest number of new customers in any quarter?

2. About how many more new customers did the *Daily Herald* get in the third quarter than the *Daily Dispatch*?

3. During which quarter was there the least difference in the numbers of new customers for the two papers? About how great was the difference that quarter?

4. How many new customers did the *Daily Dispatch* get during the second half of the year? during the first half of the year?

5. List your estimates of the number of new customers for each paper for each quarter. What is the mean number of new customers for each paper?

6. **Strategy Practice**   Rosa started a new paper route. The first week she found 1 new customer. The second week, she found 4 new customers, the third week 7 new customers, the fourth week 10 new customers, and so on. If she continued getting customers in this way, during which week did she get 30 new customers? Hint: Make a table and look for a pattern.

Interpreting Data

Work with a group. Here is this season's data for a school's top three swimmers in the 50-meter freestyle. You have been asked to analyze the data and help the coach choose one of the swimmers to enter a state meet.

50-Meter Freestyle (time in seconds)			
Date	Pat	Kim	Cory
4/7	52.8	56.6	66.7
4/14	A	A	62.8
4/21	53.1	57.3	57.5
4/28	116.4	A	59.5
5/5	53.5	56.7	55.6
5/12	51.3	51.0	52.0
5/19	54.5	57.3	53.6
5/26	A	A	52.0

A = absent

Part 1

1. Carefully consider the data for each swimmer. Look at each swimmer's fastest and slowest times and look for trends in performance.
   - Discuss why these factors might be important considerations in selecting a swimmer for the meet.
   - What do they indicate about how well a swimmer might do in the future?

2. When analyzing data, people often use a single number to represent the set of data as a whole. Discuss with your group what single number might best represent the data for each swimmer. How did you arrive at this number?

Part 2

Standard measures of central tendency are often used to summarize data.

3. Compare the methods you used in exercise 2 with the methods for finding the measures of central tendency defined in the box.

Measures of Central Tendency

Mean	the average of a set of numbers
Median	the middle number in a set of data when the numbers are arranged in order (If no one middle number exists, then the median is the average of the two middle numbers.)
Mode	the number, if any, that occurs most often in a set of data

4. Pat's data contains an extreme number—one that is quite different from the others in the set. To explore how extreme numbers affect data, consider the mean, median, and mode for each swimmer's data.

- What happens to Pat's mean, median, and mode if his extreme number is omitted?
- Suppose Kim had not been absent on 4/14, but instead he had an extremely poor time. What do you think would have happened to his mean? Median? Mode? Make up an example to verify your reasoning.
- Which measure of central tendency seems to be most affected by an extreme number? Why might this be so?

5. To keep track of his swimmers' progress, the coach calculates means every week.
   - What was Pat's mean at the end of the second week? At the end of the third week?
   - What effect did Pat's extreme score have on his mean for 4/28? For 5/26?
   - Suppose a swimmer had his or her fastest time at the beginning of the season. Would that time have a greater effect on the mean for that month or the mean for the season? How can you verify your reasoning?

6. Pat claims that his mean time is best. When he calculated the mean, he excluded his 116.4-second time because he had leg cramps that day. Is Pat's claim misleading? Why or why not?

7. Suppose a student's mean for two trials is the same as Kim's mean for the season. Which mean do you consider more reliable? Why?

8. Predict a time for each swimmer in the state meet. Give reasons for your predictions. Which swimmer's time is easiest to predict? Which is hardest to predict? Why?

9. Suppose the coach will hold one more tryout before deciding on a swimmer for the state meet. He will only consider swimmers with means of 60 seconds or less.
   - What is the slowest time each swimmer could swim and still be considered for the state meet?
   - Is it likely that all three swimmers will be considered for the state meet after this final tryout?
   - Share your reasoning with another group.

Part 3

10. With your group, decide which swimmer you think the coach should choose to enter the state meet. Be prepared to support your decision.

11. Present your case to the class and listen to each group's arguments for its swimmer. At the end of each presentation, talk about whether any of the arguments were misleading. If so, how?

Probability

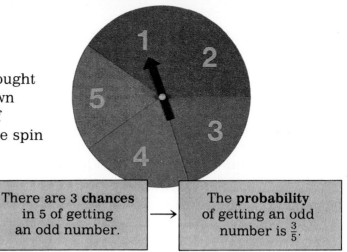

The new board game Hector bought has a spinner like the one shown here. What is the **probability** of getting an odd number with one spin of the pointer?

There are 5 **equally likely** outcomes: 1, 2, 3, 4, 5	→	There are 3 **chances** in 5 of getting an odd number.	→	The **probability** of getting an odd number is $\frac{3}{5}$.

Here are some other examples for the spinner.

A. There are 2 chances in 5 of getting an even number. ⟶ The probability of getting an even number is $\frac{2}{5}$.

B. There are 5 chances in 5 of getting a number less than 6. ⟶ The probability of getting a number less than 6 is $\frac{5}{5}$ or 1.

C. There are 0 chances in 5 of getting a number greater than 5. ⟶ The probability of getting a number greater than 5 is $\frac{0}{5}$ or 0.

Each outcome is equally likely in the following experiments.
Give the missing information in each row.

Experiment	Outcomes	Chances	Probability
1. Draw a card without looking. 〔1 2 3 4〕	1 2 3 4	There is 1 chance in ▥ of getting a 3.	The probability of getting a 3 is ▥.
2. Toss a cube with sides numbered 1–6.	1 2 3 4 5 6	There are ▥ chances in 6 of getting an odd number.	The probability of getting an odd number is ▥.
3. Toss a cube that has one of the letters A, B, C, D, E, F on each face.	A B C D E F	There are 2 chances in ▥ of getting a vowel (A or E).	The probability of getting a vowel is ▥.

Suppose you draw one of these cards without looking.

1. What are the possible outcomes?

2. Are the outcomes equally likely?

3. What is the probability of getting an odd number?

4. What is the probability of getting a red card?

Suppose you draw a marble without looking.

5. What are the possible outcomes?

6. Do you have a better chance of getting a green marble or a yellow marble?

7. What is the probability of getting a green marble?

Suppose you spin the pointer.

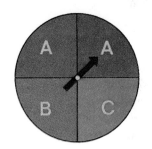

8. Which letter do you think you would get most often in 12 spins?

9. Which color do you think you would get most often in 12 spins?

10. What is the probability that you will get an A?

11. What is the probability that the pointer will stop on a red space?

Skillkeeper

Find the percent of each number.

1. 20% of 20   2. 5% of 40   3. 15% of 300   4. 75% of 160

5. 30% of 50   6. 2% of 30   7. 150% of 72   8. 29% of 200

Find the products.

9. 3.6   10. 8.7   11. 5.15   12. 4.8   13. 4.12
   × 2.4   × 6.3   × 8.4   × 0.25   × 3.20

Probability and Prediction

Work with a group. You will need a
standard deck of 52 playing cards
and index cards.

Part 1

Shuffle the deck of cards.
Pick a card without looking.
Try to predict what your card will be.

1. What is the probability of predicting the card's suit
   (spades, hearts, diamonds, or clubs)? Of predicting the
   card's rank? Of predicting both suit and rank? Discuss
   your answer.

   Have one person pick a card from
   the deck and show it to the group.
   Keep a tally of the number of
   times the card is and is not a club.
   Repeat the process 20 times.

Not a Club	Club

2. Are the results what you would expect based on the
   probabilities? Why or why not?

3. Combine your data with that of the rest of the class. Are
   the results now closer to or farther from the results you
   would expect based on the probabilities? Discuss reasons
   for your answer.

   Have one person in your group be the "dealer." The dealer
   draws one card from the deck at a time, face down. Each
   other person predicts what the suit will be. Then the dealer
   shows the card and puts it back in the deck. Each person
   tallies his or her correct and incorrect predictions. Repeat
   the procedure 20 times.

4. Are the results what you would expect based on probability? Why or why not?

5. How would the results change if all the spades were removed from the deck?

Part 2

Now you will use index cards to create your own deck of cards labeled A, B, C, and D.

6. Make a deck of 24 cards where each outcome, A, B, C, and D, is equally likely. Draw a card 24 times, remembering to return the card and shuffle after each draw. Record your results on a tally chart.

A	ⅼ ⅼ ⅼ
B	ⅼ ⅼ
C	ⅼ ⅼ ⅼ ⅼ ⅼ
D	ⅼ ⅼ ⅼ

7. Write the probability for each outcome as a fraction. Tell how these probabilities could help you decide what results to expect.

8. How could you change your deck so that you are twice as likely to select a card marked A or B as to select a card marked C or D? (You need not have 24 cards in the deck.) Change your deck and test this new deck by drawing cards and keeping a tally chart like the one above.

9. Write a probability for each outcome. Take turns predicting what the next card drawn might be. How can you use your probabilities to help you predict?

QUESTION
DATA
PLAN
ANSWER
CHECK

Applied Problem Solving

You plan to swim at a public pool during the summer. Will you pay daily fees or buy a season pass?

Some Things to Consider

- You do not know for sure how many times you will go swimming. You would like to swim an average of at least twice a week, possibly three times a week.

- You will be away at summer camp for 1 week.

- The daily fee is $0.70.

- A season pass costs $18.00. You can swim any time the pool is open with no other cost.

- Your summer season is 13 weeks long.

Some Questions to Answer

1. What would it cost to swim an average of twice a week during your summer season and pay daily fees?

2. What would it cost to swim an average of three times a week and pay daily fees?

3. How many days can you swim before paying the daily fees costs more than a season pass?

What Is Your Decision?

Will you pay daily fees or buy a season pass?

Chapter Review-Test

Use the bar graph for questions 1–3.

1. Which vegetable was selected by the most students?

2. About how many people picked yams?

3. Which two foods were picked by the same number of students?

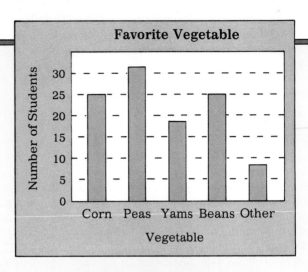

Favorite Vegetable

Use the circle graph for questions 4–6.

4. What is the sum of the percents?

5. How many people picked rock?

6. How many more people picked country music than picked jazz music?

Favorite Music of 60 People

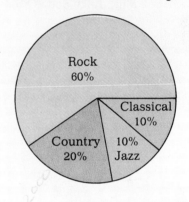

Use these test scores for questions 7–9.

83, 90, 86, 98, 98, 85, 83, 86, 88, 83

7. What is the mean of the scores?

8. What is the mode of the scores?

9. What is the median of the scores?

Use the cards for questions 10–12.

1	2	3	4	5	6	7	8

10. What is the probability of getting a 3 on one draw?

11. What is the probability of getting an even number?

12. Suppose the cards were in a hat and you drew one card. If you did this 40 times, how many times might you expect to get a 5?

13. The first five days of the week had these amounts of rain:
3 cm, 2 cm, 1 cm, 3 cm, 1 cm

What was the mean amount of rain per day?

14. Jodie made these scores on her first six health tests:
68, 76, 87, 74, 96, 82

What was Jodie's median score?

Another Look

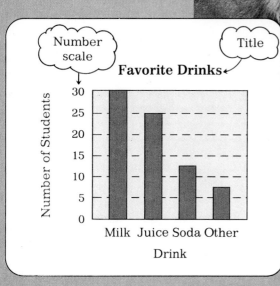

Answer these questions about the bar graph.

1. Which drink was selected by the most students?

2. About how many students picked soda?

3. How many more students picked milk than picked juice?

4. How many students does the space from one horizontal line to the next stand for?

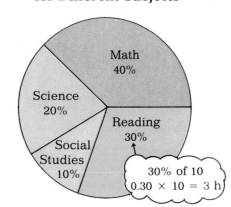

10 Hours Study Time for Different Subjects

Math 40%

Science 20%

Reading 30%

Social Studies 10%

30% of 10
0.30 × 10 = 3 h

Answer these questions about the circle graph.

5. What was the total number of hours spent studying?

6. What is the sum of the percents?

7. How many hours were spent studying math?

8. How many hours were spent studying science?

```
  77      To find the mean of a
  50      list of numbers
  60      • find their sum and
  54      • divide the sum by the
  70        number of addends.
  48
+ 54            59  ← mean
_____       7)413
Sum: 413
```

Find the mean of each list of numbers. Round to the nearest tenth when necessary.

9. 17, 14, 24, 19, 16

10. 48, 39, 42, 51, 63, 44

11. 129, 116, 133, 120, 106

Enrichment

Motion Geometry: Translations

Rectangle 2 is called a **slide image** or **translation image** of rectangle 1. Each point of the rectangle was moved **right 4, up 3.**

Copy each figure on graph paper. Make the moves as directed to draw a translation image of each figure.

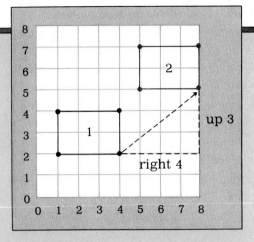

1. right 2, up 3

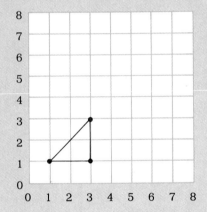

2. left 2, up 3

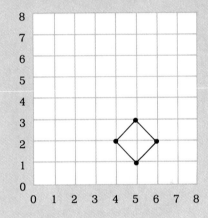

3. right 2, up 2

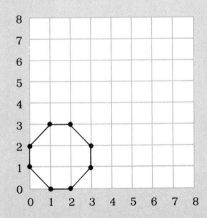

4. right 3

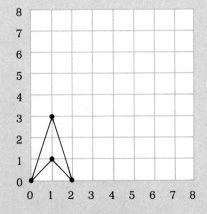

5. Draw a simple figure of your own choice on graph paper. Give instructions for making the moves for a translation image of the figure. Let a classmate try it!

343

Cumulative Review

Which word describes each triangle?

1.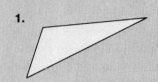
A scalene
B isosceles
C equilateral
D not given

2.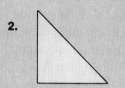
A acute
B right
C obtuse
D not given

Name each polygon.

3.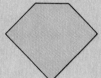
A pentagon
B hexagon
C octagon
D not given

4.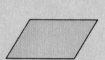
A parallelogram
B rhombus
C trapezoid
D not given

Use circle O for items 5–7.

5. Name a radius.

A $\overline{OL}$
B $\overline{MK}$
C $\overline{KJ}$
D not given

6. Name a central angle.

A ∠LOM
B ∠MKJ
C ∠K
D not given

7. Name a chord.

A $\overline{LO}$
B $\overline{MO}$
C $\overline{KO}$
D not given

8. Give a fraction for 85%.

A $\frac{19}{20}$
B $\frac{9}{10}$
C $\frac{3}{4}$
D not given

9. Give a percent for 0.67.

A 76%
B 6.7%
C 67%
D not given

10. Give a decimal for 18%.

A 1.8
B 8.1
C 18.0
D not given

11. Find 25% of 80.

A 50
B 200
C 20
D not given

12. Find 65% of 240.

A 1,560
B 156
C 305
D not given

13. Eldora's class wants to sell 70 tickets to the school carnival. They have already sold 70% of that number. How many have they sold?

A 150
B 60
C 56
D not given

14. In a survey of 120 people 45% said that they watch the news on TV every day. How many people in the group watch the TV news daily?

A 45
B 54
C 57
D not given

14

Perimeter, Area, and Volume

Looking back down the 91 steep, narrow steps she had just climbed, Erika felt a little dizzy. She was standing with her friend at the top of the Castillo, a great pyramid built hundreds of years ago by the Maya Indians in the area that is now Yucatan, Mexico. Beside Erika, atop the pyramid, was a small temple 5.8 meters long and 4.3 meters wide. Twenty-four meters below lay many other ruins of the old Maya Indian city.

Erika thought the Maya ball court was particularly interesting. There, on a field 94 meters long by 35 meters wide, teams had played a strange and difficult game. In some ways the game was like soccer; in other ways, like basketball. The teams tried to score goals by hitting a ball through a small stone ring 8 meters above the ground, without using their hands or feet. As she looked down on the ancient playing field, Erika found herself thinking about how much she would enjoy telling the other members of her soccer team about her wonderful visit to this city of the past!

Perimeter

The state of Colorado is one of the states that is nearly rectangular. It is approximately 589 km long and 456 km wide. If you could drive all the way around it, about how far would you drive?

The distance around a figure is called the **perimeter** of the figure.

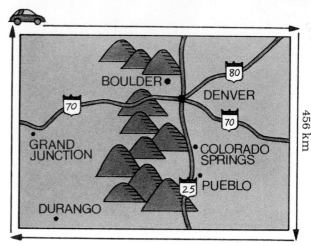

456 km

589 km

To find the perimeter, add the lengths of the sides.

$$\begin{array}{r} 589 \\ 456 \\ 589 \\ + \ 456 \\ \hline 2{,}090 \end{array}$$

When the figure is a rectangle, we can use a shortcut! We double the sum of the length and the width.

$P = 2 \times (l + w)$
$P = 2 \times (589 + 456)$
$P = 2 \times 1{,}045 = 2{,}090$

If you could drive around the perimeter of Colorado you would drive about 2,090 km.

Find the perimeter of each figure.

1.

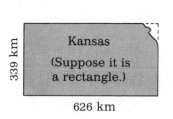

339 km

Kansas
(Suppose it is a rectangle.)

626 km

2.

Pentagon Building
Washington, D.C.

276.3 m

3.

72 m

72 m   72 m

Baseball Field

120 m   120 m

4.

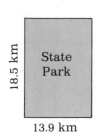

18.5 km

State Park

13.9 km

5.

3.5 km

2.5 km

Airport

6.

106.8 km

98.3 m

City Building Lot

135.7 m

94.5 m

346

Problem Solving:
Using Data from a Picture

PERIMETER PROBLEMS

Pictures are given for some of these **perimeter problems.** For others, you may need to draw a picture of your own in order to solve the problem.

1. A bulletin board has the length and width shown. What is its perimeter?

122 cm

153 cm

2. The width of a garden is 8.4 m. Its length is 16.8 m. What is the perimeter of the garden?

3. The width of a soccer field is 46 m. The length is 45 m greater than the width. What is the perimeter of the field?

27.8 m

? ?

36.6 m

4. A home is to be built on a lot shaped like a trapezoid. The parallel sides are 36.6 m and 27.8 m long. Each of the other sides is half as long as the longest side. What is the perimeter of the lot?

5. A sail for a sailboat is shaped like a right triangle. The longest side is 8.5 m. The next-longest side is 0.5 m shorter than the longest side. The third side is $\frac{1}{3}$ the sum of the lengths of the other two sides. What is the perimeter?

6. A pennant is shaped like an isosceles triangle. The short side is 24 cm and is half the length of a longer side. What is the perimeter of the pennant?

24 cm

7. A pen for a dog was made in the shape of a kite. Each of the two longer sides is 9.4 m long. Each of the two shorter sides is 2.8 m less than this. What is the perimeter of the pen?

8. Strategy Practice A picture frame is twice as long as it is wide. The perimeter of the frame is 228 cm. What are the length and the width of the picture frame?

Circumference

Work with a group. You will need
string, a centimeter ruler, and a
variety of objects with circular tops
or bottoms.

Part 1

Use objects such as paper cups, jar
lids, and cans with different
circumferences.

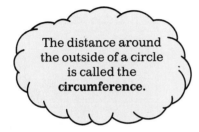

The distance around
the outside of a circle
is called the
circumference.

1. Estimate the circumference of
   each object. Record each person's
   estimate.
   - How can you use string to help
     you measure circumference?
     Find the circumference of each
     object and record it on the chart.

Object	Circumference	Diameter	$\frac{C}{d}$

2. Discuss your results.
   - How close were your estimates to the actual
     measurements?
   - Did your estimates improve as you worked?

Part 2

A straight line that passes through the center of a circle from
one side to the other is called the **diameter.** The diameter is
the longest distance across a circle.

3. Measure the diameter of each of your objects. Record your measurements on the chart.

4. With a calculator, find the ratio of circumference to **diameter** $\left(\frac{C}{d}\right)$ of each circle and record it on the chart.
   - What do you notice about the numbers in the last column?
   - Compare your results with those of another group. Did they see a similar pattern?

5. The ratio of circumference to diameter $\left(\frac{C}{d}\right)$ is called **pi** (π). The decimal value of *pi* is approximately 3.14, and its fraction value is approximately $\frac{22}{7}$.
   - If you know the circumference of a circle, can you find its diameter? How? Write an equation to show what you did.
   - If you know the diameter of a circle, can you find the circumference? How? Write an equation to show what you did.
   - Test your equations using measurements from your chart.

Part 3

You will need three cans or cylindrical objects of different sizes.

6. Measure the diameter of each object. Estimate how far you think each object will travel if you roll it so that it makes 5 complete revolutions. Explain how you made your estimates.

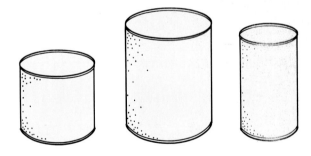

7. Now roll each object so that it makes 5 complete revolutions. Measure this distance. Discuss how your results compare with your estimates.

8. Find the circumference of each object. Compare your method with other groups' methods. Did everyone use the same method?

Area of a Rectangle

How many tiles 1 decimeter square are needed to cover the wall area behind this kitchen stove?

The **area** of a rectangular region is the number of unit squares needed to cover the region.

We can find the area in two different ways.

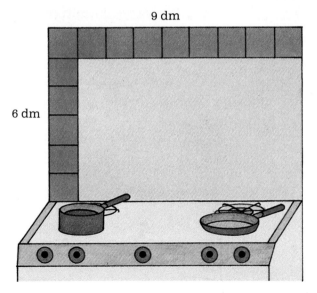

9 dm

6 dm

Thinking About Squares

There are 9 squares in each row.
There are 6 rows of squares.
There are 9 × 6, or 54 squares.

The area of the rectangle is 54 dm².
(Read **dm²** as "**square decimeters.**")

Using a Formula

Area		length		width
A	=	l	×	w
A	=	9	×	6
A	=	54 dm²		

Find the area of each rectangular region.

1.

64 cm

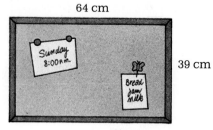

39 cm

2.

1.8 m

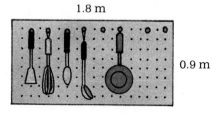

0.9 m

3.

1.24 m

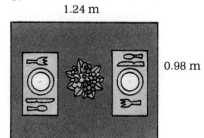

0.98 m

4. Kitchen floor
l = 6.4 m
w = 4.5 m

5. Lot for a house
l = 45 m
w = 36 m

6. Housing subdivision
l = 2.5 km
w = 4.5 km

7. City
l = 15.5 km
w = 9.5 km

8. Kitchen wall
l = 4.8 m
w = 2.5 m

9. Recipe card
l = 120 mm
w = 85 mm

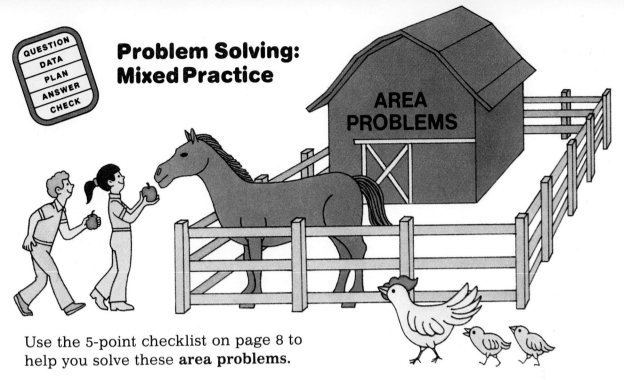

Problem Solving:
Mixed Practice

Use the 5-point checklist on page 8 to help you solve these **area problems**.

1. A rectangular room is 5.75 m long and 3.5 m wide. What is the area of the room's floor?

2. A rectangular mirror is 1.75 m long and 86 cm wide. What is its area? Note: When finding the area, be sure to use the same unit for the length and the width.

3. A rectangular lot is 36 m long and 32 m wide. A house on the lot covers 25% of the lot's area. What is the area of the house?

4. What is the area of the floor of the room pictured below?

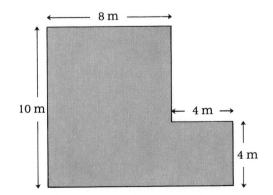

5. A rectangular room is 6.5 m long and 4.5 m wide and has 2.5 m high ceilings. What is the total area of the room's walls if the window and door use 2.75 m² of the wall space?

6. The **square root** of a number, such as 1,024, is the number that when multiplied by itself gives that number as the product. The side of a square is the square root of the area of the square. Guess and check to find the length of the sides of a square whose area is 1,024 mm².

7. **DATA HUNT** What is the area of your classroom floor in square meters? Measure to the nearest hundredth of a meter.

8. **Strategy Practice** The Handys have 36 m of fence. What is the area of the largest rectangular pen they can make? Hint: Make a table.

Area of a Triangle

Eric's teacher made puzzle boards to help the class learn about the area of a triangle.

Puzzle:
Can you make the puzzle pieces for the congruent triangles fit the rectangle?

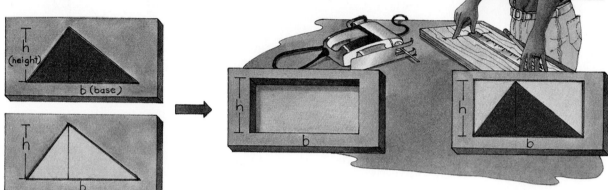

Solution

Since two congruent triangles fit into one rectangle with base and height the same as the triangles', the area of a triangle is one half the area of a rectangle.

Area of a triangle $= \frac{1}{2} \times b \times h$

Area of a rectangle

Example A

$A = \frac{1}{2} \times b \times h$

$A = \frac{1}{2} \times 8.6 \times 4.8$

height 4.8 cm
base: 8.6 cm

$A = 4.3 \times 4.8 = 20.64$ cm^2

Example B

$A = \frac{1}{2} \times b \times h$

$A = \frac{1}{2} \times 12 \times 10$

height 10 cm
base: 12 cm

$A = 6 \times 10 = 60$ cm^2

Warm Up   Find the area.

1.

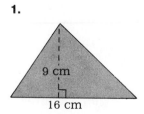

9 cm
16 cm

2.

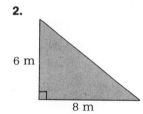

6 m
8 m

3.

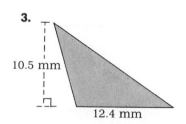

10.5 mm
12.4 mm

Practice Find the area.

1.
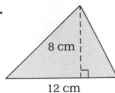
8 cm
12 cm

2.
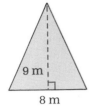
9 m
8 m

3.
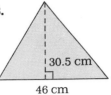
30.5 cm
46 cm

4.
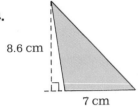
8.6 cm
7 cm

5.
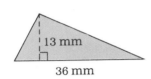
13 mm
36 mm

6.
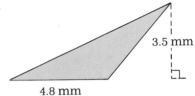
3.5 mm
4.8 mm

7.
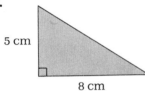
5 cm
8 cm

8.
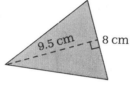
9.5 cm
8 cm

9.
12.2 mm
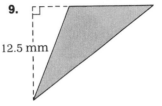
12.5 mm

10. What is the area of this triangular corner lot?

34.6 m
37.2 m

11. What is the total area of these sails?

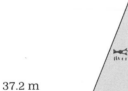
8 m
3 m
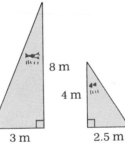
4 m
2.5 m

★ 12. What is the area of this four-sided field?

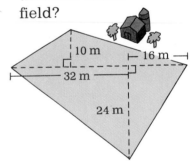
10 m
16 m
32 m
24 m

Think

Area of a Parallelogram

The puzzle pieces for the parallelogram can be made to fit into the rectangle puzzle board. Write a formula for the area of a parallelogram.

Find the area of this parallelogram.

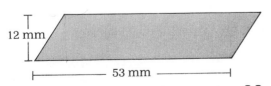
12 mm
53 mm

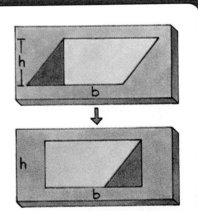

Math

353

Area of a Circle

Puzzle boards can also help you learn about the area of a circle.

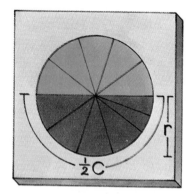

The puzzle pieces for the circle can be fitted almost exactly into the rectangle puzzle board. The area of the circle is approximately equal ($\approx$) to the area of the rectangle!

We write:
$$A = \tfrac{1}{2}C \times r$$
$$A = \pi \times r \times r$$
$$A = \pi \times r^2$$

$C = \pi \times$ diameter, so $\tfrac{1}{2}C = \pi \times$ radius.

Warm Up   Find the area of each circle.

1.

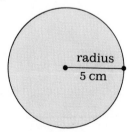

radius
5 cm

$A = 3.14 \times r \times r$
$A = 3.14 \times 5 \times 5$
$A = \text{\textbardbl} \ cm^2$

2.

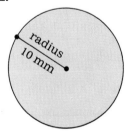

radius
10 mm

$A = 3.14 \times r \times r$
$A = 3.14 \times 10 \times 10$
$A = \text{\textbardbl} \ mm^2$

3.

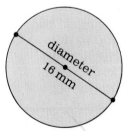

diameter
16 mm

$D = 16$, so $r = 8$
$A = 3.14 \times 8 \times 8$
$A = \text{\textbardbl} \ mm^2$

354

Practice Find the area of each circle. Use 3.14 for π. Round to the nearest hundredth when necessary.

1.
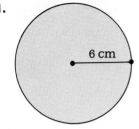
6 cm

2.
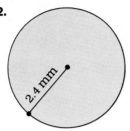
2.4 mm

3.
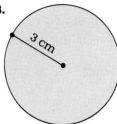
3 cm

4.
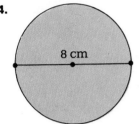
8 cm

5.
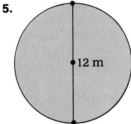
12 m

6.
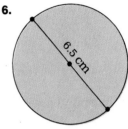
6.5 cm

7.
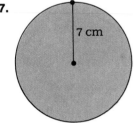
7 cm

8.
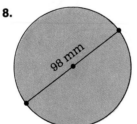
98 mm

9.
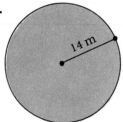
14 m

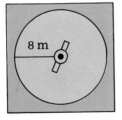
8 m

10. A rotating lawn sprinkler sprays water over the area of a circle whose radius is 8 m. What is the area of the lawn watered?

 11. Use 3.142 for π and decide how much greater the area of a 42-cm diameter pizza is than the area of a 36-cm diameter pizza.

Think

Area Estimation

Estimate the area of the circle as accurately as you can by counting square units and parts of square units.

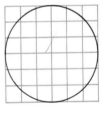

By how much does your estimate differ from the actual area? (Use 3.14 for π.)

Math

Surface Area

How many square centimeters of colored paper are needed to cover the surface of the record storage box?

The **surface area** of a figure is the sum of the areas of all its faces.

We find the surface area of the box by adding the areas of six rectangles.

Top: $65 \times 32 = 2{,}080$
Bottom: $65 \times 32 = 2{,}080$
Front: $65 \times 36 = 2{,}340$
Back: $65 \times 36 = 2{,}340$
End: $32 \times 36 = 1{,}152$
End: $32 \times 36 = \underline{1{,}152}$
$11{,}144$

The surface area of the box is 11,144 cm².

36 cm

32 cm

65 cm

Warm Up Find the surface area of each object.

1. Tool box

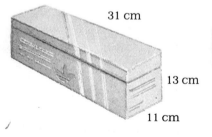

95 cm

56 cm

42 cm

2. Record box

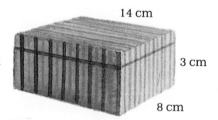

14 cm

3 cm

8 cm

3. Coin box

28 cm

7 cm

16 cm

4. Shoe box

31 cm

13 cm

11 cm

5. Cedar chest

1.2 m

0.5 m

0.45 m

6. Small refrigerator

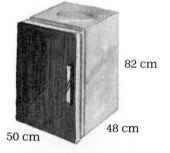

82 cm

50 cm

48 cm

Practice Find the surface area of each box.

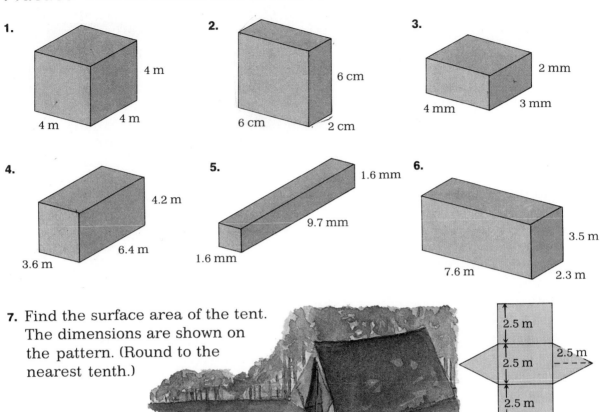

1. 4 m, 4 m, 4 m

2. 6 cm, 6 cm, 2 cm

3. 2 mm, 4 mm, 3 mm

4. 4.2 m, 6.4 m, 3.6 m

5. 1.6 mm, 9.7 mm, 1.6 mm

6. 3.5 m, 7.6 m, 2.3 m

7. Find the surface area of the tent. The dimensions are shown on the pattern. (Round to the nearest tenth.)

2.5 m, 2.5 m, 2.5 m, 2.5 m, 3.5 m

★ 8. Find the surface area of this can. The dimensions are shown on the pattern. Use 3.14 for π.

4 cm, circumference of circle, 11 cm, 4 cm

Skillkeeper

Find the mean of each list of numbers.
Round to the nearest tenth when necessary.

1. 2, 18, 13, 7

2. 22, 41, 10, 27

3. 67, 48, 53, 61, 70

4. 113, 128, 116, 132

5. 3, 8, 11, 5, 4

6. 17, 38, 51, 26, 28

7. 248, 273, 259, 263, 240

8. 74, 63, 82, 59, 91, 67

9. 298, 47, 93, 966

Volume

How many centimeter cubes will the box hold?

The **volume** of a box is the number of cubic units it will hold. We can use this unit

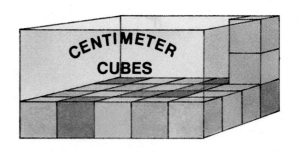

and find the volume of this box in two ways.

Thinking About Cubes

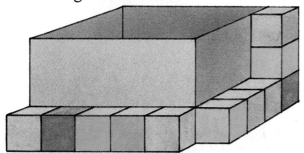

There are 5 rows of 4 cubes, or 20 cubes in each layer. The box will hold 3 layers. The volume of the box is $5 \times 4 \times 3$, or 60 cm³ (cubic centimeters).

Using a Formula

volume		length		width		height
V	$=$	l	$\times$	w	$\times$	h
$\downarrow$		$\downarrow$		$\downarrow$		$\downarrow$
V	$=$	5	$\times$	4	$\times$	3

$$V = 60 \text{ cm}^3$$

Find the volume of each box.

1.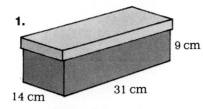
9 cm
31 cm
14 cm

2.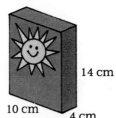
14 cm
10 cm   4 cm

3.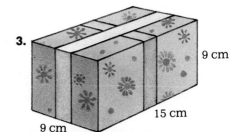
9 cm
15 cm
9 cm

4.
3 cm
3.1 cm
3.2 cm

5.
2.5 cm
3.5 cm
3 cm

6.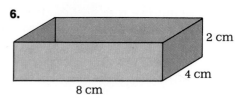
2 cm
4 cm
8 cm

7. $l = 15$ cm
$w = 3.5$ cm
$h = 10$ cm

8. $l = 4$ m
$w = 1.5$ m
$h = 2$ m

9. $l = 10.8$ cm
$w = 7.0$ cm
$h = 5.5$ cm

358

Problem Solving: Using Estimation

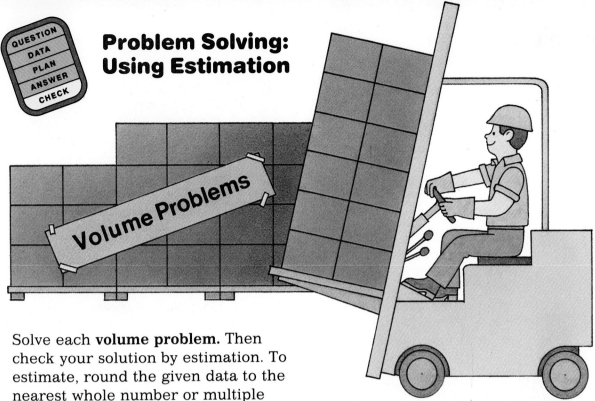

Volume Problems

Solve each **volume problem.** Then check your solution by estimation. To estimate, round the given data to the nearest whole number or multiple of 10.

1. A room is 4.2 m long, 3 m wide, and 2.8 m high. What is the volume of the room in cubic meters (m³)?

2. A flower box is 61 cm long, 32 cm wide, and 38 cm high. How many cubic centimeters of soil are needed to fill it?

3. What is the volume of a swimming pool that is 20.4 m long and 9.8 m wide, and has an average depth of 1.9 m?

4. A storage locker is 3.7 m long, 2.8 m wide, and 2.3 m deep. How much space is left after 11.75 m³ of luggage is placed in the locker?

5. A food storage freezer is 1.4 m long, 1 m wide, and 0.9 m deep. How many cubic meters less is its volume than that of a freezer with a volume of 1.75 m³?

6. A large gift box is 24.2 cm long, 17.5 cm wide, and 4.3 cm high. How many more cubic centimeters will it hold than a box 18.2 cm long, 13.3 cm wide, and 3.5 cm high?

7. **DATA BANK**   A bar of soap might be 9 cm long, 6 cm wide, and 3 cm high. Suppose you have a bar of metal this size. How many grams would it weigh if it were iron? copper? silver? gold? lead? aluminum? (See Data Bank, page 423.)

8. **DATA HUNT**   A cubic meter of air weighs about 1.29 kg. About how much does the air in your classroom weigh?

9. **Strategy Practice**   A fish tank is 60 cm long, 25 cm wide, and 20 cm high. How many times as much water will a larger tank hold if each dimension is twice as great?

Applied
Problem Solving

QUESTION
DATA
PLAN
ANSWER
CHECK

Your soccer team wants to reseed the soccer field. How many boxes of grass seed will you buy?

Blue
Grass

GRASS SEED MIXTURE

This mixture is superior to other shade brands commonly available. Remember, all grass needs some sunlight to grow.

Some Things to Consider

- The soccer field takes up an area 78 m long and 58 m wide. It has a 15 m strip of grass all around its perimeter that should also be reseeded.

- The soccer field is used for practice or games every day.

- A light cover of grass requires 1 kg of seed for every 100 m² of field. A heavy cover requires 1.5 kg of seed for every 100 m² of field.

- You live in a windy area, so some grass seed will be lost to the wind.

- You can buy grass seed only in boxes of 2 kg of seed per box.

- A box of grass seed costs $8.95.

Some Questions to Answer

1. What is the area of the grass to be reseeded including the strip around the playing field?

2. How many kilograms of seed do you need for a light cover of grass? for a heavy cover of grass?

3. How many boxes of seed do you need for a light cover of grass? for a heavy cover?

What Is Your Decision?

How many boxes of grass seed will you buy?

Chapter Review-Test

1. Find the perimeter and area of this rectangle.

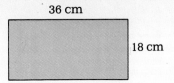

36 cm

18 cm

Find the perimeter and area of these triangles.

2.

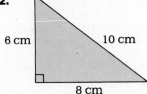

6 cm   10 cm

8 cm

3.

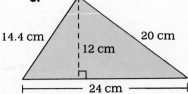

14.4 cm   20 cm

12 cm

24 cm

4.

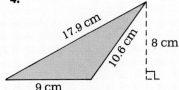

17.9 cm   10.6 cm   8 cm

9 cm

Find the circumference and area of these circles.
Use 3.14 or $3\frac{1}{7}$ for π.

5.

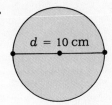

$d = 10$ cm

6.

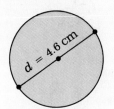

$d = 4.6$ cm

7.

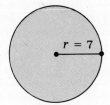

$r = 7$

Find the surface area and volume of these figures.

8.

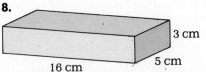

3 cm

16 cm   5 cm

9.

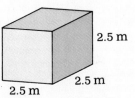

2.5 m

2.5 m

2.5 m

10.

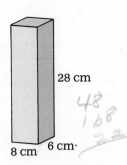

28 cm

8 cm   6 cm

Solve.

11. A parking lot is 35 m longer than it is wide. It is 45 m wide. What is the perimeter of the lot?

12. A garden is 9.5 m long. Its width is 1.5 less than its length. What is the area of the garden?

13. A storage chest has length 1.2 m, width 0.7 m, and height 0.8 m. What is the volume of the chest? What is the surface area?

Another Look

perimeter   length   width

$$P = l + w + l + w$$
$$= 15 + 6 + 15 + 6$$
$$= 42 \text{ cm}$$

area   length   width

$$A = l \times w$$
$$15 \times 6 = 90 \text{ cm}^2$$

6 cm

15 cm

area   base   height

$$A = \frac{1}{2} \times (b \times h)$$
$$= \frac{1}{2} \times (10 \times 6)$$
$$= \frac{1}{2} \times 60$$
$$= 30 \text{ cm}^2$$

h: 6 cm

b: 10 cm

Use $3\frac{1}{7}$ or 3.14.

circumference   diameter

$$C = \pi \times d$$
$$= 3.14 \times 6$$
$$= 18.84 \text{ cm}$$

d = 6 cm
r = 3 cm

area

$$A = \pi \times r \times r$$
$$= 3.14 \times 3 \times 3$$
$$= 28.26 \text{ cm}^2$$

Find the perimeter and area of each figure.

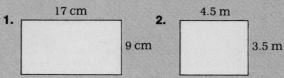

1. 17 cm, 9 cm

2. 4.5 m, 3.5 m

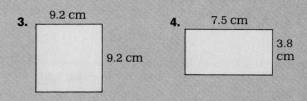

3. 9.2 cm, 9.2 cm

4. 7.5 cm, 3.8 cm

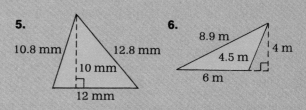

5. 10.8 mm, 12.8 mm, 10 mm, 12 mm

6. 8.9 m, 4.5 m, 4 m, 6 m

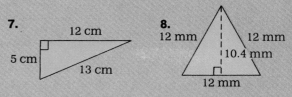

7. 12 cm, 5 cm, 13 cm

8. 12 mm, 12 mm, 10.4 mm, 12 mm

Find the circumference and area of each circle.

9.

d = 8 cm

10.

d = 2.5 m

11.

r = 14 mm

12.

r = 5 cm

362

Enrichment

Geometry Geoboard Areas

You can find the area of figures on a geoboard or dot paper by counting unit squares ☐ or by finding the area of a triangle that is half of some square or rectangle.

Geoboard

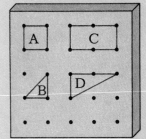

Give the number for each ▥.

1. The area of square A is 1, so the area of triangle B is ▥ square unit(s).

2. The area of rectangle C is 2, so the area of triangle D is ▥ square unit(s).

3. The area of the rectangular region is ▥ square units.

4. The area of the yellow region is ▥ square units.

5. The area of the brown region is ▥ square units.

6. The area of the blue region is ▥ square units.

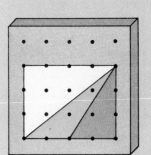

You can also find the area of any figure on a geoboard or dot paper by using **Pick's formula.**

Number of nails on the boundary of the figure

Number of nails inside the figure

$$\text{Area} = \frac{b}{2} + i - 1$$

Use Pick's formula to find the area of these figures. Check by counting squares.

7.
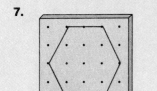

8.
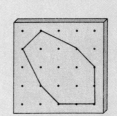

9.
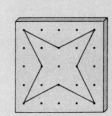

10.

11. Make some figures of your own on the geoboard or dot paper. Find their areas using Pick's formula. Check your answers by counting squares or parts of squares.

Cumulative Review

For items 1–3 use the graph below.

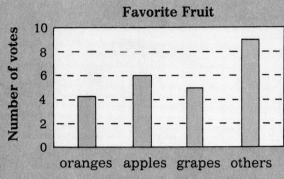

Favorite Fruit

1. How many votes were for grapes?

A 4 **B** 5
C 6 **D** not given

2. Which fruit got the least votes?

A apples **B** grapes
C oranges **D** not given

3. How many more votes did "others" get than apples?

A 2 **B** 6
C 9 **D** not given

4. Give the mean of these numbers:
56, 24, 44, 87, 44

A 44 **B** 51
C 52 **D** not given

5. Give the mean of these numbers to the nearest tenth:
145, 126, 159, 138, 130

A 138 **B** 140
C 139 **D** not given

For items 6–8 choose the fraction for each ratio.

6. 4:7 **A** 4 is to 7 **B** $\frac{7}{4}$
C $\frac{4}{7}$ **D** not given

7. 6 tickets for $5

A $\frac{6}{11}$ **B** $\frac{6}{5}$
C 6 to 5 **D** not given

8. 3 dogs to every 4 cats

A $\frac{3}{12}$ **B** $\frac{4}{3}$
C $\frac{3}{4}$ **D** not given

Solve for n.

9. $\frac{3}{8} = \frac{n}{24}$ **A** $n = 3$ **B** $n = 9$
C $n = 12$ **D** not given

10. $\frac{5}{6} = \frac{25}{n}$ **A** $n = 11$ **B** $n = 30$
C $n = 25$ **D** not given

11. $\frac{20}{28} = \frac{4}{n}$ **A** $n = 8$ **B** $n = 5$
C $n = 6$ **D** not given

12. $\frac{35}{50} = \frac{n}{10}$ **A** $n = 7$ **B** $n = 5$
C $n = 15$ **D** not given

13. There are 3 red marbles and 5 yellow marbles in a bag. If you draw 1 marble, what is the probability of getting a yellow marble?

A $\frac{3}{5}$ **B** $\frac{3}{8}$
C $\frac{5}{8}$ **D** not given

14. Glen drew a map with the scale 2 cm = 5 km. If Aton is 12 cm from Beeton on the map, how many kilometers is Aton from Beeton?

A 12 km **B** 30 km
C $\frac{5}{12}$ **D** not given

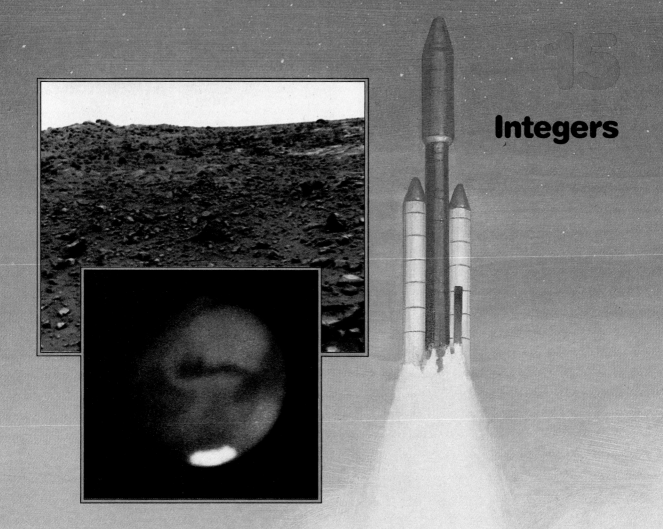

15

Integers

Martian weather report: clear and sunny but cold.

When the *Viking 1* and *Viking 2* spacecraft went to Mars, they gathered information about Martian weather and soil. The first weather report was received from *Viking 1* on July 23, 1976. The air temperature just after dawn was ⁻86°C. Later in the day, however, the temperature rose a total of 56°C—to a high of ⁻30°C! In September of the same year, *Viking 2* landed 7,400 km away from *Viking 1*. *Viking 2* reported air temperatures that ranged from a low of ⁻82°C to a high of ⁻29°C. Other studies of Mars have shown that the average yearly temperature is ⁻50°C at the planet's equator and ⁻130°C at the poles.

Although we cannot predict when astronauts of the future will make their first landing on Mars, we can safely forecast the kind of weather they will find: cold!

Positive and Negative Integers

Integers are numbers that are used to describe things that are opposites of each other. The integers include the **positive integers**, the **negative integers**, and **zero.**

A number line is one way of understanding positive and negative integers. The numbers to the right of zero are positive integers. The numbers to the left of zero are negative integers.

Work with a group.

Part 1

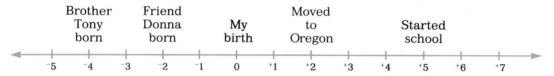

1. Susie is making a number line showing important events in her life. Talk with your group.
   - Why did Susie put her birth at zero?
   - How old was Susie when she moved to Oregon?
   - Is her brother Tony older or younger? How do you know?

2. Make a number line of your life.
   - Where will you put events that happened before you were born? Why?
   - Where will you put events that you expect to happen in the future? Why?

Part 2

3. Play an integer game with your group.
   - Draw a number line to represent distance.
   - Make the distances east of zero positive integers and the distances west of zero negative integers.

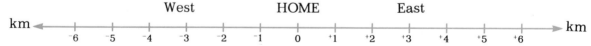

Rules
   - Start at HOME. Take turns telling each other a direction and a number of kilometers to travel.
   - Show where you land.
   - Name the point where you land. Tell where you would have landed if you had gone in the opposite direction.

4. What if you started at a different place? Play the game again.
   - Guess where you would land.
   - Draw moves on the number line to check your guesses.

5. Now give each other a starting place and a landing place. Tell how far you travel.

6. Suppose you know the landing place, the distance, and the direction traveled. Tell how you can find the starting place.

Part 3

7. With your group, think of ways we use positive and negative integers in real life.
   - List as many as you can.
   - For each way, write several examples of integers. Then write the opposite of those integers.
   - Draw diagrams or pictures.
   - Explain your work to other groups.

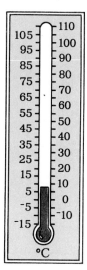

Adding Integers

Tim jogged 5 km west from his home. Then he jogged 3 km further west. How far and in what direction was he from home?

To solve this problem, we can add negative integers.

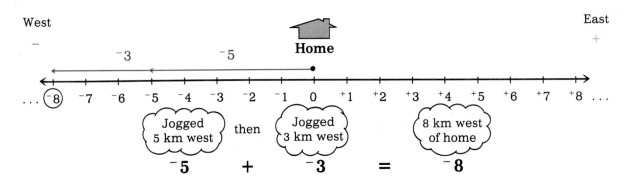

Tim was 8 km west of home.

In the situation below, we add positive integers.

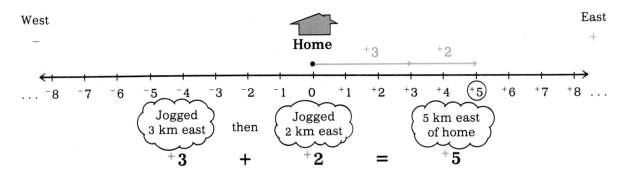

Warm Up

Find the sum. Use the number line if needed.

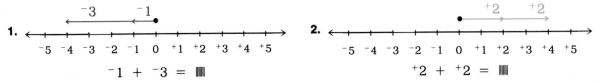

1. $^-1 + {}^-3 = $ ▦

2. $^+2 + {}^+2 = $ ▦

Practice Write an addition equation for each number line picture.

1.

2.

3.

4.

Find the sums. Think about the number line if needed.

5. $^-2 + {}^-3$ **6.** $^+4 + {}^+3$ **7.** $^+6 + {}^+1$ **8.** $^-5 + {}^-4$

9. $^+7 + {}^+3$ **10.** $^-8 + {}^-1$ **11.** $^-9 + {}^-2$ **12.** $^+6 + {}^+6$

13. $^-4 + {}^-4$ **14.** $^-8 + {}^-4$ **15.** $^+9 + {}^+3$ **16.** $^-6 + {}^-5$

17. $^-8 + {}^-7$ **18.** $^-9 + {}^-8$ **19.** $^+7 + {}^+6$ **20.** $^+4 + {}^+9$

21. The sum of two positive integers is a _?_ integer.

22. The sum of two negative integers is a _?_ integer.

23. Kate jogged 4 km west, then rested and jogged 5 more km west. How far and in what direction was she from home?

Skillkeeper

Find each area.

1. $l = 15$ cm   **2.** $l = 52$ m   **3.** $l = 9.4$ m   **4.** $l = 2.8$ cm

$w = 8$ cm $w = 10$ m $w = 6.3$ m $w = 4$ cm

$A = $ ▥ $A = $ ▥ $A = $ ▥ $A = $ ▥

Find each area. Use 3.14 for π and the formula $A = \pi \times r \times r$.

5. $r = 3$ cm   **6.** $d = 4$ m   **7.** $r = 1.5$ m   **8.** $d = 8$ cm

$A = $ ▥ $A = $ ▥ $A = $ ▥ $A = $ ▥

More Adding Integers

Here are some examples of bike trips which suggest additions involving a positive and a negative number. Study each example. Give the missing sums.

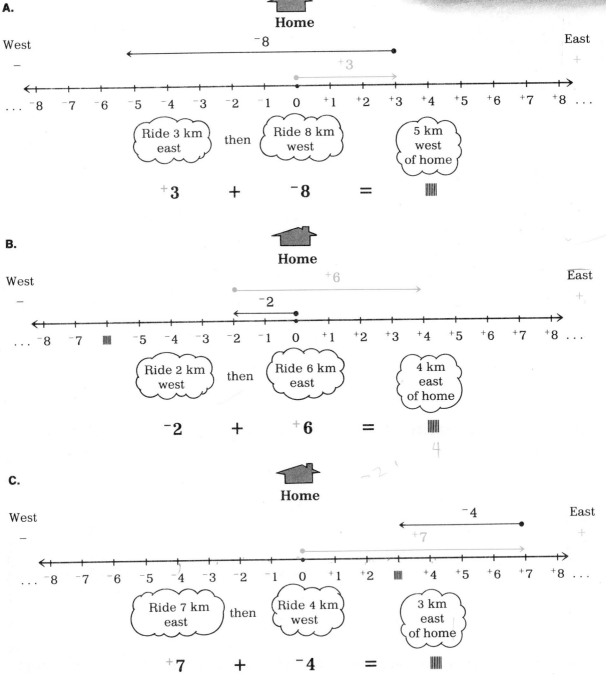

A.

Home

West — East +

... ⁻8 ⁻7 ⁻6 ⁻5 ⁻4 ⁻3 ⁻2 ⁻1 0 ⁺1 ⁺2 ⁺3 ⁺4 ⁺5 ⁺6 ⁺7 ⁺8 ...

⁻8

⁺3

(Ride 3 km east) then (Ride 8 km west) (5 km west of home)

⁺3 + ⁻8 = |||||

B.

Home

West — East +

... ⁻8 ⁻7 ||||| ⁻5 ⁻4 ⁻3 ⁻2 ⁻1 0 ⁺1 ⁺2 ⁺3 ⁺4 ⁺5 ⁺6 ⁺7 ⁺8 ...

⁺6

⁻2

(Ride 2 km west) then (Ride 6 km east) (4 km east of home)

⁻2 + ⁺6 = |||||

4

C.

Home

West — East +

... ⁻8 ⁻7 ⁻6 ⁻5 ⁻4 ⁻3 ⁻2 ⁻1 0 ⁺1 ⁺2 ||||| ⁺4 ⁺5 ⁺6 ⁺7 ⁺8 ...

⁻4

⁺7

(Ride 7 km east) then (Ride 4 km west) (3 km east of home)

⁺7 + ⁻4 = |||||

370

Write an addition equation for each number line picture.

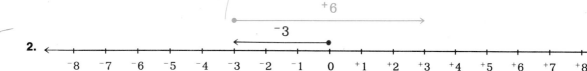

1.

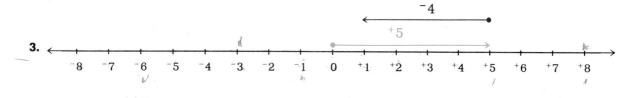

2.

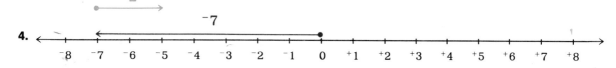

3.

4.

Find the sums. Use a number line when needed.

5. $^+7 + ^-3$ **6.** $^+6 + ^+8$ **7.** $^+4 + ^-3$ **8.** $^+6 + ^-6$

9. $^+2 + ^-6$ **10.** $^-17 + ^+8$ **11.** $^+1 + ^-9$ **12.** $^-9 + ^+4$

13. $^-6 + ^-4$ **14.** $^+9 + ^-5$ **15.** $^-2 + ^+8$ **16.** $^+9 + ^+7$

17. $^-7 + ^+16$ **18.** $^-13 + ^+6$ **19.** $^+3 + ^-8$ **20.** $^-4 + ^+13$

21. $^-8 + ^+8$ **22.** $^+13 + ^-7$ **23.** $^-14 + ^+8$ **24.** $^+7 + ^-2$

★ **25.** $^-47 + ^+23$ ★ **26.** $^+82 + ^-46$ ★ **27.** $^+23 + ^-89$ ★ **28.** $^-46 + ^+93$

Think

Discovering an Integer Pattern

Copy this grid. Find the integers for the empty squares by adding across and down. Make up some other grids like this one. What pattern do you discover?

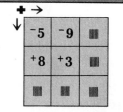

Math

Subtracting Integers

How much higher is an elevation of 6 km above sea level than an elevation of 4 km below sea level?

On the number line in the picture, we see that $^+6$ is 10 units above $^-4$, so 6 km above sea level is 10 km higher than 4 km below sea level.

Since the problem above asks us to compare two numbers ($^+6$ and $^-4$) we can also subtract to find the answer. As with whole numbers, we can think of subtracting integers as finding the missing addend.

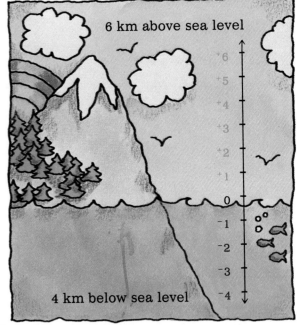

6 km above sea level

4 km below sea level

$$\begin{array}{ccc} \text{sum} & \text{addend} & \text{addend} \\ ^+6 & - & ^-4 & = & ? \end{array}$$

What integer adds to $^-4$ to give $^+6$?

Since $^+10 + {^-4} = {^+6}$,
$^+6 - {^-4} = {^+10}$

Other Examples

$^-6 - {^-4} = {^-2}$, because $^-2 + {^-4} = {^-6}$

$^+4 - {^-6} = {^+10}$, because $^+10 + {^-6} = {^+4}$

$^-6 - {^+4} = {^-10}$, because $^-10 + {^+4} = {^-6}$

$^-4 - {^-6} = {^+2}$, because $^+2 + {^-6} = {^-4}$

Warm Up   Subtract. Check by adding.

What integer adds to $^-3$ to give $^-5$?

$$\begin{array}{ccc} s & a & a \end{array}$$
1. $^-5 - {^-3} = n$

What integer adds to $^-8$ to give $^-5$?

2. $^-5 - {^-8} = n$

What integer adds to $^-3$ to give $^+1$?

3. $^+1 - {^-3} = n$

What integer adds to $^+3$ to give $^-5$?

4. $^-5 - {^+3} = n$

What integer adds to $^-2$ to give $^+4$?

5. $^+4 - {^-2} = n$

What integer adds to $^+5$ to give $^-4$?

6. $^-4 - {^+5} = n$

Practice Find the differences.
Thinking of addends and a sum may help you.

	s	a	a
1.	$^+3$	$-$ $^-5$	$= n$

	s	a	a
2.	$^-2$	$-$ $^+6$	$= n$

	s	a	a
3.	$^-2$	$-$ $^-4$	$= n$

	s	a	a
4.	$^+5$	$-$ $^-3$	$= n$

	s	a	a
5.	$^-3$	$-$ $^+8$	$= n$

	s	a	a
6.	$^+8$	$-$ $^-6$	$= n$

	s	a	a
7.	$^-8$	$-$ $^-5$	$= n$

	s	a	a
8.	$^+2$	$-$ $^+9$	$= n$

	s	a	a
9.	$^-5$	$-$ $^-4$	$= n$

	s	a	a
10.	$^+5$	$-$ $^-1$	$= n$

	s	a	a
11.	$^+2$	$-$ $^-3$	$= n$

	s	a	a
12.	$^+6$	$-$ $^-1$	$= n$

	s	a	a
13.	$^-8$	$-$ $^-8$	$= n$

	s	a	a
14.	6	$-$ $^-3$	$= n$

	s	a	a
15.	$^-9$	$-$ $^-8$	$= n$

	s	a	a
16.	$^-5$	$-$ 0	$= n$

	s	a	a
17.	$^+6$	$-$ $^+9$	$= n$

	s	a	a
18.	$^+2$	$-$ $^-4$	$= n$

19. How much higher is an elevation of 5 km above sea level ($^+5$) than an elevation of 3 km below sea level ($^-3$)?

20. Write and solve an integer equation for this problem. How much higher is an elevation of 2 km below sea level ($^-2$) than an elevation of 7 km below sea level ($^-7$)?

★ **21.** You may have discovered this rule:

> To subtract an integer, add its opposite.

Examples:

$^-1 - ^+6 = ^-1 + ^-6 = ^-7$

$^+6 - ^-4 = ^+6 + ^+4 = ^+10$

Use the rule to check the differences in exercises 1–10 above. Show your work.

Skillkeeper

Find the volume. Use the formula
$V = l \times w \times h$.

1. $l = 9$ cm
$w = 3$ cm
$h = 5$ cm
$V = $ ▦

2. $l = 7$ m
$w = 4$ m
$h = 2$ m
$V = $ ▦

3. $l = 80$ mm
$w = 70$ mm
$h - 40$ mm
$V = $ ▦

4. $l = 35$ m
$w = 2.4$ m
$h = 3$ m
$V = $ ▦

5. $l = 20$ cm
$w = 8.6$ cm
$h = 4.2$ cm
$V = $ ▦

6. $l = 18.4$ mm
$w = 10.8$ mm
$h = 6.5$ mm
$V = $ ▦

QUESTION
DATA
PLAN
ANSWER
CHECK

Problem Solving: Using Data from a Newspaper

Use the data from the "newspaper clippings" as needed to solve the problems.

1. How many more strokes did Lopez take than Nicols? (Hint: Find $^-2 - {^-8}$.)

2. How many more strokes did Gilper take than Lopez?

3. Suppose Beam had finished with 8 fewer strokes. What would Beam's score have been?

4. What was the difference between the nationwide high and low temperatures?

5. What was the difference between the nationwide low and the record local low?

6. The local low yesterday was 4°F higher than today's local low. What was yesterday's local low?

7. How much higher is the elevation of Mt. Whitney than the elevation of Death Valley?

Sports News

Nichols wins the holiday golf tournament by a big margin!

Nichols	$^-8$	(8 strokes under par*)
Lopez	$^-2$	
Gilper	$^+4$	(4 strokes over par)
Beam	$^+6$	

*8 fewer strokes than the standard number of strokes for the course.

Today's Weather

Nationwide high	75°F	(San Antonio, TX)
Nationwide low	$^-6$°F	(Bismark, N.D.)
Local high	70°F	
Local low	48°F	
Record local high	82°F	
Record local low	30°F	

Travel Section

Many of the visitors to Death Valley, California, know that at 282 ft below sea level it is the lowest point in the United States. Not so many of them know that less than 125 mi away lies Mt. Whitney. This 14,494 ft high peak is the highest point in the United States south of Alas

374

8. Antar stock had gained 5 points the day before. What was the total change for the two days?

9. What is the difference between the greatest gain and the greatest loss for a local stock?

10. Benco stock had lost 3 points the day before. What was its total change for the two days?

Stock Market Report

Local Stock	Points Gained or Lost*
Antar	⁺3
Benco	⁻4
Carbenz	⁺1
DRL	⁻2
Ensil	⁺5

On Wall Street the jump in stock prices

*Dollars per share increase or decrease

11. How many seconds after liftoff did the rocket engines run?

National News

The powerful engines on the space shuttle rocket were started 45 seconds before liftoff ($^-$45 s). They ran for a total of 360 seconds to

Late Sports Report

Football running back Tom Gallup carried the ball the last three plays to give the Eagles a 21–14 win over the Bearcats. He gained 5 yards, lost 7 yards, and gained 9 yards to cross the goal line on the final play. He

12. How many total yards did Tom Gallup gain on the last 3 plays?

13. Strategy Practice On the back of a clipping cut from a newspaper, Steve saw this picture of the top 3 layers of a monument that was to be built in the city park. How many blocks do you think are needed in all if there are to be 10 layers?

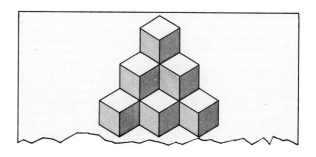

Comparing and Ordering Integers

Here are scores for a game some
students played. Negative integers
show scores "in the hole," and
positive integers show scores "to the
good." Who had a higher score, Bart
or Jeral? Can you list the scores in
order from greatest to least?

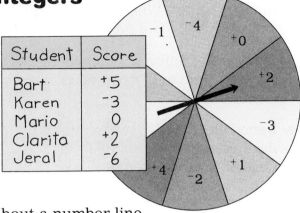

Student	Score
Bart	+5
Karen	-3
Mario	0
Clarita	+2
Jeral	-6

Comparing Integers

We can compare integers by thinking about a number line.
The integer that is farther to the right is the greater of two integers.

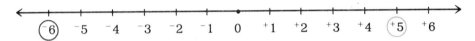

⁺5 > ⁻6   Bart's score was greater than Jeral's.

Ordering Integers

We order a list of integers by
comparing them two at a time.

Bart ⎫ ⁺5
Clarita ⎪ ⁺2
Mario ⎬ 0
Karen ⎪ ⁻3
Jeral ⎭ ⁻6

Scores ordered
from greatest
to least

Other Examples

⁻1 > ⁻2   ⁻3 < ⁺1   ⁺2 < ⁺5   0 > ⁻5   ⁻3 > ⁻20

Write > or < for each ▦

1. ⁺4 ▦ ⁻3
2. ⁺7 ▦ ⁺9
3. ⁻1 ▦ ⁺2
4. ⁺4 ▦ 0

5. ⁻5 ▦ ⁻2
6. ⁺3 ▦ ⁻3
7. ⁺1 ▦ ⁻4
8. ⁻12 ▦ ⁻35

9. 0 ▦ ⁻6
10. ⁺2 ▦ ⁻4
11. ⁻8 ▦ ⁺3
12. ⁻5 ▦ ⁺5

13. ⁻6 ▦ ⁻5
14. ⁻1 ▦ ⁻9
15. ⁺3 ▦ ⁻5
16. ⁺6 ▦ ⁻15

Order from greatest to least.

17. ⁻4, ⁺3, 0, ⁻2, ⁻6, ⁺7

18. ⁻2, ⁺7, ⁻1, ⁺1, ⁻4, ⁺3

19. ⁺16, ⁻4, ⁺3, ⁻14, ⁻17

Order from least to greatest.

20. ⁻15, ⁺6, ⁺10, 0, ⁻8, ⁻3

21. ⁺8, 0, ⁻1, ⁺1, ⁻4, ⁺14

22. ⁻89, ⁺98, ⁻99, ⁺100, ⁻86

More Practice, page 444, Set D

Problem Solving: Mixed Practice

Solve.

1. Some scientists say that the earth is about 4.5 billion years old. The first life on earth may have appeared 3.54 billion years ago. For how long was the earth without life?

2. The oldest rock found so far on earth is 0.8 times as old as the earth. Use data from problem 1 to find the age of this rock.

3. The ratio of the average diameter of the moon to the average diameter of the earth is 3 to 11. The average diameter of the moon is about 3,450 km. About what is the average diameter of the earth?

4. Water covers 71% of the earth's surface. What percent of the earth's surface does land cover?

5. Mt. Everest, the earth's highest mountain, reaches a height of 8,543 m above sea level (+8,543 m). The Mariana Trench in the Pacific Ocean, the deepest known part of any ocean, is 10,918 m below sea level (-10,918 m). What is the difference of these two elevations?

6. The highest temperature recorded on earth (in Africa) was +58°C. The lowest temperature recorded (in Antarctica) was -88°C. What is the difference between these temperatures?

7. The lowest sea temperature is -2°C (in the White Sea). The highest sea temperature is +38°C warmer than this (in the Persian Gulf). What is the highest sea temperature?

8. **DATA BANK** How many hours difference in time is there between Beijing (Peking), China, and Los Angeles, California? List the cities given from most hours earlier than GMT to most hours later than GMT. (See Data Bank, page 424.)

9. **Strategy Practice** The Pacific Ocean (with nearby seas) makes up $\frac{1}{2}$ of the total ocean area. The Indian Ocean (with nearby seas) makes up $\frac{2}{10}$ of the total ocean area. The rest is the Atlantic Ocean (with nearby seas), which covers 72 million km². What is the total ocean area?

Graphing with Integers

A spot near Lebanon, Kansas, is the geographic center of
the United States (not including Alaska and Hawaii).
We can use this center as the **origin** (0,0) and **ordered pairs**
of integers (coordinates) to show the approximate locations
of some other cities.

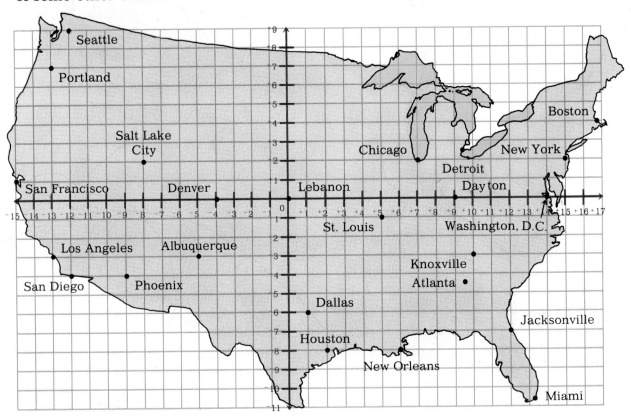

Examples

Chicago: right 7, up 2 **(⁺7,⁺2)**   Knoxville: right 10, down 3 **(⁺10,⁻3)**

Denver: left 4, up 0   **(⁻4,0)**   Phoenix: left 9, down 4   **(⁻9,⁻4)**

Use ordered pairs of integers to give the locations of these cities.

1. New York   **2.** Seattle   **3.** Dayton

4. Jacksonville   **5.** Albuquerque   **6.** New Orleans

What cities are at these locations?

7. (⁺14,0)   **8.** (⁻13,⁺7)   **9.** (⁻12,⁻4)   **10.** (⁻8,⁺2)

11. (⁺1,⁻6)   **12.** (⁻15,⁺1)   **13.** (⁺2,⁻8)   **14.** (⁺5,⁻1)

378

Use the graphs below for exercises 1–30.

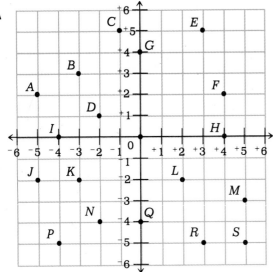

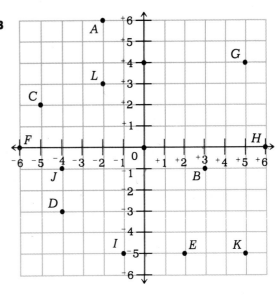

Give the ordered pair for each point on graph A.

1. A **2.** D **3.** G **4.** F **5.** I **6.** K

7. H **8.** B **9.** L **10.** R **11.** N **12.** P

13. M **14.** S **15.** E **16.** C **17.** Q **18.** J

Give the point on graph B for each ordered pair.

19. $(^+5, ^+4)$ **20.** $(^-2, ^+6)$ **21.** $(^-4, ^-3)$ **22.** $(^-6, 0)$

23. $(^+3, ^-1)$ **24.** $(^-5, ^+2)$ **25.** $(^+2, ^-5)$ **26.** $(^+6, 0)$

27. $(^-1, ^-5)$ **28.** $(^-2, ^+3)$

29. $(^+5, ^-5)$ **30.** $(^-4, ^-1)$

Graph each figure on graph paper by graphing and connecting points.

31. A kite: $(^+4, ^-3)$ $(^-3, 0)$ $(^-4, ^+5)$ $(^+1, ^+4)$

32. A triangle: $(^+2, ^-2)$ $(^-4, ^+4)$ $(^+2, ^+4)$

33. Just for fun: $(^-8, ^-1)$ $(^-3, ^+4)$ $(^-2, ^+6)$ $(^-1, ^+6)$ $(^-1, ^+4)$ $(^+7, ^-1)$ $(^+7, ^-2)$ $(^+6, ^-3)$ $(^+4, ^-2)$ $(^+6, ^-4)$ $(^+5, ^-4)$ $(^-1, ^-2)$ $(^-2, ^-8)$ $(^-8, ^-1)$. As extras, include $(^-1, ^+2)$ and $(^+6, ^-1)$.

Applied
Problem Solving

You are in Flagstaff, Arizona. You want to rent a car to do some weekday sightseeing while on vacation. Should you use the Unlimited Driving or the Per Kilometer rental plan?

Some Things to Consider

- The weekday rates for the Unlimited Driving Plan are $48 per day.

- The weekday rates for the Per Kilometer rental plan are $19 each day plus 12¢ for each kilometer.

- You are going to rent a car for 4 days.

- You may take trips from Flagstaff to these places:

  Petrified Forest, 176 km from Flagstaff

  Grand Canyon, 216 km from Flagstaff

  Meteor Crater, 64 km from Flagstaff

- You are also going to do some driving around Flagstaff.

Some Questions to Answer

1. What would be the total cost of the Unlimited Driving rate?

2. What would be the total cost, not including kilometers driven, at the Per Kilometer rate?

3. What would be the total cost at the Per Kilometer rate including round trips from Flagstaff to each of the other places listed?

What Is Your Decision?

Will you use the Unlimited Driving Plan or the Per Kilometer rental plan?

Chapter Review-Test

Give the opposite of each integer.

1. $^+4$ **2.** $^-3$ **3.** $^-8$ **4.** $^+12$ **5.** $^-72$ **6.** $^+135$

Give the integer for the point on the number line that is

7. 6 units to the left of 0.   **8.** 13 units to the right of 0.

Find the sums.

9. $^+3 + {}^+7$ **10.** $^+2 + {}^-6$ **11.** $^-4 + {}^-10$ **12.** $^-3 + {}^+9$

13. $^-12 + {}^+5$ **14.** $^+7 + {}^-3$ **15.** $^-9 + {}^-6$ **16.** $^+8 + {}^-7$

Find the differences. Thinking of addends and a sum may help.

	s	a	a
17.	$^-5$	$-$	$^-3 = n$

	s	a	a
18.	$^+4$	$-$	$^-1 = n$

	s	a	a
19.	$^-3$	$-$	$^+6 = n$

	s	a	a
20.	$^+2$	$-$	$^+8 = n$

	s	a	a
21.	$^-7$	$-$	$^-4 = n$

	s	a	a
22.	$^-3$	$-$	$^-9 = n$

Write > or < for each 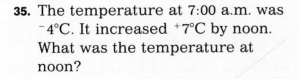 .

23. $^+12$ ⬚ $^+7$ **24.** $^-1$ ⬚ $^+3$ **25.** $^-4$ ⬚ $^-10$ **26.** $^+9$ ⬚ $^-10$ **27.** 0 ⬚ $^-5$

Give the ordered pairs for these points.

28. A   **29.** B

30. C   **31.** D

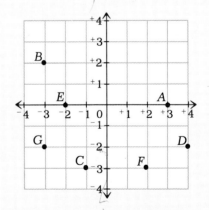

Give the points for these ordered pairs.

32. $(^-2,0)$ **33.** $(^-3,^-2)$ **34.** $(^+2,^-3)$

Solve.

35. The temperature at 7:00 a.m. was $^-4°C$. It increased $^+7°C$ by noon. What was the temperature at noon?

36. Mountain City has an elevation of $^+4$ km. Valley City has an elevation of $^-1$ km. What is the difference of these elevations?

381

Another Look

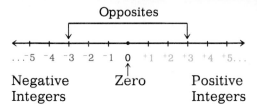

Opposites

$$\ldots \bar{}5 \quad \bar{}4 \quad \bar{}3 \quad \bar{}2 \quad \bar{}1 \quad 0 \quad {}^+1 \quad {}^+2 \quad {}^+3 \quad {}^+4 \quad {}^+5 \ldots$$

Negative   Zero   Positive
Integers   Integers

To add integers, think about the number line.

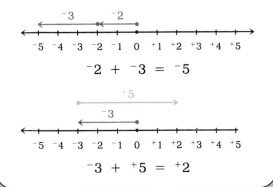

$${}^-2 + {}^-3 = {}^-5$$

$${}^-3 + {}^+5 = {}^+2$$

To subtract integers, find the missing addend.

$$\begin{array}{ccc} s & a & a \\ {}^+5 & - & {}^-3 & = & ? \end{array}$$

What integer adds to $^-3$ to give the sum $^+5$?

$^+5 - {}^-3 = {}^+8$, since
$^+8 + {}^-3 = {}^+5$

left   right

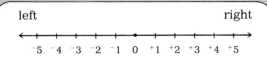

$^+1$ is to the right of $^-2$, so $^+1 > {}^-2$

$^-2$ is to the right of $^-5$, so $^-2 > {}^-5$

$^-3$ is to the left of $^+2$, so $^-3 < {}^+2$

Give the opposite of each integer.

1. $^-1$ **2.** $^+4$ **3.** $^-8$

4. $^-20$ **5.** $^+56$ **6.** $^-127$

7. $^+14$ **8.** $^-86$ **9.** $^+675$

10. $^-324$ **11.** $^+189$ **12.** $^-10$

Find the sums.

13. $^+4 + {}^+8$ **14.** $^-6 + {}^-2$

15. $^-3 + {}^-9$ **16.** $^+7 + {}^+15$

17. $^+8 + {}^-4$ **18.** $^-9 + {}^+3$

19. $^-2 + {}^+9$ **20.** $^-6 + {}^+11$

21. $^-7 + {}^-8$ **22.** $^+9 + {}^-1$

23. $^-8 + 0$ **24.** $^-16 + {}^+16$

25. $^-4 + {}^+13$ **26.** $^+2 + {}^-11$

Find the differences.

$$\begin{array}{ccc} s & a & a \end{array}$$
27. $^+4 - {}^-1 = n$ **28.** $^-8 - {}^+4 = n$

29. $^-2 - {}^+6 = n$ **30.** $^+3 - {}^-8 = n$

31. $^-7 - {}^-2 = n$ **32.** $^-4 - {}^+4 = n$

Write > or < for each ▨ .

33. $^+5$ ▨ $^-3$ **34.** $^+9$ ▨ $^+2$

35. 0 ▨ $^-3$ **36.** $^+1$ ▨ $^-1$

37. $^-8$ ▨ $^-4$ **38.** $^-2$ ▨ $^+2$

39. $^+8$ ▨ $^-12$ **40.** $^-3$ ▨ $^-18$

Enrichment

Using a Calculator to Check Integer Patterns

Push a whole number key to enter a positive integer. Push a whole number key followed by the $+/-$ key to enter a negative integer.

$^-5$ has been entered by pushing 5 $+/-$.

Push the keys shown to check these examples.

$$8 \;|+|\; 5 \;|+/-|\; |=|$$

$$8 + {}^-5 = 3$$

$$6 \;|+/-|\; |-|\; 2 \;|+/-|\; |=|$$

$$^-6 - {}^-2 = {}^-4$$

$$4 \;|\times|\; 3 \;|+/-|\; |=|$$

$$4 \times {}^-3 = {}^-12$$

Copy each column of equations. Use your calculator to solve each equation. What patterns do you see?

1.	2.	3.	4.
$5 + 4 = ?$	$4 - 4 = ?$	$4 \times 4 = ?$	$4 \times {}^-4 = ?$
$5 + 3 = ?$	$4 - 3 = ?$	$4 \times 3 = ?$	$3 \times {}^-4 = ?$
$5 + 2 = ?$	$4 - 2 = ?$	$4 \times 2 = ?$	$2 \times {}^-4 = ?$
$5 + 1 = ?$	$4 - 1 = ?$	$4 \times 1 = ?$	$1 \times {}^-4 = ?$
$5 + 0 = ?$	$4 - 0 = ?$	$4 \times 0 = ?$	$0 \times {}^-4 = ?$
$5 + {}^-1 = ?$	$4 - {}^-1 = ?$	$4 \times {}^-1 = ?$	$^-1 \times {}^-4 = ?$
$5 + {}^-2 = ?$	$4 - {}^-2 = ?$	$4 \times {}^-2 = ?$	$^-2 \times {}^-4 = ?$
$5 + {}^-3 = ?$	$4 - {}^-3 = ?$	$4 \times {}^-3 = ?$	$^-3 \times {}^-4 = ?$
$5 + {}^-4 = ?$	$4 - {}^-4 = ?$	$4 \times {}^-4 = ?$	$^-4 \times {}^-4 = ?$

5. Use your calculator to help you make up some rules for multiplying and dividing integers.

1. Give a fraction for 8%.

A $\frac{1}{10}$ **B** $\frac{8}{25}$

C $\frac{1}{8}$ **D** not given

2. Give a fraction for 80%.

A $\frac{4}{5}$ **B** $\frac{2}{3}$

C $\frac{1}{8}$ **D** not given

3. Give a percent for $\frac{3}{5}$.

A 30%   **B** 50%

C 60%   **D** not given

4. Give a decimal for 135%.

A 0.135   **B** 13.5

C 1.35   **D** not given

5. Give a percent for 1.65.

A $16\frac{1}{2}\%$ **B** 165%

C $1\frac{13}{20}\%$ **D** not given

6. Find 25% of 36.

A 8   **B** 45

C 27   **D** not given

7. Find 5% of 140.

A 7   **B** 70

C 28   **D** not given

8. Find the perimeter.

A 5.12 cm^2
B 4.8 cm
C 9.6 cm
D not given

1.6 cm   3.2 cm

9. Find the area.

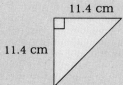

11.4 cm   11.4 cm

A 64.98 cm^2
B 129.96 cm^2
C 22.8 cm^2
D not given

10. Find the circumference.
Use 3.14 for π and $C = \pi \times d$.

$d = 6$ cm

A 9.42 cm
B 18.84 cm
C 113.04 cm
D not given

11. Find the area.
Use 3.14 for π and $A = \pi \times r \times r$.

$r = 10$ cm

A 31.4 cm^2
B 314 cm^2
C 1,256 cm^2
D not given

12. Find the volume.

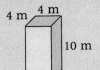

4 m   4 m   10 m

A 160 m^3
B 80 m^3
C 56 m^3
D not given

13. What is the area of a square garden if each side is 25 meters long?

A 125 m^2 **B** 500 m^2

C 100 m^2 **D** not given

14. 60% of the 125 members of a club voted for Mark for treasurer. How many members voted for Mark?

A 75   **B** 50

C 100   **D** not given

Estimating with Customary Units

First estimate the length. Then measure the length of the object.

1.

    Your estimate: ▥ in.
    Actual measure: ▥ in. (to the nearest $\frac{1}{2}$ in.)

2. Pencil Lead

    Your estimate: ▥ in.
    Actual measure: ▥ in. (to the nearest $\frac{1}{4}$ in.)

3.

    Your estimate: ▥ in.
    Actual measure: ▥ in. (to the nearest $\frac{1}{8}$ in.)

4.

    Your estimate: ▥ in.
    Actual measure: ▥ in. (to the nearest $\frac{1}{16}$ in.)

First estimate. Then measure the actual length.

5. Your arm span

    Your estimate: ▥ ft ▥ in.
    Actual measure: ▥ ft ▥ in.
    (to the nearest $\frac{1}{2}$ in.)

6. Length of your normal step

    Your estimate: ▥ ft ▥ in.
    Actual measure: ▥ ft ▥ in.
    (to the nearest inch)

★ **7.** Estimate a distance of 50 ft by stepping it off. Measure to see by how many feet or inches your estimate varies from the measured distance.

Problem Solving: Using Data from a Picture

QUESTION
DATA
PLAN
ANSWER
CHECK

Solve. Use data from the pictures as needed.

1. What is the area of the garden in square feet?

12 ft

15 ft

2. How many feet of fencing are needed to build a fence around the garden?

3. What is the area of the picture in square inches?

4. How much framing board would be needed to go around the picture? Give the answer in feet and inches.

5. The furniture in the room pictured at the right uses about 39 yd^2 of floor area. How much open floor space is left in the room?

6. Baseboard is needed to go around all except the fireplace side of the room. How many yards will be needed?

7. A bike path equal in total length to the perimeter of the park is to be made around the park. How long will the path be?

8. The park has 8 mi^2 of lakes. What is the land area of the park?

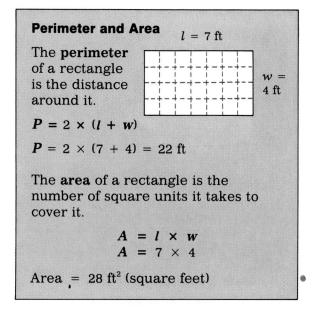

Perimeter and Area

$l = 7$ ft

The **perimeter** of a rectangle is the distance around it.

$w = 4$ ft

$P = 2 \times (l + w)$

$P = 2 \times (7 + 4) = 22$ ft

The **area** of a rectangle is the number of square units it takes to cover it.

$$A = l \times w$$
$$A = 7 \times 4$$

Area = 28 ft^2 (square feet)

16 in.

24 in.

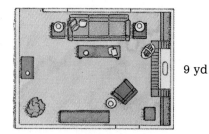

9 yd

12 yd

9 mi

14 mi

9. What is the volume of the storage chest?

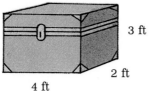

3 ft

2 ft

4 ft

10. How many square feet of decorative paper will it take to cover it?

11. How much paper would it take to cover the surface of the shipping box?

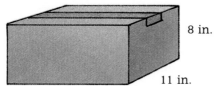

8 in.

11 in.

16 in.

12. What is the volume of the shipping box above?

13. How many cubic inches of space will the stereo speaker use when it is packed for shipping?

14. All faces of the stereo speaker except the front and back are to be varnished. How many square inches is this?

★ **15.** Concrete is often sold by the cubic yard. About how many cubic yards of concrete are needed for a sidewalk 40 ft long, 3 ft wide, and 4 in. thick (high)?

16. DATA HUNT How many cubic feet of air are in your classroom for each person in your class?

17. Strategy Practice A cord of wood is enough wood to make a stack 8 ft by 4 ft by 4 ft. Mr. Woodburner was charged $120 per cord for a load of wood. The load of wood made a stack 12 ft long, 3 ft wide, and 4 ft high. How much should Mr. Woodburner have paid for this much wood?

Volume and Surface Area

The **volume** of a box is the number of unit cubes it takes to fill it.

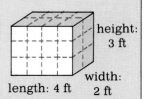

height: 3 ft

length: 4 ft

width: 2 ft

$V = l \times w \times h$

$V = 4 \times 2 \times 3$

Volume = 24 ft³ (cubic feet)

The **surface area** of a box is the sum of the areas of each of its faces.

s.a. = 12 + 12 + 6 + 6 + 8 + 8
s.a. = 52 ft²

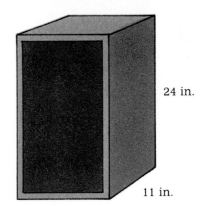

24 in.

11 in.

14 in.

Capacity

A **fluid ounce** (oz) is a basic customary unit of capacity.

2 tablespoons = 1 ounce

A **cup** (c) holds 8 oz.

1 cup = 8 ounces

A **pint** (pt) holds 2 c.

1 pint = 2 cups

A **quart** (qt) holds 2 pt.

1 quart = 2 pints

A **gallon** (gal) holds 4 qt.

1 gallon = 4 quarts

Give the missing numbers.

1. 2 oz = ▦ tablespoons

2. 2 c = ▦ oz

3. 2 qt = ▦ pt

4. 3 pt = ▦ c

5. 2 gal = ▦ qt

6. 1 qt = ▦ c

7. 1 gal = ▦ pt

8. 1 gal = ▦ c

9. 8 qt = ▦ gal

10. 4 c = ▦ qt

11. $\frac{1}{2}$ pt = ▦ c

12. $\frac{1}{2}$ gal = ▦ qt

13. 1 cup of cooking oil fills ▦ tablespoons.

14. A quart of milk fills ▦ cups.

15. 1 gallon and 2 pints of limeade fill ▦ cups.

16. 1 pint of cough syrup fills ▦ tablespoons.

17. A gallon of honey fills ▦ pint jars.

18. 2 pints and 2 cups of tomato juice fill ▦ quarts.

Problem Solving: Mixed Practice

Solve.

1. Ned bought 6 pint bottles of grape juice. How many quarts of grape juice was this?

2. How many cups of lemonade are in six 12-oz cans of lemonade?

3. Milk costs $2.24 a gallon. Is this more than or less than 49¢ per quart? How much more or less per quart is it?

4. A container holds $1\frac{1}{2}$ gal of apple juice. How many quarts does it hold?

5. A can holds 1 qt of orange juice. Another can holds 28 oz of juice. Which can holds more juice? How many ounces more does it hold?

6. Estela paid 20¢ for $\frac{1}{2}$ pt of milk for her lunch. Her mother paid $1.12 for $\frac{1}{2}$ gal of milk. How much more or less per quart did Estela pay than her mother?

7. A storage can measures 1 ft by 1 ft by 1 ft. If a gallon has a volume of 231 in.^{3}, how many gallons does the can hold? (Round the answer to the nearest tenth.)

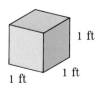

8. **Strategy Practice** Suppose you have a 4-qt jar and an 11-qt jar and a barrel of apple cider. There are no markings on either jar. How can you use these jars to get 5 qt of cider in the larger jar?

Weight

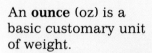

An **ounce** (oz) is a basic customary unit of weight. 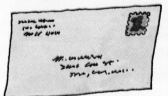 A letter might weigh 1 ounce.	A **pound** (lb) is 16 oz. A football boxed for mailing 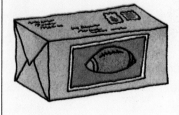 1 pound = 16 ounces	A **ton** (T) is 2,000 lb. A small mail delivery truck  1 ton = 2,000 pounds

Give the missing numbers.

1. 1 lb = ▨ oz

2. 1 T = ▨ lb

3. 3 lb = ▨ oz

4. 4 T = ▨ lb

5. $\frac{3}{4}$ lb = ▨ oz

6. $\frac{1}{2}$ T = ▨ oz

7. 32 oz = ▨ lb

8. 10,000 lb = ▨ T

9. 18 oz = ▨ lb

10. 5,000 lb = ▨ T

11. 30 T = ▨ lb

12. 256 oz = ▨ lb

Complete each sentence. Write **oz**, **lb**, or **T**.

13. A tennis ball weighs about 2 __?__.

14. A person might weigh 140 __?__.

15. A large whale might weigh 160 __?__.

16. An automobile might weigh $1\frac{1}{2}$ __?__.

17. A book might weigh 28 __?__.

18. A loaf of bread might weigh 1 __?__.

19. A large elephant might weigh 5 __?__.

Problem Solving: Mixed Practice

Solve.

1. A package weighs 56 oz. How many pounds does it weigh?

2. A wooden gift box containing 12 large apples was mailed to a friend. The empty box weighed 2 lb. When filled, the box weighed 8 lb. About how much did one of the apples weigh?

3. A company shipped 10,000 boxes of softballs weighing 8 oz per box. How many tons were shipped?

4. In a recent year the postal rate on first class letters was 20¢ for the first ounce and 17¢ for each additional ounce. How much did it cost to mail an 8-ounce letter?

5. To mail books in a recent year it cost 63¢ for the first pound, 23¢ for each additional pound through 7 lb, and 14¢ for each pound over 7 lb. What did it cost to mail a box of books that weighed 144 oz?

6. **DATA BANK**   How many pounds does a basketball weigh? Give your answer as a mixed number. List the weights of other balls used for sports from lightest to heaviest. (See Data Bank, p. 426.)

7. **DATA HUNT**   Is the total weight of the students in your class more than or less than a ton? How many pounds more or less?

8. **Strategy Practice**   Jed weighs 3 times as much as Luis. Together the two boys weigh 180 lb. What is the weight of each boy?

Temperature

The degree Fahrenheit (°F) is the basic customary unit of temperature.

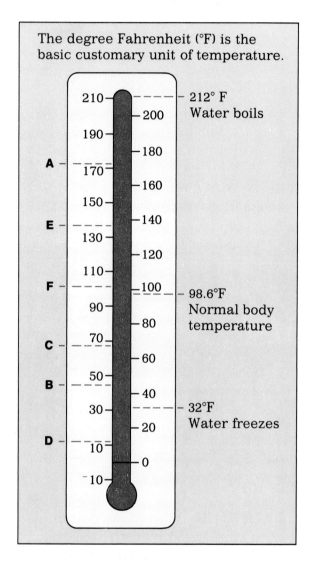

210 —
212° F
Water boils
200
190 —
180
A
170
160
150 —
E
140
130
120
110 —
F
100
98.6°F
Normal body
temperature
90
80
70
C
60
50 —
B
40
30 —
32°F
Water freezes
20
D
10
0
-10

Give the letter on the thermometer that is the best estimate for the temperature suggested by each picture.

1. Hottest recorded U.S. temperature

2. Hot cocoa (not quite boiling)

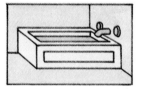

3. Warm bath water

4. Cold water

5. Room temperature

6. Frozen custard

Choose the most reasonable temperature for each.

7. Melting lead
A 99°F
B 212°F
C 621°F

8. Ice water
A 60°
B 33°F
C 0°F

9. Hot summer day
A 95°F
B 55°F
C 35°F

10. Inside a freezer
A 125°F
B 25°F
C 50°F

11. Slight fever
A 100°F
B 95°F
C 105°F

12. Hot soup
A 180°F
B 100°F
C 50°F

13. Cool fall day
A 50°F
B 90°F
C 10°F

14. Hot faucet water
A 60°F
B 90°F
C 150°F

15. DATA HUNT What is the difference between today's indoor temperature and today's outdoor temperature in °F?

Problem Solving: Using a Calculator

Use a calculator to solve each problem below.

1. A dollar bill is 6 in. long. How much money would you have if you had a string of dollar bills laid end to end for 1 mile?

2. A small car costs $5,695. The car weighs 2,654 lb. What is the cost for each pound of car?

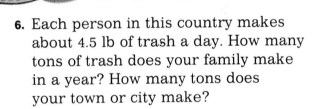

6. Each person in this country makes about 4.5 lb of trash a day. How many tons of trash does your family make in a year? How many tons does your town or city make?

3. Suppose you could drive the 238,866 miles from the earth to the moon in an automobile at 55 miles per hour. How many hours, to the nearest whole number of hours, would it take you to drive there and back? How many days?

4. How many years would it take you to walk the 24,901 miles around the earth if you walked at a rate of 12 miles a day?

5. An ounce of nickels contains 6 nickels. An 85-lb student has a bag of nickels that weighs the same as she does. What is the value of the money in the bag?

7. **DATA HUNT** Find your pulse rate. If your heart has beaten at this rate ever since you were born, about how many times had your heart beaten when you had your last birthday?

8. **Strategy Practice** Suppose a rich king gave his favorite daughter 1 oz of gold the first day, 2 oz the second, 4 oz the third, 8 oz the fourth, and so on. If the gold was worth $489 an ounce, what was the value of all her gold after 10 days?

Mixed Skills Practice

Computation

Find the answers.

1. $138{,}201 - 56{,}849$

2. $3{,}157 \times 268$

3. $94\overline{)56{,}163}$

4. $865{,}462 \\ 49{,}786 \\ + 8{,}458$

5. $537.55 - 46.263$

6. 236.5×3.07

7. $0.06\overline{)0.0546}$

8. 76% of 98

9. $\frac{5}{6} = \frac{75}{n}$ $n = ?$

10. $4\frac{2}{3} \div 3\frac{5}{8}$

11. $54\frac{5}{8} + 39\frac{7}{10}$

12. $34\frac{2}{7} - 19\frac{3}{5}$

13. $\frac{7}{12} \times 144$

14. $^-15 + {}^+8$

15. $\overset{s}{^-4} - \overset{a}{^-6} = \overset{a}{n}$

16. $94{,}683 + 48{,}577$

17. $67\overline{)27{,}403}$

18. $6.2\overline{)215.6}$

19. 47.8×98.3

20. $6\frac{4}{5} \times 3\frac{3}{8}$

Mental Math

Write only the answers.

21. $4{,}000 + 9{,}000$

22. $5{,}200 - 900$

23. 500×700

24. $24{,}000 \div 80$

25. 75.3×10

26. 56.84×100

27. $7.234 \times 1{,}000$

28. $674 \div 10$

29. $865.2 \div 100$

30. $9{,}374 \div 1{,}000$

31. 25% of 32

32. 50% of 126

33. $3 \times 5\frac{1}{3}$

34. $19.5 + 3.5$

35. $^-12 + {}^+5$

36. $2.4 \div 6$

Estimation

Estimate.

37. $9{,}879 + 4{,}068$

38. $89.56 - 44.18$

39. 8.29×5.98

40. $53.87 \div 5.89$

41. $484 \div 7$

42. $713 \div 8$

43. 52% of 64

44. 24% of 124

45. $849 + 781 + 957$

46. $3.73 + 8.28 + 7.24$

47. $8.49 + 5.36 + 9.58 + 6.75$

48. $4{,}976 + 5{,}174 + 4{,}965$

49. $8.24 + 7.95 + 7.79 + 8.06$

50. $6{,}926 + 7{,}352 + 6{,}966 + 7{,}085 + 7{,}218$

Applied Problem Solving

You are going to build a clubhouse. You need to decide whether to build the floor from $\frac{3}{4}$-in. plywood or from 1 by 6 boards.

Some Things to Consider

$\frac{3}{4}$ in.

$5\frac{1}{2}$ in.

- The floor is to be a 6 ft by 8 ft rectangle.

- A 1 by 6 board is actually $\frac{3}{4}$ in. thick by $5\frac{1}{2}$ in. wide. These boards come in lengths of 8, 10, 12, 14, 16, 18, and 20 ft. They cost 29¢ for each foot of length.

- The $\frac{3}{4}$ in. plywood comes in 4 ft by 8 ft pieces. Plywood of average quality costs 50¢ a square foot. You cannot buy just a part of a 4 by 8 ft piece.

- You want to build the clubhouse as cheaply and as quickly as possible.

Some Questions to Answer

1. How many full sheets of plywood would it take to build the floor? How many square feet is that? What would the cost be?

2. How many inches wide is the floor?

3. What is the smallest number of 1 by 6 boards that will be needed?

4. How long must each board be? How many ft of boards are needed?

5. What would be the total cost for the boards?

What Is Your Decision?

Will you use plywood or will you use 1 by 6 boards?

401

Problem Solving:
Using the Strategies

Use one or more of the strategies listed to help you solve each problem below.

Choose the Operations
Guess and Check
Draw a Picture
Make a Table
Make an Organized List
Use Logical Reasoning
Work Backward
Solve a Simpler Problem
Find a Pattern

1. Joe decided to start a 10-day exercise program, gradually increasing the number of push-ups he did each day. The first day he would do 1, the next day 2, the next day 4, the next day 8, and so on. If Joe tried to do this, how many push-ups would he have to do the last day of his program?

2. Luz Maria and 6 friends decide that each person will take a roller coaster ride with each of the others. How many rides will it take to do this?

3. In a class 100-m run, Ken, Mindy, Brad, and Emily finished first, second, third, and fourth (not in that order). Emily was neither second nor third. Mindy was neither first nor second. If Brad was third, what was the order of finish?

4. On a trip to Europe, 3 out of every 4 seats on an airplane were filled. If there were 150 passengers, how many seats were on the plane?

Chapter Review-Test

Give the missing numbers.

1. 6 ft = ▥ in.

2. 5 yd = ▥ ft

3. 3 yd = ▥ in.

4. 3 mi = ▥ ft

5. $1\frac{1}{2}$ mi = ▥ yd

6. 24 in. = ▥ ft

7. 21 ft = ▥ yd

8. 36 in. = ▥ yd

9. 72 in. = ▥ yd

10. Estimate the length of this segment. Then give the length to the nearest $\frac{1}{2}$ in., $\frac{1}{4}$ in., and $\frac{1}{8}$ in.

Add, subtract, or multiply.

11.
```
   6 ft 9 in.
+  3 ft 7 in.
```

12.
```
   8 yd 1 ft
-  2 yd 2 ft
```

13.
```
   4 ft 5 in.
×        3
```

Give the missing numbers.

14. 1 c = ▥ oz

15. 1 pt = ▥ c

16. 1 gal = ▥ qt

17. 1 qt = ▥ pt

18. 1 oz = ▥ tablespoons

19. 12 qt = ▥ gal

20. 1 T = ▥ lb

21. 1 lb = ▥ oz

22. 32 oz = ▥ lb

Choose the best estimate for each.

23. Weight

6 oz   4 lb $\frac{1}{8}$ T

24. Weight

4 oz   2 lb $\frac{1}{4}$ T

25. Temperature

cold faucet water

10°F   45°F   90°F

26. Temperature

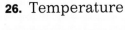
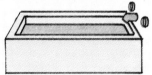

hot bath water

65°F   130°F   210°F

Solve.

27. How many cups are in six 12-oz cans of pineapple juice?

28. A house covers $\frac{1}{4}$ the area of a lot 42 yd long and 36 yd wide. How many square yards does it cover? How many feet of fencing are needed to put a fence around the lot?

Another Look

Length

12 inches (in.) = 1 foot (ft)

3 ft = 1 yard (yd)

36 in. = 1 yd

5,280 ft = 1 mile (mi)

1,760 yd = 1 mi

Length = 4 in. to the nearest $\frac{1}{2}$ in.

Length = $6\frac{1}{2}$ in. to the nearest $\frac{1}{4}$ in.

Length = $1\frac{3}{8}$ in. to the nearest $\frac{1}{8}$ in.

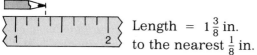

5 ft 6 in.
+ 7 ft 9 in.

15 in. is 1 ft 3 in.

12 ft 15 in., or 13 ft 3 in.

Capacity
8 fluid ounces (oz) = 1 cup (c)
2 cups = 1 pint (pt)
2 pt = 1 quart (qt)
4 qt = 1 gallon (gal)

Weight
16 ounces (oz) = 1 pound (lb)
2,000 lb = 1 ton (T)

Temperature
Water freezes at 32° Fahrenheit (32°F) and boils at 212°F.

Give the missing numbers.

1. 4 ft = ▨ in.
2. 6 yd = ▨ ft
3. 5 yd = ▨ in.
4. 3 mi = ▨ ft
5. 2 mi = ▨ yd
6. $3\frac{1}{2}$ ft = ▨ in.
7. $1\frac{3}{4}$ yd = ▨ in.
8. $2\frac{1}{3}$ yd = ▨ ft
9. 72 in. = ▨ ft
10. 24 ft = ▨ yd

Measure to the unit shown.

11.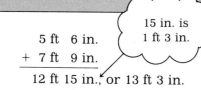
nearest $\frac{1}{2}$ in.

12.
nearest $\frac{1}{4}$ in.

13.
nearest $\frac{1}{8}$ in.

Add, subtract, or multiply.

14.   7 ft 10 in.
     + 3 ft 8 in.

15.   6 yd 24 in.
     + 3 yd 30 in.

16.   12 ft 3 in.
     − 4 ft 9 in.

17.   6 yd 2 ft
     ×   4

Give the missing numbers.

18. 4 c = ▨ oz
19. 3 pt = ▨ c
20. 5 qt = ▨ pt
21. 2 gal = ▨ qt
22. 3 lb = ▨ oz
23. 2 T = ▨ lb
24. 2 qt = ▨ c
25. 48 oz = ▨ lb
26. 1 gal = ▨ pt
27. 12 qt = ▨ gal

Enrichment

Large Numbers and Scientific Notation

Try this quiz about large numbers!

Match the questions with the answers.

ANSWERS	QUESTIONS
1. 1,000 (or 10 hundreds)	**A** About how many seats are there in a large stadium?
2. 10,000 (or 100 hundreds)	**B** About how many pages are there in a thick telephone book?
3. 100,000 (or 1,000 hundreds)	**C** About how many grains of sand are there in a cup?
4. 1,000,000 (or 1,000 thousands)	**D** About how many minutes are there in 2,000 years?
5. 1,000,000,000 (or 1,000 millions)	**E** How many centimeters do you run in a 100 m dash?

*See upside down answers to check your score.

Here are some period names to help you read a very large number.

Sextillions	Quintillions	Quadrillions	Trillions	Billions	Millions	Thousands	Ones
↓	↓	↓	↓	↓	↓	↓	↓
4 7 6 ,	5 8 7 ,	3 1 9 ,	6 0 8 ,	7 4 2 ,	8 7 1 ,	0 2 3 ,	9 6 4

Scientific notation is often used to write very large numbers. Here is an example.

Distance from the earth to the sun:

93,000,000 miles
(to the nearest million)

Distance in scientific notation:

$$\underline{9.3} \times \underline{10^7}$$

a number between 1 and 10   a power of 10

Can you read these numbers and write them in scientific notation?

1. Recent estimation of world's population: 4,000,000,000

2. Distance across the Milky Way Galaxy: 6,000,000,000,000,000,000 miles

3. Distance from the earth to the sun and back: 186,000,000 miles

Cumulative Review

1. Find the perimeter.

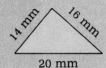

A 50 mm
B 2,240 mm^2
C 25 mm
D not given

2. Find the circumference.
Use 3.14 for π and $C = \pi \times d$.

A 6.28 m
B 12.56 m
C 25.12 m
D not given

3. Find the area.

A 3.24 m^2
B 1.62 m^2
C 3.6 m^2
D not given

4. Find the surface area.

A 200 m^2
B 125 m^2
C 20 m^2
D not given

Find the sum or difference.

5. $^+6 + {}^-4$

A $^+2$ B $^-2$
C $^+10$ D not given

6. $^-9 + {}^+14$

A $^+5$ B $^+23$
C $^-23$ D not given

7. $^-6 - {}^-3$

A $^-3$ B $^-9$
C $^+3$ D not given

Which symbol ($>$, $<$, or $=$) goes in each ▦ ?

8. $^+3$ ▦ $^-7$

A $>$ B $<$ C $=$

9. $^-6$ ▦ $^+6$

A $>$ B $<$ C $=$

Give the missing numbers.

10. 3 ft = ▦ in.

A 4   B 24
C 36   D not given

11. 4 pt = ▦ c

A 2   B 8
C 16   D not given

12. 2 lb = ▦ oz

A 8   B 16
C 32   D not given

13. Randy used 16 fluid ounces of milk in a recipe. How many cups of milk did he use?

A 8   B 4
C 2   D not given

14. Indra needs 6 yd of rope. She has 3 yd 2 ft. How much more rope does she need?

A 3 yd 1 ft   B 2 yd 1 ft
C 2 yd 2 ft   D not given

TECHNOLOGY RESOURCE BANK

Giving Input to a Computer

A set of instructions for a computer is often developed first in flowchart form. Then it is typed into the computer as a computer program. A simple example is given below.

Flowchart

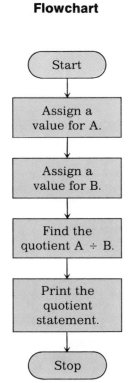

Computer Program
(typed into a computer)

```
10 PRINT "COMPUTERS CAN
   DIVIDE."
20 LET A = 625
30 LET B = 5
40 PRINT "625 DIVIDED
   BY 5 = "; A/B
50 END
```

When you type RUN and press RETURN , the computer shows ⟶

Review

PRINT instructs the computer to print what is inside the quotes.

LET A = 625 gives the letter A a value of 625.

A/B means A ÷ B. Since A/B is not inside quotes, the computer shows the quotient when A is divided by B.

```
COMPUTERS CAN DIVIDE.
625 DIVIDED BY 5 = 125
```

INPUT is another useful word in computer programming. It allows you to respond to a computer question by typing in data. Study the example below.

Computer Program

```
10 PRINT "HOW TALL ARE YOU (IN CM)?"
20 INPUT H
30 PRINT "I GUESS YOUR WEIGHT (IN KG)"
40 PRINT "TO BE "; (4 * H-390)/5
50 END
```

This signals you to type in a number for H.

When you type RUN and press RETURN, the computer shows

```
HOW TALL ARE YOU (IN CM)?
?
```

If you type 144 and press RETURN, the computer shows

```
I GUESS YOUR WEIGHT (IN KG)
TO BE 37.2
```

In the program above, what would be the computer's final statement if you type in 150? if you type in 138?

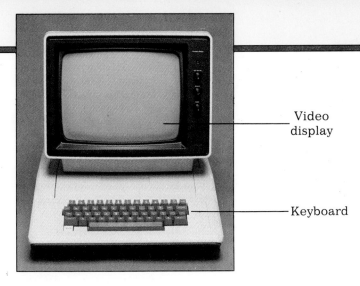

Video display

Keyboard

Give a RUN for each program. Choose your own INPUT numbers.

1.
```
10 PRINT "GIVE THE LENGTH OF"
20 PRINT "A SIDE OF A SQUARE."
30 INPUT S
40 PRINT "THE SQUARE'S AREA
   IS "; S * S
50 END
```

2.
```
10 PRINT "CHOOSE A NUMBER."
20 INPUT N
30 PRINT "WE SAY THAT"
40 PRINT N; " SQUARED IS ";
   N * N
50 END
```

3.
```
10 PRINT "GIVE THE LENGTH OF"
20 PRINT "THE SIDE OF A CUBE."
30 INPUT S
40 PRINT "THE CUBE'S VOLUME
   IS "; S * S * S
50 END
```

4.
```
10 PRINT "CHOOSE A NUMBER."
20 INPUT N
30 PRINT "WE SAY THAT"
40 PRINT N; " CUBED IS ";
   N * N * N
50 END
```

5.
```
10 PRINT "NUMBER OF LETTERS
   IN FIRST NAME?"
20 INPUT F
30 PRINT "NUMBER OF LETTERS
   IN LAST NAME?"
40 INPUT L
50 PRINT "YOUR LUCKY NUMBER
   IS "; F * L
60 END
```

6.
```
10 PRINT "TO THE NEAREST TENTH"
20 PRINT "HOW MANY CM LONG IS"
30 PRINT "YOUR MIDDLE FINGER?"
40 INPUT M
50 PRINT "I GUESS YOUR HEIGHT"
60 PRINT "IN CM TO BE "; 20 * M
70 END
```

7. Use INPUT to write a computer program that will find the product of any two numbers the program's user chooses.

8. Write a program that will find the area of any rectangle the program's user chooses.

Decisions in a Computer Program

Sometimes a computer program is written so that the computer must make a **decision** about a situation. The IF-THEN statement in a program is like a decision box in a flowchart.

Air traffic controllers use computers to make many decisions each day.

Flowchart

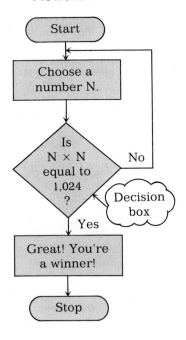

Computer Program

```
10 PRINT "CHOOSE A NUMBER."
20 INPUT N
30 IF N * N = 1024 THEN 50
40 GOTO 10
50 PRINT "GREAT! YOU'RE
   A WINNER!"
60 END
```

If $N \times N = 1{,}024$, the computer skips to line 50. If $N \times N$ is not equal to 1,024, the next step is line 40.

When you type RUN and press RETURN, the computer shows ⟶

```
CHOOSE A NUMBER.
?
```

If you type 28, the computer asks you to choose again.

If you type 32, the computer shows ⟶

```
GREAT! YOU'RE A
WINNER!
```

1. In the program above, what decision must the computer make?

2. What would happen if line 40 were left out?

3. When you have found 32, the "game" is over. Change the program to produce a new "game."

Answer the questions about each flowchart program.

Flowchart

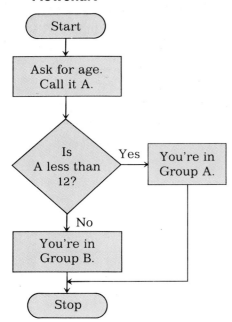

Computer Program

```
10 PRINT "WHAT IS YOUR AGE?"
20 INPUT A
30 IF A < 12 THEN 60
40 PRINT "YOU'RE IN GROUP B."
50 GOTO 70
60 PRINT "YOU'RE IN GROUP A."
70 END
```

1. What line in the program relates to the flowchart decision box?

2. What is the RUN (output) for your age?

3. Jim is 9 years old. He typed the program. What was the RUN?

Flowchart

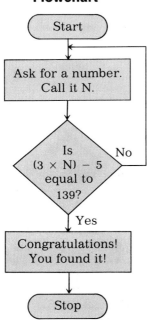

Computer Program

```
10 PRINT "CHOOSE A NUMBER."
20 INPUT N
30 IF (3 * N) - 5 = 139 THEN 50
40 GOTO 10
50 PRINT "CONGRATULATIONS!
   YOU FOUND IT!"
60 END
```

4. What decision must the computer make?

5. What happens if you choose the wrong number?

6. What is the correct number? What is the RUN if you choose this number?

Using Strings in Computer Programs

For some computer programs it is useful to have a simple symbol to stand for a name, an address, a license plate number or a **string** of printed characters.

A symbol such as **A$,** called a **string variable,** is used for this purpose.

Police departments use computers to keep accurate records and find information quickly.

Study these examples.

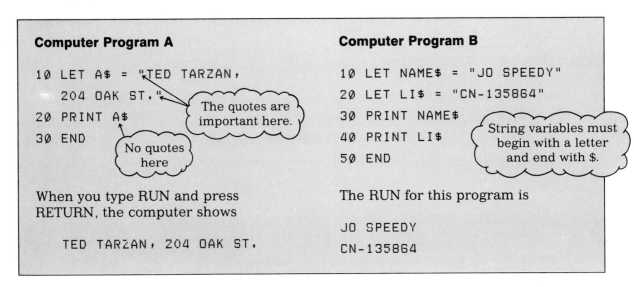

Computer Program A

```
10 LET A$ = "TED TARZAN,
   204 OAK ST,"
20 PRINT A$
30 END
```

The quotes are important here.

No quotes here

When you type RUN and press RETURN, the computer shows

```
   TED TARZAN, 204 OAK ST,
```

Computer Program B

```
10 LET NAME$ = "JO SPEEDY"
20 LET LI$ = "CN-135864"
30 PRINT NAME$
40 PRINT LI$
50 END
```

String variables must begin with a letter and end with $.

The RUN for this program is

```
JO SPEEDY
CN-135864
```

Each program below contains errors. Write the corrected lines for the program and give the RUN for each.

1.
```
10 LET A$ = HI
20 LET B$ = THERE
30 PRINT A$
40 PRINT B$
50 END
```

2.
```
10 LET NAME$ = "BILL"
20 LET AGE$ = "12 YEARS OLD"
30 PRINT "NAME$"
40 PRINT "AGE$"
50 END
```

Give the RUN for each program.

1.
```
10 LET N$ = "IKE"
20 LET PH$ = "452-5909"
30 PRINT N$
40 PRINT PH$
50 END
```

2.
```
10 PRINT "WHAT'S YOUR NAME?"
20 INPUT N$
30 PRINT "HI " N$     Use your name.
40 PRINT "IT'S NICE TO WORK
   FOR YOU."
50 END
```

3.
```
10 LET A$ = "ONE"
20 LET B$ = "TWO-"
30 LET C$ = "THREE-"
40 LET D$ = "FOUR-"
50 PRINT D$; C$; B$; A$
60 END
```

4.
```
10 LET T1$ = "SCALENE "
20 LET T2$ = "ISOSCELES "
30 LET T3$ = "EQUILATERAL"
40 PRINT "3 TYPES OF TRIANGLES"
50 PRINT T1$; T2$; T3$
60 END
```

5.
```
10 PRINT "LET'S ESTIMATE
   YOUR ADULT HEIGHT."
20 PRINT "HOW MANY CM TALL
   ARE YOU NOW?"
30 INPUT H
40 PRINT "ARE YOU A BOY OR
   A GIRL?"
50 INPUT X$
60 IF X$ = "GIRL" THEN 90
70 PRINT "YOUR ADULT HEIGHT
   (CM) WILL BE ABOUT ";
   (5 * H)/4
80 GOTO 100
90 PRINT "YOUR ADULT HEIGHT
   (CM) WILL BE ABOUT ";
   (10 * H)/9
100 END
```

6. A computer can "add words." What do you think the RUN for this program will be?

```
10 LET A$ = "MICKEY-"
20 LET B$ = "MOUSE"
30 PRINT A$ + B$
40 END
```

★ **7.** Write a program of your own that uses a string variable.

Computer Graphics—Using Logo Commands

A computer can draw geometric shapes on the computer screen. A special computer language, called **Logo,** can be used to give the computer the desired commands. A small triangle, called a **turtle,** moves around the screen to make the geometric drawings. Some examples of Logo commands are shown in the table.

Logo Command	Turtle Movement	Picture
FD 40	Draws a segment 40 units FORWARD.	↑
BK 30	Draws a segment 30 units BACK.	
RT 60	Turns to the RIGHT (clockwise) 60°.	60°
LT 90	Turns to the LEFT (counterclockwise) 90°.	90°
REPEAT	Repeats a command, as: REPEAT 2 [FD 20 RT 90]	

At the start the turtle is in the middle of the screen and points up. Turns (RT or LT) totaling 360° are needed to turn the turtle completely around.

To draw the regular hexagon at the right, the turtle must draw 6 segments each 30 units long. After drawing each segment, the turtle must turn right 60°. To make the turtle draw the hexagon, you can type this command 6 times:

    FD 30 RT 60

or you can type this REPEAT command once:

    REPEAT 6 [FD 30 RT 60]

What REPEAT command would you use to make the turtle draw an equilateral triangle with each side 40 units long?

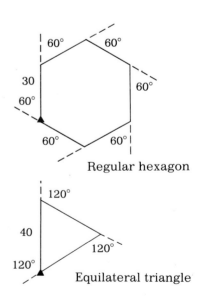

Regular hexagon

Equilateral triangle

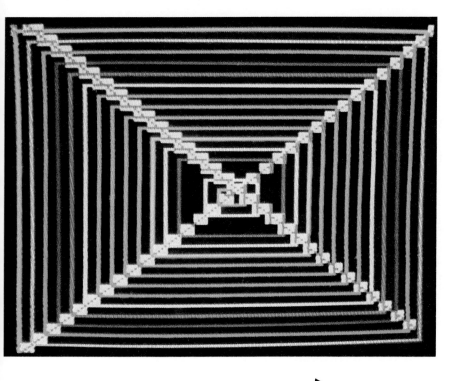

Copy and complete the Logo command for each picture.

1.

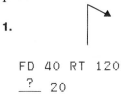

FD 40 RT 120
_?_ 20

2.

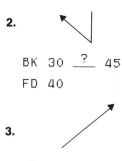

BK 30 _?_ 45
FD 40

3.

_?_ 45 FD 60

4.

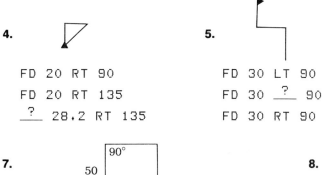

FD 20 RT 90
FD 20 RT 135
_?_ 28.2 RT 135

5.

FD 30 LT 90
FD 30 _?_ 90
FD 30 RT 90

6.

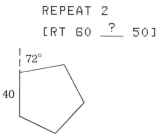

REPEAT 2
[RT 60 _?_ 50]

7.

90°

50

Write a command using REPEAT that will make the turtle draw a square 50 units long on each side.

8.

72°

40

Write a command using REPEAT that will make the turtle draw a regular pentagon 40 units long on each side.

9. Draw the figure that the turtle would draw in response to this Logo command:
REPEAT 8 [FD 30 RT 45]

10. Write a Logo command of your own. Draw the picture that the turtle would draw for your command.

Problem 1 (For use after page 49)

Play Addition Tic-Tac-Toe with a partner. Players 1 and 2 take turns entering two numbers from the addend list. Each tries to pick numbers whose sum is on the grid shown. If a player is correct, the computer replaces the sum with a 1 or 2. You lose a turn if you choose numbers whose sum is already marked. The first player to get three in a row, column, or diagonal wins. No pencils, please! Use your mental math and estimation skills.

Program 1

```
 10   REM ADDITION TIC-TAC-TOE
 20   DIM A$(3,3): P=1
 30   FOR R = 1 TO 3 : FOR C = 1 TO 3
 40   READ A(R,C): NEXT C: NEXT R
 50   T = T + 1 : GOSUB 210
 60   PRINT: PRINT "ADDEND LIST: 29, 38,
      41, 56, 79 "
 70   PRINT "PLAYER "P" : CHOOSE 2
      ADDENDS ": INPUT A, B
 80   PRINT: N = A + B
 90   FOR R = 1 TO 3: FOR C = 1 TO 3
100   IF A(R,C) < > N THEN 120
110   IF A(R,C) = N THEN A(R,C) = P
120   NEXT C: NEXT R
130   IF P = 1 THEN 160
140   P = P - 1
150   GOTO 170
160   P = P + 1
170   IF T = 12 THEN 200
180   GOTO 50
190   DATA 135, 117, 79, 94, 85, 120, 67,
      108, 97
200   END
210   FOR R = 1 TO 3: FOR C = 1 TO 3
220   PRINT A(R,C),: NEXT C
230   PRINT: NEXT R : PRINT
240   RETURN
```

Problem 2 (For use after page 133)

The scores for a game were 678, 634, 726, 653, 704, and 695. What is your estimate for the average of these scores? Use Program 2 to compare your estimate with the actual average.

Program 2

```
 10   REM ESTIMATING AVERAGES
 20   PRINT: INPUT "HOW MANY NUMBERS DO
      YOU WANT TO AVERAGE? "; N
 30   PRINT "TYPE EACH NUMBER AND PRESS
      <RETURN>. "
 40   T = 0
 50   FOR X = 1 TO N: INPUT E: T = T + E:
      NEXT X
 60   PRINT: INPUT "ESTIMATED
      AVERAGE? ";A: PRINT
 70   PRINT "ESTIMATE " A, "AVERAGE "
      T/N, "DIFFERENCE " ABS(T/N-A)
 80   PRINT: INPUT "MORE NUMBERS TO
      AVERAGE? ";Y$
 90   IF LEFT$(Y$,1) = "Y" THEN 20
100   END
```

Problem 3 (For use after page 75)

If pencils are $0.25 each and pens are $0.49 each, what can you buy for $2.00 or less? Use Program 3 to make a chart showing the total cost for different numbers of pencils and pens.

Program 3

```
 10   REM PENCILS AND PENS
 20   PRINT: INPUT "PENCILS NEEDED? ";X
 30   PRINT: INPUT "PENS NEEDED? ";Y
 40   T = X* .25 + Y* .49
 50   IF T < = 2 THEN 70
 60   PRINT: PRINT "THE TOTAL COST IS
      MORE THAN $2.00. ": GOTO 20
 70   PRINT: PRINT "THE TOTAL COST IS
      $"T " FOR ":PRINT X " PENCILS AND "Y
      "PENS. "
 80   PRINT: INPUT "MORE NUMBERS? ";Y$
 90   IF LEFT$(Y$,1) = "Y" THEN 20
100   END
```

Problem 4 (For use after page 273)
The computer will give you an angle. Estimate the measure of the angle in degrees. Begin the Logo program by typing ANGLE and pressing Return.

Program 4
```
TO ANGLE
CS
RT 90
FD 80
BK 80
MAKE "X RANDOM 180 + 1
LT :X
FD 80
HT
PR [ESTIMATE THE MEASURE]
PR [OF THE ANGLE]
PR [IN DEGREES.]
MAKE "ANS READLIST
PR :X
PR [DEGREES]
END
```

Problem 5 (For use after page 341)
Use Program 5 to help you draw regular polygons with 5, 6, and 8 sides. Experiment with the outside angle used to draw the polygon. Try typing in PENTAGON 80. See page 414 for help.

Program 5
```
TO PENTAGON :ANGLE
CLEARSCREEN
HIDETURTLE
REPEAT 5[FD 50 RT :ANGLE]
END
TO HEXAGON :ANGLE
CLEARSCREEN
HIDETURTLE
REPEAT 6 [FD 50 RT :ANGLE]
END
TO OCTAGON :ANGLE
CLEARSCREEN
HIDETURTLE
REPEAT 8 [FD 50 RT:ANGLE]
END
```

Problem 6 (For use after page 247)
Play this game with a classmate. You are each given a different 2-digit number for a divisor. You each choose a 3-digit dividend. The student with the largest remainder for the division problem wins.

Program 6
```
10  REM LARGEST REMAINDER
20  D( 1) = INT(79*RND( 1)+ 15):D(2)=
    D( 1) + INT( 10*RND( 1)-6)
30  IF D( 1) = D(2) THEN 20
40  FOR N = 1 TO 2: GOSUB 160: NEXT N
50  PRINT: PRINT "HERE ARE THE
    REMAINDERS: "
60  PRINT: PRINT "PLAYER 1 " ,
    "PLAYER 2 "
70  FOR N = 1 TO 2: PRINT R(N)
80  NEXT N
90  PRINT: PRINT
100 IF R ( 1 )>R(2) THEN PRINT "PLAYER 1
    WINS, ": GOTO 130
110 IF R( 1 )=R(2) THEN PRINT "YOU
    TIE! ": GOTO 130
120 PRINT "PLAYER 2 WINS! "
130 INPUT "WANT TO PLAY AGAIN? "; Y$
140 IF LEFT$(Y$,1) = "Y" THEN 20
150 END
160 PRINT: PRINT "PLAYER "N" YOUR
    DIVISOR IS " D(N)
170 INPUT "TYPE A 3-DIGIT NUMBER: ";
    K(N)
180 IF K(N)< 100 OR K(N)>999 THEN PRINT
    "3 DIGITS PLEASE! ": GOTO 170
190 Q(N) = K(N)/D(N): S(N) = INT(Q(N)):
    R(N) = K(N) - S(N)*D(N)
200 RETURN
```

Problem 7 (For use after page 361)
A machine makes a box by cutting equal square pieces from the four corners of a 12-inch square. What size square should be cut from the corners to make a box that will hold the largest amount? Use Program 7.

Program 7

```
10   REM LARGEST VOLUME
20   PRINT: INPUT "ENTER THE SIDE: "; L
30   W = L: PRINT: INPUT "CUT WHAT SIZE
     PIECE?"; C
40   IF C > = L / 2 THEN PRINT "
     CUT IS NOT POSSIBLE.": GOTO 30
50   V = (L - 2*C) * (W - 2*C) * C
60   PRINT: PRINT "VOLUME IS: "V" CUBIC
     INCHES."
70   PRINT: PRINT "RECORD THE RESULT IN
     A TABLE."
80   PRINT: INPUT "CUT ANOTHER SIZE?
     (Y/N) ";Y$
90   IF LEFT$(Y$,1) = "Y" THEN 30
100  END
```

Problem 8 (For use after page 317)

The computer chooses a fraction between 0 and 1. The denominator is less than 9 and is never 7. Use mental math to discover the fraction the computer has chosen.

Program 8

```
10   REM GUESS MY FRACTION
20   D = INT (12 * RND (1) - 3): IF D <
     2 THEN 20
30   IF D = 7 OR D = 9 THEN 20
40   N = INT (12 * RND (1) - 3)
50   C = 1: IF N > = D THEN 30
60   IF N < 2 THEN 40
70   PRINT : INPUT "NUMERATOR ";N1
80   INPUT "DENOMINATOR ";D1
90   IF N / D = N1 / D1 THEN PRINT
     "RIGHT! YOU TOOK "C"
     GUESSES.": GOTO 140
100  IF N / D < N1 / D1 THEN PRINT
     "TOO HIGH.":C = C + 1: GOTO 120
110  PRINT "TOO LOW.":C = C + 1: GOTO
     120
120  PRINT : INPUT "TRY AGAIN?
     (Y/N)";Y$
130  IF LEFT$ (Y$,1) < > "N" THEN 70
140  PRINT "THE FRACTION IS "N"/" D
150  END
```

Problem 9 (For use after page 17)

Three people were invited to a party. They each brought 1 friend and each of these friends brought 2 of their friends. How many people went to the party? Use Program 9 to help you make a table showing the results for 3, 4, 5, 6, and 100 invited people.

Program 9

```
10   REM COUNTING FRIENDS
20   PRINT: INPUT "NUMBER ORIGINALLY
     INVITED? "; P
30   PRINT: PRINT "NUMBER OF THEIR
     FRIENDS: " P
40   PRINT: PRINT "NUMBER OF FRIENDS'
     FRIENDS: " P*2
50   PRINT: PRINT "TOTAL NUMBER AT THE
     PARTY: " P*4
60   PRINT: INPUT "TRY AGAIN? "; Y$
70   IF LEFT$(Y$,1) = "Y" THEN 20
80   END
```

Problem 10 (For use after page 189)

Can you use a unit segment and estimate the length of a given segment to the nearest unit? Try Program 10.

Program 10

```
10   REM ESTIMATING LENGTH
20   U = INT(6*RND(1)+3)
30   FOR N = 1 TO U: PRINT "_";: NEXT N:
     PRINT " 1 UNIT "
40   PRINT: PRINT
50   S = INT(78*RND(1) + 1)
60   L = INT(S/U*10)/10
70   FOR N= 1 TO S: PRINT "_"; :NEXT N
80   PRINT: PRINT: INPUT "ESTIMATE THE
     LENGTH "; E
90   PRINT "LENGTH " , "EST." , "DIFF."
100  PRINT L , E , ABS(L-E)
110  INPUT "TRY AGAIN?(Y/N) ";Y$: PRINT
120  IF LEFT$(Y$,1) = "Y" THEN 20
130  END
```

Problem 11 (For use after page 221)
A survey showed that 9,240 persons in a city of 30,800 were Cub fans. First estimate what fraction of the people this was. Then use Program 11 to help you find the actual lowest-terms fraction. Be sure to continue dividing until the numerator and denominator have only 1 as a common factor.

Program 11
```
10   REM LOWEST-TERMS FRACTIONS
20   PRINT: INPUT "ENTER NUMERATOR: "; N
30   PRINT: INPUT "ENTER DENOMINATOR: "
     ; D
40   PRINT: PRINT "WHAT NUMBER CAN
     DIVIDE BOTH "N" AND "D" EVENLY? "
     : INPUT X
50   A = N/X: IF INT(A) <> N/X THEN PRINT
     X " WILL NOT DIVIDE "N" EVENLY. TRY
     AGAIN. ": GOTO 40
60   B = D/X: IF INT(B) <> D/X THEN PRINT
     X " WILL NOT DIVIDE "D" EVENLY. TRY
     AGAIN. ": GOTO 40
70   PRINT "THE NEW FRACTION IS "
     A"/"B"."
80   PRINT "REDUCE "A"/"B" AGAIN?
     (Y OR N)": INPUT Y$
90   N= A: D = B: IF LEFT$(Y$,1) = "Y"
     THEN 40
100  PRINT: INPUT "REDUCE A NEW
     FRACTION?(Y/N) ";Y$
110  IF LEFT$(Y$,1) = "Y" THEN GOTO 20
     : PRINT
120  END
```

Problem 12 (For use after page 403)
You want to buy some material by the yard. The computer will tell you how many inches you need. Estimate the length in yards. The computer will tell you how close you were to the next whole number of yards. Choose a partner and see who can make the closer estimate. Take turns and keep score for ten tries.

Program 12
```
10   REM ESTIMATING YARDS
20   PRINT: I = INT(400*RND(1) + 499)
30   PRINT "YOU NEED "I " INCHES OF
     MATERIAL. "
40   PRINT: INPUT "ESTIMATE THE NUMBER
     OF YARDS: "; E
50   Q = INT(I/36): IF Q <> I/36 THEN
     Q = Q + 1
60   PRINT: PRINT "YOU WILL NEED "Q "
     YARDS. "
70   IF Q = E THEN PRINT "YOUR ESTIMATE
     IS CORRECT. ": GOTO 90
80   PRINT "YOU MISSED BY " ABS(Q-E)
     "YARD(S). "
90   INPUT "TRY AGAIN?(Y/N) ";Y$
100  IF LEFT$(Y$,1) = "Y" THEN 20
110  END
```

Problem 13 (For use after page 103)
How many different ways can you make change for a $0.50 coin without using pennies? Try Program 13.

Program 13
```
10   REM MAKING CHANGE
20   PRINT: INPUT "HOW MANY
     QUARTERS? ";Q
30   PRINT: INPUT "HOW MANY DIMES? ";D
40   PRINT: INPUT "HOW MANY
     NICKELS? ";N
50   T = Q*.25 + D*.1 + N*0.05
60   IF T = 0.5 THEN 140
70   IF T>0.5 THEN 110
80   PRINT:PRINT "YOU NEED MORE COINS. "
90   PRINT "YOUR TOTAL IS $"T
100  PRINT "TRY AGAIN. ":GOTO 20
110  PRINT:PRINT "YOU HAVE TOO MANY
     COINS. "
120  PRINT "YOUR TOTAL IS $"T
130  PRINT "TRY AGAIN. ":GOTO 20
140  PRINT:PRINT "YOU CORRECTLY MADE
     CHANGE FOR $0.50. "
150  PRINT: INPUT "TRY AGAIN? ";Y$
160  IF LEFT$(Y$,1) = "Y" THEN 20
170  END
```

COMPUTER-ASSISTED PROBLEM SOLVING

Problem 14 (For use after page 381)

Suppose your grandmother agreed to give you $1.00 for your sixth birthday, $2.00 on your seventh birthday, $4.00 on your eighth birthday, and so on, doubling the amount each year. Guess the amount of your gift on your 15th and 21st birthdays. Check your guesses using Program 14.

Program 14

```
 10  REM DOUBLE YOUR MONEY
 20  S = 0: T = 1: PRINT: INPUT "FOR
     WHICH BIRTHDAY WOULD YOU LIKE
     TO SEE THE TOTAL GIFT?" ;G
 30  PRINT: IF G < 6 THEN PRINT "AT " G "
     YEARS OLD, YOU ARE TOO YOUNG. ":
     PRINT : GOTO 20
 40  PRINT "AGE","PRESENT" ,"TOTAL"
 50  FOR I = 6 TO G
 60  T = T * 2:S = S + T / 2: PRINT
     " "I," $"T / 2," $"S
 70  NEXT I
 80  PRINT : PRINT "WHEN YOU ARE "G "
     YEARS OLD,"
 90  PRINT "YOUR GRANDMOTHER'S GIFT
     WILL BE $"T / 2","
100  END
```

Problem 15 (For use after page 163)

Program 15 can assist you to find the prime factors of 80, 270, 399, 180, 325, and 858. Use the rules for divisibility to choose prime number divisors. Good first choices are 2 or 3.

Program 15

```
 10  REM FINDING PRIME FACTORS
 20  INPUT "FIND PRIME FACTORS OF WHAT
     NUMBER? ";X : X 1 = X
 30  PRINT : PRINT "DIVIDE "X " BY WHAT
     PRIME NUMBER? "
 40  INPUT D : IF D = 1 THEN 160
 50  IF D = 2 THEN 70
 60  GOSUB 120
 70  Q = X/D
 80  IF Q <> INT(Q) THEN PRINT D " DOES
     NOT DIVIDE "X : GOTO 30
 90  N = N + 1 : F(N) = D
100  PRINT X"/"D" = "Q : IF Q=1 THEN 170
110  X = Q : GOTO 30
120  FOR C = 2 TO D-1
130  IF D/C = INT(D/C) THEN 160
140  NEXT C
150  RETURN
160  PRINT D " IS NOT A PRIME NUMBER. " :
     GOTO 30
170  PRINT "THE PRIME FACTORS OF "X 1
     "ARE: "
180  FOR J = 1 TO N : PRINT F(J) " "; :
     NEXT J
190  END
```

Problem 16 (For use after page 295)

The ratio of the circumference (C) of a circle to the diameter (d) is the same for all circles. It is a number written as π and called pi. Find an approximate decimal value for π by measuring circular objects. Program 16 will help you.

420

Program 16

```
10  REM RATIO OF CIRCUMFERENCE TO
    DIAMETER
20  INPUT "HOW MANY OBJECTS DID YOU
    MEASURE? "; N
30  S = 0 : FOR X = 1 TO N
40  PRINT : PRINT "OBJECT "X
50  INPUT "CIRCUMFERENCE = ";C(X)
    : INPUT " DIAMETER = ";D(X)
60  P(X) = C(X)/D(X)
70  P(X) = INT( 100*P(X)+.005)/100
80  S = S + P(X) : NEXT X
90  FOR X = 1 TO N: PRINT :PRINT C(X)
    "/" D(X)" = "P(X) : NEXT X
100 PRINT: PRINT "AVERAGE VALUE FOR
    THE RATIO OF THE " :PRINT
    "CIRCUMFERENCE TO THE DIAMETER
    IS " S/N ", "
110 END
```

Calculator-Assisted Problem Solving

Problem 17 (For use with page 308)
What would you buy if you had $80 to spend for items you could order? Use a catalog or advertisement to select the items, and the Data Bank, page 425, to figure the tax. List the items and their prices, including tax.

Problem 18 (For use with page 398)
What is the difference between the highest recorded temperature in North America and the highest recorded temperature in Europe in degrees Celsius? in degrees Fahrenheit?

Use the Data Bank, page 424, for needed data. Use this formula to find degrees Fahrenheit when degrees Celsius is known:

Degrees Fahrenheit = 1.8 × Celsius temperature + 32

Problem 19 (For use with page 349)
The distance a bike travels when the pedals go around once is found by multiplying the gear ratio by the circumference of the wheel. As a rider changes gears on a 10-speed bike, the gear ratios change. First find the circumference of a wheel with a diameter of 2.17 feet. Use that figure to find the distance traveled for each gear ratio. Then solve:

How many feet farther do you travel with one turn of the pedal in gear 7 than in gear 1? How many times as far?

Gear number	Gear ratio	Distance traveled when pedal goes around once
1	1.36	
2	1.58	
3	1.86	
4	2.00	
5	2.17	
6	2.38	
7	2.71	
8	2.74	
9	3.25	
10	3.71	

Problem 20 (For use with page 311)
The Rule of 72 is used to estimate how long it takes money to double when it is earning interest at a certain rate. Divide 72 by the interest rate number to get the number of years required for doubling. Suppose an investor puts $28,000 in a savings bank account. If the bank pays 5% interest per year, how much will be in the savings account at the end of the first year? How long will it be before the amount of money is doubled, assuming it earns 5% interest each year?

Problem 21 (For use with page 118)

A *batting average* is found by comparing the number of hits a player gets to the number of times the player is officially at bat. Another interesting baseball statistic is found by first multiplying the number of singles a player has by 1, the number of doubles by 2, triples by 3, and home runs by 4. The sum of these products divided by the number of official at-bats is the *slugging average* (slugging percentage).

Figure the batting averages and slugging averages of the players listed below. What is the order of the players according to batting average? What is the order according to slugging average?

Players

	1	2	3	4	5
At bats	615	644	596	607	585
Hits	238	206	192	188	199
Singles	163	117	127	115	119
Doubles	42	29	26	32	37
Triples	15	17	14	18	12
Home runs	18	43	25	23	31

Problem 22 (For use with page 143)

Copy and complete this table to find the cost of using these appliances for the number of hours given, if the cost per kilowatt-hour (kWh) is $0.072. Then answer the following questions: Which costs more to operate for a month, a stove or refrigerator? How much more?

Appliances

	Refrigerator	TV	Stove
kW used/h	0.62	0.33	12.2
Hrs used/mo	720	125	14
kWh/mo			
Cost/mo			

kW stands for kilowatt. kWh stands for kilowatt-hour. A kilowatt-hour is a measure of electrical energy used per hour.

Problem 23 (For use with page 161)

Complete the table to find the cost per gram or kilogram (cost/unit weight). Which costs less per kilogram, steak or fish? How much less? Which costs more per gram, apples or peanuts? How much more?

Item	Cost	Weight	Cost/unit weight
Steak	$7.15	1.25 kg	
Fish	2.29	0.45 kg	
Apples	0.45	315 g	
Peanuts	1.99	340 g	

Problem 24 (For use with page 227)

An automobile loses value each year. This loss of value might be estimated by subtracting $\frac{5}{30}$ of the original cost from its value at the end of the first year, $\frac{4}{30}$ of the original cost from its value the second year, $\frac{3}{30}$ of its original cost from its value the third year, $\frac{2}{30}$ the fourth year, and $\frac{1}{30}$ the fifth year. What is the value after 5 years of an automobile that cost $7,500 new? Make a chart to show the loss in value for the first five years.

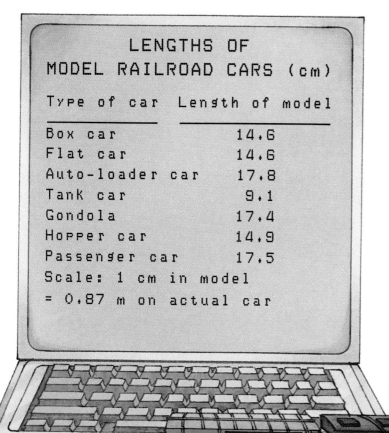

LENGTHS OF MODEL RAILROAD CARS (cm)

Type of car	Length of model
Box car	14.6
Flat car	14.6
Auto-loader car	17.8
Tank car	9.1
Gondola	17.4
Hopper car	14.9
Passenger car	17.5

Scale: 1 cm in model = 0.87 m on actual car

Weight of a Cubic Centimeter of Selected Metals

Metal	Weight, in grams, of 1 cm^3
Aluminum	1.7
Chromium	7.1
Copper	8.96
Gold	19.3
Iron	7.9
Lead	11.3
Nickel	8.9
Silver	10.5
Tin	7.3

U.S. TRANSPORT PLANES

Kind of Plane	Number of Passengers	Maximum Speed (km/h)	Usual Gross Weight (kg)	Maximum Length (m)
707 (120B)	181	966	117,030	44
727 (100)	131	982	77,110	41
737 (100)	112	943	50,350	27
747 (100B)	442	1,030	332,490	71
DC-8 (Series 40)	176	982	142,880	46
DC-9 (Series 40)	125	927	54,890	38
DC-10 (Series 40)	345	982	259,460	56
L-1011 (100)	400	1,006	211,380	54

TEMPERATURE RECORDS

Record Description	Place Recorded	Temperature
Hottest on Earth	Al Aziziyah, Libya	58°C
Hottest in North America	Death Valley, Calif., (USA)	56.7°C
Hottest in Australia	Cloncurry, Queensland	53.1°C
Hottest in Europe (not including Russia)	Córdoba, Spain	46°C
Coldest on Earth	Vostok, Antarctica	⁻88.3°C
Coldest outside Antarctica	Oymyakon, Siberia (Russia)	⁻68°C
Coldest in North America	Floeberg Bay, Canada	⁻58.3°C
Coldest in Europe (not including Russia)	Sodankylä, Finland	⁻45°C

THE SIX SUNNIEST CITIES IN THE UNITED STATES

City	Number of Clear Days in a Year
Las Vegas, NV	216
Phoenix, AZ	214
Bakersfield, CA	202
Tucson, AZ	198
El Paso, TX	194
Sacramento, CA	193

Time in Major World Cities Compared to Greenwich Mean Time (GMT)

City	Hours earlier (−) or later (+) than GMT
Baghdad	⁺3
Beijing (Peking)	⁺8
Brussels	⁺1
Buenos Aires	⁻3
Cairo	⁺2
Caracas	⁻4
Chicago	⁻6
Djakarta	⁺7
London	0
Los Angeles	⁻8
Ottawa	⁻5
Tokyo	⁺9

The World's 5 Largest Passenger Ships

Ship	Length (feet)	Width (feet)
Norway	1,035	110
United States	990	101
Queen Elizabeth 2	963	105
Canberra	818	102
Oriana	804	97

Central Florida

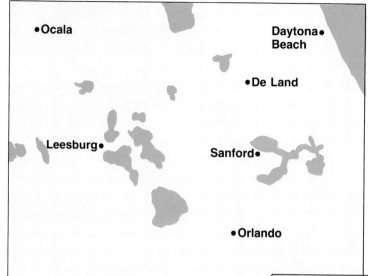

- •Ocala
- Daytona• Beach
- •De Land
- Leesburg•
- Sanford•
- •Orlando

Map Scale: $\frac{1}{4}$ inch = 5 miles

Most Common Adult Fears
(from a survey of 10,000 United States adults)

Fear	Percent naming
1. Speaking in front of a group	41
2. Heights	32
3. Insects and bugs	22
4. Money problems	22
5. Deep water	22

$0.05 SALES TAX TABLE

Amount of Sale	Tax	Amount of Sale	Tax
$77.90—78.09	$3.90	$79.50—79.69	$3.98
78.10—78.29	3.91	79.70—79.89	3.99
78.30—78.49	3.92	79.90—80.09	4.00
78.50—78.69	3.93	80.10—80.29	4.01
78.70—78.89	3.94	80.30—80.49	4.02
78.90—79.09	3.95	80.50—80.69	4.03
79.10—79.29	3.96	80.70—80.89	4.04
79.30—79.49	3.97	80.90—81.09	4.05

Recent Record Altitudes for Hot Air Balloons

Type	Pilot	Date of Record	Record Altitude (meters)
AX-1, AX-2	Katherine E. Boland	Nov., 1978	3,477
AX-3	Brian Boland	Nov., 1978	4,642
AX-4	Geoff Green	Oct., 1978	6,797
AX-5, AX-6	Carol Davis	Mar., 1980	9,690
AX-7	Julian Nott	Jan., 1976	11,286
AX-8	Kingswood Sprott, Jr.	Sept., 1975	11,823
AX-9	Chauncey Dunn	Aug., 1979	16,154
AX-10	Chauncey Dunn	Aug., 1979	16,215

Lengths of Some Prehistoric Reptiles

Reptile	Length	Shape
Pteranodon	8.2 m	
Ichthyosaur	12.8 m	
Plesiosaur	12.2 m	
Mosasaur	9.1 m	
Eogyrinus	4.5 m	

United States INDIAN TRIBES

Tribe	Population
CHIPPEWA	92,377
CHEROKEE	66,150
NAVAHO	96,743
CREE	72,572
PUEBLO	30,971

Approximate Weights of Balls Used in Popular Sports

Ball	Weight (oz)
Baseball	5
Basketball	22
Bowling ball	256
Football	15
Golf ball	$1\frac{1}{2}$
Soccer ball	16
Table tennis ball	$\frac{1}{12}$
Tennis ball	2
Volleyball	$9\frac{1}{2}$

BOWLING ALLEY MEASUREMENTS

Length of lane................19.17 m
Width of lane.................1.06 m
Length of approach area.................4.6 m
Width of gutter ....0.23 m

APPENDIX

Set A   For use after page 3

Find the sums or differences.

1.	3	2.	5	3.	3	4.	4	5.	0	6.	6	7.	8
	+ 0		+ 3		+ 5		+ 6		+ 7		+ 8		+ 6

8.	9	9.	12	10.	10	11.	5	12.	7	13.	0	14.	13
	− 9		− 0		− 1		− 5		− 0		− 0		− 3

15.	3	16.	6	17.	3	18.	5	19.	3	20.	1	21.	4
	2		1		8		7		3		5		2
	+ 4		+ 2		+ 3		+ 4		+ 3		+ 9		+ 8

Set B   For use after page 5

Find the products.

1.	3	2.	0	3.	2	4.	3	5.	9	6.	1	7.	4
	× 0		× 7		× 3		× 2		× 1		× 9		× 7

8.	7	9.	1	10.	3	11.	0	12.	5	13.	3	14.	6
	× 4		× 3		× 1		× 8		× 3		× 5		× 1

15. $(5 \times 2) \times 3$ **16.** $5 \times (2 \times 3)$ **17.** $(3 \times 2) \times 5$

Set C   For use after page 7

Divide. Check by multiplying.

1. $8\overline{)8}$ **2.** $2\overline{)2}$ **3.** $1\overline{)2}$ **4.** $1\overline{)5}$ **5.** $3\overline{)3}$ **6.** $1\overline{)3}$

7. $3\overline{)6}$ **8.** $4\overline{)0}$ **9.** $1\overline{)6}$ **10.** $6\overline{)0}$ **11.** $1\overline{)1}$ **12.** $2\overline{)8}$

13. $6\overline{)24}$ **14.** $6\overline{)30}$ **15.** $7\overline{)21}$ **16.** $2\overline{)14}$ **17.** $5\overline{)25}$ **18.** $6\overline{)36}$

Set D   For use after page 11

Do the operations in the order shown by the parentheses.

1. $(8 + 3) − 2$ **2.** $(21 \div 3) \times 2$ **3.** $5 + (8 − 4)$

4. $(9 \div 3) \times 5$ **5.** $(9 − 1) \times 4$ **6.** $3 + (3 \times 3)$

Set A For use after page 29

Write > (greater than) or < (less than) for each ⦀ .

1. 251 ⦀ 261

2. 6,900 ⦀ 6,799

3. 5,055 ⦀ 5,505

4. 10,901 ⦀ 11,009

5. 32,018 ⦀ 31,801

6. 658,334 ⦀ 659,000

Order from least to greatest.

7. 3,191; 3,011; 3,121; 3,111

8. 28,303; 29,003; 28,330; 28,033

Set B For use after page 31

Round to the nearest ten. Then round to the nearest hundred.

1. 841

2. 513

3. 1,458

4. 8,325

5. 5,899

6. 9,431

7. 15,235

8. 11,129

9. 32,623

10. 51,174

Round to the nearest thousand.

11. 2,542

12. 18,033

13. 10,501

14. 61,399

15. 120,760

Round to the nearest ten thousand.

16. 7,026

17. 23,360

18. 182,300

19. 909,090

20. 750,990

Set C For use after page 33

Estimate by rounding to the nearest ten.

1.	2.	3.	4.	5.
21 + 54	86 + 93	72 − 47	128 − 69	135 − 91

Estimate by rounding to the nearest thousand.

6.	7.	8.	9.	10.
11,873 − 9,260	3,866 + 2,149	23,788 − 14,022	5,870 + 4,366	18,625 − 10,440

Estimate by rounding to the nearest dollar.

11.	12.	13.	14.	15.
$6.50 + 3.25	$19.52 − 12.80	$13.60 + 5.80	$6.49 + 3.71	$20.89 + 3.90

428

Set A For use after page 37

Add.

1.	291 + 439	2.	875 + 327	3.	266 + 478	4.	893 + 653	5.	1,257 + 3,669

6.	8,575 + 3,446	7.	$27.93 + 17.58	8.	3,497 + 928	9.	28,735 + 16,884	10.	$789.79 + 251.88

Set B For use after page 39

Add.

1.	239 87 + 125	2.	521 893 + 326	3.	1,297 793 + 3,442	4.	10,926 6,337 + 15,488	5.	$872.50 36.77 + 96.48

6.	1,175 228 312 + 1,480	7.	13,396 18,472 16,585 + 21,929	8.	28,194 61,462 31,221 + 29,967	9.	$125.79 89.62 105.37 + 74.43	10.	$312.99 287.43 364.31 + 289.36

Set C For use after page 41

Subtract.

1.	611 − 329	2.	471 − 393	3.	1,952 − 1,899	4.	3,926 − 477	5.	5,855 − 3,286

6.	$23.25 − 14.87	7.	13,341 − 9,755	8.	23,113 − 14,754	9.	$251.14 − 147.92	10.	88,753 − 87,995

Set D For use after page 43

Subtract.

1.	803 − 125	2.	980 − 297	3.	1,208 − 543	4.	2,004 − 1,885	5.	3,080 − 1,762

6.	3,000 − 1,793	7.	4,080 − 1,296	8.	$33.00 − 25.87	9.	35,008 − 14,397	10.	$40.00 − 23.12

Set A   For use after page 44

Estimate. Use the front-end method.

1.	317 + 985	2.	442 + 365	3.	224 + 977	4.	$6.31 + 4.72	5.	$10.68 + 5.35

6.	219 572 + 605	7.	843 902 + 256	8.	$5.21 8.03 + 6.78	9.	97 232 + 569	10.	$4.76 2.03 + 4.28

Set B   For use after page 59

Write >, <, or = for each ▓ .

1. 0.9 ▓ 0.09   **2.** 3.2 ▓ 3.32   **3.** 68.1 ▓ 68.11   **4.** 0.303 ▓ 0.033

5. 4.51 ▓ 4.510   **6.** 0.105 ▓ 0.099   **7.** 0.999 ▓ 1   **8.** 0.0009 ▓ 0.001

9. 2.0004 ▓ 1.999   **10.** 0.0304 ▓ 0.340   **11.** 8.891 ▓ 8.918   **12.** 0.05103 ▓ 0.05310

Order the numbers from least to greatest.

13. 0.0312; 0.039; 0.0041; 0.0301; 0.0049   **14.** 0.1043; 0.0976; 0.0909; 0.1100; 0.1009

Set C   For use after page 61

Round to the nearest tenth.

1. 3.25   **2.** 0.064   **3.** 12.503   **4.** 0.882   **5.** 5.742

Round to the nearest hundredth.

6. 1.983   **7.** 6.0451   **8.** 0.057   **9.** 1.1192   **10.** 20.022

Round to the nearest whole number.

11. 8.5   **12.** 3.27   **13.** 16.0003   **14.** 54.587   **15.** 0.54

Set A   For use after page 65

Add.

1.	5.8 + 3.2	**2.**	19.03 + 3.45	**3.**	$19.52 + 89.78	**4.**	3.497 + 0.095	**5.**	$355.85 + 576.92
6.	6.2 3.3 + 4.8	**7.**	99.32 3.18 + 101.9	**8.**	$33.25 9.85 + 62.15	**9.**	$69.75 5.28 + 14.63	**10.**	0.30883 1.09203 + 0.35104

Set B   For use after page 67

Subtract.

1.	9.6 − 3.8	**2.**	80.71 − 16.25	**3.**	0.33 − 0.26	**4.**	1.511 − 0.367	**5.**	1.813 − 0.098
6.	$0.92 − 0.87	**7.**	30.226 − 5.908	**8.**	$100.05 − 87.66	**9.**	$0.89 − 0.05	**10.**	5.3321 − 3.9874

Set C   For use after page 72

Estimate. Look for compatible numbers.

1. 63 + 199 + 38

2. $2.15 + $4.88 + $3.06

3. 273 + 92 + 30 + 9

4. 426 + 309 + 573

5. $19.27 + $99.80 + $80.55

6. 17 + 298 + 82

Set D   For use after page 85

Multiply.

1.	42 × 2	**2.**	91 × 3	**3.**	27 × 7	**4.**	79 × 4	**5.**	57 × 8
6.	125 × 6	**7.**	723 × 4	**8.**	615 × 8	**9.**	$2.59 × 7	**10.**	2,183 × 8
11.	4,619 × 3	**12.**	$23.34 × 8	**13.**	$87.95 × 7	**14.**	51,622 × 8	**15.**	31,409 × 4

Set A For use after page 89

Multiply.

1.	2.	3.	4.	5.
29 × 19	35 × 27	61 × 23	127 × 17	342 × 63

6.	7.	8.	9.	10.
1,205 × 21	2,267 × 73	$9.54 × 63	$17.84 × 76	$39.98 × 82

Set B For use after page 95

Multiply.

1.	2.	3.	4.	5.
205 × 124	334 × 106	218 × 292	455 × 265	807 × 700

6.	7.	8.	9.	10.
469 × 239	625 × 304	289 × 378	567 × 899	692 × 475

11.	12.	13.	14.	15.
1,021 × 205	2,416 × 315	4,877 × 129	6,697 × 872	5,833 × 475

Set C For use after page 97

Estimate the answers. Use clustering.

1. 58 + 61 + 59

2. 79 + 82 + 78

3. 97 + 102 + 106

4. 27 + 34 + 29 + 31

5. 2,984 + 3,114 + 3,080

6. 319 + 291 + 295 + 308

Set D For use after page 110

Estimate these quotients. Choose numbers so that you can use a basic fact.

1. 284 ÷ 7

2. 555 ÷ 8

3. 535 ÷ 61

4. 398 ÷ 84

5. 71)284

6. 54)295

7. 93)814

8. 63)1,781

9. 48)2,457

10. 587)4,217

11. 575)5,377

12. 921)8,079

Set A   **For use after page 115**

Divide and check.

1. $7\overline{)652}$ 2. $8\overline{)238}$ 3. $6\overline{)558}$ 4. $5\overline{)3,182}$ 5. $7\overline{)6,118}$

6. $8\overline{)4,282}$ 7. $5\overline{)9,877}$ 8. $8\overline{)\$36.48}$ 9. $7\overline{)\$65.87}$ 10. $5\overline{)12,284}$

11. $6\overline{)43,026}$ 12. $9\overline{)61,911}$ 13. $8\overline{)45,336}$ 14. $7\overline{)31,283}$ 15. $6\overline{)20,489}$

Set B   **For use after page 123**

Divide and check.

1. $42\overline{)381}$ 2. $62\overline{)546}$ 3. $23\overline{)218}$ 4. $45\overline{)360}$ 5. $72\overline{)655}$

6. $95\overline{)760}$ 7. $59\overline{)413}$ 8. $61\overline{)317}$ 9. $75\overline{)450}$ 10. $99\overline{)912}$

11. $26\overline{)236}$ 12. $41\overline{)333}$ 13. $67\overline{)206}$ 14. $85\overline{)512}$ 15. $49\overline{)147}$

Set C   **For use after page 124**

Divide. Watch for estimates that need to be changed.

1. $52\overline{)315}$ 2. $58\overline{)563}$ 3. $26\overline{)210}$ 4. $53\overline{)368}$ 5. $84\overline{)589}$

6. $36\overline{)183}$ 7. $68\overline{)333}$ 8. $43\overline{)426}$ 9. $73\overline{)442}$ 10. $56\overline{)506}$

11. $23\overline{)206}$ 12. $38\overline{)267}$ 13. $69\overline{)278}$ 14. $93\overline{)553}$ 15. $54\overline{)436}$

Set D   **For use after page 127**

Divide and check.

1. $23\overline{)1,035}$ 2. $56\overline{)952}$ 3. $61\overline{)1,586}$ 4. $39\overline{)1,992}$ 5. $54\overline{)1,404}$

6. $57\overline{)3,881}$ 7. $35\overline{)4,486}$ 8. $53\overline{)21,889}$ 9. $86\overline{)36,378}$ 10. $87\overline{)49,245}$

11. $69\overline{)24,702}$ 12. $59\overline{)\$316.24}$ 13. $48\overline{)\$428.16}$ 14. $36\overline{)19,052}$ 15. $62\overline{)54,384}$

Set A   For use after page 128

Divide.

1. $36\overline{)2{,}880}$ **2.** $56\overline{)2{,}270}$ **3.** $25\overline{)777}$ **4.** $23\overline{)2{,}392}$ **5.** $21\overline{)10{,}626}$

6. $57\overline{)11{,}630}$ **7.** $41\overline{)21{,}735}$ **8.** $13\overline{)1{,}380}$ **9.** $26\overline{)13{,}026}$ **10.** $32\overline{)1{,}643}$

11. $22\overline{)26{,}510}$ **12.** $28\overline{)58{,}912}$ **13.** $14\overline{)78{,}834}$ **14.** $41\overline{)43{,}043}$ **15.** $35\overline{)105{,}160}$

Set B   For use after page 129

Divide.

1. $126\overline{)1{,}134}$ **2.** $523\overline{)4{,}184}$ **3.** $329\overline{)2{,}303}$ **4.** $488\overline{)2{,}932}$

5. $255\overline{)2{,}300}$ **6.** $417\overline{)3{,}344}$ **7.** $536\overline{)2{,}687}$ **8.** $369\overline{)2{,}796}$

9. $584\overline{)3{,}237}$ **10.** $214\overline{)7{,}490}$ **11.** $364\overline{)9{,}464}$ **12.** $599\overline{)38{,}935}$

Set C   For use after page 139

Estimate the products by rounding so that you can
use a basic fact.

1. $\begin{array}{r} 4.8 \\ \times\ 3.2 \\ \hline \end{array}$ **2.** $\begin{array}{r} 5.34 \\ \times\ \ \ 3 \\ \hline \end{array}$ **3.** $\begin{array}{r} 9.26 \\ \times\ 3.44 \\ \hline \end{array}$ **4.** $\begin{array}{r} 8.65 \\ \times\ 3.87 \\ \hline \end{array}$ **5.** $\begin{array}{r} 2.042 \\ \times\ \ 3.24 \\ \hline \end{array}$

6. $\begin{array}{r} 31.54 \\ \times\ \ \ 7.3 \\ \hline \end{array}$ **7.** $\begin{array}{r} 83.64 \\ \times\ \ 4.12 \\ \hline \end{array}$ **8.** $\begin{array}{r} 72.29 \\ \times\ 65.89 \\ \hline \end{array}$ **9.** $\begin{array}{r} \$26.67 \\ \times\ \ \ \ 4.9 \\ \hline \end{array}$ **10.** $\begin{array}{r} \$214.85 \\ \times\ \ \ \ \ 8.7 \\ \hline \end{array}$

Estimate the quotients by rounding so that you can
use a basic fact.

11. $6\overline{)289.41}$ **12.** $5.8\overline{)476.44}$ **13.** $8.7\overline{)541.92}$ **14.** $4.6\overline{)248.11}$

15. $5.4\overline{)\$286.25}$ **16.** $8.3\overline{)724.36}$ **17.** $8.8\overline{)814.46}$ **18.** $2.3\overline{)\$136.42}$

Set A   For use after page 141

Multiply.

1. $\begin{array}{r} 4.5 \\ \times\ 2.8 \\ \hline \end{array}$	**2.** $\begin{array}{r} 7.9 \\ \times\ 8.4 \\ \hline \end{array}$	**3.** $\begin{array}{r} 0.23 \\ \times\ \ \ 5 \\ \hline \end{array}$	**4.** $\begin{array}{r} 3.79 \\ \times\ \ \ 4 \\ \hline \end{array}$	**5.** $\begin{array}{r} 1.29 \\ \times\ 0.27 \\ \hline \end{array}$
6. $\begin{array}{r} 34.5 \\ \times\ \ 3.7 \\ \hline \end{array}$	**7.** $\begin{array}{r} 9.24 \\ \times\ \ \ 5.8 \\ \hline \end{array}$	**8.** $\begin{array}{r} 0.46 \\ \times\ 0.35 \\ \hline \end{array}$	**9.** $\begin{array}{r} \$3.52 \\ \times\ \ \ 7.4 \\ \hline \end{array}$	**10.** $\begin{array}{r} \$102.12 \\ \times\ \ \ \ \ 0.4 \\ \hline \end{array}$
11. $\begin{array}{r} 32.4 \\ \times\ 1.37 \\ \hline \end{array}$	**12.** $\begin{array}{r} 1.334 \\ \times\ \ \ 0.9 \\ \hline \end{array}$	**13.** $\begin{array}{r} 91.45 \\ \times\ \ \ 8.1 \\ \hline \end{array}$	**14.** $\begin{array}{r} 5.47 \\ \times\ \ 3.1 \\ \hline \end{array}$	**15.** $\begin{array}{r} \$209.25 \\ \times\ \ \ \ 1.13 \\ \hline \end{array}$

Set B   For use after page 143

Multiply.

1. $\begin{array}{r} 0.2 \\ \times\ 0.9 \\ \hline \end{array}$	**2.** $\begin{array}{r} 0.05 \\ \times\ 0.03 \\ \hline \end{array}$	**3.** $\begin{array}{r} 6.8 \\ \times\ 0.7 \\ \hline \end{array}$	**4.** $\begin{array}{r} 3.08 \\ \times\ 0.07 \\ \hline \end{array}$	**5.** $\begin{array}{r} 12.26 \\ \times\ 0.005 \\ \hline \end{array}$
6. $\begin{array}{r} 25.03 \\ \times\ \ \ 0.2 \\ \hline \end{array}$	**7.** $\begin{array}{r} \$5.79 \\ \times\ \ 0.06 \\ \hline \end{array}$	**8.** $\begin{array}{r} 89.22 \\ \times\ \ \ 0.13 \\ \hline \end{array}$	**9.** $\begin{array}{r} 0.062 \\ \times\ \ 0.07 \\ \hline \end{array}$	**10.** $\begin{array}{r} 124.3 \\ \times\ 0.006 \\ \hline \end{array}$
11. $\begin{array}{r} 324.7 \\ \times\ \ 0.09 \\ \hline \end{array}$	**12.** $\begin{array}{r} 85.3 \\ \times\ 13.4 \\ \hline \end{array}$	**13.** $\begin{array}{r} \$17.69 \\ \times\ \ \ 0.08 \\ \hline \end{array}$	**14.** $\begin{array}{r} 0.032 \\ \times\ 0.051 \\ \hline \end{array}$	**15.** $\begin{array}{r} 0.091 \\ \times\ 0.012 \\ \hline \end{array}$

Set C   For use after page 144

Multiply. Write only the answers.

1. 8.51×10 **2.** 0.03×10 **3.** 10×5.921 **4.** 10×89.06

5. 0.029×10 **6.** 100×7.54 **7.** 12.3×100 **8.** 0.1×100

9. 100×5.003 **10.** 100×45.95 **11.** $1,000 \times 0.07$ **12.** $3.245 \times 1,000$

13. $0.29 \times 1,000$ **14.** $1,000 \times 4.6$ **15.** $1,000 \times 0.79$ **16.** $1,000 \times 5.9$

Set A For use after page 149

Divide. Check your answers.

1. $7\overline{)5.81}$ **2.** $5\overline{)13.30}$ **3.** $9\overline{)27.45}$ **4.** $4\overline{)121.6}$ **5.** $7\overline{)36.61}$

6. $8\overline{)751.2}$ **7.** $5\overline{)0.310}$ **8.** $6\overline{)324.6}$ **9.** $7\overline{)65.87}$ **10.** $6\overline{)1.338}$

11. $23\overline{)94.53}$ **12.** $15\overline{)76.80}$ **13.** $24\overline{)77.28}$ **14.** $21\overline{)14.49}$ **15.** $54\overline{)46.98}$

16. $42\overline{)22.26}$ **17.** $36\overline{)122.76}$ **18.** $12\overline{)\$63.72}$ **19.** $14\overline{)\$173.32}$ **20.** $52\overline{)\$117.52}$

Set B For use after page 151

Find the quotients. Round to the nearest tenth.

1. $4\overline{)13}$ **2.** $6\overline{)25}$ **3.** $7\overline{)62}$ **4.** $9\overline{)3.8}$ **5.** $14\overline{)72}$

6. $7\overline{)122}$ **7.** $23\overline{)89}$ **8.** $12\overline{)3.49}$ **9.** $15\overline{)61.2}$ **10.** $16\overline{)145}$

Find the quotients. Round to the nearest hundredth or cent.

11. $8\overline{)3}$ **12.** $7\overline{)15}$ **13.** $13\overline{)20}$ **14.** $11\overline{)65}$ **15.** $15\overline{)25.3}$

16. $6\overline{)\$2.98}$ **17.** $6\overline{)\$50.18}$ **18.** $8\overline{)\$12.85}$ **19.** $14\overline{)\$32.67}$ **20.** $12\overline{)\$27.44}$

Set C For use after page 152

Divide. Write only the answers.

1. $3.7 \div 10$ **2.** $12.19 \div 10$ **3.** $7.05 \div 10$ **4.** $126 \div 10$ **5.** $28.3 \div 10$

6. $61.9 \div 100$ **7.** $0.7 \div 100$ **8.** $652.3 \div 100$ **9.** $12 \div 100$ **10.** $903 \div 100$

11. $500 \div 1,000$ **12.** $169 \div 1,000$ **13.** $3.9 \div 1,000$ **14.** $38 \div 1,000$ **15.** $457 \div 1,000$

Set A   For use after page 157

Divide. Round to the nearest hundredth
when necessary.

1. $5.6\overline{)17.92}$ 2. $2.1\overline{)8.61}$ 3. $0.32\overline{)1.968}$ 4. $0.04\overline{)0.2092}$

5. $4.7\overline{)2.444}$ 6. $0.6\overline{)1.908}$ 7. $4.6\overline{)8.694}$ 8. $0.85\overline{)2.856}$

9. $0.05\overline{)1.237}$ 10. $0.9\overline{)3.667}$ 11. $0.004\overline{)0.014}$ 12. $0.08\overline{)0.536}$

Set B   For use after page 159

Divide. Check by multiplying.

1. $0.06\overline{)2.88}$ 2. $0.003\overline{)0.078}$ 3. $0.012\overline{)6.24}$ 4. $0.09\overline{)86.4}$

5. $2.6\overline{)130}$ 6. $6.1\overline{)244}$ 7. $0.015\overline{)1.2}$ 8. $0.28\overline{)140}$

9. $0.043\overline{)9.89}$ 10. $1.5\overline{)8.4}$ 11. $2.9\overline{)20.3}$ 12. $0.044\overline{)35.2}$

Set C   For use after page 197

Find the missing numerator or denominator.

1. $\frac{2}{3} = \frac{\text{▥}}{18}$ 2. $\frac{1}{8} = \frac{\text{▥}}{32}$ 3. $\frac{3}{5} = \frac{24}{\text{▥}}$ 4. $\frac{4}{9} = \frac{\text{▥}}{45}$ 5. $\frac{5}{6} = \frac{35}{\text{▥}}$

6. $\frac{2}{7} = \frac{12}{\text{▥}}$ 7. $\frac{4}{5} = \frac{\text{▥}}{20}$ 8. $\frac{3}{16} = \frac{\text{▥}}{32}$ 9. $\frac{7}{10} = \frac{21}{\text{▥}}$ 10. $\frac{11}{12} = \frac{55}{\text{▥}}$

Write one fraction equivalent to the given fraction.

11. $\frac{3}{10}$ 12. $\frac{4}{9}$ 13. $\frac{1}{6}$ 14. $\frac{4}{7}$ 15. $\frac{4}{11}$ 16. $\frac{3}{5}$ 17. $\frac{9}{10}$

Set D   For use after page 198

Find the greatest common factor for each pair of numbers.

1. $\begin{array}{c}8\\20\end{array}$ 2. $\begin{array}{c}6\\26\end{array}$ 3. $\begin{array}{c}20\\16\end{array}$ 4. $\begin{array}{c}35\\50\end{array}$ 5. $\begin{array}{c}16\\48\end{array}$ 6. $\begin{array}{c}7\\15\end{array}$

7. $\begin{array}{c}21\\28\end{array}$ 8. $\begin{array}{c}6\\32\end{array}$ 9. $\begin{array}{c}8\\52\end{array}$ 10. $\begin{array}{c}21\\56\end{array}$ 11. $\begin{array}{c}24\\60\end{array}$ 12. $\begin{array}{c}18\\54\end{array}$

Set A   For use after page 199

Write each fraction in lowest terms.

1. $\frac{6}{21}$ 2. $\frac{9}{30}$ 3. $\frac{8}{28}$ 4. $\frac{25}{40}$ 5. $\frac{15}{35}$ 6. $\frac{14}{42}$

7. $\frac{12}{32}$ 8. $\frac{18}{45}$ 9. $\frac{20}{42}$ 10. $\frac{36}{60}$ 11. $\frac{16}{20}$ 12. $\frac{24}{30}$

Set B   For use after page 200

Write each improper fraction as a mixed number or whole number.

1. $\frac{10}{3}$ 2. $\frac{22}{5}$ 3. $\frac{22}{6}$ 4. $\frac{33}{2}$ 5. $\frac{56}{8}$ 6. $\frac{67}{10}$

7. $\frac{37}{15}$ 8. $\frac{29}{4}$ 9. $\frac{28}{13}$ 10. $\frac{44}{9}$ 11. $\frac{95}{5}$ 12. $\frac{49}{6}$

Set C   For use after page 201

Write each mixed number as an improper fraction.

1. $2\frac{4}{5}$ 2. $1\frac{7}{10}$ 3. $5\frac{2}{9}$ 4. $3\frac{4}{7}$ 5. $5\frac{3}{8}$ 6. $4\frac{1}{10}$

7. $9\frac{5}{8}$ 8. $2\frac{7}{11}$ 9. $7\frac{3}{5}$ 10. $6\frac{5}{9}$ 11. $7\frac{2}{3}$ 12. $10\frac{1}{5}$

Set D   For use after page 202

Write $>$, $<$, or $=$ for each ▓ .

1. $\frac{5}{8}$ ▓ $\frac{7}{12}$ 2. $\frac{2}{3}$ ▓ $\frac{4}{9}$ 3. $\frac{4}{10}$ ▓ $\frac{6}{15}$ 4. $\frac{2}{5}$ ▓ $\frac{3}{7}$

5. $2\frac{2}{3}$ ▓ $2\frac{3}{4}$ 6. $1\frac{8}{10}$ ▓ $1\frac{12}{15}$ 7. $5\frac{5}{9}$ ▓ $5\frac{4}{7}$ 8. $3\frac{3}{5}$ ▓ $3\frac{4}{7}$

Compare the fractions or mixed numbers two at a time.
Then list them in order from least to greatest.

9. $\frac{3}{10}, \frac{2}{7}, \frac{2}{5}$ 10. $2\frac{4}{7}, 2\frac{1}{3}, 2\frac{9}{14}$ 11. $\frac{2}{3}, \frac{5}{9}, \frac{4}{7}$ 12. $2\frac{1}{7}, \frac{7}{8}, 1\frac{1}{4}$

Set A   For use after page 205

Add or subtract.

1. $\frac{5}{6}$
$+ \frac{1}{6}$

2. $\frac{3}{11}$
$+ \frac{2}{11}$

3. $\frac{4}{5}$
$+ \frac{3}{5}$

4. $1\frac{4}{9}$
$+ 3\frac{2}{9}$

5. $2\frac{3}{10}$
$+ 4\frac{1}{10}$

6. $\frac{7}{8}$
$- \frac{6}{8}$

7. $\frac{9}{10}$
$- \frac{3}{10}$

8. $1\frac{7}{9}$
$- 1\frac{5}{9}$

9. $5\frac{4}{11}$
$- 3\frac{2}{11}$

10. $10\frac{4}{5}$
$- 3\frac{1}{5}$

11. $\frac{3}{8}$
$- \frac{1}{8}$

12. $\frac{4}{11}$
$+ \frac{3}{11}$

13. $6\frac{5}{16}$
$+ 3$

14. $2\frac{11}{16}$
$- 1\frac{7}{16}$

15. $3\frac{17}{30}$
$+ 4\frac{7}{30}$

Set B   For use after page 207

Find the least common denominator of these fractions.

1. $\frac{3}{8}, \frac{1}{16}$

2. $\frac{5}{12}, \frac{1}{3}$

3. $\frac{3}{4}, \frac{2}{7}$

4. $\frac{1}{2}, \frac{3}{5}$

5. $\frac{5}{8}, \frac{1}{6}, \frac{2}{3}$

6. $\frac{3}{10}, \frac{3}{4}$

7. $\frac{1}{2}, \frac{3}{20}$

8. $\frac{5}{24}, \frac{7}{8}$

9. $\frac{4}{5}, \frac{3}{7}$

10. $\frac{2}{3}, \frac{7}{12}, \frac{4}{5}$

Set C   For use after page 209

Add.

1. $\frac{1}{8}$
$+ \frac{3}{4}$

2. $\frac{2}{3}$
$+ \frac{1}{6}$

3. $\frac{1}{10}$
$+ \frac{2}{5}$

4. $\frac{5}{12}$
$+ \frac{1}{6}$

5. $\frac{1}{4}$
$+ \frac{7}{8}$

6. $\frac{1}{3}$
$+ \frac{2}{9}$

7. $\frac{3}{8}$
$+ \frac{1}{10}$

8. $\frac{2}{5}$
$+ \frac{3}{15}$

9. $\frac{3}{20}$
$+ \frac{4}{5}$

10. $\frac{3}{4}$
$+ \frac{4}{5}$

11. $\frac{1}{8}$
$+ \frac{1}{6}$

12. $\frac{3}{5}$
$+ \frac{2}{3}$

Subtract.

13. $\frac{7}{12}$
$- \frac{1}{2}$

14. $\frac{9}{20}$
$- \frac{2}{10}$

15. $\frac{4}{9}$
$- \frac{1}{3}$

16. $\frac{3}{4}$
$- \frac{7}{16}$

17. $\frac{4}{5}$
$- \frac{3}{4}$

18. $\frac{5}{6}$
$- \frac{5}{18}$

Set A For use after page 211

Find the sums.

1. $3\frac{1}{2}$
   $+\ 2\frac{3}{8}$

2. $10\frac{1}{6}$
   $+\ \ 3\frac{1}{12}$

3. $1\frac{4}{5}$
   $+\ 3\frac{2}{15}$

4. $10\frac{7}{9}$
   $+\ 25\frac{2}{3}$

5. $16\frac{4}{5}$
   $+\ 17\frac{3}{20}$

6. $1\frac{1}{2}$
   $3\frac{5}{8}$
   $+\ 7\frac{3}{16}$

7. $24\frac{5}{9}$
   $14\frac{1}{3}$
   $+\ \ 6\frac{1}{6}$

8. $33\frac{1}{5}$
   $2\frac{1}{2}$
   $+\ 17\frac{1}{6}$

9. $15\frac{1}{3}$
   $41\frac{5}{6}$
   $+\ 29\frac{1}{6}$

10. $68\frac{2}{3}$
    $9\frac{1}{4}$
    $+\ 10\frac{5}{12}$

Set B For use after page 213

Subtract.

1. $6\frac{5}{6}$
   $-\ 5\frac{1}{3}$

2. $10\frac{3}{4}$
   $-\ \ 7\frac{1}{8}$

3. $13\frac{4}{5}$
   $-\ \ 5\frac{3}{10}$

4. $11\frac{7}{8}$
   $-\ \ 6\frac{5}{16}$

5. $5\frac{5}{9}$
   $-\ 4\frac{1}{3}$

6. $20\frac{11}{12}$
   $-\ 15\frac{3}{4}$

7. $16\frac{4}{9}$
   $-\ \ 7\frac{1}{6}$

8. $12\frac{4}{5}$
   $-\ 12\frac{2}{3}$

9. $8\frac{3}{4}$
   $-\ 3\frac{2}{5}$

10. $9\frac{5}{6}$
    $-\ 7\frac{3}{4}$

11. $27\frac{3}{5}$
    $-\ 17\frac{1}{7}$

12. $19\frac{3}{10}$
    $-\ 17\frac{1}{5}$

13. $27\frac{7}{8}$
    $-15\frac{1}{3}$

14. $11\frac{5}{6}$
    $-\ 10\frac{1}{12}$

15. $9\frac{5}{6}$
    $-\ 8\frac{7}{9}$

Set C For use after page 215

Subtract.

1. $3\frac{1}{7}$
   $-\ 1\frac{5}{7}$

2. $4\frac{1}{5}$
   $-\ 2\frac{3}{10}$

3. 7
   $-\ 3\frac{5}{6}$

4. $10\frac{3}{8}$
   $-\ \ 9\frac{3}{4}$

5. $15\frac{2}{9}$
   $-\ \ 8\frac{5}{6}$

6. $11\frac{1}{4}$
   $-\ \ 8\frac{5}{6}$

7. $10\frac{3}{10}$
   $-\ \ 7\frac{7}{10}$

8. $20\frac{2}{5}$
   $-\ \ 9\frac{2}{3}$

9. $17\frac{3}{5}$
   $-\ 13\frac{5}{6}$

10. $30\frac{1}{12}$
    $-\ \ 2\frac{2}{9}$

Set A   For use after page 231

Find the product in lowest terms.

1. $\frac{9}{20} \times \frac{2}{9}$ 2. $\frac{4}{5} \times \frac{1}{2}$ 3. $\frac{2}{5} \times \frac{5}{6}$ 4. $\frac{2}{3} \times \frac{5}{6}$ 5. $\frac{10}{9} \times \frac{9}{10}$

6. $\frac{2}{3} \times \frac{12}{19}$ 7. $\frac{4}{9} \times \frac{27}{28}$ 8. $\frac{3}{5} \times \frac{10}{27}$ 9. $\frac{3}{2} \times \frac{6}{7}$ 10. $\frac{3}{14} \times 7$

11. $\frac{3}{7} \times \frac{14}{15}$ 12. $\frac{2}{17} \times \frac{34}{35}$ 13. $9 \times \frac{5}{81}$ 14. $\frac{5}{3} \times \frac{33}{35}$ 15. $\frac{39}{49} \times \frac{7}{13}$

Set B   For use after page 233

Find the product in lowest terms.

1. $1\frac{1}{3} \times 4\frac{1}{2}$ 2. $1\frac{3}{8} \times 1\frac{3}{5}$ 3. $2\frac{2}{3} \times 3$ 4. $4\frac{2}{7} \times \frac{2}{5}$

5. $1\frac{5}{9} \times 3\frac{6}{7}$ 6. $12 \times 1\frac{5}{6}$ 7. $3\frac{1}{3} \times 1\frac{3}{5}$ 8. $2\frac{2}{5} \times 20$

9. $3\frac{3}{7} \times 3\frac{1}{2}$ 10. $2\frac{1}{3} \times 1\frac{5}{28}$ 11. $18 \times 2\frac{1}{9}$ 12. $3\frac{3}{5} \times 5\frac{1}{2}$

Set C   For use after page 236

Write the lowest-terms fraction or mixed number for each decimal.

1. 0.2   2. 0.15   3. 3.65   4. 0.01   5. 7.02

6. 5.075   7. 0.045   8. 8.062   9. 9.55   10. 2.6

11. 75.085   12. 0.001   13. 3.24   14. 0.128   15. 0.012

Set D   For use after page 237

Write a decimal for each fraction.

1. $\frac{3}{5}$ 2. $\frac{3}{10}$ 3. $\frac{37}{100}$ 4. $\frac{7}{4}$ 5. $\frac{9}{5}$ 6. $\frac{7}{10}$

7. $\frac{1}{20}$ 8. $\frac{5}{2}$ 9. $\frac{9}{8}$ 10. $\frac{1}{5}$ 11. $\frac{91}{100}$ 12. $\frac{13}{8}$

13. $\frac{9}{4}$ 14. $\frac{5}{16}$ 15. $\frac{9}{20}$ 16. $\frac{9}{16}$ 17. $\frac{23}{20}$ 18. $\frac{189}{100}$

Set A   For use after page 241

Find the quotients.

1. $\frac{1}{3} \div \frac{1}{6}$ **2.** $8 \div \frac{4}{5}$ **3.** $\frac{11}{12} \div \frac{11}{12}$ **4.** $\frac{4}{3} \div \frac{5}{12}$ **5.** $\frac{4}{5} \div 6$

6. $\frac{3}{8} \div \frac{3}{16}$ **7.** $\frac{2}{3} \div \frac{4}{15}$ **8.** $\frac{4}{5} \div 12$ **9.** $\frac{7}{20} \div \frac{14}{15}$ **10.** $\frac{5}{8} \div \frac{5}{6}$

11. $\frac{2}{7} \div \frac{3}{14}$ **12.** $3 \div \frac{9}{10}$ **13.** $\frac{4}{9} \div \frac{5}{12}$ **14.** $\frac{3}{10} \div \frac{9}{40}$ **15.** $\frac{9}{8} \div \frac{3}{16}$

Set B   For use after page 243

Divide and check.

1. $1\frac{2}{3} \div 3\frac{3}{4}$ **2.** $6\frac{1}{8} \div 1\frac{3}{4}$ **3.** $9 \div 3\frac{3}{8}$ **4.** $2\frac{1}{3} \div 4\frac{2}{3}$ **5.** $4\frac{1}{6} \div 2\frac{1}{2}$

6. $1\frac{3}{7} \div 2\frac{6}{7}$ **7.** $6\frac{3}{8} \div 5\frac{2}{3}$ **8.** $\frac{9}{10} \div 3\frac{3}{5}$ **9.** $4\frac{4}{5} \div 12$ **10.** $4\frac{2}{7} \div 2\frac{1}{7}$

11. $9\frac{1}{7} \div 2\frac{2}{7}$ **12.** $3\frac{5}{9} \div 5\frac{1}{3}$ **13.** $7\frac{1}{2} \div 2\frac{2}{5}$ **14.** $2\frac{1}{5} \div \frac{11}{15}$ **15.** $3\frac{3}{4} \div 1\frac{9}{16}$

Set C   For use after page 303

Write each decimal as a percent.

1. 0.36   **2.** 0.28   **3.** 0.02   **4.** 0.17   **5.** 0.07   **6.** 0.92

Write each fraction as a percent.

7. $\frac{13}{100}$ **8.** $\frac{79}{100}$ **9.** $\frac{85}{100}$ **10.** $\frac{1}{100}$ **11.** $\frac{25}{100}$ **12.** $\frac{112}{100}$

Write each percent as a decimal.

13. 89%   **14.** 54%   **15.** 12%   **16.** 60%   **17.** 39%   **18.** 99%

Write each percent as a fraction in lowest terms.

19. 80%   **20.** 11%   **21.** 24%   **22.** 46%   **23.** 75%   **24.** 90%

Set A   For use after page 305

Find an equivalent fraction with denominator 100.
Then write a percent for each fraction.

1. $\frac{9}{10}$ **2.** $\frac{3}{4}$ **3.** $\frac{11}{50}$ **4.** $\frac{4}{5}$ **5.** $\frac{17}{20}$ **6.** $\frac{4}{25}$

7. $\frac{4}{20}$ **8.** $\frac{15}{30}$ **9.** $\frac{9}{15}$ **10.** $\frac{42}{56}$ **11.** $\frac{12}{40}$ **12.** $\frac{20}{25}$

Divide to find a decimal or mixed decimal for each
fraction. Then write the decimal as a percent.

13. $\frac{1}{3}$ **14.** $\frac{3}{8}$ **15.** $\frac{2}{5}$ **16.** $\frac{3}{10}$ **17.** $\frac{4}{7}$ **18.** $\frac{4}{9}$

19. $\frac{5}{6}$ **20.** $\frac{9}{8}$ **21.** $\frac{5}{16}$ **22.** $\frac{4}{3}$ **23.** $\frac{1}{11}$ **24.** $\frac{1}{12}$

Set B   For use after page 306

Write a decimal and a lowest-terms fraction
for each percent.

1. 25%   **2.** 30%   **3.** 14%   **4.** 43%   **5.** 32%

6. 85%   **7.** $6\frac{1}{2}$%   **8.** 48%   **9.** 115%   **10.** $3\frac{2}{5}$%

11. $20\frac{1}{2}$%   **12.** 64%   **13.** $\frac{1}{2}$%   **14.** $21\frac{1}{5}$%   **15.** 144%

Set C   For use after page 309

Find the percent of each number.

1. 75% of 20   **2.** 21% of 13   **3.** $12\frac{1}{2}$% of 400   **4.** 67% of 35

5. 60% of 30   **6.** 72% of 150   **7.** $37\frac{1}{2}$% of 24   **8.** 25% of 160

Estimate the percent of each number.

9. 24% of 80   **10.** 34% of 300   **11.** 9% of 70   **12.** 19% of 50

13. 52% of 140   **14.** 26% of 200   **15.** 48% of 500   **16.** 11% of 150

Set A   For use after page 369

Find the sums.

1. $^-4 + {}^-7$ 2. $^+3 + {}^+5$ 3. $^-2 + {}^-8$ 4. $^+8 + {}^+5$

5. $^-3 + {}^-8$ 6. $^-7 + {}^-9$ 7. $^+4 + {}^+10$ 8. $^+5 + {}^+1$

9. $^+6 + {}^+4$ 10. $^-3 + {}^-12$ 11. $^-1 + {}^-7$ 12. $^-10 + {}^-2$

Set B   For use after page 371

Find the sums.

1. $^+8 + {}^-3$ 2. $^-3 + {}^-8$ 3. $^+11 + {}^+2$ 4. $^-9 + {}^+3$

5. $^+2 + {}^-4$ 6. $^-15 + {}^+8$ 7. $^-7 + {}^-2$ 8. $^+10 + {}^+5$

9. $^-7 + {}^-9$ 10. $^+5 + {}^+6$ 11. $^+3 + {}^-11$ 12. $^-5 + {}^-7$

Set C   For use after page 373

Find the differences. Thinking of addends and a sum may help you.

	s	a	a
1.	$^+3$	$-$	$^-9 = n$

	s	a	a
2.	$^-2$	$-$	$^+5 = n$

	s	a	a
3.	$^+2$	$-$	$^-5 = n$

	s	a	a
4.	$^-1$	$+$	$^+7 = n$

	s	a	a
5.	$^+3$	$-$	$^+8 = n$

	s	a	a
6.	$^+6$	$-$	$^-8 = n$

	s	a	a
7.	$^+2$	$-$	$^+7 = n$

	s	a	a
8.	$^+5$	$-$	$^-5 = n$

	s	a	a
9.	$^-5$	$+$	$^+6 = n$

Set D   For use after page 376

Write > or < for each ▦ .

1. $^+5$ ▦ $^-3$ 2. $^-8$ ▦ $^-7$ 3. $^-2$ ▦ $^+4$ 4. $^-5$ ▦ $^-9$

5. $^+3$ ▦ $^-4$ 6. $^+6$ ▦ $^-5$ 7. $^-7$ ▦ $^-20$ 8. $^+1$ ▦ $^-12$

9. $^-10$ ▦ $^-2$ 10. $^+2$ ▦ $^-1$ 11. $^-4$ ▦ $^+3$ 12. 0 ▦ $^-7$

Order from greatest to least.

13. $^-10, {}^-18, {}^+5, {}^+1, {}^+12, 0$ 14. $^+1, {}^-4, {}^+8, {}^+4, {}^-10, {}^+2$ 15. $^-12, {}^-15, {}^-6, {}^-30, {}^-10, {}^-8$

TABLE OF MEASURES

Metric System		Customary System	

Length

1 centimeter (cm)	10 millimeters (mm)	1 foot (ft)	12 inches (in.)
1 decimeter (dm)	100 millimeters (mm) 10 centimeters (cm)	1 yard (yd)	36 inches (in.) 3 feet (ft)
1 meter (m)	1,000 millimeters (mm) 100 centimeters (cm) 10 decimeters (dm)	1 mile (m)	5,280 feet (ft) 1,760 yards (yd)
1 kilometer (km)	1,000 meters (m)		

Area

1 square meter (m^2)	100 square decimeters (dm^2) 10,000 square centimeters (cm^2)	1 square foot (ft^2)	144 square inches $(in.^2)$

Volume

1 cubic decimeter (dm^3)	1,000 cubic centimeters (cm^3) 1 liter (L)	1 cubic foot (ft^3)	1,728 cubic inches $(in.^3)$

Capacity

1 teaspoon	5 milliliters (mL)	1 cup (c)	8 fluid ounces (fl oz)
1 tablespoon	12.5 milliliters (mL)	1 pint (pt)	16 fluid ounces (fl oz) 2 cups (c)
1 liter (L)	1,000 milliliters (mL) 1,000 cubic centimeters (cm^3) 1 cubic decimeter (dm^3) 4 metric cups	1 quart (qt)	32 fluid ounces (fl oz) 4 cups (c) 2 pints (pt)
		1 gallon (gal)	128 fluid ounces (fl oz) 16 cups (c) 8 pints (pt) 4 quarts (qt)

Weight

1 gram (g)	1,000 milligrams (mg)	1 pound (lb)	16 ounces (oz)
1 kilogram (kg)	1,000 grams (g)		

Time

1 minute (min)	60 seconds (s)		365 days
1 hour (h)	60 minutes (min)	1 year (yr)	52 weeks
1 day (d)	24 hours (h)		12 months
1 week (w)	7 days (d)	1 decade	10 years
1 month (mo)	about 4 weeks	1 century	100 years

GLOSSARY

a.m. A way to indicate time from 12:00 midnight to 12:00 noon.

acute angle An angle that has a measure less than 90°.

acute triangle A triangle in which each angle has a measure less than 90°.

addend One of the numbers to be added.

Example:
$$\begin{array}{r} 3 \\ + \ 5 \\ \hline 8 \end{array} \quad \text{addends}$$

addition An operation that gives the total number when two or more numbers are put together.

angle Two rays from a single point.

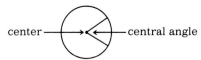

area The measure of a region, expressed in square units.

average The quotient obtained when the sum of a set of numbers is divided by the number of addends.

bit Binary digit, 0 or 1.

capacity The volume of a space figure given in terms of liquid measurement.

central angle An angle whose vertex is the center of a circle.

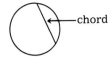

center —— central angle

chord A segment containing any two points of a circle.

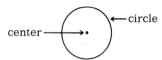

chord

circle A plane figure in which all the points are the same distance from a point called the center.

center —— circle

circumference The distance around a circle.

common factor A number that is a factor of two different numbers is a common factor of those two numbers.

common multiple A number that is a multiple of two different numbers is a common multiple of those two numbers.

compass An instrument used to make circles.

composite number A whole number greater than 1 that has more than two factors.

cone A space figure with one circular face and one vertex.

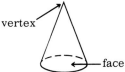

vertex

face

congruent figures Figures that have the same size and shape.

coordinates Number pair used in graphing.

cross products Products obtained by multiplying the numerator of one fraction by the denominator of a second fraction, and the denominator of the first fraction by the numerator of the second fraction.

cube A space figure whose faces are all squares.

customary units of measure See Table of Measures, page 429.

data Information.

data bank A place where information is stored.

decagon A polygon with 10 sides.

decimal Any base-ten numeral written using a decimal point.

3.2 ← decimal

↑
decimal point

degree A unit of angle measure.

degree Celsius (°C) A metric unit for measuring temperature.

degree Fahrenheit (°F) A customary unit for measuring temperature.

denominator The number below the line in a fraction.

$\frac{3}{4}$ ← denominator

diagonal A segment, other than a side, connecting two vertices of a polygon.

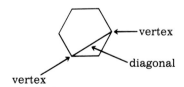

vertex

diagonal

vertex

diameter A chord that passes through the center of a circle.

difference The number obtained by subtracting one number from another.

Example:
$$\begin{array}{r} 9 \\ -\ 4 \\ \hline 5 \end{array} \leftarrow \text{difference}$$

digits The symbols used to write numerals: 0, 1, 2, 3, 4, 5, 6, 7, 8, and 9.

dividend A number to be divided.

$$7\overline{)\overset{4}{28}} \leftarrow \text{dividend}$$

division An operation that tells how many sets or how many in each set.

divisor The number by which a dividend is divided.

$$\text{divisor} \longrightarrow 7\overline{)\overset{4}{28}}$$

edge One of the segments making up any of the faces of a space figure.

←edge

END An instruction in a computer program that tells the computer to stop.

equality (equals, or =) A mathematical relation of being exactly the same.

equally likely outcomes Outcomes that have the same chance of occurring.

equal ratios Ratios that give the same comparison. $\frac{9}{27}$ and $\frac{1}{3}$ are equal ratios.

equation A number sentence involving the use of the equality symbol.

Example: $9 + 2 = 11$

equilateral triangle A triangle with all 3 sides the same length and all angles the same measure.

equivalent fractions Fractions that name the same amount.

Example: $\frac{1}{2}$ and $\frac{2}{4}$

estimate To find an answer that is close to the exact answer.

even number A whole number that has 0, 2, 4, 6, or 8 in the ones place.

expanded form A way to write numbers that shows the place value of each digit.

Example: $9,000 + 300 + 20 + 5$

exponent A number that tells how many times another number is to be used as a factor

$$5 \cdot 5 \cdot 5 = 5^3 \begin{array}{l} \leftarrow \text{exponent} \\ \leftarrow \text{base} \end{array}$$

face One of the plane figures (regions) making up a space figure.

face→

factors Numbers that are combined in the multiplication operation to give a number called the product.

$$6 \times 7 = 42$$
$$\nwarrow \nearrow$$
$$\text{factors}$$

flowchart A chart that shows a step-by-step way of doing something.

fraction A number that expresses parts of a whole or a set.

Example: $\frac{3}{4}$

GOTO An instruction in a computer program that causes the computer to skip to a specified line in the program.

graph A picture that shows information in an organized way.

greater than (>) The relationship of one number being larger than another number.

Example: $6 > 5$, read "6 is greater than 5."

greatest common factor (GCF) The greatest number that is a factor of each of two numbers.

grouping (associative) property When adding (or multiplying) three or more numbers, the grouping of the addends (or factors) can be changed and the sum (or product) is the same.

Examples: $2 + (8 + 6) = (2 + 8) + 6$
$3 \times (4 \times 2) = (3 \times 4) \times 2$

hexagon A polygon with six sides.

improper fraction A fraction in which the numerator is greater than or equal to the denominator.

INPUT An instruction in a computer program that causes the computer to stop and request data while running a program.

integers The whole numbers together with their negatives.

Examples: 5, 0, 23

isosceles triangle A triangle with at least 2 sides the same length and at least 2 angles the same measure.

least common denominator (LCD) The least common multiple of two denominators.

least common multiple (LCM) The smallest nonzero number that is a multiple of each of two given numbers.

less than (<) The relationship of one number being smaller than another number.

      Example: 5 < 6, read "5 is less than 6."

line A straight path that is endless in both directions.

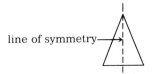

line of symmetry A line on which a figure can be folded so that the two parts fit exactly.

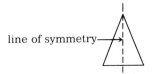

line of symmetry

LIST A copy of a set of instructions that tells a computer what to do.

Logo A computer language that can be used for computer graphics.

lowest terms A fraction is in lowest terms if the numerator and denominator have no common factor greater than 1.

mean The quotient obtained when the sum of two or more numbers is divided by the number of addends.

median The middle number of a set of numbers that are arranged in order.

metric units of measure See Table of Measures, page 429.

mixed decimal A combination of a decimal and a fraction, such as $0.4\frac{1}{3}$.

mixed number A number that has a whole number part and a fraction part, such as $2\frac{3}{4}$.

mode In a list of data, the number or item that occurs most often. There may be more than one mode.

multiple A number that is the product of a given number and a whole number.

multiplication An operation that combines two numbers, called factors, to give one number, called the product.

negative integer Any number in the set { ⁻1, ⁻2, ⁻3, . . . }

number line A line that shows numbers in order.

    Example:

      7   8   9   10

numeral A symbol for a number.

numerator The number above the line in a fraction.

    $\frac{3}{4}$ ⟵ numerator

obtuse angle An angle with a measure greater than 90° and less than 180°.

obtuse triangle A triangle with one angle measuring more than 90°.

octagon A polygon with 8 sides.

odd number A whole number that has 1, 3, 5, 7, or 9 in the ones place.

one property In multiplication, when either factor is 1, the product is the other factor.

order (commutative) property When adding (or multiplying) two or more numbers, the order of the addends (or factors) can be changed and the sum (or product) is the same.

    Examples: $4 \times 5 = 5 \times 4$
                  $2 \times 3 = 3 \times 2$

ordered pair Two numbers that are used to give the location of a point on a graph.

origin The intersection of the coordinate axes; the point associated with the ordered pair (0,0).

outcome A possible result in a probability experiment.

p.m. A way to indicate time from 12:00 noon to 12:00 midnight.

parallel lines Two lines that lie in the same plane and do not intersect.

parallelogram A quadrilateral with two pairs of parallel sides.

pentagon A polygon with five sides.

percent (%) Per 100; a way to compare a number with 100.

perimeter The distance around a figure.

perpendicular lines Two lines that intersect at right angles.

pi (π) The ratio of the circumference of a circle to its diameter. $\pi \approx 3.14$.

place value The value given to the place a digit occupies in a number.

Example: 3   5   6

hundreds place ⅃
tens place ———⅃
ones place ————⅃

plane figure A figure that lies on a flat surface.

Examples:

□   △   ○

square   triangle   circle

point A single, exact location, often represented by a dot.

polygon A closed figure formed by line segments.

polyhydron A space figure whose faces are polygons.

positive integer Any number in the set {1, 2, 3, ... }

prime number A number that has exactly 2 factors (the number itself and 1).

PRINT An instruction in a computer program that tells a computer to type something.

prism A space figure whose bases are congruent polygons in parallel planes and whose faces are parallelograms.

probability The probability that an event will occur in a set of equally likely outcomes is the number of ways the event can occur divided by the total number of possible outcomes.

product The result of the multiplication operation.

Example: $6 \times 7 = 42$
                              ↑
                       product

program A set of instructions that tells a computer what to do.

proportion A statement that two ratios are equal.

Example: $\frac{6}{9} = \frac{2}{3}$

protractor An instrument used for measuring angles.

pyramid A space figure whose base is a polygon and whose faces are triangles with a common vertex.

quotient The number (other than the remainder) that is the result of the division operation.

                          quotient
                              ↓
Examples: $45 \div 9 = 5$ $7)\overline{42}$ ← quotient

radius A segment from the center of a circle to a point on the circle.

radius

ratio A pair of numbers used in making certain comparisons. The ratio of 3 to 4 can be written $\frac{3}{4}$.

ray A part of a line, having only one end point.

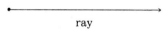
ray

reciprocal Two numbers are reciprocals if their product is 1. 5 and $\frac{1}{5}$ are reciprocals.

rectangle A quadrilateral that has four right angles.

regular polygon A polygon with all sides the same length and all angles the same measure.

remainder The number less than the divisor that remains after the division process is completed.

Example: $7)\overline{47}$ ⟵ 6

                      $\underline{42}$
                        5 ← remainder

repeating decimal A decimal with digits which from some point on repeat periodically. 6.2835835 . . . and 0.33333 . . . are repeating decimals. They may also be written $6.2\overline{835}$ and $0.\overline{3}$ respectively.

rhombus A quadrilateral with all sides the same length.

right angle An angle that has a measure of 90°.

right triangle A triangle that has one right angle.

Roman numerals   Numerals used by the Romans.

Examples: I = 1, V = 5, VI = 6

rounding   Replacing specific numbers with numbers expressed in even units, such as tens, hundreds, or thousands.

Example: 23 rounded to the nearest 10 is 20.

RUN   A command that tells the computer to execute a program.

scale drawing   A drawing of an object made so that distances in the drawing are proportional to actual distances.

scalene triangle   A triangle with no sides the same length and no angles the same measure.

scientific notation   A system of writing a number as the product of a power of 10 and a number between 1 and 10.

Example: $2{,}300{,}000 = 2.3 \times 10^6$

segment   A straight path from one point to another.

similar figures   Two figures that have the same shape.

space figure   A figure that has volume.

Examples:

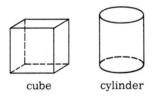

cube   cylinder

sphere   A space figure in which all the points are the same distance from a center point.

square   A quadrilateral with four right angles and all sides the same length.

subtraction   An operation that tells the difference between two numbers, or how many are left when some are taken away.

sum   The number obtained by adding numbers.

Example:
```
      3
    + 2
    ————
      5  ← sum
```

surface area   The sum of the areas of all the faces of a space figure.

symmetric figure   A plane figure that can be folded in half so that the two halves match.

trading   To make a group of ten from one of the next highest place value, or one from ten of the next lowest place value. Examples: one hundred can be traded for ten tens; ten ones can be traded for one ten.

trapezoid   A quadrilateral with one pair of parallel sides.

triangle   A polygon with three sides.

unit   An amount or quality used as a standard of measurement. See Table of Measures, page 429.

vertex (vertices)   The point that the two rays of an angle have in common. Also, the common point of any two sides of a polygon.

volume   The number of cubic units of space that a space figure holds.

whole number   Any number in the set {0, 1, 2, 3, . . .}.

zero property   In addition, when one addend is 0, the sum is the other addend. In multiplication, when either factor is 0, the product is 0.

Photograph Acknowledgments

Animals Animals: 404
Art Resource: 107
Craig Aurness/West Light: 108 top
Frank Balthis: 293
Tom Bean/Tom Stack & Associates: 380 center
Bill Benoit/Atoz Images: 119
Marc Bernheim/Woodfin Camp & Associates: 345
L. Blair/Woodfin Camp & Associates: 164
Elihu Blotnick*: 380 top
Sisse Brimberg/Woodfin Camp & Associates: 64
James Broderick/International Stock Photography Ltd.: 58
Frank Cezus/Atoz Images: 34
© Jerry Cooke/Earth Scenes: 325
Gerald A. Corsi/Tom Stack & Associates: 377 center
Culver Pictures: 88
© De Beers Consolidated Mines Limited: 45
J. DiMaggio/Focus On Sports: 98
N. Elahi/Taurus Photos: 241
Fawcett/Animals Animals: 342
Focus On Sports: 120, 187, 193, 306, 340
Stephen Frisch: 40, 41, 328, 425
Stephen Frisch*: 1, 35, 47, 51, 79, 94, 109, 113, 170, 185, 210, 214, 215 top, 225, 226, 244, 245, 251, 263, 277, 332, 368, 374 top, 385, 388 top, 410, 412
George B. Fry III*: 409
Mickey Gibson/Animals Animals: 318
Stewart Green/Tom Stack & Associates: 236 top
Tom & Michele Grimm/International Stock Photography Ltd.: 114
Bob Hamburgh/Tom Stack & Associates: 308
Phil & Loretta Herman/Tom Stack & Associates: 274
Randall Hyman: 53
Jet Propulsion Lab: 62
Breck P. Kent/Animals Animals: 167
Wayland Lee*/Addison-Wesley Publishing Company: 6, 7, 11, 15, 28, 55, 56, 72, 97, 135, 144, 149 right, 161, 181, 184, 196, 198, 203, 209, 215 bottom, 219, 227, 266, 282, 283, 302, 315, 334, 336, 337, 360, 380 bottom, 383, 388 bottom, 394, 401, 407
Zig Leszczynski/Animals Animals: 248
Library of Congress: 125
Willard Luce/Animals Animals: 104
David Manzonowicz/Monkmeyer Press Photo Service: 36, 37
Steve Martin/Tom Stack & Associates: 152
Fred Mayer/Woodfin Camp & Associates: 382

Robert McClanahan/International Stock Photography Ltd.: 84
Dan McConnell/Atoz Images: 23
Dan McCoy/Rainbow: 415
R. Mendonca/Tom Stack & Associates: 121
Stephen Meyers/Animals Animals: 153
Gary Milburn/Tom Stack & Associates: 296
Warren Morgan/Focus On Sports: 158, 159
Kal Muller/Woodfin Camp & Associates: 76
Keith Murami/Tom Stack & Associates: 149 left
NASA: 63, 142, 236 – 237 bottom, 365 top, 365 center, 375
Mark Newman/Tom Stack & Associates: 321 bottom
Marvin Newman/Woodfin Camp & Associates: 148
Charles O'Rear/West Light: 108 center
Brian Parker/Tom Stack & Associates: 190, 321 top, 377 top
Stacy Pick/Stock, Boston: 57
Richard Pilling/Focus On Sports: 29, 131
Scott Ransom/Taurus Photos: 362
Ed Robinson/Tom Stack & Associates: 2
Ed Rooney/International Stock Photography Ltd.: 73
Bill Ross/West Light: 115
L. L. Rue III/Atoz Images: 18, 222
Kevin Schafer/Tom Stack & Associates: 134
Sepp Seitz/Woodfin Camp & Associates: 299
Elliott Varner Smith*: 101
Souricat/Animals Animals: 50
Tom Stack/Tom Stack & Associates: 10, 237 top
Bill Stanton/International Stock Photography Ltd.: 99
Bob Stern/International Stock Photography Ltd.: 156
Scott Thode/International Stock Photography Ltd.: 96
Bruce M. Willman/Tom Stack & Associates: 137
Rollie Wilson/Focus On Sports: 324
Chuck Wise/Earth Scenes: 374 bottom
Ed Wolff/Earth Scenes: 330
Jim Yuskovitch/Tom Stack & Associates: 21

Special thanks to Mount Zion Hospital and Medical Center, San Francisco, for the use of their facilities for the photograph taken for page 185 and to the Federal Aviation Administration, San Francisco Airport Tower, for the use of their facilities for the photograph taken for page 410.

*Photographs provided expressly for the publisher.

Cover Photograph
©Baron Wolman